Isabella Salas

Miss Hughes

Grammar and Writing 7

Student Edition

First Edition

Christie Curtis

Mary Hake

Hake Publishing

Grammar and Writing 7

First Edition

Student Edition

Copyright ©2011 by Hake Publishing

Printed in the United States of America

ISBN: 978-1-935839-15-6

Hake Publishing
P. O. Box 662061
Arcadia, CA 91066
www.studygrammar.com

Printing History:
2 3 4 5 6 7 8 9 10   15 14 13 12 11

CPSIA Tracking and Labeling Information:
Printed by Bang Printing, Brainerd, MN, USA; Job # 314536, 9/26/11

Contents

Introduction

Welcome to a language arts program devised for easy reading and instruction. Behind this program is a team of dedicated teachers who care about your success and desire to present incremental teaching material in a simple format.

This program consists of a series of **daily lessons**, **review sets**, and **tests** that are carefully sequenced to develop a variety of skills and concepts. We include lessons on capitalization, punctuation, parts of speech, sentence structure, spelling rules, and correct word usage, all with a focus on improving your writing.

To increase our understanding, we will learn to diagram sentences. Diagramming a sentence, like doing a puzzle, exercises your brain and helps you to see the structure of the sentence and the function of its parts. Knowing how to diagram an English sentence will make your future study of foreign languages much easier. It will also help you with correct word usage and punctuation as you write.

Because of the incremental nature of this program, **it is essential that the lessons be taught in order, that all practice and review sets be completed, and that no lessons be skipped.**

In addition to the daily lessons, the program includes a series of **writing lessons**. These are designed to guide you through the process of composing a complete essay. Also included are weekly **dictations** for practice in spelling and punctuation. You will also be asked to keep a journal; the program contains suggested **journal topics**.

Before you start your lesson, you need not wait for teacher instruction because you know how to begin each day:

> MONDAY—Find your weekly dictation in the appendix and copy it to practice for your Friday test.
>
> TUESDAY, WEDNESDAY, THURSDAY—Find your journal topic in the appendix and begin writing.
>
> FRIDAY—Look over your dictation to prepare for your dictation test.

No matter your goals, mastery of the English language is one of the most valuable tools you can possess. It is our hope that this program provides you with a strong foundation not only for future language arts studies but for a lifetime of satisfying and successful writing.

Best wishes!

LESSON 1

Four Types of Sentences

> **Dictation or Journal Entry**
>
> **Vocabulary:**
> We will learn the definitions of three words that look similar: *adapt, adept,* and *adopt.*
>
> *Adapt* means to adjust, accommodate, or modify to fit. If we move from one climate to another, we must *adapt* to the changes.
>
> *Adept* means expert or proficient. The *adept* painter depicted the landscape realistically.
>
> *Adopt* means to embrace, espouse, or take by choice. People often *adopt* the religion of their parents.

A group of words that expresses a complete thought is called a sentence. A capital letter begins each sentence. There are **four types of sentences.**

Declarative   A **declarative sentence** makes a statement and ends with a period.

We fly the American flag from sunrise until sunset.

The flag flies both day and night above the Capitol.

No flag is flown at the White House when the President is absent.

Interrogative   An **interrogative sentence** asks a question and ends with a question mark:

When should we take down the American flag?

Why is that flag at half mast?

Why must the flag not touch the ground?

Imperative   An **imperative sentence** expresses a command or a request and ends with a period:

Raise the American flag at sunrise.

Take down the American flag at sundown.

Please treat the flag with highest respect.

Exclamatory   An **exclamatory sentence** shows excitement or strong feeling and ends with an exclamation point:

Wow, that is the biggest flag I've ever seen!

I can't wait until the Fourth of July!

Hurrah, thousands of flags are waving to honor the United States of America!

Example Tell whether the following sentences are declarative, interrogative, imperative, or exclamatory.

(a) Can any birds fly from the moment they hatch?

(b) Don't drop that bird egg.

(c) Some birds are born fully feathered and able to fly.

(d) That eagle has such a huge wingspan!

Solution (a) This is an **interrogative** sentence because it asks a question and ends with a question mark.

(b) This sentence commands you to do something, and it ends with a period. Therefore, it is **imperative.**

(c) This **declarative** sentence makes a statement and ends with a period.

(d) This **exclamatory** sentence shows strong feeling and ends with an exclamation point.

Practice Identify the sentence type. Write "declarative," "interrogative," "imperative," or "exclamatory."

a. The ornithologist was a genius!

b. Birds with large feet are called megapods.

c. Please study megapods for tomorrow's quiz.

d. Do you know where the mound builders lay their eggs?

e. Most species lay their eggs in large mounds of leaves, twigs, loose soil, and grass.

Replace each blank with *adapt, adept,* or *adopt.*

f. Will you _____ a new pet from the humane society?

g. I hope my new German shepherd will _____ quickly to our home.

h. The dog is quite _____ at jumping over fences and digging under them.

Review set 1 Replace each blank with the correct word to complete sentences 1–10.

1. A sentence begins with a _____ letter.

2. A declarative sentence makes a _____ and ends with a period.

3. A group of words that expresses a complete _____ is called a sentence.

4. A(n) _____ sentence ends with an exclamation point.

5. An imperative sentence expresses a _____ or a request.

6. A(n) _____ sentence ends with a question mark.

7. A _____ expresses a complete thought.

8. A(n) _____ sentence shows strong feeling.

9. Declarative and imperative sentences end with a _____.

10. An interrogative sentence asks a _____.

For 11–24, write whether each sentence is declarative, interrogative, exclamatory, or imperative.

11. Do you know when Aesop lived?

12. Aesop lived between 620 and 560 B.C.

13. King Croesus of Lydia appointed Aesop as his ambassador to other countries.

14. Wow! Aesop wrote his fables a long time ago!

15. While fulfilling his duties as ambassador, Aesop gained recognition for his stories.

16. What a talented storyteller!

17. Please listen carefully to these details.

18. Bring your notes tomorrow.

19. Did you know that storytellers did not write down their stories during Aesop's time?

20. For homework, read one of *Aesop's Fables*.

21. Anything can happen in a fable!

22. Can a goose really lay a golden egg?

23. Are you familiar with the interesting characters in these fables?

24. Each of Aesop's tales ends with a moral—a rule to live by.

For 25–27, replace each blank with the correct vocabulary word.

25. Will you _____ Aesop's moral to "be yourself"?

26. I wish I were more _____ at remembering words of wisdom.

27. I am trying to _____ my lifestyle to "slow and steady wins the race."

28. Unscramble these words to make a declarative sentence:

    Fables   readers   still   *Aesop's*   enjoy

29. Unscramble these words to make an exclamatory sentence:

    huge   that   look   at   bullfrog

30. Unscramble these words to make an interrogative sentence:

    you   "The Crow and the Pitcher"   read   have

LESSON
2

Simple Subject • Simple Predicate

> **Dictation or Journal Entry**
>
> **Vocabulary:**
> Many of our English prefixes originate from the Greek language. One such prefix, *macro-*, means *large* or *long*. We use our prefix knowledge to help us with the definitions of the following words:
>
> The *macrocosm* is the entire world or the universe, or a system that contains subsystems.
>
> A *macrofossil* is a fossil large enough to see with the naked eye.
>
> A *macron* is the symbol placed over a vowel to indicate a "long" vowel sound.

A sentence has two main parts: (1) the subject and (2) the predicate. The subject is the part that tells who or what the sentence is about. The predicate is the part that tells something about the subject. The sentences below have been divided into their two main parts—subjects and predicates.

COMPLETE SUBJECT	COMPLETE PREDICATE
Dark, ominous clouds	gather.
The freezing rain	is pounding our roof.
A man in black boots	stomps through puddles.
I	like this inclement weather.

The complete (whole) subject or predicate may consist of a single word or of many words. However, a subject or predicate consisting of many words always has an essential part that we call the *simple subject* or *simple predicate*.

SIMPLE SUBJECT	SIMPLE PREDICATE
clouds	gather
rain	is pounding
man	stomps
I	like

Simple Subject

The main word or words in a sentence that tell *who* or *what* is doing or being something is called the **simple subject.** In the sentences below, we have italicized the simple subjects.

The *woman* behind the podium began to address the assembly.

Citizens will vote in November.

The *creator* of the painting donated it to the charity auction.

Drivers must respect the speed limit.

Understood Subject In an imperative sentence, the subject, you, is understood:

(You) Drive carefully.

(You) Please help me.

(You) Drink plenty of water.

Example 1 Write the simple subject of each sentence.

(a) Corn grows most rapidly on warm nights.

(b) Please give me your name and address.

Solution (a) Who or what grows rapidly? Corn does, so **corn** is the simple subject.

(b) This is an imperative sentence. Therefore, the subject, **you,** is understood.

Simple Predicate The **simple predicate** is the verb. A verb expresses action or being. We have underlined the simple predicates of the sentences below.

BEING: The macron <u>is</u> a pronunciation tool.

ACTION: The school <u>adopted</u> a new textbook.

ACTION: Yiddish <u>evolved</u> from a German dialect.

ACTION: Eventually, we <u>adapt</u> to changes.

Notice that sometimes the simple predicate contains more than one word as in the sentences below. We call this the *verb phrase.*

Many plants <u>can grow</u> after dark.

Yiddish <u>has developed</u> under Slavic influences.

Debby <u>has been adopting</u> stray cats for many years.

Example 2 Write the simple predicate of this sentence:

Spanish explorers named the plain.

Solution We examine the sentence and discover that the explorers "named." Therefore, **named** is the simple predicate.

Sometimes the order of the subject and predicate is reversed, as in the sentences below:

On the plain <u>grow</u> many *yuccas.*

Here <u>comes</u> the *band.*

There <u>were</u> several *people* in line.

Example 3   Give the simple subject and the simple predicate of this sentence:

Through the gate galloped the stallion.

Solution   We remember that sometimes the predicate comes before the subject. The simple subject of this sentence is **stallion.** What did the stallion do? It "galloped," so the simple predicate is **galloped.**

Split Predicate   In interrogative sentences, we usually find parts of the predicate split by the subject, as in these sentences:

<u>Did</u> *you* <u>see</u> the Spanish bayonets and daggers?

<u>Shall</u> *we* <u>visit</u> the museum tomorrow?

<u>Will</u> the *man* with the beard <u>come</u> with us?

Example 4   Give the simple predicate of this sentence:

Would you recognize Spanish bayonets or daggers?

Solution   The subject is *you.* "Would recognize" describes the action of the subject, so the simple predicate is **would recognize.**

Practice   For a–d, write the simple subject of each sentence.

a. Did Mrs. O'Leary's cow really start the Chicago Fire of 1871?

b. The yucca plants are called Spanish bayonets and daggers.

c. At the bottom of this rumor is a dishonest newspaper reporter.

d. Study your dictation carefully.

For e–g, write the simple predicate of each sentence.

e. Do horses graze in pastures?

f. Wildflowers (are) not common in winter.

g. Over the ice fields (ran) the penguin.

For h–j, replace each blank with the correct vocabulary word.

h. Please place a _____ over the *a* in "stake."

i. We classify dinosaur fossils as _____.

j. A _____ of peace requires the cooperation of the entire world.

More Practice   See Master Worksheets.

Review set 2   Replace each blank with the correct word to complete sentences 1–5.

1. A complete sentence has a _____ and a predicate.
(2)

2. The simple predicate is the _____ phrase.
(2)

3. The simple _____ is the main word in a sentence
(2) that tells who or what is doing something.

4. A verb expresses _____ or being.
(2)

5. The verb phrase is called the simple _____.
(2)

Write the simple subject of sentences 6–14.

6. Aesop told a story about a crow and a pitcher.
(2)

7. Please explain the moral of that story.
(2)

8. The thirsty crow searches for water.
(2)

9. A pitcher holds a few inches of water.
(2)

10. Can the crow drink it?
(2)

11. Unfortunately, there is a problem.
(2)

12. The bird's beak is too short.
(2)

13. Should he break the pitcher?
(2)

(2) **14.** No, the water will spill.

For 15–23, write the simple predicate of each sentence.

15. The mouth of the pitcher is too narrow.
(2)

16. Along comes a hint.
(2)

17. A bird lands in a birdbath.
(2)

18. The water overflows the rim of the bath.
(2)

19. Aha, the crow has discovered a solution.
(2)

20. The crow drops pebbles into the pitcher.
(2)

21. With each pebble, the water level rises.
(2)

22. Soon, the water reaches the top of the pitcher.
(2)

23. Now, the crow can drink the water.
(2)

24. Unscramble these words to make a declarative sentence:
(1)

    problem   smart   solved   a   crow   a

25. Unscramble these words to make an interrogative
(1) sentence:

    problems   can   solve   you

26. Unscramble these words to make an exclamatory
(1) sentence:

    solution   have   perfect   the   I

27. Unscramble these words to make an imperative sentence:
(1)

    the   not   break   pitcher   do

For 28–30, replace each blank with the correct vocabulary word from Lesson 1 or 2.

28. The word "rise" should have a _____ over the *i*.
(2)

29. Was the crow _____ at problem solving?
(1)

30. In troublesome situations, we can _____ and gain
(1) what at first seems impossible.

LESSON 3

Complete Sentences, Sentence Fragments, and Run-on Sentences

Dictation or Journal Entry

Vocabulary:
Notice the difference between two similar words, *human* and *humane*.

Human, an adjective, means characteristic of man. To make a mistake is only *human*.

Humane, also an adjective, means kind or compassionate. Removing the thorn from the dog's paw was the *humane* thing to do.

Complete Sentences   A **complete sentence** expresses a complete thought. It has both a subject and a predicate. The following are **complete sentences**. Simple subjects are italicized, and simple predicates are underlined.

> The large *end* of an egg <u>contains</u> an air sac.

> The unhatched *chick* <u>can breathe</u> from the air sac.

> In a normal egg, the chick's *head* <u>points</u> toward the large end of the egg.

> Please <u>hold</u> the chick carefully.

Notice that the sentence above, "Please hold the chick carefully," does not appear to have a subject. It is an imperative sentence, a command. The subject, you, is understood.

> (*You*) Please <u>hold</u> the chick carefully.

Sentence Fragments   A **fragment** is a piece of a sentence that lacks a subject or a verb or both. When a sentence fragment fails to tell us who or what is doing the action, it is missing the subject:

> Returned to normal breathing. (who or what?)

If we identify the subject, and we do not know what it is doing, the expression is missing a verb:

> A temporary loss of breath. (does what?)

Another error that results in fragments is using the *to* form and *ing* form of the verb, as in these sentences:

> The runner catching his breath. (*ing* form of verb)

> Three friends to run a marathon. (*to* form of verb)

We can correct these sentence fragments by adding subjects and/or verbs.

Example 1 Make a complete sentence from this sentence fragment: Returned to normal breathing.

Solution We add a subject to tell who or what returned to normal breathing. There is more than one correct answer.

The *athlete* returned to normal breathing.

Example 2 Make a complete sentence from this sentence fragment: A temporary loss of breath.

Solution We add an action verb telling what "a temporary loss of breath" does. Again, there are various ways to correct this fragment.

A temporary loss of breath <u>results</u> in the increase of lactic acid in muscles.

We could also add a being verb to tell what "a temporary loss of breath" is.

A temporary loss of breath <u>is</u> short-lived and uncomfortable.

Example 3 Make a complete sentence from this sentence fragment: The runner catching his breath.

Solution Without a helping verb, the *ing* verb form, *catching*, creates a sentence fragment. So, we add a helping verb, <u>is</u>.

The runner <u>is catching</u> his breath.

Run-on Sentences A sentence is complete only if it expresses a complete thought. Two complete thoughts, written or spoken as one sentence without proper punctuation or connecting words, are called a **run-on sentence**.

RUN-ON SENTENCE:
Second wind is the name given to the return of normal breathing this occurs after a temporary loss of breath.

TWO COMPLETE SENTENCES:
Second wind is the name given to the return of normal breathing. This occurs after a temporary loss of breath.

If we use a comma instead of a period, or if we omit the joining words or punctuation between sentences, we have a run-on sentence.

RUN-ON SENTENCE:
The runner's heart will beat faster, the nervous system will adjust to the higher speed.

ONE COMPLETE SENTENCE:
The runners' heart will beat faster, and the nervous system will adjust to the higher speed.

We correct run-on sentences by adding punctuation and/or connecting words.

Example 4 Correct this run-on sentence:

Many people supposed that Henry Hudson was Dutch he was really English.

Solution We add a comma and a connecting word to make this a complete sentence.

Many people supposed that Henry Hudson was Dutch, but he was really English.

Solution We can also correct this run-on sentence by adding a period and a capital letter to make two complete sentences.

Many people supposed that Henry Hudson was Dutch. He was really English.

Practice For a–d, tell whether each expression is a sentence fragment, run-on sentence, or complete sentence.

a. The life of Henry Hudson is obscure historians agree that he was an Englishman by birth.

b. His voyage in the *Half Moon*.

c. In 1609, Henry Hudson explored New York Bay and the Hudson River.

d. Rewrite and correct this run-on sentence. There is more than one answer.
The engagement ring is worn on the fourth finger ancient people believed that a vein runs directly from that finger to the heart.

    e. Rewrite and correct this sentence fragment. There is more than one answer.

The bride in the long white gown.

Replace each blank with the correct vocabulary word.

    f. The _____ body requires sleep, food, water, and exercise.

    g. We owe _____ treatment to animals as well as to people.

More Practice

For 1–14, write "yes" if the sentence is complete; write "no" if it is not.

1. The black and white car with a light on top.

2. John slept.

3. A red pickup truck with a heavy load.

4. Over the fence and into the neighbor's yard.

5. The zucchini grew quickly.

6. Running, leaping, and shouting, "Hooray!"

7. I've read the book.

8. Barked all night long.

9. Listen to me.

10. Listening to soothing piano music.

11. I laughed.

12. Come here.

13. Painted the tall white fence.

14. In the late afternoon before dark.

For 15–20, write whether each expression is a complete sentence, a sentence fragment, or a run-on sentence.

15. Hudson sailed.

16. An early explorer of North America.

17. Captain John Smith was born in 1580, he bravely crossed the Atlantic Ocean.

18. His adventures in France, Hungary, and Turkey, as well as in the New World.

19. Captain John Smith founded Jamestown, Virginia.

20. John Smith had many adventures later he wrote a book about them.

For 21–23, make a complete sentence from each sentence fragment. Answers will vary.

21. Sailed around the world.

22. Approaching an iceberg.

23. The ice-covered Arctic Ocean around the North Pole.

For 24–26, rewrite and correct each run-on sentence. Answers will vary.

24. Glaciers are large masses of ice and packed snow they form icebergs and ice shelves.

25. The Arctic Ocean is the smallest ocean it is also the coldest.

26. I saw an iceberg did you?

Review set 3 Replace each blank with the correct word to complete sentences 1–6.

1. A sentence _____ is a piece of a sentence.
(3)

2. If we identify the subject, and it is not doing anything,
(3) the expression is missing a _____.

3. When a group of words fails to tell who or what is doing
(3) the action, it is missing a _____.

4. A _____ sentence has both a subject and a
(3) predicate.

5. More than one complete thought written as one sentence
(3) is called a _____ sentence.

6. A complete sentence expresses a _____ thought.
(1)

7. Which sentence is imperative? Choose A or B.
(1)   A. Have you read Aesop's "The Fox and the Grapes"?
   B. Read Aesop's "The Fox and the Grapes."

8. Unscramble these words to make an interrogative
(1) sentence:

we   shall   for   meanings   look   deeper

9. Unscramble these words to make a declarative sentence:
(1)

moral   fable   a   has   this

For 10–12, write whether the expression is a complete
sentence or a sentence fragment.

10. Wandering through the countryside, a fox spies some
(3) grapes.

11. Grapes as big as saucers and as purple as amethysts.
(3)

12. An especially attractive bunch, large in size and
(3) appealing in color.

For 13 and 14, write whether each sentence is a complete
sentence or a run-on sentence.

13. The fox never misses a chance to eat the grapes will make
(3) a delicious breakfast.

14. Morning dew glistens on the grapes like diamonds in the
(3) sunlight.

Write the simple subject of sentences 15–19.

15. Eat some juicy grapes.
(2)

16. Jumping high in the air, the fox tries to grab some.
(2)

17. Frustration grips the fox.
(2)

18. The fox pretends disinterest in the grapes.
(2)

19. We can't have everything.
(2)

Write the simple predicate in sentences 20–24.

20. The fox paces back and forth.
(2)

21. The grapes lie beyond the fox's grasp.
(2)

22. Giving up, the fox snarls.
(2)

23. Do those grapes look sour?
(2)

24. They probably would taste bad anyway.
(2)

For 25 and 26, write which sentence is complete. Choose A or B.

25. A. Speaking badly of things beyond his reach.
(2) B. He had an attitude of sour grapes.

26. A. To know the old, familiar phrase, "sour grapes."
(2) B. The phrase originated with this story.

For 27–30, choose the best word to complete each sentence.

27. What kind of attitude did the fox (adapt, adept, adopt)?
(1)

28. Frustration is a (humane, human) reaction to a difficult
(3) situation.

29. The prefix *macro-* means (tasty, large, tiny).
(2)

30. Sometimes we must (adapt, adept, adopt) to changes in
(1) our lives.

LESSON 4   Action Verbs • Diagramming the Simple Subject and Simple Predicate

---

Dictation or Journal Entry

Vocabulary:
The prefix *micro-* originates from the Greek language and means small or minute.

A *microbus* is a small vehicle in the shape of a bus. The automobile corporation designed a *microbus* to seat ten people.

A *microcosm* is a little world. The invalid could not leave home; she felt she lived in a *microcosm*.

A *microscope* is an instrument used to view very small objects. The scientist viewed the blood cells through a *microscope*.

Action Verbs   We remember that a complete sentence contains a subject and a verb. The verb tells what the subject is or does. An **action verb** describes what the subject does or did. *Runs* is the action verb in the sentence below. It tells what the cheetah does.

> The cheetah <u>runs</u> faster than any other four-footed animal in the world.

Sometimes a sentence contains more than one action verb. In the sentence below, *chases* and *captures* are two action verbs telling what the cheetah does.

> The cheetah <u>chases</u> and <u>captures</u> its prey.

Example 1   Identify each action verb in these sentences.

(a) The swiftest greyhounds race at more than sixty miles per hour.

(b) A cheetah strikes its prey with its paw.

Solution   (a) The action verb, **race,** tells what greyhounds do.

(b) The action verb, **strikes,** tells what a cheetah does.

Improving Our Writing   We can make our writing more vivid and accurate by using descriptive and precise action verbs. Consider these two sentences:

> The squirrel <u>went</u> up the tree.

> The squirrel <u>scurried</u> up the tree.

We notice that the verb *scurried* gives a clearer picture of how the squirrel went up the tree. *Scampered, dashed,* and *rushed* are also descriptive action verbs. We try to choose the action verb with the truest, most precise meaning.

Example 2   Replace the action verb in this sentence with one that might be more precise or descriptive. Consider the different possibilities.

The panther <u>goes</u> after its prey.

Solution   Our answers will vary. Here are some possibilities:

The panther **sprints** after its prey.

The panther **races** after its prey.

The panther **leaps** after its prey.

Diagramming Simple Subjects and Simple Predicates   In Lesson 2, we identified simple subjects and simple predicates. Now, we will learn to **diagram** the simple subject and simple predicate of a sentence according to this pattern:

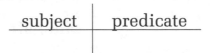

Below, we diagram the simple subject and simple predicate of this sentence: Sopranos sing the high parts.

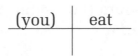

We place the simple subject on the left and the simple predicate on the right. We separate the subject and predicate with a vertical line.

If the subject is understood, as in an imperative sentence, we place *you* in parentheses on the left like this:

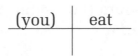

Eat your spinach.

Example 3   Diagram the simple subject and simple predicate of this sentence: Owls catch mice in the fields.

Solution   The "who or what" (subject) of the sentence is *owls*, so we place it on the left. "Catch" tells what the owls do; it is the simple predicate, so we place it on the right.

$$\overline{\text{Owls} \quad | \quad \text{catch}}$$

We remember that a simple predicate is not always an action verb. It can also show "being."

Dad <u>was</u> an army lieutenant.

Some simple predicates consist of more than one word.

Eagles <u>had been soaring</u> overhead.

Example 4   Diagram the simple subject and simple predicate of this sentence:

The first domesticated animals might have been dogs.

Solution   The simple predicate of this sentence is "might have been." We ask ourselves, "*What* might have been?" The answer is the subject, *animals*. Our diagram looks like this:

$$\overline{\textbf{animals} \quad | \quad \textbf{might have been}}$$

Practice   Write each action verb in sentences a and b.

    a. The book of *Job* lists camels, oxen, sheep, and donkeys as domesticated too.

    b. Abel fed and guarded his sheep.

    c. Write an action verb that might be more descriptive to replace the underlined verb in this sentence: Fido <u>ate</u> the bone.

Diagram the simple subject and simple predicate of sentences d and e.

    d. A disabled woman invented the toy bear.

    e. The bear was called Teddy for Theodore Roosevelt.

For f–h, replace each blank with the correct vocabulary word.

    f. A small world is a _____.

    g. Our team will travel on the _____ to the game.

h. The snowflake's crystalline structure was revealed in the
_____.

More Practice   Write each action verb in sentences 1–5.

1. My friend wrote a poem about promises.

2. We read poems by Robert Frost.

3. Jayne writes poetry.

4. Jasmine washed and dried the dishes.

5. Listen to this poem by William Wordsworth.

Diagram the simple subject and simple predicate of sentences 6–16.

6. James swam sixty laps of the pool.

7. Have you swum today?

8. Diagram this sentence.

9. Tom has been studying German.

10. Did Christina pass her test?

11. Omar had been the team's most valuable player.

12. Tell the truth.

13. Was Miss Wu teasing?

14. I will adapt my schedule to these changes.

15. Gloria became adept at photography.

16. Mountains surrounded the quiet town.

Review set 4   Write each action verb in sentences 1–5.

1. Long ago Aesop told a story about a city mouse and a
(4) country mouse.

2. A city mouse travels to the country.
(4)

3. His cousin, a country mouse, lives in a barn.
(4)

4. Normally, the city mouse eats gourmet foods.
(4)

5. The country mouse prepares a simple supper for his
(4) cousin.

For 6–8, replace the action verb in each sentence with one that might be more accurate or descriptive. There are many possibilities.

6. The city mouse dislikes the meal.
(4)

7. Crickets come out at night.
(4)

8. The sound of the crickets soothes the country mouse.
(4)

For 9–11, make a complete sentence from each sentence fragment. Answers will vary.

9. The crickets' noise bothering the city mouse.
(3)

10. To hear horrible screeching sounds.
(3)

11. The city mouse in the country.
(3)

For 12–14, correct each run-on sentence. Answers may vary.

12. The city mouse finally dozes off then a rooster crows.
(3)

13. The city mouse detests the country the country mouse
(3) will visit the city.

14. The carpet and woodwork impress the country mouse
(3) maybe the city is better than the country.

For 15–17, write whether the expression is a sentence fragment, a run-on sentence, or a complete sentence.

15. What would you like to eat?
(3)

16. A mouse in the chaos of the noisy, busy city streets.
(3)

17. Streets are dangerous the mouse is frightened.
(3)

For 18–21, write whether each sentence is declarative, interrogative, imperative, or exclamatory.

18. Wait a minute.
(1)

19. There's a cat!
(1)

20. The mice feast on party leftovers.
(1)

21. Does the dog scare the mice?
(1)

Diagram the simple subject and simple predicate of sentences 22–26.

22. Do cats threaten the mice?
(2, 4)

23. Bubble gum sticks to the country mouse's leg.
(2, 4)

24. The streets smell bad.
(2, 4)

25. Listen to me!
(2, 4)

26. Does the mouse like the city?
(2, 4)

For 27–30, choose the best word to complete each sentence.

27. A complete sentence has a (verb, subject, pronoun) and a
(3) predicate.

28. A macrocosm is a (large, small, imaginary) world.
(2)

29. (Human, Humane) means kind or compassionate.
(3)

30. A microscope is used to view very (large, small, cold)
(4) items.

LESSON 5

Capitalizing Proper Nouns

Dictation or Journal Entry

Vocabulary:

We remember that homophones are words with the same pronunciation but different spellings and meanings. *Waive* and *wave* are homophones.

Waive means to relinquish or give up voluntarily. The defendant decided to *waive* the right to a trial by jury.

A *wave* (noun) is a moving swell on the surface of water. The ocean's *waves* were five feet high today. To *wave* (verb) is to greet or signal with a hand motion. Let's *wave* goodbye to our friends.

Proper Nouns

We remember that a noun is a person, place, or thing. A noun may be common or proper. A common noun does not name a specific person, place, or thing. A **proper noun** does name a specific person, place, or thing and requires a capital letter.

COMMON NOUN	PROPER NOUN
country	Great Britain
lake	Lake Michigan
day	Friday
month	January
girl	Shirley Temple
book	*David Copperfield*

Common Nouns Within Proper Nouns

When a common noun such as "lake," "river," "mountain," "street," or "school" is a part of a proper noun, we capitalize it as in the examples below.

COMMON NOUN	PROPER NOUN
boulevard	Hollywood Boulevard
university	Boston University
ocean	Mediterranean Sea
family	Martinez Family
canal	Panama Canal
mountains	Appalachian Mountains
hemisphere	Western Hemisphere

Small Words Within Proper Nouns

When the following small words are parts of a proper noun, we do not capitalize them unless they are the initial or final word:

a, an, and, at, but, by, for, from,

if, in, into, of, on, the, to, with

Notice the following examples.

> *The Adventures of Tom Sawyer*
> Bank of America
> Straits of Gibraltar
> House of Commons
> Richard the Lionhearted
> "The Battle Hymn of the Republic"

Example   Capitalize proper nouns in these sentences as needed.

(a) One of the main characters is huckleberry finn.

(b) Have you read *where the red fern grows?*

(c) The sciarrotta family cruised from catalina island to ensenada, mexico.

(d) The irish celebrate st. patrick's day.

Solution   (a) We capitalize **Huckleberry Finn** because it is a specific person.

(b) **Where, Red, Fern,** and **Grows** are capitalized because they are words of a book title. The small word *the* is not capitalized.

(c) **Sciarrotta Family** is a specific family and needs capital letters. Also, **Catalina Island** is a specific island, and **Ensenada, Mexico** is a specific city in a specific country.

(d) **Irish** is capitalized because it is a group of people from a specific country. **St. Patrick's Day** is a specific day.

Practice   Rewrite sentences a–e, capitalizing each proper noun.

a. charles dickens gained fame for his memorable characters.

b. uriah heep devised a scheme to capture agnes wickfield as his wife.

c. charles dickens wrote a novel called *a tale of two cities.*

d. During the victorian age, some english writers traveled to the united states to read their novels to american audiences.

e. Excellent swimmers attempt to swim the english channel.

For f–i, replace each blank with *wave* or *waive*.

    f. Local surfers hoped for a big _____ on the day of the surfing competition.

    g. Prince Charles will _____ enthusiastically at his supporters as he tours the streets of London.

    h. Every camper will sign a document to _____ the right to sue the campground.

    i. The American Flag will _____ proudly in the wind.

More Practice   See Master Worksheets.

Review set 5   Write and capitalize each proper noun in sentences 1–10.

    1. henry david thoreau was born in concord, massachusetts,
    (5) on july 12, 1817.

    2. ralph waldo emerson and nathaniel hawthorne also lived
    (5) in this community near boston, massachusetts.

    3. thoreau's descendants were protestants who fled france
    (5) because of catholic persecution.

    4. cynthia dunbar, thoreau's wife, descended from a
    (5) grandfather who favored the british in the american revolutionary war.

    5. thoreau attended harvard university in cambridge,
    (5) massachusetts, along the charles river.

    6. His ideas impressed horace greeley, the editor of the *new*
    (5) *york herald.*

    7. thoreau's masterpiece, *walden*, focuses on the variety of
    (5) nature.

    8. He visited cape cod and maine for their vast beauty.
    (5)

    9. Please, aunt yumi, take me to the yard sale on maple
    (5) street.

    (5) **10.** Is it difficult to wake up on monday mornings?

Choose the best word to complete sentences 11–13.

11. Even though Dad was driving, he (waved, waived) his
 (5) right to choose the radio station.

12. We measure (large, small, heavy) things with a
 (2, 4) micrometer.

13. Every (human, humane) experiences pain at times.
 (3)

Write the action verb from sentences 14 and 15.

14. The country mouse consumes a sugar frosting rose.
 (4)

15. Even the candle tastes good.
 (4)

For 16 and 17, replace the action verb with one that might be more precise or descriptive.

16. The mice eat cheese.
 (4)

17. A dog scares the mice.
 (4)

For 18–21, write whether the sentence is declarative, interrogative, exclamatory, or imperative.

18. Country mice hate the city!
 (1)

19. Go back to the country.
 (1)

20. The country mouse prefers simple meals, peace, and
 (1) quiet.

21. Do you understand the moral, "to each his own"?
 (1)

For 22–24, write whether the expression is a sentence fragment, run-on sentence, or complete sentence.

22. A swallow and a crow argue over something silly who is
 (3) finer?

23. The swallow's feathers are prettier and finer.
 (3)

24. Appearance not worth much in a winter snow storm.
 (3)

25. Make a complete sentence from this sentence fragment:
 (3)
    The meaning of "fair-weather friends."

For 26 and 27, correct each run-on sentence.

26. We value our friendships we might need a friend's help
(3)   someday.

27. Don't be a "fair-weather friend" a good friend is loyal in
(3)   good weather and bad.

Diagram the simple subject and simple predicate of sentences
28–30.

28. Have you read "The Swallow and the Crow"?
(2, 4)

29. High in the tree sits the crow.
(2, 4)

30. The silly birds' argument escalates.
(2, 4)

LESSON 6

Present and Past Tense of Regular Verbs

> **Dictation or Journal Entry**
>
> **Vocabulary:**
> The words *climactic* and *climate* look similar but have different meanings.
>
> *Climactic* refers to the climax or culmination. The *climactic* portion of the plot generally occurs about two-thirds of the way into the story.
>
> *Climate* is the general weather of a region over a period of years. Deserts are famous for their arid *climate*.

Tense means time. Verbs tell us not only what action is occurring but also when it is occurring. The form of a verb, or the verb tense, changes in order to show when the action takes place. Three simple verb tenses are present, past, and future. In this lesson, we will talk about the present and past tense of regular verbs. Later, we will review the many irregular verbs.

Present Tense

The **present tense** refers to action that is happening now. We add an *s* when the subject is singular, except for when the pronoun is *I* or *you*.

PLURAL SUBJECTS AND PRONOUNS *I* AND *YOU*	SINGULAR SUBJECTS
Cats <u>meow</u>.	The cat <u>meows</u>.
I <u>snack</u>.	He <u>snacks</u>.
We <u>glance</u>.	She <u>glances</u>.
They <u>own</u>.	Lance <u>owns</u>.
You <u>bristle</u>.	Gretchen <u>bristles</u>.
Kari and Matt <u>crawl</u>.	Nathan <u>crawls</u>.

When a verb ends in *s, x, z, ch,* or *sh,* we add *es* when the subject is singular.

PLURAL SUBJECTS AND PRONOUNS *I* AND *YOU*	SINGULAR SUBJECTS
We <u>blush</u>.	Robert <u>blushes</u>.
Sodas <u>fizz</u>.	A soda <u>fizzes</u>.
Pitchers <u>pitch</u>.	A pitcher <u>pitches</u>.
People <u>kiss</u>.	Mom <u>kisses</u>.
Trainers <u>coax</u>.	A trainer <u>coaxes</u>.

When a verb ends in a consonant and a *y*, we change the *y* to *i* and add *es* for the singular form.

PLURAL SUBJECTS AND PRONOUNS *I* AND *YOU*	SINGULAR SUBJECTS
I seldom <u>cry</u>.	He seldom <u>cries</u>.
They <u>rely</u> on you.	Elspeth <u>relies</u> on you.

Example 1   Replace each blank with the singular present tense form of the verb.

(a) You <u>reply</u>. He _____.

(b) Nosy neighbors <u>pry</u>. A nosy neighbor _____.

(c) Children <u>play</u>. A child _____.

(d) Darryl and Carol <u>boss</u>. She _____.

(e) People <u>switch</u>. George _____.

Solution   (a) **replies** (Since the verb ends in *y*, we change the *y* to *i* and add *es*.)

(b) **pries** (Since the verb ends in *y*, we change the *y* to *i* and add *es*.)

(c) **plays** (We add an *s* when the subject is singular.)

(d) **bosses** (The verb ends in *s*, so we add *es*.)

(e) **switches** (The verb ends in *ch*, so we add *es*.)

Past Tense   The **past tense** shows action that has already occurred. To form the past tense of regular verbs, we add *ed*.

squawk—squawked

toss—tossed

When a one-syllable verb ends in a consonant, we double the consonant and add *ed*.

rub—rubbed

mop—mopped

When a verb ends in *e*, we drop the *e* and add *ed*.

bake—baked

writhe—writhed

When the verb ends in *y*, we change the *y* to *i* and add *ed*.

dry—dried

apply—applied

Example 2 Write the past tense form of each verb.

(a) slap   (b) share   (c) reply

(d) pat   (e) study   (f) shove

Solution (a) **slapped** (Since this is a short verb ending in a consonant, we double the consonant and add *ed*.)

(b) **shared** (The verb ends in *e*, so we drop the *e* and add *ed*.)

(c) **replied** (The verb ends in *y*, so we change the *y* to *i* and add *ed*.)

(d) **patted** (Since this is a short verb ending in a consonant, we double the consonant and add *ed*.)

(e) **studied** (The verb ends in *y*, so we change the *y* to *i* and add *ed*.)

(f) **shoved** (The verb ends in *e*, so we drop the *e* and add *ed*.)

Errors to Avoid Do not use the present tense form for the past tense.

NO: Last week, I <u>hook</u> a trout.
YES: Last week, I <u>hooked</u> a trout.

NO: Yesterday, I <u>drop</u> by Udi's house.
YES: Yesterday, I <u>dropped</u> by Udi's house.

NO: Timothy <u>fries</u> doughnuts earlier this morning.
YES: Timothy <u>fried</u> doughnuts earlier this morning.

Do not shift from past to present in the same phrase.

NO: She <u>stepped</u> out and <u>slips</u> on the ice.
YES: She <u>stepped</u> out and <u>slipped</u> on the ice.

NO: Yesterday, he <u>raised</u> the flag at daybreak and <u>lowers</u> it at sundown.

YES: Yesterday, he <u>raised</u> the flag at daybreak and <u>lowered</u> it at sundown.

Example 3   Choose the correct form of the verb to complete each sentence.

(a) Geraldine baked vanilla cupcakes and (frosts, frosted) them with chocolate icing.

(b) While watching the video, we (pop, popped) popcorn and ate it.

Solution   (a) Geraldine baked vanilla cupcakes and **frosted** them with chocolate icing.

(b) While watching the video, we **popped** popcorn and ate it.

Practice   For a–d, replace each blank with the singular present tense form of the underlined verb.

a. Many parrots <u>screech</u> shrilly. That parrot _____ shrilly.

b. Nine players <u>walk</u> proudly onto the field. The pitcher _____ proudly onto the field.

c. Clerks <u>box</u> groceries. The clerk _____ groceries.

d. Students <u>try</u> to learn the material. A student _____ to learn the material.

For e–l, write the past tense form of each verb.

e. plop   **f.** bully   **g.** knit   **h.** place

i. comply   **j.** rake   **k.** slip   **l.** bat

For m and n, choose the correct verb form.

m. A few days ago, the moths (chew, chewed) a hole in my best wool sweater.

n. The umpire claimed that the pitcher (balks, balked) on his last pitch.

For o–r, replace each blank with the correct vocabulary word.

o. That ninth-inning home run was a _____ way to win the game.

p. The Mediterranean _____ with its mild temperatures appeals to many.

q. The movie's _____ action enthralled the audience.

r. Alaska's _____ does not appeal to those who dislike the cold.

Review set 6   For 1–5, replace each blank with the singular present tense form of the verb.

1. Cows supply milk. The cow _____ milk.
(4, 6)

2. Soda and root beer fizz when poured on ice cream. Root
(4, 6) beer _____ when poured on ice cream.

3. Tailors patch holes in jeans. The tailor _____
(4, 6) holes in jeans.

4. Cats hiss at dogs. My cat _____ at dogs.
(4, 6)

5. People yawn when they are bored. Dr. Gnu _____
(4, 6) when she is bored.

For 6–10, replace each blank with the past tense form of the verb.

6. Louisa May Alcott (cry) _____ out for her sisters to
(4, 6) help her save a half-starved bird.

7. The girls (trap) _____ the bird in order to save it.
(4, 6)

8. Louisa May Alcott (base) _____ her stories on her
(4, 6) own family life.

9. Bill (talk) _____ about his favorite book.
(4, 6)

10. A fireman (pry) _____ the door open to rescue
(4, 6) someone.

For 11–13, write and correctly capitalize each proper noun.

11. In march of 1840, louisa may alcott wrote her first poem,
(5) entitled "to the first robin."

12. *little women*, her first book, was about four sisters living
(5) in new england.

13. louisa may alcott's home, orchard house, remains one of
(5) new england's most popular tourist attractions.

Choose the correct verb form for sentences 14 and 15.

14. Long ago, Louisa May Alcott (suffers, suffered) numerous
(4, 6) physical ailments.

15. During the 1800s, she (pens, penned) stories about the
(4, 6) domestic life of young girls.

16. Make a complete sentence from this sentence fragment:
(1, 3) Did not receive much literary credit during her life.

17. Rewrite and correct this run-on sentence:
(1, 3) Aesop told a fable it was about a donkey and a
grasshopper.

For 18–20, write whether each expression is a sentence
fragment, run-on sentence, or complete sentence.

18. Hearing the interesting sound of some grasshoppers
(1, 3) chirping.

19. The donkey wants to chirp like the grasshoppers.
(1, 3)

20. The grasshoppers say that drinking dew is their secret the
(1, 3) donkey will try it.

For 21–24, write whether the sentence is declarative,
interrogative, imperative, or exclamatory.

21. How stupid it was for the donkey to think that he could
(1) chirp like a cricket!

22. Can a donkey survive on dew alone?
(1)

23. One person's meat is another's poison.
(1)

24. Do not be foolish in your desires.
(1)

Diagram the simple subject and simple predicate of sentences
25–27.

25. Eat sensibly.
(2, 4)

26. Without food, a donkey will die.
(2, 4)

27. Within the story lies a moral.
(2, 4)

Choose the best word to complete sentences 28–30.

28. A little world is a (microcosm, macrocosm).
(2, 4)

29. It is not (human, humane) to mistreat animals.
(3)

30. Will Mrs. Smith (adapt, adept, adopt) another tortoise?
(1)

LESSON 7

Concrete, Abstract, and Collective Nouns

Dictation or Journal Entry

Vocabulary:

Miso-, meaning hatred, is another prefix of Greek origin. Words like *misogynist, misoneism,* and *misogamist* indicate some type of hatred.

Misogynist, a noun, refers to one who hates or distrusts women. The employer, a *misogynist,* wanted to hire only men.

Misoneism is the hatred or intolerance of change. The company's *misoneism* caused its eventual downfall.

A *misogamist* hates marriage. Clarence, a *misogamist,* preferred the single life.

Concrete Nouns

A **concrete noun** names a person, place, or thing. It may be either common or proper.

CONCRETE COMMON	CONCRETE PROPER
ship	*Queen Mary*
doctor	Dr. Dinwitty
river	Amazon River

Abstract Nouns

An **abstract noun** names something that cannot be seen or touched. It names something that you can think about. An abstract noun can be common or proper as well.

ABSTRACT COMMON NOUNS	ABSTRACT PROPER NOUNS
month	August
religion	Catholicism
holiday	Easter
nationality	Japanese
language	Portuguese
philosophy	Platonism

Example 1

For sentences a–c, write each noun and label it *C* for concrete or *A* for abstract.

(a) The doctrines of Islam call for justice and peace among all people of the world.

(b) With courage and determination, Olaf climbed Mount Everest.

(c) Does Onping speak Cantonese as well as English?

Solution (a) **doctrines—A;   Islam—A;   justice—A;   peace—A; people—C; world—C**

(b) **courage—A;   determination—A;   Olaf—C;   Mount Everest—C**

(c) **Onping—C;   Cantonese—A;   English—A**

Collective Nouns   A **collective noun** names a collection of persons, places, animals, or things. We list a few examples below.

PERSONS: clan, congregation, team, panel, jury, family

ANIMALS: pack, herd, flock, litter, gaggle (geese), swarm

PLACES: United Kingdom, South America, Southeast Asia

THINGS: collection, assortment, batch, bunch, selection

Example 2   Write the collective noun from each sentence.
(a) The selection of desserts tempted the hungry diner.

(b) The patriotic crowd waived American flags in support of the President.

(c) Central America includes countries such as El Salvador, Costa Rica, Nicaragua, Guatemala, and Honduras.

(d) The school of goldfish fled from the wader.

Solution   (a) **selection**   (b) **crowd**

(c) **Central America**   (d) **school**

Practice   For a–d, tell whether each noun is abstract or concrete.
a. computer disk   **b.** integrity

c. philosophy   **d.** cell phone

For sentences e–g, write each noun and label it *C* for concrete or *A* for abstract.

e. Without fear, the paramedic climbed a high fence and rescued the lady in distress.

f. Misoneism prevents growth and progress.

g. Mr. Jansen drove his microbus down the narrow alley.

Write each collective noun that you find in sentences h–j.

h. The diners chose from an assortment of fruit.

i. A gaggle of geese frightened the zoo visitors.

j. That bunch of bananas satisfied the hungry monkey.

For k–m, replace each blank with the correct vocabulary word.

k. Sometimes a divorced person becomes a bitter _____.

l. The _____ avoided contact with women as much as possible.

m. Is _____ more common among the elderly than the younger generation, or do people of all ages dislike change?

More Practice   For 1–12, tell whether each noun is abstract or concrete.

1. generosity   **2.** misogamist   **3.** forgiveness   **4.** knee

5. backpack   **6.** sympathy   **7.** misoneism   **8.** pizza

9. moose   **10.** mustard   **11.** peace   **12.** lettuce

For sentences 13–18, write each noun and label it *C* for concrete or *A* for abstract.

13. Bryon played the piano with skill and enthusiasm.

14. With rhythm and zeal, John strummed the guitar.

15. Accuracy is crucial in mathematics.

16. Henry spoke the truth with grace.

17. David spoke about the integrity of his friend.

18. The prisoner pleaded for justice and mercy.

Write each collective noun that you find in sentences 19–21.

19. The Ingalls clan raised a herd of cattle on the Dakota prairie.

20. The congregation prayed that the team would have safe travel.

21. James donated a batch of drawings from his collection to his art class.

Review set 7
1. Write the concrete nouns from this list: courage, notebook, curtain, bench, amazement.
   (7)

2. Write the abstract nouns from this list: garden, relaxation, consternation, orchids, ledger
   (7)

3. Write the collective nouns from this list: litter, bouquet, pedal, celery, brood
   (7)

For sentences 4 and 5, write each noun and label it *C* for concrete or *A* for abstract.

4. Emily Dickinson wrote poems filled with humor and originality.
   (5, 7)

5. However, her life was full of unhappiness and disappointment.
   (7)

6. Write each collective noun from this sentence: In 1890, Emily's sister compiled a collection of Emily's poems.
   (7)

Choose the best word to complete sentences 7–9.

7. Although early historians once considered Edward Dickinson, Emily's father, a (macron, macrofossil, misoneist), newly discovered letters reveal a flexible father and husband.
   (2, 7)

8. Emily's loneliness at Mount Holyoke Female Seminary was only (human, humane, adept).
   (1, 3)

9. The intellectual (climactic, climate, macrocosm) of the Dickinson home encouraged Emily to pursue poetry.
   (2, 6)

For 10–12, replace each blank with the singular present tense form of the verb.

10. Ministers preach. A minister _____.
    (4, 6)

11. Doorbells buzz. A doorbell _____.
    (4, 6)

12. Puddles muddy shoes. A puddle _____ shoes.
    (4, 6)

For 13–15, replace each blank with the past tense form of the verb.

13. A gnat (talk) _____ to a bull.
(4, 6)

14. He (try) _____ to apologize to the bull for
(4, 6) bothering him.

15. Finally, the gnat (rap) _____ on the bull's horn to
(4, 6) get his attention.

For 16–19, write each proper noun that requires capitalization.

16. Was edward dickinson really reminiscent of the original
(5) new england puritans?

17. The *springfield republican* printed some of emily
(5) dickinson's poems.

18. Her poem "i'm nobody" playfully describes a frog.
(5)

19. On may 15, 1886, at the age of fifty-five, emily dickinson
(5) died in amherst, massachusetts.

For 20 and 21, choose the correct verb form.

20. A gnat buzzes around the head of a bull for several
(4, 6) minutes, and then it (lands, landed) on the bull's horn.

21. Now, the gnat (apologizes, apologized), for he does not
(4, 6) wish to disturb the bull.

22. Rewrite and correct this run-on sentence: The gnat says
(1, 3) that he is sorry for causing the bull any inconvenience he
will be off the horn in a moment.

23. Make a complete sentence from this sentence
(1, 3) fragment: Is making a formal apology to the bull.

For 24–26, write whether each expression is a sentence fragment, run-on sentence, or complete sentence:

24. The gnat thinks that his weight will bother the bull of
(1, 3) course it won't.

25. The bull has not noticed the tiny gnat.
(1, 3)

26. The gnat's inflated ego, or his erroneous perception of his
(1, 3) own size and importance.

Diagram the simple subject and simple predicate of sentences 27 and 28.

27. Does the bull answer the foolish, self-absorbed gnat?
(2, 4)

28. Have you heard this story before?
(2, 4)

For 29 and 30, tell whether the sentence is declarative, interrogative, imperative, or exclamatory.

29. The fable teaches, "The smaller the mind, the greater the
(1) conceit."

30. Does the gnat understand this moral?
(1)

LESSON 8

Helping Verbs

Helping Verbs   We know that every predicate contains a verb. Sometimes, the verb is more than one word in the sentence. The main verb may have one or more **helping verbs.** The main verb shows the action; the helping verbs do not show action, but they help to form the verb tense.

> You <u>might have wondered</u> about the origin of teddy bears.

In the sentence above, "wondered" is the main verb, and "might" and "have" are helping verbs. "Might have wondered" is the entire verb phrase.

Memorize these common helping verbs:

is, am, are, was, were, be, being, been,

has, have, had, may, might, must,

can, could, do, does, did,

shall, will, should, would

Example   Write the entire verb phrase and underline the helping verbs in these sentences.

was invented

(a) The toy bear, or teddy bear, <u>was</u> invented by Margarete Steiff in Germany.

had used

(b) Margarete Steiff <u>had used</u> leftover material for the bear.

must have wanted

(c) Other children in the village <u>must have wanted</u> rag bears too.

may have marketed

(d) Margarete's brother, Richard Steiff, <u>may have</u> marketed these bears in the United States.

Solution   (a) <u>**was** invented</u> ("Was" is a helping verb for the main verb "invented.")

(b) <u>had</u> **used**

(c) <u>must</u> <u>have</u> **wanted**

(d) <u>may</u> <u>have</u> **marketed**

Practice   **a.** Study the helping verbs listed in this lesson. Memorize them one line at a time. Practice saying them *in order* (perhaps to your teacher or friend). Then write as many as you can from memory.

For sentences b–e, write the entire verb phrase and underline the helping verbs.

has served

   b. Only one Catholic priest <u>has</u> served in Congress.

had been elected

   c. Father Gabriel Richard <u>had been</u> elected by the people of the Territory of Michigan in 1823.

might have been hoping

   d. Father Richard <u>might have been</u> hoping for two terms in Congress.

must have dissappointed

   e. His defeat in the election for a second term <u>must have</u> disappointed him.

For f–i, replace each blank with the correct vocabulary word.

   f. Great Britain remains a strong _____ of the United States.

   g. Please park your cars in the _____ behind the house.

   h. Trying to knock down all ten pins, a bowler rolls his ball down a long _____.

   i. Lucy's most dependable _____ is her husband.

More Practice   See Master Worksheets.

Review set 8   **1.** Write from memory the common helping verbs listed in
(8)   this lesson. Check your list by referring to the lesson.

For 2–6, write the entire verb phrase and underline each helping verb.

2. Theodore Dreiser was born into a poor German family.
(4, 8)

3. Shall I read more about Theodore Dreiser?
(4, 8)

4. The family must have suffered cold and hunger.
(4, 8)

5. Did Theodore Dreiser begin his career as a newspaper
(4, 8) reporter?

6. Some people might have objected to his novels.
(4, 8)

For 7 and 8, write and capitalize each proper noun.

7. By the end of april, we shall have read *an american*
(5, 7) *tragedy,* by theodore dreiser.

8. In 1930, dreiser received a nobel prize in literature.
(5, 7)

For 9–11, write whether the expression is a complete sentence, a sentence fragment, or a run-on sentence.

9. Please read "The Goose Who Laid the Golden Eggs."
(1, 3)

10. A poor farmer and his wife selling eggs and butter.
(1, 3)

11. This would hardly support them they struggled to
(1, 3) survive.

For 12 and 13, replace each blank with the singular present tense form of the verb.

12. They worry. The wife _____.
(4, 6)

13. You miss the boat. She _____ the boat.
(4, 6)

For 14 and 15, replace each blank with the past tense form of the verb.

14. A miracle (occur) _____ as they gathered eggs.
(4, 6)

15. Unfortunately, greed (trap) _____ them in its
(4, 6) snare.

For 16–19, write whether the noun is concrete or abstract.

16. egg   **17.** greed   **18.** gold   **19.** miracle
(7)   *(7)*   *(7)*   *(7)*

20. Choose the correct verb form for this sentence:
(4, 6) Last night, they (collect, collected) a particularly heavy egg from the goose.

21. Rewrite and correct this run-on sentence:
(1, 3)　　The egg was made of gold it made them rich.

22. Write each collective noun from this list: swarm, geese, (7) colony (ants), hens.

For 23–25, tell whether the sentence is declarative, exclamatory, imperative, or interrogatory.

23. The couple began wearing expensive clothes and hiring (1) servants.

24. Were they spending money wisely?
(1)

25. Beware of greed.
(1)

Diagram the simple subject and simple predicate of sentences 26 and 27.

26. The couple owed everyone money.
(2, 4)

27. Sadly, the goose was slaughtered for its golden eggs.
(2, 4)

Choose the best word to complete sentences 28–30.

28. The farmer was his wife's (alley, ally, macron) in a greedy (2, 8) scheme.

29. They did not (adopt, adapt, adept) well to the change in (1) their income.

30. We can easily see a (macrofossil, microfossil) with the (2) naked eye.

LESSON 9   Singular, Plural, Compound, and Possessive Nouns • Noun Gender

---

Dictation or Journal Entry

Vocabulary:

The prefix *ortho-* comes from the Greek language and means straight, upright, and vertical.

An *orthodontist* is a dentist who straightens teeth. The *orthodontist* straightened the girl's crooked teeth.

Orthograde, an adjective, means walking with the body upright or vertical. Human beings move in an *orthograde* manner.

Orthotics are supports or braces to straighten weak joints or muscles. The specialist gave the injured athlete *orthotics* to correct his weak ankles.

Singular or Plural   Nouns are either singular or plural. A **singular noun** names only one person, place, or thing. A **plural noun** names more than one person, place, or thing.

SINGULAR NOUNS	PLURAL NOUNS
wagon	wagons
wrench	wrenches
cliff	cliffs
hero	heroes

Example 1   Tell whether each noun is singular or plural.

(a) fax   (b) lashes   (c) chips

(d) pennies   (e) knee   (f) vacation

Solution   (a) **singular**   (b) **plural**   (c) **plural**

(d) **plural**   (e) **singular**   (f) **singular**

Compound   A noun made up of two or more words is a **compound noun.** Sometimes we write a compound noun as one word:

anybody, classroom, treetop

Often we write compound nouns as two words:

computer disk, cassette tape, snow tire

Other compound nouns are hyphenated:

jack-o-lantern, brother-in-law, over-the-counter

There is no pattern for determining whether to spell a compound noun as one word, two separate words, or one hyphenated word. We must use the dictionary.

Example 2   Write each compound noun from this list:

cell phone	hippopotamus	compact disk
great-aunt	basketball	encyclopedia

Solution   The compound nouns from the list above are **cell phone, compact disk, great-aunt,** and **basketball.**

Possessive   A **possessive noun** tells "who" or "what" owns something. Possessive nouns can be either singular or plural. The possessive form of nouns have an apostrophe and an *s* added to them:

a *doctor's* stethoscope   the *pier's* railing
the *surfer's* board   the *computer's* monitor
anybody's guess   a *box's* lid
someone's address   a *toddler's* mess
James's backpack   the *boss's* desk

Usually only an apostrophe is added to plural nouns when they end with the letter *s*:

the *Newkirks'* apartment   those *waitresses'* aprons
those *elephants'* trunks   these *nurses'* credentials
some *churches'* pews   the *bosses'* schedules

Example 3   Write the possessive noun from each sentence.

(a) The monkey's habit of searching through its hair is not to find fleas, lice, or other body parasites.

(b) Watching monkeys play added to the children's excitement.

(c) The boys' response was to behave like monkeys.

(d) The primates' antics entertain zoo curators.

Solution   (a) **monkey's**   (b) **children's**   (c) **boys'**   (d) **primates'**

Noun Gender   We also group nouns according to gender. In English there are four **genders:** Masculine, feminine, indefinite (either sex), and neuter (no sex). Below are examples of each gender of nouns.

MASCULINE	FEMININE	INDEFINITE	NEUTER
uncle	aunt	relative	bologna
brother	sister	sibling	socks
stallion	mare	horse	bicycle
buck	doe	deer	gasoline

Example 4 Tell whether each noun is masculine, feminine, indefinite, or neuter.

(a) paintbrush   (b) bull   (c) child   (d) hen

Solution   (a) **neuter**   (b) **masculine**   (c) **indefinite**   (d) **feminine**

Practice For a–d, tell whether each noun is singular or plural.

a. women   **b.** tangerine

c. Venus   **d.** boysenberries

e. Write each compound noun from this list:
briefcase   attorneys-at-law
undergraduate   university

Write each possessive noun from sentences f–i.

f. A brother-in-law is the brother of one's husband or wife.

g. Neither the rhinoceros's hide nor the hunter's windshield were bullet-proof.

h. The bridesmaids' dresses and the groomsmen's vests were maroon and blue plaid.

i. The men's breakfast included Mom's scrambled eggs, bacon, and country potatoes.

For j–m, tell whether each noun is masculine, feminine, indefinite, or neuter.

j. curtain   **k.** rooster   **l.** professor   **m.** daughter

Replace each blank with the correct vocabulary word to complete sentences n–q.

n. The dentist recommended that the patient see an _____ to straighten his teeth.

o. The prefix *ortho-* means _____, upright, or vertical.

p. One might wear _____ on their feet to correct falling arches.

q. A tiger does not walk in an _____ manner.

Review set 9

1. Write from memory the common helping verbs.
(8)

2. Write each plural noun from this list: urchin, aliens,
(9) autos, wrench

3. Write each compound noun from this list: hot air
(9) balloon, snorkel, soapbox, vehicle

4. Write each possessive noun from this sentence: My
(9) sister-in-law's ideas and my brother's illustrations made our family's scrap book very entertaining.

5. Write and correctly capitalize each proper noun in this
(5) sentence: "the mouse and the frog" is another of aesop's fables.

For 6–9, write whether the noun is masculine, feminine, indefinite, or neuter.

6. mouse   **7.** actress   **8.** water   **9.** son
(9)   (9)   (9)   (9)

For 10 and 11, write the entire verb phrase and underline each helping verb.

10. In "The Mouse and the Frog," a mouse will become
(4, 8) friendly with a frog.

11. The frog might extend friendship and hospitality to the
(4, 8) mouse.

Diagram the simple subject and simple predicate of sentences 12 and 13.

12. The sun has risen on an ill-fated day for the mouse.
(2, 4)

13. Into the pond leaps the frog.
(2, 4)

For 14–16, write whether the expression is a complete sentence, a sentence fragment, or a run-on sentence.

14. The frog ties the mouse's foot to its own hind leg this is to
(1, 3) keep the mouse safe.

15. Now, the frog is swimming across the pond and dragging
(1, 3) the mouse along behind.

16. Plunging to the bottom of the pond with the overly-
(1, 3) trusting mouse in tow.

17. Make a complete sentence from this sentence
(1, 3) fragment: Now, the drowning mouse attracting much attention.

18. Rewrite and correct this run-on sentence: A hungry
(1, 3) hawk spies the struggling mouse the hawk pounces on the mouse and carries it away.

For 19–21, tell whether the noun is concrete or abstract.

19. hawk   **20.** treachery   **21.** danger
(7)   *(7)*   *(7)*

22. Write each collective noun from this list:
(7)
armada   troop   frogs   mice

For 23 and 24, write whether the sentence is declarative, imperative, interrogative or exclamatory.

23. The mouse is still tied to the frog.
(1)

24. Aha, the frog suffers the same fate as the mouse!
(1)

Choose the best word to complete sentences 25–27.

25. A wide (ally, alley, macrocosm) between the buildings
(2, 8) provided access for emergency vehicles.

26. Michael waited on his surfboard for the perfect (waive,
(5) wave).

27. The (misogynistic, climactic, humane) man ignored all
(3, 7) the women.

For 28 and 29, write the singular present tense form of the verb.

28. Frogs catch flies. This frog _____ flies.
(4, 6)

29. Mice scurry. The mouse _____ .
(4, 6)

30. Replace the blank with the past tense form of the
(4, 6) verb: An old toad (nap) _____ in the sun.

LESSON 10

Future Tense

The **future tense** refers to action that has not yet occurred. The future tense is usually formed with the helping verbs *shall* or *will*. With the pronouns *I* and *we*, the use of *shall* is preferable in formal writing.

He *will* adapt.	We *shall* adapt.
They *will* wave.	I *shall* wave.
You *will* cooperate.	We *shall* cooperate.
Zachary *will* return.	She and I *shall* return.
Kayla *will* struggle.	We *shall* struggle.
Bruce and John *will* laugh.	I *shall* laugh.

Example 1   Complete the future tense verb form by replacing each blank with *will* or *shall*, as you would do in formal writing.

(a) I _____ research that topic.

(b) Rich _____ investigate previous members of Congress.

(c) The three Washburn brothers _____ remain famous for serving in Congress at the same time.

(d) We _____ never know for certain where houseflies go for the winter.

Solution   (a) I **shall** research that topic.

(b) Rich **will** investigate previous members of Congress.

(c) The three Washburn brothers **will** remain famous for serving in Congress at the same time.

(d) We **shall** never know for certain where houseflies go for the winter.

In informal writing, the helping verb *shall* is sometimes used with pronouns other than *I* and *we* in order to show strong emotion or to imply a threat or command.

You <u>shall</u> visit the doctor today.

He <u>shall</u> pay back every cent!

Andrea <u>shall</u> finish her homework before playing!

Errors to Avoid   Do not use the present for the future tense.

NO: Next week, I <u>give</u> my persuasive speech.
YES: Next week, I <u>shall give</u> my persuasive speech.

NO: They <u>finish</u> the project next month.
YES: They <u>will finish</u> the project next month.

NO: Later, they <u>announce</u> the winners of the contest.
YES: Later, they <u>will announce</u> the winner of the contest.

Example 2   Identify the following underlined verbs as present, past or future tense.

(a) A generation <u>lasts</u> thirty to thirty-three years.

(b) With a telescope, Galileo <u>discovered</u> sunspots, lunar mountains and valleys, and Jupiter's four largest satellites.

(c) Stars <u>revolve</u> around the centers of galaxies.

(d) <u>Will</u> you <u>explore</u> space through the huge Hale telescope on top of Mount Palomar in California?

Solution   (a) **present**   (b) **past**   (c) **present**   (d) **future**

Example 3   Write the correct form of the verb.

(a) Ralph (past of *study*) astronomy last semester.

(b) Tonight, we (future of *see*) the Little Dipper and the North Star.

(c) Astronauts (past of *land*) on the Moon.

(d) Light (present of *travel*) at the speed of about 300,000 kilometers per second.

Solution (a) Ralph **studied** astronomy last semester.

(b) Tonight, we **shall see** the Little Dipper and the North Star.

(c) Astronauts **landed** on the Moon.

(d) Light **travels** at the speed of about 300,000 kilometers per second.

Practice For sentences a–d, tell whether the underlined verb is present, past, or future tense.

a. We shall learn about the first flight across the Atlantic.

b. The United States Navy seaplane *NC-4* made the first trip across the Atlantic.

c. Shall I tell you the actual distance of the flight?

d. The distance between Rockaway, New York, and Plymouth, England, is 3,925 nautical miles.

For e–g, write the correct form of the verb.

e. Amelia Earhart and Charles Lindbergh (past of *share*) a love for flying.

f. Someday, I (future of *enjoy*) flying.

g. In flight school, a student (present of *learn*) all about the instrument panel of the aircraft.

For h–k, replace each blank with *will* or *shall*, as you would do in formal writing, in order to complete the future tense form of the verb.

h. Jeff _____ supervise the trainees.

i. I _____ adopt two tortoises next month.

j. _____ we change our names?

k. In your science class, you _____ examine a glass prism splitting light into its primary colors.

For l–o, replace each blank with the correct vocabulary word.

   l. The new _____ written by the school governing board states that all students must wear uniforms.

   m. The man's tall _____ made him stand out in the crowd.

   n. In the park stood a marble _____ of an early pioneer.

   o. The spectators were amazed by Bobo the elephant's imposing _____.

More Practice   See "Slapstick Story #1" with Master Worksheets.

Review set 10   For 1–3, write the verb phrase and indicate whether it is past, present, or future tense.

   1. The frog's treachery against the mouse caused the frog's
(6, 10) own downfall.

   2. Lamar chooses "The Monkey and the Camel" as his
(6, 10) favorite fable.

   3. We shall read "The Monkey and the Camel" for
(6, 10) homework.

For 4–6, write the correct form of the italicized verb.

   4. The animals (future of *convene*) for a great meeting.
(8, 10)

   5. A monkey (past of *dance*) for entertainment at the
(4, 6) meeting.

   6. The audience (present of *applaud*) the monkey's
(4, 6) performance.

For 7 and 8, replace each blank with *will* or *shall* to complete the future tense form of the verb.

   7. We _____ observe the jealousy of the camel.
(10)

   8. The monkey _____ receive praise for dancing.
(10)

For sentences 9 and 10, write each noun and label it singular or plural.

9. The envious camel is dancing.
(9)

10. The beasts shake their heads and laugh.
(9)

For 11–14, write each noun and label it feminine, masculine, indefinite, or neuter.

11. The camel is driven away. **12.** A bull laughs.
(9)   (9)

13. A lioness jeers.   **14.** The meeting adjourns.
(9)   (9)

15. Write the possessive noun in this sentence: Indeed, the
(9) camel's dance seems ridiculous.

16. Write the compound noun in this sentence: His phony
(9) behavior brings his downfall.

17. From memory, write the twenty-three helping verbs.
(8)

18. Write the entire verb phrase from this sentence, and
(4, 8) underline each helping verb.

O. Henry has become one of the most famous pseudonyms in American literature.

Diagram the simple subject and simple predicate of sentences 19 and 20.

19. O. Henry's real name was William Sydney Porter.
(2, 4)

20. Might Nam have known him?
(2, 4)

21. Choose the correct verb form for this sentence: When he
(4, 6) was fifteen, O. Henry (works, worked) in a drugstore.

22. Write whether this expression is a sentence fragment,
(1, 3) run-on sentence, or complete sentence: Displaying an interesting snake in a bottle of alcohol.

23. Rewrite and correct this run-on sentence: O. Henry's
(1, 3) father was a well-known physician he often treated the poor for free.

For sentences 24 and 25, write each noun and label it concrete or abstract.

24. O. Henry pitched horseshoes for fun.
(7)

25. This man also found enjoyment in books.
(7)

26. Write and capitalize each proper noun from this
(5) sentence: Next tuesday, in gramercy park, new york, mr. bigglesworth will reveal the details of o. henry's personal life.

27. Unscramble these words to make an interrogative
(1) sentence.

> failure   life   a   his   was

Choose the best word to complete sentences 28–30.

28. The prefix (*miso-*, *ortho-*, *macro-*) means straight and
(7, 9) upright.

29. A misogamist (loves, hates, desires) marriage.
(7)

30. Climactic refers to the (weather, climax, climate).
(6)

LESSON 11

Capitalization: Sentence, Pronoun *I*, Poetry

Dictation or Journal Entry

Vocabulary:

The Greek prefix *caco-* means something bad or vile.

Cacography is bad handwriting or spelling. The writer's *cacography* was impossible to read.

Cacophony is disagreeable or discordant sound. Hundreds of parrots created a *cacophony* of squawking in the pecan tree.

The reasons for capitalizing words are many. Since proper nouns name a specific person, place, or thing, we capitalize them. We also remember that a common noun linked with a proper noun requires a capital letter. For example, the word "boulevard" is capitalized in "Hollywood Boulevard."

However, little words such as *a*, *of*, *the*, *an*, and *in* are not capitalized when they are part of a proper noun (as in the United States of America).

Now, we will learn more about capitalization.

First word of every sentence   The **first word of every sentence** requires a capital letter.

> The practice of giving certain gifts on designated wedding anniversaries began in Germany.
>
> The silver anniversary occurs after twenty-five years.
>
> The golden anniversary marks fifty years of marriage.

The pronoun *I*   The **pronoun *I*** is always capitalized, no matter where it is placed in the sentence.

> I shall carve a statue of magnificent stature!
>
> Shall I call the orthodontist about my crooked teeth?
>
> No one needs orthotics as much as I.

First word in a line of poetry   The **first words of each line in most poetry** are usually capitalized. For example, Ogden Nash writes the following:

> The Panther is like a leopard,
> Except it hasn't been peppered.
> Should you behold a panther crouch,
> Prepare to say Ouch.
> Better yet, if called by a panther,
> Don't anther.

However, some poets, for effect, purposely do not capitalize the first words of every line of their poetry. For example, Myra Cohn Livingston writes this poem:

> Jennifer's my other name
> (It's make-believe
> and just a game.)
> I'm really Anne,
> But just the same
> I'd much
> much
> rather
> have a name
> like Jennifer
> (So, if you can
> don't call me Anne.)

Example Write each word that is missing a capital letter in these sentences.

(a) Cape Morris K. Jesup, i believe, is the most northern point of land.

(b) this cape is located on the northeastern extremity of Greenland.

(c) Eve Miriam capitalized the first word of each line in her poem, "Me Myself and I":

> isn't it strange
> that however i change,
> i still keep on being me.

Solution (a) The pronoun *I* is capitalized in this sentence.

(b) We capitalize the first word of every sentence, so we write, "This cape is located on the northeastern extremity of Greenland."

(c) We capitalize the first word of each line of the poem as well as the pronoun *I,* so we write,

> Isn't it strange
> That however **I** change,
> **I** still keep on being me.

Practice Write each word that should be capitalized in a–c.

    a. Rules for capitalization, i think, are easier than rules for punctuation.

    b. fright causes hair to rise, especially on cats.

    c. Dorothy Aldis follows traditional capitalization rules in her poem "Everybody Says":

> everybody says
> i look just like my mother.
> everybody says
> i'm the image of Aunt Bee.
> everybody says
> my nose is like my father's
> but i want to look like me.

Replace each blank with the correct word to complete sentences d–f.

    d. The Greek prefix *caco-* means _____ or vile.

    e. An example of _____ is a noisy cat fight.

    f. The pharmacist could not read the patient's prescription because of the physician's _____.

Review set
11

For 1–3, write each word that should be capitalized.

    1. Emily Dickinson capitalized the first word in each line of
    (11) her verses. Here are some familiar lines from "I'm Nobody":

> how dreary—to be—Somebody!
> how public—like a Frog—
> to tell one's name—the livelong June—
> to an admiring Bog!

    2. shall i read aesop's "the fox and the mask"?
    (5, 11)

    3. a fox breaks into the home of an actor.
    (11)

For 4–6, write the verb phrase and name its tense as present, past, or future.

4. The fox rummages through the actor's belongings.
(6, 10)

5. Finally, he encountered the mask of a human head.
(6, 10)

6. Will the fox appear wise with this mask on his face?
(6, 10)

For 7–9, write the correct form of the verb.

7. He (present of *wish*) to give intelligent advice.
(6)

8. I (future of *remember*) the fox's words.
(10)

9. Unfortunately, the mask (present of *lack*) brains.
(6)

For 10 and 11, write each noun and label it singular or plural.

10. The mask looks truly remarkable.
(9)

11. Looks are worthless without good sense.
(9)

For 12 and 13, write each noun and label it masculine, feminine, neuter, or indefinite.

12. The fine-looking mask proves worthless.
(9)

13. Does the fox demonstrate wisdom?
(9)

For 14 and 15, replace each blank with the singular present tense form of the verb.

14. Athletes pass footballs. Lucy _____ a football.
(6)

15. People wax their cars. Lucy _____ her car.
(6)

16. Write the compound noun from this list:
(9)
        saxophone   mother-in-law   brontosaurus

17. Write the possessive noun from this sentence: Mr.
(9) Smith's dog won a blue ribbon in the purebred class at the local fair.

18. From memory, write the twenty-three helping verbs from
(8) Lesson 8.

For 19 and 20, write the entire verb phrase and underline each helping verb.

19. After the fair, Mr. Smith had achieved respect for mixed
(4, 8) breed dogs.

20. He may have decided to adopt a homeless pup.
(4, 8)

Diagram the simple subject and simple predicate of sentences 21–23.

21. Jack London was the Prince of the Oyster Pirates in San
(2, 4) Francisco Bay.

22. Did pirates steal oysters from privately owned oyster
(2, 4) beds?

23. With borrowed money, Jack had purchased a tall-masted
(2, 4) sailing sloop.

24. Make a complete sentence from this sentence fragment:
(1, 3)   The tall-masted sailing sloop.

For 25 and 26, write each noun and label it concrete or abstract.

25. French Frank was another pirate who stole oysters.
(7)

26. Youth and success gave Jack London popularity.
(7)

27. Unscramble these words to make an imperative
(1, 3) sentence:

        oysters   not   do   steal

Choose the best word to complete sentences 28–30.

28. The camel was not (adept, adapt, adopt) at dancing.
(1)

29. Walking in an *orthograde* manner means walking with
(9) the body (horizontal, upright, bent).

30. A (statue, stature, statute) is a rule or law.
(10)

LESSON 12

Irregular Plural Nouns, Part 1

Dictation or Journal Entry

Vocabulary:
Let us examine the words *confidently* and *confidentially*. Although similar in spelling, they differ in meaning.

Confidently means to do something with full assurance or strong belief. The computer technician *confidently* took apart the computer to fix the problem.

Confidentially, however, means secretly or privately. The doctor spoke *confidentially* to the nurse about the patient's illness.

Plural Nouns

We never form a plural with an apostrophe. In most cases, we make a singular noun plural by adding an *s*.

SINGULAR	PLURAL
face	faces
truth	truths
form	forms
mistake	mistakes

Irregular Forms

Some nouns have irregular plural forms. We must learn these. We add *es* to a singular noun ending in the following letters: *s, sh, ch, x, z.*

SINGULAR	PLURAL
watch	watches
glass	glasses
Agnes	Agneses
Perez	Perezes
tax	taxes
rash	rashes
Baltz	Baltzes

We add an *s* when a singular noun ends with *ay, ey, oy,* or *uy.*

SINGULAR	PLURAL
tray	trays
turkey	turkeys
buoy	buoys
guy	guys

We change *y* to *i* and add *es* when a singular noun ends in a consonant plus *y*, unless it is someone's name.

SINGULAR	PLURAL
library	libraries
reply	replies
sky	skies
penny	pennies
Jenny	Jennys

Example   For a–p, write the plural form of each singular noun.

(a) rug   (b) patch   (c) box   (d) ray

(e) guess   (f) drawer   (g) party   (h) bush

(i) alley   (j) boy   (k) waltz   (l) fracas

(m) buy   (n) worry   (o) toss   (p) Jerry

Solution   (a) **rugs** (regular)   (b) **patches** (ends in *ch*)

(c) **boxes** (ends in *x*)   (d) **rays** (ends in *ay*)

(e) **guesses** (ends in *ss*)   (f) **drawers** (regular)

(g) **parties** (ends in consonant plus *y*)

(h) **bushes** (ends in *sh*)   (i) **alleys** (ends in *ey*)

(j) **boys** (ends in *oy*)   (k) **waltzes** (ends in *z*)

(l) **fracases** (ends in *s*)   (m) **buys** (ends in *uy*)

(n) **worries** (ends in consonant plus *y*)

(o) **tosses** (ends in *ss*)   (p) **Jerrys** (someone's name)

Practice   For a and b, replace each blank with the correct vocabulary word.

a. The courageous student spoke _____ in front of the class.

b. He whispered _____ that he had declared bankruptcy and moved to another state.

For c–r, write the plural form of each singular noun.

    c. play   **d.** rope   **e.** donkey   **f.** slash

    g. decoy   **h.** pass   **i.** tricycle   **j.** pantry

    k. crutch   **l.** fax   **m.** cherry   **n.** box

    o. body   **p.** mystery   **q.** Larry   **r.** Mary

More Practice

Write the plural of each singular noun.

    1. watch   **2.** way   **3.** country   **4.** inch

    5. birthday   **6.** jelly   **7.** church   **8.** play

    9. Nancy   **10.** fox   **11.** holiday   **12.** Freddy

    13. wrench   **14.** delay   **15.** Monty   **16.** perch

    17. monkey   **18.** Allison   **19.** grass   **20.** blue jay

    21. Tommy   **22.** ax   **23.** finch   **24.** pony

    25. Debby   **26.** miss   **27.** summary   **28.** prefix

    29. suffix   **30.** journey   **31.** discovery **32.** fly

Review set 12

For 1–4, write the plural of each singular noun.

    1. key   **2.** Cindy   **3.** torch   **4.** stencil
    (9, 12)   *(9, 12)*   *(9, 12)*   *(9, 12)*

    5. Write each concrete noun from this list: fears, pears,
    (7, 9) hopes, ropes, truths, booths, beliefs, trees, thoughts, cots

For 6–8, replace each blank with the singular present tense form of the verb.

    6. Peng and Eng box. Weng _____.
    (4, 6)

    7. Marika and Emika comply. Mika _____.
    (4, 6)

    8. Artists paint. An artist _____.
    (4, 6)

For 9–11, write the past tense of each verb.

    9. whip   **10.** crash   **11.** pry
    (4, 6)   *(4, 6)*   *(4, 6)*

    12. Write each possessive noun from this list: cats, cat's,
    (9, 12) grooms, groom's, ladies, ladies', lady's, Wallys, Wally's

13. Write whether the following sentence is a complete
(1, 3) sentence, run-on sentence, or sentence fragment.

   Speaking to me confidentially in a hushed voice.

14. Write each word that should be capitalized in this
(5, 11) sentence:

   last tuesday, i read louisa may alcott's poem about
   spring, "to the first robin."

For 15–17, write the verb phrase and tell whether it is
present, past, or future tense.

15. I shall read "The Cat and the Bell," one of Aesop's
(8, 10) fables.

16. Sometimes mice live in haylofts.
(4, 6)

17. A group of mice discussed the farmer's cat.
(4, 6)

For 18–20, write the correct form of the verb.

18. A cat generally (present of *torment*) mice.
(4, 6)

19. We (future of *discuss*) the experiences of the hayloft
(8, 10) mice.

20. The farmer's cat (past of *trap*) the mice inside.
(4, 6)

21. Write the collective noun from this sentence: A group of
(7) mice found the perfect solution for a problematic cat.

22. Write the noun from this sentence that is indefinite in
(9) gender: Was the cat a tom or a female?

23. Write the compound noun from this sentence: Did the
(9) hayloft provide a safe haven for the community of mice?

24. From memory, write the twenty-three helping verbs from
(8) Lesson 8.

25. Diagram the simple subject and simple predicate of this
(2, 4) sentence:

   One mouse had been thinking of the perfect solution.

26. Rewrite the following run-on sentence, using a period
(1, 3)   and a capital letter to correct it: The mice discussed many different plans then they decided to tie a bell around the cat's neck.

27. Write the abstract noun from this sentence: The mouse's
(7)   brilliance astounded the other mice.

Choose the best word to complete sentences 28–30.

28. With a loud voice, the young mouse (confidently,
(12)   confidentially) announced his idea.

29. However, a wise old mouse spoke (confidentially,
(12)   confidently) and quietly to another mouse, saying that it is easy to think of impossible solutions.

30. The prefix (*miso-*, *caco-*, *ortho-*) means bad or vile.
(9, 11)

LESSON
13

Irregular Plural Nouns, Part 2

Dictation or Journal Entry

Vocabulary:
The prefix *eu-* means "good."

Euphony is pleasant or harmonious sound. The euphony of Mozart's music appeals to many.

Euphoria is a feeling of well-being or elation. Theresa felt *euphoria* when her little sister was born.

A *eulogy* is a written or spoken commendation of a person or thing. Often, it is a tribute to a deceased person. A minister or friend may give a *eulogy* at a funeral.

We continue our study of plural nouns.

Irregular Forms   Some singular nouns change completely in their plural forms.

SINGULAR	PLURAL
child	children
goose	geese
octopus	octopi
vertebra	vertebrae
man	men
woman	women

Other nouns are the same in their singular and plural forms.

SINGULAR	PLURAL
sheep	sheep
deer	deer
trout	trout

Dictionary   When we are uncertain, it is very important that we use a dictionary to check plural forms. If the plural form of the noun is regular (only add *s* to the singular noun), then the dictionary will not list it. Sometimes the dictionary will list two plural forms for a noun. The first one listed is the preferred one. (Example: vertebra *n., pl.* vertebrae, vertebras)

Example 1   Write the plural form of each of the following singular nouns. Use a dictionary if you are in doubt.

(a) gentleman   (b) mouse   (c) trout   (d) syllabus

Solution   (a) **gentlemen** (irregular form) (b) **mice** (irregular form)

(c) We check the dictionary and find that the plural of trout is **trout.**

(d) We check the dictionary and find that the preferable plural for syllabus is **syllabi.**

Nouns Ending in *f, ff, fe* For most nouns ending in *f, ff,* and *fe,* we add *s* to form the plural.

SINGULAR	PLURAL
cliff	cliffs
roof	roofs
safe	safes

However, for some nouns ending in *f,* and *fe,* we change the *f* to *v* and add *es.*

SINGULAR	PLURAL
scarf	scarves
life	lives
elf	elves

Nouns Ending in *o* We usually add *s* to form the plurals of nouns ending in *o,* especially if they are musical terms.

SINGULAR	PLURAL
soprano	sopranos
solo	solos
alto	altos
piano	pianos
banjo	banjos
radio	radios

However, the following are important exceptions:

SINGULAR	PLURAL
hobo	hoboes
tomato	tomatoes
mango	mangoes
potato	potatoes
torpedo	torpedoes
mosquito	mosquitoes
echo	echoes

...and many more!

Since there are many more exceptions, we must check the dictionary to be sure of the correct spelling.

Example 2   Write the plural form of each singular noun. Use the dictionary if you are unsure.

(a) waif   (b) tangelo   (c) leaf   (d) piccolo

Solution   (a) **waifs** (word ending in *f*)

(b) **tangelos** (We check the dictionary and find that the plural of tangelo is not irregular, so we just add an *s*.)

(c) We check the dictionary and find that the plural of leaf is **leaves.**

(d) **piccolos** (musical term)

Compound Nouns   We make the main element plural in a compound noun.

SINGULAR	PLURAL
daughter-in-law	daughters-in-law
attorney-at-law	attorneys-at-law
bellman	bellmen
maid-of-honor	maids-of-honor
power of attorney	powers of attorney
justice of the peace	justices of the peace
Prince of Wales	Princes of Wales
songbird	songbirds

Nouns Ending in *ful*   We form the plurals of nouns ending in *ful* by adding an *s* at the end of the word.

SINGULAR	PLURAL
plateful	platefuls
earful	earfuls

Example 3   Write the plural form of each of the following singular nouns. Use a dictionary if you are in doubt.

(a) teaspoonful   (b) commander in chief

Solution   (a) **teaspoonfuls** (word ending in *ful*)

(b) **commanders in chief** (compound noun)

Practice   For a–l, write the plural form of each singular noun. Use the dictionary if you are in doubt.

    a. cupful   **b.** brother-in-law   **c.** handkerchief

    d. hoof   **e.** vermin   **f.** ox

    g. goose   **h.** tooth   **i.** soprano

    j. tomato   **k.** wolf   **l.** half

For m–o, replace each blank with the correct vocabulary word.

    m. The fans experienced _____, or elation, when their team swept the playoffs.

    n. The sopranos, altos, and tenors blended in a _____ of harmonious voices.

    o. The President spoke a _____ honoring those who had died in the war.

More Practice   Write the plural of each noun.

    1. thief   **2.** wife   **3.** shelf   **4.** knife

    5. calf   **6.** foot   **7.** cactus   **8.** louse

    9. sheep   **10.** man   **11.** handful   **12.** woman

   13. child   **14.** mouse   **15.** goose   **16.** cupful

   17. life   **18.** loaf   **19.** piano   **20.** potato

   21. sister-in-law   **22.** gentleman

Review set 13   For 1–8, write the plural form for each singular noun.

    1. cartful   **2.** counselor-at-law
    (12, 13)   *(12, 13)*

    3. portfolio   **4.** fungus
    (12, 13)   *(12, 13)*

    5. donkey   **6.** arch
    (12, 13)   *(12, 13)*

7. prefix
(12, 13)

8. raspberry
(12, 13)

For 9–11, tell whether each noun is feminine, masculine, indefinite, or neuter.

9. damsel   **10.** prince   **11.** castle
(9)   *(9)*   *(9)*

12. Write each abstract noun from this list: devotion, moat,
(7) chivalry, flag, javelin

Choose the correct verb form for sentences 13 and 14.

13. Yesterday Annie Mae washed the car and (rinses, rinsed)
(4, 6) it with the hose.

14. Last night, she (cleans, cleaned) the garage too.
(4, 6)

For 15 and 16, replace the blank with the singular present tense form of the verb.

15. Monkeys munch on bananas. The monkey _____
(4, 6) on bananas.

16. Siti and Roesli fry bananas. Johnny _____
(4, 6) bananas.

17. Replace the blank with the past tense form of the
(4, 6) verb: The groomer (snip) _____ the dog's nails too
short.

18. Write each possessive noun from this list: orthodontists',
(9) orthodontist's, orthodontists, sisters, sisters', sister's,
monkey's, monkeys

19. Write each word that should be capitalized in the
(5, 11) sentence below.

edgar allen poe's poem "annabel lee" begins, "it was
many and many a year ago, in a kingdom by the
sea..."

For 20–22, write the correct form of the verb.

20. In Aesop's "The Bull and the Bullfrog," a young bullfrog
(4, 6) (present of *explore*) the far end of a pond.

21. The bullfrog (future of *meet*) a bull drinking water from
(8, 10) the pond.

22. The bull's size (past of *amaze*) the bullfrog.
(4, 6)

23. Write the collective noun from this sentence: An army of
(7) frogs would not equal the size of this bull!

24. Write whether this expression is a sentence fragment,
(3) run-on sentence, or complete sentence: The old bullfrog
took big gulps of air this puffed him up.

Diagram the simple subject and simple predicate of sentences
25 and 26.

25. Did the old bullfrog grow as big as the bull?
(2, 4)

26. He may have exploded from all that puffing!
(2, 4)

Choose the best word to complete sentences 27–30.

27. At the end of this fable, the young bullfrog might have
(11, 13) given a (cacophony, eulogy, macrocosm) for the old
bullfrog.

28. A (stature, statute, statue) prohibited dogs from being off-
(10) leash on the beaches.

29. A cacophony is a (melodic, discordant, pleasant) sound.
(11)

30. Misoneism is the (love, hatred, opposite) of change.
(7)

LESSON 14

Irregular Verbs, Part 1: *To Be, Have, Do*

Dictation or Journal Entry

Vocabulary:

Notice the difference between the verbs *allude* and *elude*.

Allude means to refer to something indirectly or casually. The clerk's letter of resignation only *alluded* to his illness as a reason for leaving.

Elude means to escape by trickery, speed, or cleverness. The fugitive *eluded* the police for many days.

To be, have, and *do* are three of the most frequently used verbs in the English language. The tenses of these verbs are irregular; they do not fit the pattern of the regular verbs. Therefore, we must memorize them now if we have not done so already.

Points of View   Verb forms often change according to three points of view: First person (*I* or *we*), second person (*you*), and third person (*he, she, it, they,* and singular or plural nouns). Below are charts showing the verb forms of *to be, have,* and *do*.

To Be

	PRESENT		PAST	
	SINGULAR	PLURAL	SINGULAR	PLURAL
1ST PERSON	I <u>am</u>	we <u>are</u>	I <u>was</u>	we <u>were</u>
2ND PERSON	you <u>are</u>	you <u>are</u>	you <u>were</u>	you <u>were</u>
3RD PERSON	he <u>is</u>	they <u>are</u>	he <u>was</u>	they <u>were</u>

Have

	PRESENT		PAST	
	SINGULAR	PLURAL	SINGULAR	PLURAL
1ST PERSON	I <u>have</u>	we <u>have</u>	I <u>had</u>	we <u>had</u>
2ND PERSON	you <u>have</u>	you <u>have</u>	you <u>had</u>	you <u>had</u>
3RD PERSON	he <u>has</u>	they <u>have</u>	he <u>had</u>	they <u>had</u>

Do

	PRESENT		PAST	
	SINGULAR	PLURAL	SINGULAR	PLURAL
1ST PERSON	I <u>do</u>	we <u>do</u>	I <u>did</u>	we <u>did</u>
2ND PERSON	you <u>do</u>	you <u>do</u>	you <u>did</u>	you <u>did</u>
3RD PERSON	he <u>does</u>	they <u>do</u>	he <u>did</u>	they <u>did</u>

Example   Complete each sentence with the correct form of the verb.

(a) Even a small galaxy (present of *have*) billions of stars.

(b) Long ago, Arab shepherds (past of *to be*) fearful of the winking star, *Algol*.

(c) I (present of *to be*) keenly interested in pulsar stars, which send out beams of radio waves at regular intervals.

(d) We (past of *have*) studied the movements of snakes.

(e) How (present of *do*) the snake propel itself?

(f) They (past of *do*) not see the rattlesnake in the path ahead.

Solution   (a) Even a small galaxy **has** billions of stars.

(b) Long ago, Arab shepherds **were** fearful of the winking star, *Algol*.

(c) I **am** keenly interested in pulsar stars, which send out beams of radio waves at regular intervals.

(d) We **had** studied the movements of snakes.

(e) How **does** the snake propel itself?

(f) They **did** not see the rattlesnake in the path ahead.

Practice   Write the correct verb form to complete sentences a–f.

a. Indian summer (present of *to be*) the name given in America to mild, calm weather occurring in the fall.

b. Old wives' tales (past of *have*) claimed that Indian summer followed a spell of wintry weather called squaw winter.

c. Sheung and Ting (past of *to be*) not familiar with the term Indian summer.

d. In 1978, the Einstein Observatory satellite (past of *to be*) launched into space.

e. The planet Jupiter (present of *have*) many satellites.

f. (present of *Do*) light take some time to travel?

For g–j, replace each blank with *allude* or *elude.*

g. Sometimes a mouse can _____ a cat for a long time.

h. Although they don't call him a liar, they _____ to his dishonesty.

i. Will the rabbit be able to _____ the fox?

j. If you refer to something indirectly, you _____ to it.

More Practice   Choose the correct verb form for each sentence.

1. Mrs. Yu (do, does) fifty sit-ups every morning.

2. Jupiter (have, has) at least twenty-eight satellites.

3. Those macrofossils (was, were) huge!

4. (Do, Does) he give his dog humane treatment?

5. The main characters (was, were) humans, not animals.

6. We (was, were) studying the underwater macrocosm.

7. Under a microscope, they (was, were) examining microcosms of fungi and bacteria.

8. Ilbea and Jerry (is, are) waving from the cruise ship.

9. (Was, Were) you eluding the orthodontist yesterday?

10. (Was, Were) your brother with you?

11. Flora (have, has) an alley behind her house.

12. (Do, Does) Flora like this warm climate?

13. Flora is hinting; she (am, are, is) alluding to her fear of flying.

14. The desert climate (is, are) warm and dry.

15. I (are, is, am) waiting for a climactic ending of this basketball season.

16. A misogamist (have, has) a hatred of marriage.

17. We (have, has) many faithful allies around the world.

19. That ancient statue (do, does) not remind me of anyone in particular.

20. The old woman stooped; she (do, did) not have an orthograde posture.

Review set 14

For 1–3, write whether the sentence is declarative, imperative, interrogative, or exclamatory.

1. Has the old bullfrog gulped down too much air?
(1)

2. The ending of this fable astounds me!
(1)

3. Stretch your arm no farther than your sleeve will reach.
(1)

For 4–7, choose the correct form of the verb.

4. Some old bullfrogs (is, am, are) vain and ignorant.
(8, 14)

5. I believe that bullfrog (have, has) exploded.
(8, 14)

6. He (do, does) things for attention.
(8, 14)

7. They (was, were) shocked by his abrupt demise.
(8, 14)

Write the correct verb form for sentences 8–13.

8. Jack London (present of *to be*) still one of the most popular American writers around the world.
(8, 14)

9. By the age of fifteen, Jack London (past of *have*) a reputation for stealing oysters.
(8, 14)

10. Young Jack (present of *have*) an experience at sea that causes him to give up crime and drinking.
(8, 14)

11. His adventures at sea (past of *furnish*) him with material for his novel *The Sea Wolf*.
(4, 6)

12. Next week, we (future of *read*) Jack London's *The Call of the Wild*.
(4, 10)

13. Meg (present of *do*) each daily reading assignment.
(8, 14)

For 14–19, write the plural for each noun.

14. ferry
(12, 13)

15. tankful
(12, 13)

16. grotto
(12, 13)

17. roof
(12, 13)

18. hoof
(12, 13)

19. turnkey
(12, 13)

20. Replace the blank with the singular present tense form of
(4, 6) the verb: Dry winds parch throats. The dry wind
_____ throats.

21. Write the possessive noun from this sentence: The
(9) fairies' wings glistened in the moonlight.

22. Replace the blank with the past tense form of the verb.
(4, 6) The gymnast (flip) _____ off the trampoline.

23. Write each word that should be capitalized in this
(5, 11) sentence: edgar allen poe's poem "the raven" begins,
"once upon a midnight dreary, while i pondered, weak
and weary…"

24. Write the collective noun in this sentence: A cacophony
(7) of squawks came from a company of parrots flying
overhead.

25. Write each noun from the sentence below and label it
(9) masculine, feminine, neuter, or indefinite.

The child wandered aimlessly on the playground.

26. Diagram the simple subject and simple predicate of this
(2, 4) sentence: The bus had been waiting for me.

27. Write whether this expression is a sentence fragment,
(3) run-on sentence, or complete sentence: A young man of
much talent and ambition.

Choose the best word to complete sentences 28–30.

28. The prefix (*caco-, eu-, miso-*) means "good."
(11, 13)

29. The noise from crows might be a (eulogy, cacophony,
(11, 13) humane).

30. The artist carved a (stature, statue, statute) of a giant
(10) pelican.

LESSON 15

Four Principal Parts of Verbs

Dictation or Journal Entry

Vocabulary:
Notice the difference between the words *heresy* and *hypocrisy*.

Heresy is an opinion or doctrine that disagrees with the doctrine of a church or deviates from accepted beliefs or standards. The perceived *heresy* of Martin Luther infuriated the Roman Catholic Church.

Hypocrisy is pretending to follow religious, moral, upright, or virtuous beliefs when one does not really possess them. The treasurer's claim that he was guarding the funds was *hypocrisy*, for in reality he was embezzling money.

Four Principal Parts

Every verb has **four** basic forms, or **principal parts.** In order to form all the tenses of each verb, we need to learn these principal parts: (1) the verb, (2) the present participle, (3) the past, and (4) the past participle.

Present Tense

The first principal part is the singular verb in its **present tense** form, which is used to express *present time*, something that is *true at all times*, and *future time*:

adapt   elude   wave

Present Participle

The second principal part, the **present participle**, is used to form the progressive tenses (continuing action). The present participle is formed by adding *ing* to the singular verb. It is preceded by a form of the *to be* helping verb:

(is) adapting   (are) eluding   (is) waving

Past Tense

The third principal part of a verb, used to express *past time*, is the **past tense,** which we form by adding *ed* to most verbs.

adapted   eluded   waved

Past Participle

The fourth principal part of a verb, used to form the *perfect* tenses, is the **past participle.** It is preceded by a form of the *to have* helping verb. For regular verbs, the past and the past participle are the same.

PAST	PAST PARTICIPLE
adapted	(have) adapted
eluded	(has) eluded
waved	(have) waved

Example

Complete the chart by writing the second, third, and fourth principal parts (present participle, past tense, and past participle) of each verb.

VERB	PRESENT PARTICIPLE	PAST TENSE	PAST PARTICIPLE
adopt	(is) adopting	adopted	(has) adopted
(a) allude	_____	_____	_____
(b) waste	_____	_____	_____
(c) affect	_____	_____	_____
(d) trip	_____	_____	_____
(e) accept	_____	_____	_____

Solution

VERB	PRESENT PARTICIPLE	PAST TENSE	PAST PARTICIPLE
(a) allude	**(is) alluding**	**alluded**	**(has) alluded**
(b) waste	**(is) wasting**	**wasted**	**(has) wasted**
(c) affect	**(is) affecting**	**affected**	**(has) affected**
(d) trip	**(is) tripping**	**tripped**	**(has) tripped**
(e) accept	**(is) accepting**	**accepted**	**(has) accepted**

Practice   For a–e, complete the chart by writing the second, third, and fourth principal parts (present participle, past tense, and past participle) of each verb.

VERB	PRESENT PARTICIPLE	PAST TENSE	PAST PARTICIPLE
a. honor	_____	_____	_____
b. cry	_____	_____	_____
c. clip	_____	_____	_____
d. pitch	_____	_____	_____
e. substitute	_____	_____	_____

For f–h, replace each blank with *hypocrisy* or *heresy*.

f. Saying you have no money to help a needy family and then taking a luxurious vacation might be an example of _____.

g. A Christian, Jew, or Muslim who believed there was no God could be accused of _____.

h. Miss Gossip displayed _____ by heaping compliments on her guests while making sarcastic remarks about them behind their backs.

More Practice   Write the present participle, past tense, and past participle of each verb.

1. pour   **2.** adjust

3. maltreat   **4.** advise

5. learn   **6.** imply

7. pass   **8.** allow

9. pare   **10.** remember

Review set 15   For 1 and 2, write the present participle, past tense, and past participle for each verb.

1. waive   **2.** spot
(8, 15)   *(8, 15)*

For 3–10, choose the correct form of the verb.

3. I (is, am, are) now reading Aesop's "The Stag and His
(8, 14) Antlers."

4. The stag (is, am, are) admiring his own reflection in the
(8, 14) water.

5. They (is, am, are) such splendid antlers!
(8, 14)

6. (Have, Has) you ever seen antlers so large and so elegant?
(6, 14)

7. The stag (have, has) not yet discovered the importance of
(8, 14) usefulness rather than beauty.

8. (Do, Does) the stag appreciate his knobby knees and long,
(8, 14) thin legs?

(8, 14) **9.** (Do, Does) the hunters see the stag?

10. His fine antlers (was, were) now tangled in a tree.
(8, 14)

Write the entire verb phrase and underline each helping verb in sentences 11 and 12.

11. Hunters might have shot the entangled stag.
(4, 8)

12. In the end, however, the stag's long, thin legs will have
(4, 8) carried him to safety.

For 13–15, write the correct form of the verb.

13. I (future of *critique*) Mark Twain's *The Adventures of*
(4, 10) Huckleberry Finn.

14. This story (present of *look*) back to Mark Twain's
(4, 6) boyhood.

15. Mark Twain (present of *speak*) to and for the common
(4, 6) man.

For 16–19, write the plural of each singular noun.

16. cargo   **17.** Ramirez
(12, 13)   *(12, 13)*

18. wolf   **19.** steamboat
(12, 13)   *(12, 13)*

20. Write each word that should be capitalized in this
(5, 11) sentence: a famous restaurant called bamboo buffet, on
peck road in el monte, serves chinese fortune cookies.

21. Write each possessive noun in this list: antlers, antlers',
(7, 9) businessmen, businessman's, stags, stag's, stags'

22. Tell whether this expression is a complete sentence,
(1, 3) run-on sentence, or sentence fragment: An entire float of
crocodiles moved stealthily down the river I screamed.

23. Write each compound noun from this sentence: Mom
(9) appreciates her appliances, for her grandmother used a
washboard for the laundry.

24. Write each noun from the sentence below and label it
(9) masculine, feminine, neuter, or indefinite.

The protective red hen guarded her six chicks in the
coop.

Diagram the simple subject and simple predicate of sentences 25 and 26.

25. They should have been wearing their raincoats.
(2, 4)

26. Remember your umbrella.
(2, 4)

27. Tell whether this sentence is declarative, interrogative,
(1, 3) exclamatory, or imperative: After forty days, Noah sent out a raven from the ark that he had built.

Choose the best word to complete sentences 28–30.

28. A marble (statue, stature, statute) of a national hero
(10) guards the park's entrance.

29. Cacography is (proper, good, bad) handwriting or
(11) spelling.

30. Christina skated gracefully and (confidently,
(12) confidentially) over the ice.

LESSON 16

Simple Prepositions

Dictation or Journal Entry

Vocabulary:

The Greek root *mania* means passion or madness.

A *maniac* is a raving, insane person. The reckless driver drove like a *maniac*.

Megalomania is a mental disorder characterized by delusions of greatness and power. The patient's claim to be Julius Caesar was symptomatic of his *megalomania*.

Bibliomania is an excessive desire to possess or acquire books. *Bibliomania* attacks some avid readers.

Prepositions   **Prepositions** are words belonging to the part of speech that shows the relationship between a noun or pronoun and another word. Notice how a preposition (italicized) shows the relationship between a bug and the straw:

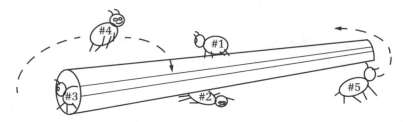

Bug #1 is *on* the straw. Bug #2 is *under* the straw. Bug #3 is *inside* the straw. Bug #4 is jumping *over* the straw. Bug #5 is walking *around* the straw.

Besides defining spatial relationships, prepositions also define temporal and abstract relationships. Below is a list of common prepositions.

aboard	because of	excepting	off	since
about	before	for	on	through
above	behind	from	on account of	throughout
according to	below	from among	on behalf of	till
across	beneath	from between	on top of	to
across from	beside	from under	onto	toward
after	besides	in	opposite	under
against	between	in addition to	out	underneath
along	beyond	in behalf of	out of	until
alongside	but	in front of	outside	unto
alongside of	by	in place of	outside of	up
along with	by means of	in regard to	over	up to
amid	concerning	in spite of	over to	upon
among	considering	inside	owing to	via
apart from	despite	inside of	past	with
around	down	into	prior to	within
aside from	down from	like	regarding	without
at	during	near	round	
away from	except	near to	round about	
back of	except for	of	save	

Simple Prepositions Notice that some prepositions in the list above are single words while others are groups of words. In this lesson we will learn to recognize single-word prepositions, **simple prepositions,** which we list alphabetically here. To help you memorize these, we list them in four columns.

1	2	3	4
aboard	*beside*	*inside*	*since*
about	*besides*	*into*	*through*
above	*between*	*like*	*throughout*
across	*beyond*	*near*	*till*
after	*but*	*of*	*to*
against	*by*	*off*	*toward*
along	*concerning*	*on*	*under*
alongside	*considering*	*onto*	*underneath*
amid	*despite*	*opposite*	*until*
among	*down*	*out*	*unto*
around	*during*	*outside*	*up*
at	*except*	*over*	*upon*
before	*excepting*	*past*	*via*
behind	*for*	*regarding*	*with*
below	*from*	*round*	*within*
beneath	*in*	*save*	*without*

Simple prepositions are underlined in the sentences below. Notice how they show the relationship between "find" and "islands."

Divers find abalone <u>around</u> islands.

Divers find abalone <u>near</u> islands.

A person, place, or thing always follows a preposition. We call this word the object of the preposition. In the first sentence, we see that *islands* is the object of the preposition *around.* In the second sentence, *islands* is the object of the preposition *near.* We will practice this concept more in a later lesson.

Example Underline each preposition in sentences a–c.

(a) White abalone are endangered throughout Southern and Baja California.

(b) Ninety-nine percent of abalone are eaten by predators during the larvae phase of development.

(c) All filter-feeding animals, from baleen whales to sea anemones, prey on white abalone.

Solution   (a) White abalone are endangered **throughout** Southern and Baja California.

(b) Ninety-nine percent **of** abalone are eaten **by** predators **during** the larvae phase **of** development.

(c) All filter-feeding animals, **from** baleen whales **to** sea anemones, prey **on** white abalone.

Practice   **a.** Memorize the first column of prepositions on the preceeding page: Study the column for a moment, then cover it, and say the prepositions to yourself or to a friend. Repeat this until you can say all the preposition in the first column.

b. Now follow the instructions for Practice "a" in order to memorize the next three columns of prepositions, and say them to yourself or to a friend.

c. Have a "preposition contest" with yourself or with a friend to see how many prepositions you can write in one minute.

List each preposition that you find in sentences d–i.

d. The white abalone is at the top of the endangered list for marine invertebrates.

e. Like its red, pink, green, and black cousins, the white abalone has been hunted without limits.

f. In 1997, California authorities banned commercial harvest of these mollusks.

g. Planted one hundred feet below the surface of the ocean, the abalone are safe from poachers.

h. Alongside the pier, a giant sea bass hovered hungrily around the abalone.

i. Beneath a ship at sea, an octopus drilled holes into an abalone shell despite the law against the destruction of these creatures.

For j–m, replace each blank with the correct vocabulary word.

j. The librarian's obsession with acquiring books causes the patrons to suspect _____.

k. The Greek suffix meaning "madness" or "passion" is _____.

l. A wild-eyed _____ threw rocks at the swarm of bumble bees.

m. Adolph Hitler's quest for power could be called _____.

More Practice

Write each preposition that you find in these sentences.

1. Even before the break of day, the rooster in my neighbor's yard crows with gusto.

2. Amid the confusion at breakfast, I ate my toast without butter.

3. What happened to Daniel on the school bus?

4. Jen's latest artwork is stuck to the refrigerator with magnets.

5. Despite his best efforts, Jacob couldn't lift the sack of concrete from the bed of the truck.

6. With her friends around her, Maya celebrated her thirteenth birthday.

7. Micah spent only three minutes inside the hall of mirrors.

8. During his adult years, Mr. Klein lived in London and traveled to Paris on weekends.

9. Before the meeting at Patty's, we made oatmeal cookies with raisins.

10. After the meeting, Sarah would not leave without our recipe.

Review set For 1–4, replace each blank with the missing preposition
16 from your alphabetical list.

1. aboard, _____, above, across, after, _____,
(16) along, _____ amid, among, around, _____,
before, behind, below, _____

2. Beside, _____, between, _____, but, by,
(16) concerning, _____, despite, down, during,
_____, excepting, for, from, _____

3. Inside, _____, like, near, _____, off,
(16) _____, into, opposite, out, _____,
_____, past, regarding, round, save

4. Since, through, _____, till, _____, toward,
(16) under, _____, until, not, _____ upon, via,
with, _____, without

5. Write each preposition from this sentence: Looking into
(16) the water, the silly dog in Aesop's fable thought that
another dog had a juicy steak in his mouth.

For 6 and 7, tell whether the expression is a complete
sentence, run-on sentence, or sentence fragment.

6. An impulsive, and perhaps greedy, little dog with a large,
(3) juicy steak in his mouth.

7. When he barked at his reflection, he dropped the steak
(1, 3) into the water and lost it.

8. Write the present participle, past tense, and past
(6, 15) participle of the verb *flap.*

9. For a–d, choose the correct present tense form of the verb.
(6, 14) (a) We (have, has)   (b) You (am, are, is)
(c) He (do, does)   (d) I (am, are, is)

10. For a–d, choose the correct past tense form of the verb.
(6, 14) (a) They (was, were)   (b) It (have, had)
(c) He (was, were)   (d) She (do, did)

Write the correct verb form for sentences 11–14.

11. The biography of Walt Whitman (future of *interest*) most
(4, 10) readers.

12. We (future of *discuss*) his childhood and early adulthood.
(4, 10)

13. Walt Whitman (present of *remain*) one of America's
(4, 6) greatest poets.

14. As a young boy, Walt (past of *enjoy*) everything he saw
(4, 6) and did.

For 15–18, write the plural of each noun.

15. tempo
(12, 13)

16. shelf
(12, 13)

17. bluff
(12, 13)

18. fax
(12, 13)

19. Write each word that should be capitalized in this
(5, 11) sentence: walt whitman, a poet and journalist, was born
into a quaker family in long island, new york.

Choose the correct verb form for 20 and 21.

20. He studied literature before he (produces, produced) any
(4, 6) of his own.

21. The man (publishes, published) his own newspaper and
(4, 6) delivers it by horseback.

22. Write each abstract noun from this list: ambition,
(7) lighthouse, heresy, hypocrisy, saddle

23. From this sentence, write each noun and label it
(9) masculine, feminine, neuter, or indefinite: My brother
and sister-in-law live with their beagle in a two-story
house with a spacious yard.

For 24–27, refer to this sentence:

Has Walt Whitman composed free-flowing lines with
a rhythm of their own?

24. Write the verb phrase, underlining the helping verb and
(4, 8) circling the past participle.

25. Write each preposition in the sentence.
(16)

26. Diagram the simple subject and simple predicate of the
(2, 4) sentence.

27. Tell whether the sentence is declarative, interrogative,
(1, 3) imperative, or exclamatory.

Choose the best word to complete sentences 28–30.

28. A eulogy is a written or spoken (commendation,
(13) criticism, complaint) about a person or thing.

29. I believe his statement was (alluding, eluding) to
(14) something that happened in the past.

30. (Alleys, Allies) are narrow, back streets.
(8)

LESSON 17

Complex Prepositions

Complex Prepositions

We have reviewed the simple (single word) prepositions and identified them in sentences. In this lesson, we will learn to recognize **complex prepositions,** which contain more than one word. Let us memorize the following:

according to	in behalf of
across from	in front of
alongside of	in place of
along with	in regard to
apart from	in spite of
aside from	inside of
away from	next to
because of	on account of
by means of	on behalf of
down from	on top of
except for	outside of
from among	over to
from between	owing to
from under	prior to
in addition to	round about

Example Underline each complex preposition in sentences a and b.

(a) According to Mrs. Haroon, the neighbor who lived next to her mansion moved away from Smudgeville because of the smog.

(b) On behalf of the PTA, Mrs. Haroon stood next to the podium in front of the crowd in place of the president and presented me my plaque along with a trophy on account of all my hard work.

Solution (a) **According to** Mrs. Haroon, the neighbor who lived **next to** her mansion moved **away from** Smudgeville **because of** the smog.

(b) **On behalf of** the PTA, Mrs. Haroon stood **next to** the podium **in front of** the crowd **in place of** the president and presented me my plaque **along with** a trophy **on account of** all my hard work.

Practice   **a.** Study the first column of prepositions for a moment, then cover it, and say the prepositions to yourself or to a friend. Repeat this until you can say all the prepositions in the first column.

b. Follow the instructions above to memorize the second column of prepositions.

c. Have a "preposition contest" with yourself or with a friend to see how many prepositions you can write in one minute.

Write each complex preposition that you find in sentences d–i.

d. Because of archaeology, we know that there are buried cities.

e. In addition to tree-dating, scientists use radiocarbon (C14) dating.

f. Scientists can tell how much C14 remains by means of measuring.

g. The archaeologists gathered their maps and tools prior to their expedition.

h. According to archaeological findings, our ancestors tamed animals, built houses, and made rough cooking pots.

i. In spite of the heat, Mr. Futterer hiked down from Mount Hermon along with his friend Aaron.

For j–m, replace each blank with the correct vocabulary word.

j. The Greek prefix _____ means large or great.

k. The _____ of Chicago, Illinois, attracts many tourists.

l. The doctor's explanation for the patient's chest pain was _____.

m. Suffering from _____, the deluded man thought he was Napoleon.

More Practice

Write each simple or complex preposition that you find in these sentences.

1. According to Agnes, the pomegranate trees will adapt to their new location alongside of the stream.

2. In addition to other pronunciation aids, a macron was placed on top of each long vowel.

3. The track team had no transportation except for the microbus.

4. Aside from a slight earthquake in 1902, the Hatfield-McCoy wedding was the only climactic event in the town's history.

5. Confidentially, I'm glad they married in spite of their families' ongoing rivalry.

6. Round about the construction site on Fifth Avenue, people could not hear each other's voices because of the cacophony of saws, hammers, and drills.

7. I spoke to the orthodontist in regard to his comments about my friend's teeth.

8. Along with two violinists on violins, Dan played the viola, which created a euphony under the tent at the Aspen music festival.

9. In front of those gathered at the funeral, Josef gave a eulogy on behalf of his family regarding all the kind deeds of his deceased father.

10. Sneaking over to the neighbor's house and hiding behind their refrigerator, Yoshinaga eluded the persistent solicitor.

Review set 17

Write each preposition from sentences 1–5.

1. A hare challenges a tortoise to a race for exercise.
(16, 17)

2. I heard the story according to the tortoise.
(16, 17)

3. Because of his slow speed, the tortoise isn't a likely
(16, 17) winner.

4. The hare is in front of the tortoise for most of the race.
(16, 17)

5. The tortoise thinks of nothing except the finish line.
(16, 17)

For 6 and 7, write each noun and label it concrete or abstract.

6. The tortoise exhibits persistence, perseverance, and
(7) discipline.

7. Butch carries his house on his back.
(7)

8. Write each helping verb from this sentence: The hare
(4, 8) could have won the race.

9. Write the present participle, past tense, and past
(6, 15) participle of the verb *whiz*.

10. Write three helping verbs that begin with the letter *m*.
(8)

11. For a–d, choose the correct present tense form of the verb.
(6, 14)
   (a) He (am, are, is)   (b) They (do, does)

   (c) I (have, has)   (d) You (am, are, is)

12. For a–d, choose the correct past tense form of the verb.
(6, 14)
   (a) We (did, does)   (b) It (was, were)

   (c) She (do, did)   (d) They (was, were)

Write the correct verb form to complete sentences 13 and 14.

13. The hare (present of *eat*) lunch during the race.
(4, 6)

14. The tortoise (future of *celebrate*) at the end of the race.
(4, 10)

15. Tell whether this expression is a complete sentence,
(1, 3) sentence fragment, or run-on sentence: A huge pile of
lettuce and vegetables for the hare's victory salad.

16. Rewrite and correct this run-on sentence: The hare
(1, 3) becomes drowsy after such a big meal he searches for
shade for a nap.

For 17 and 18, write the plural of each noun.

17. goose
(12, 13)

18. moose
(12, 13)

19. Write each word that should be capitalized in this
(5, 11) sentence:

> langston hughes moved to harlem, new york, in november of 1924 and published his first book of poetry, *the weary blues*, in 1926.

20. Write each possessive noun from this list: tortoises,
(9) tortoise's, men, man's, siblings', sibling's

21. Unscramble these words to make an imperative sentence:
(1, 3)   mind   finish   keep   line   the   in

22. Write each noun from the sentence below and label it
(9) feminine, masculine, neuter, or indefinite.

> My siblings have vowed to live like the tortoise.

Diagram the simple subject and simple predicate of sentences 23 and 24.

23. The slow, steady tortoise will triumph over the confident,
(2, 4) distracted hare.

24. Here comes the tortoise!
(2, 4)

Choose the correct verb form for sentences 25 and 26.

25. The tortoise carries his house on his back and (plods,
(4, 6) plodded) steadily along the race course.

26. Earlier, the hare stopped to eat and (naps, napped) for a
(4, 6) while.

Choose the best word to complete sentences 27–30.

27. A misogynist (loves, hates, trusts) women.
(7)

28. Last night, I heard cats fighting in the (alley, ally) behind
(8) my home.

29. (Confidently, Confidentially) means secretly or privately.
(12)

30. To (allude, elude) is to escape by trickery, speed, or
(14) cleverness.

LESSON 18

The Perfect Tenses

Dictation or Journal Entry

Vocabulary:

The words *Calvary* and *cavalry* are frequently confused.

Calvary, a proper noun, refers to the site of Jesus' crucifixion. Jesus Christ died at *Calvary.*

A *cavalry* is a military troop on horseback. The Canadian Mounties are a respected *cavalry.*

We have reviewed the simple present, past, and future verb tenses. In this lesson, we will examine the three **perfect tenses**—present perfect, past perfect, and future perfect. The perfect tenses show that an action has been completed or "perfected." To form these tenses, we add a form of the helping verb *have* to the past participle.

Present Perfect   The present perfect tense describes an action that occurred in the past and is complete or continuing in the present. We add the present forms of the verb *have* to the past participle.

PRESENT PERFECT TENSE = HAVE OR HAS + PAST PARTICIPLE

Archaeologists <u>have unearthed</u> the remains of one of the oldest towns in the world near the modern city of Jericho.

One excavation <u>has identified</u> Catal Huyuk as the largest ancient settlement.

Past Perfect   The past perfect tense describes past action completed before another past action. We use the helping verb *had* before the past participle.

PAST PERFECT TENSE = HAD + PAST PARTICIPLE

Today's Iraq <u>had been</u> the ancient Greek's "Mesopotamia."

Sumerians <u>had lived</u> in the southern part of Mesopotamia.

Future Perfect   The future perfect tense describes future action to be completed before another future action. We add the future form of the helping verb *have* to the past participle.

FUTURE PERFECT TENSE = <u>WILL HAVE</u> OR <u>SHALL HAVE</u> + <u>PAST PARTICIPLE</u>

By next summer, archaeologists <u>will have uncovered</u> more information about the ziggurats, or temple-towers.

Soon we <u>shall have deciphered</u> the Rosetta Stone entirely.

By the end of seventh grade, I <u>shall have learned</u> much ancient history.

Example   For sentences a–d, write the verb phrase, and tell whether it is present perfect, past perfect, or future perfect.

(a) Sumerians had used a counting system based on units of sixty, which we use today for measuring time.

(b) Before they are young men, these Sumerian boys will have completed an education in reading, writing, and arithmetic.

(c) Has the professor explained the cylinder seals used by the Sumerians?

(d) Before Thanksgiving vacation, we shall have studied the invention of writing.

Solution   (a) **had used**—We notice the past tense form of the helping verb *have* (had), so we know that the tense is **past perfect.**

(b) **will have completed**—We see the future tense form of *have* (will have), so we know that the tense is **future perfect.**

(c) **Has explained**—The present tense form of *have* (has) is used, so the know that the tense is **present perfect.**

(d) **shall have studied**—The helping verb *have* is in future tense (shall have), so we know that the tense is **future perfect.**

Practice   For a–c, write the verb phrase, and tell whether it is present perfect, past perfect, or future perfect.

     a. Historians have visited Egypt for clues to their civilization.

     b. Settlers had migrated to Egypt from the Sahara in search of water.

     c. By next week, we shall have completed our study of ancient Egypt.

For d and e, replace each blank with the correct vocabulary word.

     d. The _____ controlled the unruly mob.

     e. Many historic paintings depict Jesus at _____.

More Practice   Diagram the simple subject and simple predicate of each sentence.

     1. Wild parrots have adapted to Southern California.

     2. In the year 2000, Nancy had adopted Gracie.

     3. By next year, the lawmakers will have waived the former requirements.

     4. Tomorrow, I shall have finished my report.

     5. Has Uncle Bill arrived from Hawaii?

     6. Have you seen the Statue of Liberty?

Review set 18   Write each preposition that you find in sentences 1–3.

     1. In the race with the tortoise, the hare lost because of his
(16, 17)arrogance.

     2. Across from the post office stands a statue of an early
(16, 17)settler.

     3. I went over to Mrs. Gutierrez's house and gave her
(16, 17)flowers on behalf of my family.

For 4–6, write the entire verb phrase and label it present perfect, past perfect, or future perfect.

     4. Hopefully, the hare will have learned his lesson.
(14, 18)

5. Had the tortoise wished for less weight on his back?
(14, 18)

6. The slow and steady tortoise has won the race.
(14, 18)

For 7–10, write the verb phrase and name its tense.

7. A mouse will discover a sleeping lion.
(8, 10)

8. The mouse had wandered aimlessly through the jungle.
(14, 18)

9. The lion has noticed the mouse!
(14, 18)

10. At the sound of the lion's roar, the little mouse trembles.
(6, 15)

11. For a–d, choose the correct present tense form of the verb.
(14)
  (a) You (am, are, is)   (b) He (am, are, is)
  (c) We (have, has)   (d) I (do, does)

12. Write whether this expression is a complete sentence,
(1, 3) sentence fragment, or run-on sentence: The lion's sharp teeth glistened in the sun.

13. Rewrite and correct this run-on sentence: The lion lifted
(1, 3) the mouse to his mouth the mouse begged for mercy.

14. Write the present participle, past tense, and past
(6, 15) participle of the verb *tickle.*

Write the correct verb form to complete sentences 15–17.

15. The mouse (present perfect of *offer*) to save the lion's life
(14, 18) in the future.

16. This offer (present of *amuse*) the lion.
(6, 15)

17. The mouse (future of *rescue*) the lion from a hunter's
(4, 10) trap.

For 18–21, write the plural for each noun.

18. handful   **19.** tornado
(12, 13)   (12, 13)

20. wrench   **21.** tray
(12, 13)   (12, 13)

22. Langston Hughes capitalized the first word of each line in
(5, 11) his poem below. Write each word that needs a capital letter in the following:

on the shoals of Nowhere
wasted my song
yet taken by the sea wind
and blown along.

Diagram the simple subject and simple predicate of sentences 23 and 24.

23. Will the mouse keep his promise to the lion?
(2, 4)

24. In spite of his smallness, the mouse could gnaw through
(2, 4) the trap.

25. Write each noun from this sentence and label it abstract
(7) or concrete: Somehow, the mouse has survived his fear of the lion.

26. Write each possessive noun from this list: lionesses,
(9) lions', cities, city's, mansion's, buildings

Choose the best word to complete sentences 27–30.

27. A newcomer, Claxton had to (adapt, adept, adopt) to
(1) different rules and unfamiliar faces.

28. A person with delusions of (greatness, smallness) suffers
(17) from megalomania.

29. (Heresy, Hypocrisy) is pretending to be moral, upright, or
(15) religious when you are not.

30. A euphony is a (discordant, pleasant, bothersome)
(13) sound.

**LESSON
19**

Verbals: The Gerund as a Subject

Dictation or Journal Entry

Vocabulary:

Let us review the homophones *their, there,* and *they're.*

Their is the possessive form of they. *Their* car is blue, but ours is red.

There means "at" or "in that place." I placed my keys over *there.*

They're is the contraction for "they are." *They're* a happy family.

Verbals   A **verbal** is a verb form that does not function as a verb. Rather, a verbal may function as a noun, an adjective, or an adverb. There are three kinds of verbals: the gerund, the infinitive, and the participle. In this lesson, we shall study the gerund.

The Gerund   A **gerund** ends in *ing* and functions as a noun. A noun can function as the subject of a sentence, a direct object, an object of a preposition, or a predicate noun. In this lesson, we shall see how the gerund can be used as the subject of a sentence.

To determine if a verb ending in *ing* is a gerund, we must see how it is used in the sentence. We follow these steps:

1. Find the simple predicate.
2. Find the simple subject.

If the *-ing* form of the verb is the simple subject, then the subject of the sentence is a **gerund.** Gerunds used as sentence subjects are italicized below. Notice that we diagram the gerund on a "stair-step" line above the base line on "stilts."

Writing is fun.

*Distance *running* requires diligence.*

Her *laughing* distracted me.

Example 1   Underline each gerund used as a subject in sentences a–c.

(a) In the land of Sumer, farming proved worthwhile.

(b) Gradually, writing developed in Sumer.

(c) Irrigating provided water for Sumerian crops.

Solution   (a) In the land of Sumer, <u>**farming**</u> proved worthwhile.

(b) Gradually, <u>**writing**</u> developed in Sumer.

(c) <u>**Irrigating**</u> provided water for Sumerian crops.

The gerund has two tenses: present and perfect.

PRESENT: studying, researching, serving

PERFECT: having studied, having researched, having served

Perfect tense gerunds are italicized in these sentences:

Having studied four hours prepared me for the exam.

Having researched every source assured my success.

Having served the volleyball well gave me more confidence.

Example 2   Diagram the simple subject and simple predicate of this sentence: Smiling improved her disposition.

Solution   We diagram the gerund, *smiling,* on a stair-step line above the base line on stilts in the location of the sentence subject.

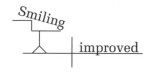

Example 3   For sentences a and b, tell whether the italicized gerund is present or perfect tense.

(a) *Having learned* the helping verbs improved my grammar.

(b) *Memorizing* exercises our brains.

Solution   (a) We notice the helping verb *have,* so we recognize that the gerund *having learned* is **perfect tense.**

(b) Since there is no helping verb *have,* we know that the gerund *memorizing* is **present tense.**

Practice Write the gerund used as a subject in sentences a–d.

     a. Hunting provided food for the Egyptians.

     b. During ancient times in Egypt, wine-making began.

     c. Praying was commonplace among Egyptians.

     d. Embalming preserved dead Egyptian noblemen.

For e–h, tell whether the italicized gerund is present or perfect tense.

     e. *Having used* many types of fluids for centuries to embalm bodies made the Egyptians expert in this practice.

     f. *Using* the mineral natron prevented decay.

     g. *Building* challenged the ancient people.

     h. *Having explored* the pyramids for years provided the archaeologists with a picture of Egyptian culture.

For i–k, replace each blank with *their, there,* or *they're.*

     i. Yes, they are related; I believe _____ cousins.

     j. The cousins rode _____ bikes to the park.

     k. They stayed _____ for four hours.

     l. Diagram the simple subject and simple predicate of this sentence: Exercising will increase your strength.

More Practice Diagram the simple subject and simple predicate of each sentence.

     1. Waving is a friendly gesture.

     2. Waiting requires patience.

     3. Eulogizing honors the deceased.

     4. Sewing is a useful skill.

     5. Does singing raise your spirits?

     6. Has counseling encouraged him?

     7. Having studied gave me confidence.

Review set   Diagram the simple subject and simple predicate of sentences
19   1–4.

1. Waxing protects wood floors.
(4, 19)

2. Listening improves our relationships.
(4, 19)

3. Traitors might expect treachery in return for their own
(4, 19) disloyalty.

4. About what did Diogenes speak?
(4, 19)

For sentences 5 and 6, write the gerund and label it present
tense or present perfect tense.

5. Having freed the lion made the mouse a lifelong friend.
(19)

6. Gnawing ropes requires sharp, strong teeth.
(19)

7. From memory, write five complex prepositions.
(17)

8. For a–f, tell whether each word is a helping verb or a
(8, 16) preposition. Write "HV" for helping verb or "P" for
preposition.

(a) among   (b) is   (c) beside

(d) been   (e) does   (f) toward

9. Write each preposition from this sentence: On account of
(16, 17) the pitiful moans, the mouse discovered the lion in the
rope trap set by some hunters.

For sentences 10–12, write the verb phrase and label it
present perfect, past perfect, or future perfect tense.

10. A little friend has developed into a great friend.
(14, 18)

11. By next week, we shall have read all about the donkey,
(10, 18) the fox, and the lion.

12. The donkey and the fox had partnered in hunting.
(14, 18)

13. Write each noun from the sentence below and circle the
(7, 9) one that is collective.

By the end of the year, our club will have discussed
several different philosophies of life.

14. For a–d, choose the correct present tense form of the verb.

(14)   (a) He (am, are, is)   (b) We (have, has)

(c) I (do, does)   (d) You (am, are, is)

15. Rewrite and correct this run-on sentence: While hunting,
(1, 3) a fox and a donkey encounter a lion the fox betrays the
donkey.

16. Tell whether this expression is a complete sentence,
(1, 3) sentence fragment, or run-on sentence: Offering to help
the lion capture the donkey.

17. Write the present participle, past tense, and past
(6, 15) participle of the verb *capture*.

Write the correct verb form to complete sentences 18–20.

18. The lion (present perfect of *promise*) not to hurt the fox.
(14, 18)

19. The donkey (present of *succumb*) to the lion's treachery.
(6, 15)

20. In the end, the lion (future perfect of *betray*) the fox just
(10, 18) as the fox betrayed the donkey.

For 21–24, write the plural for each noun.

21. tablespoonful   **22.** cargo
(12, 13)   (12, 13)

23. clutch   **24.** donkey
(12, 13)   (12, 13)

25. Write each word that should be capitalized in this
(5, 11) sentence: langston hughes, a poet and novelist, finished
his college education at lincoln university in
pennsylvania.

Choose the correct verb form for sentences 26 and 27.

26. The fox acted friendly toward the donkey and then
(6, 15) (betrays, betrayed) him.

27. The exasperated editor threw her pencil down and
(6, 15) (stomps, stomped) her foot.

Choose the best word to complete sentences 28–30.

28. Pretending friendship is an example of (hypocrisy,
(15) misoneism, heresy).

29. Wave and waive are (synonyms, antonyms,
(5) homophones).

30. (Bibliography, Bibliomania) is an excessive desire to
(16) possess books.

LESSON 20

Capitalization: Titles, Outlines, Quotations

Dictation or Journal Entry

Vocabulary:

Let us examine the similarly spelled words *imminent, immanent,* and *eminent.*

Imminent means "likely to happen at any moment." The atmosphere was tense, and war appeared *imminent.*

Immanent means innate, inborn, or indwelling. Some psychologists believe that one's personality is *immanent.*

Eminent means distinguished or prominent. The President of the United States is *eminent* around the world.

We have learned to capitalize the following: proper nouns, common nouns when they are a part of proper nouns, the pronoun *I,* the first word of every sentence, and the first word in every line of most poetry. We have also learned that little words like *of, and,* and *an* are not capitalized when part of a proper noun.

Titles   **Titles** require special capitalization. In titles, we capitalize the following:

1. The first and last words of a title

2. All verbs (action or being words)

3. All other words in the title except certain short words

4. A preposition with five or more letters (such as outside, underneath, between, etc.)

The Aeneid

The Emperor's New Clothes

The Waste Land

Unless located first or last in the title, words like *a, an, and, the, but, or, for, nor,* and prepositions with four letters or fewer do not need a capital letter. Here are some examples of properly capitalized titles:

Alice in Wonderland

The Fall of the House of Usher

Antony and Cleopatra

"America the Beautiful"

Outlines   We learn to organize written material by outlining. **Outlines** require capital letters for the Roman numerals and for the letters of the first major topics. We also capitalize the first letter of the first word in the outline.

     I. Tragedies by William Shakespeare
         A. *Antony and Cleopatra*
         B. *Julius Caesar*
     II. Comedies by William Shakespeare
         A. *The Taming of the Shrew*
         B. *The Merchant of Venice*

Quotations   We capitalize the first word of a dialogue **quotation,** as shown below.

Professor Falstaff inquired, "Have you finished reading *The Old Curiosity Shop*?"

Nell quipped, "Of course not. It's one thousand pages long!"

Example   Provide capital letters as needed.

(a) *king lear*

(b) *the two gentlemen of verona*

(c)   i. novels by jane austen
         a. *pride and prejudice*
         b. *sense and sensibility*
   ii. novels by charles dickens
         a. *the old curiosity shop*
         b. *bleak house*

(d) the old man cried, "she was always cheerful—very cheerful."

Solution   (a) *King Lear.* We capitalize the first and last words in a book title.

(b) *The Two Gentlemen of Verona* is also a long play. The preposition *of* is not capitalized. The first and last words as well as the important words require a capital letter.

(c) We remember that outlines require capital letters for their Roman numerals, major topics, and first words.

     I. Novels by Jane Austen
         A. *Pride and Prejudice*
         B. *Sense and Sensibility*
     II. Novels by Charles Dickens
         A. *The Old Curiosity Shop*
         B. *Bleak House*

(d) **T**he old man cried, "**S**he was always cheerful—very cheerful."

Practice   Rewrite a–d, using correct capitalization.

    a. i. patriotic symbols
            a. american flag
            b. eagle
      ii. patriotic songs
            a. "america"
            b. "god bless america"

    b. *beauty and the beast*

    c. Concerning grief, C. S. Lewis wrote, "children suffer not (I think) less than their elders, but differently."

    d. C. S. Lewis commented, "they [cats] very seldom seem to like one another."

Replace each blank with the correct vocabulary word.

    e. The arrival of the Boeing 737 was _____.

    f. The _____ Pope John Paul represented the voice of the Catholic church.

    g. Some of the _____ needs of a young child are touch, sleep, food, and water.

More Practice   See Master Worksheets.

Review set 20   **1.** For one minute, study the lists of prepositions from
   (16, 17) Lessons 16 and 17. Then write as many as you can from memory.

                15+ = good
                25+ = excellent
                35+ = superb
                45+ = genius
                 55 = photographic memory!

    2. Write each preposition from this sentence: In the battle
   (16, 17) between the beasts and the birds, the bat joined on behalf of the beasts.

For 3 and 4, write each book title using correct capitalization.

3. *mrs. frisbee and the rats of n.i.m.h.*
(11, 20)

4. *otto of the silver hand*
(11, 20)

Rewrite 5 and 6 using correct capitalization.

5.   i. pearl s. buck
(5, 20)   a. nobel prize in literature
     b. bridge between two civilizations

6. when others insisted that pearl s. buck did not deserve
(11, 20) the nobel prize, she agreed, saying, "oh what a pity they
didn't give it to theodore dreiser."

For 7 and 8, write the verb phrase and label it present perfect, past perfect, or future perfect.

7. Pearl S. Buck has remained a popular American author.
(14, 18)

8. Racial prejudice in China had affected Pearl S. Buck at a
(14, 18) young age.

For 9 and 10, write the gerund used as a subject.

9. Writing provided an escape from loneliness for Pearl S.
(19) Buck.

10. After college, teaching challenged her mind.
(19)

For 11 and 12, write the gerund and label it present or perfect tense.

11. Having absorbed Chinese culture enabled her to write a
(19) cookbook for Chinese food.

12. Divorcing one's husband was unacceptable to Pearl S.
(19) Buck's parents.

Write the correct verb form for sentences 13–15.

13. At first, the bat (present of *choose*) neutrality in the war
(6, 15) between the birds and the beasts.

14. The beasts (present perfect of *slap*) viciously at the birds.
(14, 18)

(6, 15) **15.** The birds (past of *rally*) successfully.

Diagram the simple subject and simple predicate in sentences 16 and 17.

16. Fighting can ruin relationships.
(4, 19)

17. Finally, the bat will have ended the battle on the
(2, 4) victorious side.

18. Unscramble these words to make an imperative sentence:
(1, 3)
          deceit   practice   never

19. Write the present participle, past tense, and past
(6, 15) participle of the verb *conclude*.

For 20–23, write the plural of each noun.

20. scarf
(12, 13)

21. shelf
(12, 13)

22. banjo
(12, 13)

23. mandolin
(12, 13)

24. From the sentence below, write each noun and label it
(7) concrete or abstract.

        The bat has an ambiguous nature.

25. Rewrite and correct this run-on sentence: After a while,
(1, 3) it appeared the beasts would win the battle then the bat
joined their side.

Choose the best word to complete sentences 26–30.

26. The perfect verb tense shows action that has been
(18) perfected or (continuing, completed).

27. The end of the battle appeared (immanent, eminent,
(20) imminent) to the bat.

28. They expressed (they're, there, their) disapproval of the
(19) bat's deceit.

29. The Greek root meaning passion or madness is (biblio,
(2, 16) macro, mania).

30. The child grew in wisdom and in (statue, stature, statute).
(10)

LESSON 21

The Progressive Verb Forms

Dictation or Journal Entry

Vocabulary:

Let us examine three words that look and sound similar: *consul, council,* and *counsel.*

A *consul* is an official appointed by a government to look after the welfare and commercial interests of its citizens in foreign countries. The President sent a *consul* to Mexico to facilitate communication.

A *council* is an assembly of persons convened for advice. The dairy *council* suggested four to six servings of milk products per day.

To *counsel* someone is to give them advice. Please *counsel* the students concerning their classes for next year. *Counsel* is also a noun meaning advice. Her parents gave her wise *counsel.*

We have learned the six main verb tenses:

1.	present	*adapt(s)*
2.	past	*has/have adapted*
3.	future	*will/shall adapt*
4.	present perfect	*have adapted*
5.	past perfect	*had adapted*
6.	future perfect	*will/shall have adapted*

All six of these main verb tenses also have a **progressive form.** A progressive verb phrase shows action in "progress" or continuing action.

Present progressive tense	=	action still in progress at the time of speaking
Past progressive	=	action in progress throughout a specific time in the past
Future progressive	=	action that will be in progress in the future
Present perfect progressive	=	action begun in the past and still continuing in the present
Past perfect progressive	=	past action begun, continued, and terminated in the past
Future perfect progressive	=	continuous future action completed at some time in the future

Progressive verb forms are expressed with some form of the verb *to be* and the present participle ("ing" added to the main verb).

Present Progressive The present progressive form consists of the appropriate present tense of *to be* (am/is/are) plus the present participle (verb + *ing*).

PRESENT PROGRESSIVE = AM, IS, OR ARE + PRESENT PARTICIPLE

The panther <u>is adapting</u> to its new environment at the zoo.

The pet lovers <u>are adopting</u> stray cats and dogs.

I <u>am adapting</u> to my new daily schedule.

Past Progressive The past progressive form consists of a past form of *to be* (was/were) plus the present participle.

PAST PROGRESSIVE – WAS OR WERE + PRESENT PARTICIPLE

The injured whale <u>was adapting</u> to captivity.

The walruses <u>were adapting</u> well to their new home.

Future Progressive We form the future progressive by adding the present participle to the future of the *to be* verb (shall be/will be).

FUTURE PROGRESSIVE = SHALL BE OR WILL BE + PRESENT PARTICIPLE

Our family <u>will be going</u> to the beach on Saturday.

I <u>shall be celebrating</u> my twenty-first birthday this year.

Present Perfect Progressive We form the present perfect progressive by using *has* or *have*, *been*, and the present participle.

PRESENT PERFECT PROGRESSIVE = HAS BEEN OR HAVE BEEN + PRESENT PARTICIPLE

The caretakers <u>have been preparing</u> for the arrival of several injured sea lions.

Corky, a killer whale, <u>has been living</u> in captivity for the last ten years.

Past Perfect Progressive The past perfect progressive consists of *had*, *been*, and the present participle.

PAST PERFECT PROGRESSIVE = HAD BEEN + PRESENT PARTICIPLE

The grandfather <u>had been caring</u> for his grandson until the young boy left home.

Madison <u>had been reading</u> a poem by William Blake when the phone rang.

Future Perfect Progressive   We form the future perfect progressive with *will* or *shall have been*, and the present participle.

FUTURE PERFECT PROGRESSIVE = <u>WILL/SHALL HAVE BEEN</u> + <u>PRESENT PARTICIPLE</u>

At graduation time, Oscar <u>will have been attending</u> this grammar school for nine years.

The couples <u>will have been dancing</u> for sixteen hours by the end of the dance marathon.

Example   For sentences a–f, write the verb phrase, and tell whether the progressive verb form is present, past, future, present perfect, past perfect, or future perfect.

(a) This June, I shall have been reading the stories of Hans Christian Andersen to my classes for twenty years.

(b) The victim was exhibiting symptoms of amnesia, a condition of memory loss.

(c) He will be entertaining his party guests with the music of Ludwig von Beethoven.

(d) Thomas A. Edison had been experimenting with electricity for many years.

(e) My sisters are visiting the Empire State Building in New York City.

(f) Since its inception, the Bill of Rights has been guiding our legislators.

Solution   (a) **shall have been reading**—The verb phrase "shall have been" is a future perfect form, so the entire phrase is **future perfect progressive.**

(b) **was exhibiting**—We notice that "was" is the past tense form of *to be*, so we know that "was exhibiting" is the **past progressive.**

(c) **will be entertaining**—"Will be" is the future form of *to be*, so the verb phrase is **future progressive.**

(d) **had been experimenting**—"Had been" is the past perfect form, so the verb phrase is **past perfect progressive.**

(e) **are visiting**—"Are" is a present form of *to be*, so the verb phrase is **present progressive.**

(f) **has been guiding**—The verb phrase "has been" indicates the present perfect tense, so the entire verb phrase is **present perfect progressive.**

Practice For sentences a–c, write the verb phrase and tell whether it is present progressive, past progressive, or future progressive.

a. The group was learning the difference between aerobic and anaerobic exercise.

b. I shall be exercising aerobically at six a.m.

c. The aerobics instructor <u>is performing</u> rhythmic arm movements.

For sentences d–f, write the verb phrase and tell whether it is present perfect progressive, past perfect progressive, or future perfect progressive.

d. The fitness leader had been instructing at the gym for five years before he quit last year.

e. In January, Matilda will have been seeing her orthodontist for two years.

f. The neighbor's dog has been howling all day.

Choose the correct word to complete sentences g and h.

g. The (progressive, perfect) tense shows action that is continuing.

h. To make the progressive tense, we use some form of the verb *to be* plus the (present, past) participle, which ends in *ing*.

For i–k, replace each blank with *consul, council,* or *counsel.*

i. A _____ of several Native American chiefs agreed to the terms of the peace treaty.

j. Mr. Green, _____ to Canada, explained the process of exchanging American dollars for Canadian money.

k. Will the minister _____ the engaged couple before they are married?

l. Diagram the simple subject and simple predicate of this sentence: Lazy Susan had been lying around all day.

More Practice Diagram the simple subject and simple predicate of each sentence.

1. This October, Dominic will have been working for the company for thirty years.

2. Sophia had been swimming for two hours.

3. I have been waiting for you since ten o'clock.

4. Have you been watching the news?

Review set 21

1. Write each preposition in this sentence:
[16, 17] In spite of their free and easy life, the frogs became disgruntled over the chaos around them.

2. Diagram the simple subject and simple predicate of this
[4, 19] sentence: Reading has given me new insights.

3. Rewrite and correct this run-on sentence: The frogs
[1, 3] wanted order in their lives they asked Jupiter, the mighty god, for a king.

Rewrite sentences 4 and 5, adding capital letters where they are needed.

4. "the frogs who desired a king" is another of aesop's
[11, 20] fables.

5. jupiter threw a log into the lake, saying, "there is your
[11, 20] king."

6. Write the word from this list that is *not* a helping
[8, 16] verb: is, am, are, was, were, be, being, been, has, have, had, do, does, did, shall, will, should, outside, would, can, could, may, might, must

7. From the sentence below, write each noun and label it
[7, 9] masculine, feminine, neuter, or indefinite.

Did the god provide a queen for the frogs?

8. Write each noun from the sentence below and circle the
(7, 9) one that is collective: An army of frogs approached Jupiter a third time.

9. Write the present participle, past tense, and past participle
(6, 15) of the verb *petition*.

10. Replace each blank with the missing prepositions from
(16, 17) your memorized list (from page 65).

aboard, about, _____, across, after, against, _____, alongside, amid, among, around, _____, before, behind, below, beneath

For 11–13, choose the correct verb form.

11. She (do, does) her chores faithfully.
(6, 14)

12. (Has, Have) Benito and Molly arrived?
(6, 14)

13. (Is, Am, Are) they coming soon?
(6, 14)

For 14 and 15, write the plural of each noun.

14. hoax
(12, 13)

15. Nancy
(12, 13)

16. Write the verb phrase from this sentence and label it past
(8, 18) perfect, present perfect, or future perfect: Jupiter will have provided the frogs three kings.

For 17–19, write the verb phrase and label it present progressive, past progressive, or future progressive.

17. The frogs were treating the log with contempt.
(8, 21)

18. We shall be learning the tragedy of the second king.
(8, 21)

19. The second king, a stork, is devouring the frogs.
(8, 21)

For 20 and 21, write the verb phrase and label it present perfect progressive, past perfect progressive, or future perfect progressive.

20. Next July, they will have been croaking in that bog for
(18, 21) three years.

(18, 21) **21.** The frogs had been begging Jupiter for a king.

For 22 and 23, write the gerund and label it present or perfect tense.

22. Having received a king did not improve the frogs' lives.
(6, 19)

23. Receiving our wishes can bring disaster.
(6, 19)

Choose the best word to complete sentences 24–28.

24. The (present, past) participle ends in *ing*.
(6, 15)

25. The (perfect, progressive) tense shows continuing action.
(18, 21)

26. A (counsel, council, consul) of frogs petitions Jupiter for
(21)   a king.

27. The (imminent, immanent, eminent) god Jupiter ruled
(20)   the frogs.

28. A megalopolis is a very (small, noisy, large) city.
(17)

Write the correct verb form to complete sentences 29 and 30.

29. The fifth cavalry division (present of *march*) every day at
(4, 6)   sunrise.

30. The toad (past perfect of *hop*) across the boulevard before
(6, 18) the parade started.

LESSON 22

Linking Verbs

> **Dictation or Journal Entry**
> **Vocabulary:**
> The prefixes *a-* and *an-* originate in the Greek language and mean "not," "without," or "lacking."
>
> *Aerobic* refers to the presence of oxygen, so *anaerobic* means without oxygen. The *anaerobic* activity of non-stop sprinting left me breathless.
>
> Since *phonic* means "with sound," the word *aphonic* means "without sound," or silent. When one mouths the words to a song, we say it is *aphonic*.

Linking Verbs

A **linking verb** "links" the subject of a sentence to the rest of the predicate. It does not show action, and it is not "helping" the action verb. Its purpose is to connect a name or description to the subject.

> Jimmy Carter <u>was</u> President of the United States.

In the sentence above, *was* links "Jimmy Carter" with "President." The word *President* renames Jimmy Carter.

> Jimmy Carter <u>is</u> admirable.

In the sentence above, *is* links "Jimmy Carter" with "admirable." The word *admirable* describes Jimmy Carter.

Watch out!

We must carefully examine our sentences. Some verbs can be used as either linking or action verbs, as shown in the two sentences below.

> Boomer <u>smells</u> musty after four weeks without a bath. (*Smells* is a linking verb. It links "Boomer" with "musty.")

> Boomer <u>smells</u> his food before he devours it. (*Smells* is an action verb, not a linking verb. Boomer is doing something—smelling.)

Common Linking Verbs

Common linking verbs include all of the "to be" verbs:

> *is, am, are, was, were, be, being, been*

The following are also common linking verbs. Memorize these:

> *look, feel, taste, smell, sound*
>
> *seem, appear, grow, become*
>
> *remain, stay*

Identifying Linking Verbs   To determine whether a verb is a linking verb, we replace it with a form of the verb "to be"—*is, am, are, was, were, be, being, been*, as in the example below.

> The fireman *feels* anxious about the burn victim.

We replace *feels* with *is*:

> The fireman *is* anxious about the burn victim.

Since the sentence still makes sense, we know that *feels* is a linking verb in this sentence. Now let us examine the word *feels* in the sentence below.

> The fireman *feels* the heat of the fire.

We replace *feels* with *is*:

> The fireman *is* the heat of the fire.

The sentence no longer makes sense, so we know that *feels* is not a linking verb in this sentence.

Example   Identify and write the linking verb, if any, in each sentence.

(a) The hero of Homer's *Illiad* is Achilles.

(b) Achilles became the greatest Greek warrior in the Trojan War.

(c) Achilles looked at Hector.

(d) Achilles appeared invincible.

(e) Achilles felt pain in his heel.

Solution   (a) The linking verb **is** links "Achilles" to "hero."

(b) The verb **became** links "Achilles" to "warrior."

(c) We replace the verb *looked* with *was*: Achilles *was* at Hector. The sentence no longer makes sense, so we know that the word *looked* is not a linking verb in this sentence. It is an action verb. There are **no linking verbs** in this sentence.

(d) The verb **appeared** links "Achilles" to "invincible."

(e) We replace the verb *felt* with *was*: Achilles *was* pain. The sentence no longer makes sense, so we know that the word *felt* is not a linking verb in this sentence. There are **no linking verbs** in this sentence.

Practice   **a.** Study the linking verbs (including the "to be" verbs) listed in this lesson. Memorize them line by line. Then say them to your teacher or to a friend.

b. Have a "linking verb contest" with yourself or with a partner. Write as many as you can from memory in one minute.

Write the linking verbs, if any, from sentences c–j.

c. Lady Dedlock appears mysterious in Charles Dickens's *Bleak House.*

d. Mr. Tulkinghorn appeared before the Lord Chancellor in *Bleak House.*

e. Jenny seemed fascinated by the grotesque and humorous characters in *Bleak House.*

f. Charles Dickens remains famous for his story, "A Christmas Carol."

g. Ebenezer Scrooge sounded stingy and grouchy.

h. In the end, Scrooge felt generous and cheerful.

i. Scrooge smelled the fresh-baked bread.

j. The fresh-baked bread smelled delicious.

For k–o, replace each blank with the correct vocabulary word.

k. Running, biking, and jogging are examples of exercise requiring oxygen; they are forms of _____ exercise.

l. The silent movie was _____.

m. A power lift and a sprint do not require steady oxygen uptake, so they are _____ exercises.

n. The videographer added sound to create _____ tapes.

o. The prefixes *a* and *an* mean "no" or _____ .

More Practice Write each linking verb from sentences 1–15.

1. Yes, my dog seemed nervous about the storm.

2. Of course, Blanca remains the best cook in El Monte.

3. That statue appears life-like.

4. That night, Tony felt lonely in the big, creaky, old house.

5. Among religious and political leaders, hypocrisy remains a problem.

6. After many long hours of work, Dale grew weary.

7. The two sisters stayed loyal to one another through the years.

8. Lavender plants smell potent and sweet.

9. Last year, Miss Farris became a high-school English teacher.

10. Christie's voice sounded hoarse after the aerobics class.

11. Wassim looks handsome.

12. Allies are friends.

13. Their cousins were dairy farmers.

14. The unripe grapes taste sour.

15. Gaius Marius was an eminent Roman general.

For 16–20, write the verb and label it action or linking.

16. Gaius tastes the bread.   **17.** The bread tastes fresh.

18. Joshua sounds the alarm.   **19.** The cry sounds urgent.

20. Before dinner, Blanca smelled the hot beef stew.

Review set 22

1. Write all the linking verbs, including the "to be" verbs, (22) listed in this lesson.

For 2–7, write the verb and label it linking or action.

2. The author appears imaginative.
(4, 22)

3. A Fairy Grandmarina appears to King Watkins.
(4, 22)

4. Seventeen children tasted the broth of onions, carrots,
(4, 22) barley, and turnips.

5. Charles Dickens is the author of "The Magic Fishbone."
(4, 22)

6. The salmon tasted delicious.
(4, 22)

7. Robert sounded the trumpet blast.
(4, 22)

Write each preposition from sentences 8 and 9.

8. Apart from the king, no one else pestered Princess Alicia
(16, 17) about the magic fishbone.

9. In addition to nursing the queen, Princess Alicia cared
(16, 17) for the needs of her brothers and sisters.

10. Rewrite this sentence, adding capital letters where they
(11, 20) are needed: dr. h. r. diogenes calls the jerusalem cricket a
potato bug.

For 11 and 12, tell whether the expression is a sentence
fragment, run-on sentence, or complete sentence.

11. Fairy Grandmarina told the king exactly how to use the
(1, 3) magic fishbone.

12. The fishbone will grant Princess Alicia one wish she
(1, 3) keeps it in her pocket.

Diagram the simple subject and simple predicate of sentences
13–15.

13. Will we discover the fishbone's secret?
(2, 4)

14. Always do your best.
(2, 4)

15. Giving brings happiness.
(4, 19)

16. Tell whether this sentence is declarative, imperative,
(1, 3) interrogative, or exclamatory: Princess Alicia heeded the
wise counsel of the Duchess.

For 17 and 18, write the plural of each noun.

17. wedding
(13, 14)

18. syllabus
(13, 14)

19. Write the present participle, past tense, and past
(6, 15) participle of the verb *hitch.*

20. Replace each blank with the missing preposition from
(16) column 2 in Lesson 16: beside, _____, between,
beyond, _____, by concerning, considering,
despite, _____, during, except, _____, for,
from

21. Write the correct form of the verb for a–c.
(6, 14) (a) She (do, does) (b)They (have, has)(c)I (was, were)

For 22–24, write the verb phrase and label it present perfect,
past perfect, or future perfect.

22. Princess Alicia had comforted her youngest brother.
(8, 18)

23. The king and his family have experienced the need for
(8, 18) others.

24. The Fairy Grandmarina will have accomplished her
(8, 18) purpose.

Write the progressive tense verb phrase from sentences 25
and 26.

25. Princess Alicia had been waiting for the appropriate time
(8, 21) to use her magic fishbone.

26. This tale is underscoring our need for patience.
(8, 21)

27. Write the gerund from this sentence and label it present
(8, 19) or perfect tense: Having nursed the queen back to health
gave Princess Alicia a sense of accomplishment.

Choose the best word to complete sentences 28–30.

28. The caring family plans to (adapt, adept, adopt) two
(1) orphans.

29. Megalocardia is an abnormally (large, small, tender)
(17) heart.

30. (Imminent, Immanent, Eminent) means "likely to happen
(20) at any moment."

LESSON
23

The Infinitive as a Subject

Dictation or Journal Entry

Vocabulary:
Let us review the present and past tense of the verbs *lie* and *lay*.

To *lie* means to recline, rest, or remain. I like to *lie* on the floor. The past tense of *lie* is *lay*. Last night, I *lay* on the floor for hours.

To *lay* means to put or place something. I will *lay* plates on the table while you *lay* the baby in his crib. The past tense of *lay* is *laid*. He *laid* his backpack on the floor. The robin *laid* an egg.

The Infinitive The **infinitive,** like the gerund, is a verbal—a word that is formed from a verb but does not function as one. The infinitive is the basic form of the verb, usually preceded by the preposition "to."

> to glance   to bristle
>
> to squander   to coax

The infinitive may function as a noun, an adjective, or an adverb. In this lesson, we will identify infinitives used as nouns and as sentence subjects. Notice that we diagram the infinitive on "stilts" above the base line.

To bristle at the sight of a dog is normal for a cat.

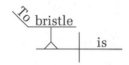

To coax the horse into the corral proved difficult.

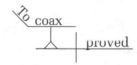

Example 1 Write each infinitive from sentences a–d.

(a) To memorize poems is difficult for some students.

(b) To organize one's room requires patience and time.

(c) To amend the Constitution involves a lengthy process.

(d) To review a teacher's notes improves exam scores.

Solution (a) **To memorize** is an infinitive used as the subject of the sentence.

(b) **To organize** is an infinitive used as the subject of the sentence.

(c) **To amend** is an infinitive used as the subject of the sentence.

(d) **To review** is an infinitive used as the subject of the sentence.

Example 2 Diagram the simple subject and simple predicate of this sentence: To smile seemed impossible.

Solution We diagram the infinitive, *to smile*, above the base line on stilts in the location of the sentence subject.

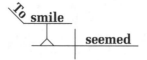

Like the gerund, the infinitive has two tense forms: present and perfect.

PRESENT: *to walk, to eat, to speak*

PERFECT: *to have walked, to have eaten, to have spoken*

Present tense infinitives are italicized here:

To speak in front of an audience makes me nervous.

To apologize demands humility.

Perfect tense infinitives are italicized here:

To have glanced both ways might have prevented the accident.

To have squandered the money would have ruined our reputations.

Example 3 For sentences a and b, tell whether the italicized infinitive is present or perfect tense.

(a) *To have captured* the criminal gave the detective satisfaction.

(b) *To succumb* to fatigue frustrates athletes.

Solution (a) The action is completed, so we know that it is **perfect tense.**

(b) The action is **present tense.**

Practice Write each infinitive that you find in sentences a–c.

a. To discover Lady Dedlock's secret becomes Mr. Tulkinghorn's passion.

b. To weave the story lines together coherently challenges Charles Dickens.

c. To have grown into a respectable woman would have satisfied Esther.

For d and e, tell whether the italicized infinitive is present or perfect tense.

d. *To have hidden* her secret for so long must have been difficult for Lady Dedlock.

e. *To forgive* Lady Dedlock was not difficult for Sir Leicester Dedlock.

For f–l, replace each blank with *lie, lay* (past tense of *lie*), *lying, lay* (present tense), or *laid.*

f. At the beach, I will _____ on the sand.

g. Yesterday, he _____ in bed all day.

h. Let us _____ these papers on the desk.

i. Last night, I _____ my keys on the dresser.

j. Now, my keys are _____ on the carpet.

k. The past tense of *lie* is _____.

l. The past tense of *lay* is _____.

m. Diagram the simple subject and simple predicate of this sentence: To toil will make you stronger.

More Practice Diagram the simple subject and simple predicate of each sentence.

1. To have finished showed her endurance.

2. To race requires courage.

3. To have studied raised their confidence.

4. To cook is a pleasure for some people.

5. To whisper might attract attention.

6. To have quit would have signaled defeat.

Review set Choose the best word to complete sentences 1–6.
23
1. In Hans Christian Andersen's "The Princess and the Pea,"
(23) the Princess (lied, laid, lay) awake all night because of the pea under her mattress.

2. A(n) (infinitive, gerund) ends in *ing* and functions as a
(19, 23) noun.

3. A(n) (infinitive, gerund) is the basic form of the verb,
(19, 23) usually preceded by the preposition "to."

4. A (perfect, progressive) tense verb shows completed
(18, 21) action.

5. To (consul, council, counsel) someone is to give advice.
(21)

6. Johnny Appleseed planted trees here and (there, their,
(19) they're).

7. Tell whether this sentence is declarative, interrogative,
(1, 3) imperative, or exclamatory: How did the old Queen determine that the young girl was a true princess?

8. Tell whether this group of words is a fragment, run-on, or
(1, 3) complete sentence: To have been infected with incurable talkativeness.

9. Write each noun from the following sentence and label it
(5, 7) abstract or concrete: While looking for a princess, the Prince experienced discouragement.

For 10–13, write the plural of each noun.
10. match   **11.** bedchamber   **12.** fray   **13.** nucleus
(12, 13)   *(12, 13)*   *(12, 13)*   *(12, 13)*

Write each word that should be capitalized in sentences 14 and 15.

14. At age nine, willa cather moved from the beautiful
(5, 11) shenandoah valley of virginia to the empty prairie of nebraska.

15. her *o pioneers!* is the best book i have read about the
(11, 20) actual soil of our country.

16. Rewrite this outline using correct capitalization:
(5, 20)

        i. willa cather

          a. childhood

          b. young adulthood

17. Replace each blank with the missing prepositions from
(16) the third column in Lesson 16.

inside, into, _____, near, _____ off, on, onto, opposite, _____, outside, _____ past, regarding, round, save

18. Replace the blank with the singular present tense form of
(6, 15) the verb: Tailors patch. A tailor _____.

19. For a–c, choose the correct form of the verb.
(6, 14) (a) I (am, are, is) (b) They (was, were)(c)You (was, were)

20. Write the present participle, past tense, and past
(6, 15) participle of the verb *preach*.

For 21–23, write the verb phrase and name its tense.

21. The old Queen has tested the Princess's character.
(8, 18)

22. On top of the many mattresses, the Princess is lying
(8, 21) awake.

23. For a long, long time, the Prince had been searching for a
(8, 21) real princess.

24. For a and b, write the verb and label it action or linking.
(4, 22)
    (a) The Princess felt the pea under her mattress.

    (b) She felt miserable and uncomfortable.

For 25 and 26, write the gerund and label its tense present or perfect.

25. Fishing was a wonderful pastime for Willa Cather.
(18, 19)

26. Having discovered a real princess delighted the Prince.
(18, 19)

Write the infinitive in sentences 27 and 28, and label its tense present or perfect.

27. To have conceived a fairy tale like "The Princess and the
(18, 23) Pea" required a vivid imagination.

28. To prove the authenticity of a princess seems silly to me.
(18, 23)

Diagram the simple subject and simple predicate of sentences 29 and 30.

29. To have slept would have disqualified her.
(4, 23)

30. Sleeping might have ruined her future.
(4, 19)

LESSON 24

Phrases and Clauses

> **Dictation or Journal Entry**
> **Vocabulary:**
> Let us review the present and past tense of the verbs *sit* and *set*.
>
> *Sit* means "to put the body in a seated position." Please *sit* in a chair or lie on the floor. The past tense of *sit* is *sat*. Last night, I *sat* at my desk for two hours.
>
> *Set* means "to place something." Please *set* your dishes on the table and lay the napkins beside them. The past tense of *set* is also *set*. Yesterday, I *set* the lamp on the desk.

Phrases   A **phrase** is a group of words used as a single word in a sentence. A phrase may contain nouns and verbs, but it does not have both a subject and a predicate. Phrases are italicized below.

PREPOSITIONAL PHRASES:

> *under a bridge*
> *after World War II*
> *in case of emergency*

VERB PHRASES:

> *should have accomplished*
> *would have adopted*
> *might have finished*

GERUND PHRASES:

> *exercising for hours*
> *skating on ice*
> *speaking effectively*

INFINITIVE PHRASES:

> *to influence one's peers*
> *to start a new project*
> *to be a good friend*

Clauses   A **clause** is a group of words with a subject and a predicate. In the clauses below, we have italicized the simple subjects and underlined the simple predicates.

> as the *climber* ascended Mount Everest
>
> since the *geographer* had mapped the terrain
>
> but *Mount Everest* is higher than Mount McKinley
>
> (*you*) Imagine the height of that mountain!

Example 1   Tell whether each group of words is a phrase or a clause.

     (a) to daydream all day

     (b) in the Himalayan heights

     (c) after we locate Nepal and Tibet

     (d) searching for Southeast Asia

     (e) if he followed the guide

Solution   (a) This group of words is an infinitive **phrase.** It does not have a subject or predicate.

     (b) This word group is a prepositional **phrase.** It does not have a subject or predicate.

     (c) This word group is a **clause.** Its subject is *we*; its predicate is <u>locate</u>.

     (d) This is a gerund **phrase.** It does not have a subject or predicate.

     (e) This word group is a **clause.** Its subject is *he*; its predicate is <u>followed</u>.

Every complete sentence has at least one clause. Some sentences have more than one clause. We have italicized the simple subjects and underlined the simple predicates in each clause of the sentence below. Notice that it contains four clauses (four subject and predicate combinations).

     After *I* <u>arrived</u> at the summit, but before *I* <u>descended</u>, *I* <u>left</u> a note that *I* <u>had been</u> there.

Below, we have diagrammed the simple subjects and simple predicates of each clause from the sentence above.

     1. After I arrived at the summit,   I | arrived

     2. but before I descended,   I | descended

     3. I left a note   I | left

     4. that I had been there.   I | had been

Example 2 Diagram the simple subjects and simple predicates of the clauses in this sentence:

Until Ada studied geography, she had no idea that Mount Kilimanjaro was the highest mountain in Africa.

Solution We examine the sentence and find that there are three clauses:

1. Until *Ada* <u>studied</u> geography,   <u>Ada</u> | <u>studied</u>

2. *she* <u>had</u> no idea   <u>she</u> | <u>had</u>

3. that *Mount Kilimanjaro* <u>was</u> the highest mountain....

<u>Mount Kilimanjaro</u> | <u>was</u>

Practice For a–d, tell whether the group of words is a phrase or a clause.

a. because mapping mountains fascinates him

b. on an active volcanic mountain in Tanzania

c. if we ascend more than two thousand feet

d. to climb Mount Whitney

Diagram each simple subject and simple predicate in clauses e–g.

e. for Mount McKinley is located in Alaska

f. since the trail led us upward

g. to laugh might be rude

For h–k, replace each blank with *sit, sat,* or *set.*

h. You may _____ beside me.

i. I'll _____ my books over there.

j. Yesterday, Molly and Polly _____ together in class.

k. Oh dear, I _____ my books on wet paint!

More Practice   Write whether each word group is a phrase or a clause.

1. after the Native Americans signed a peace treaty

2. with the Pilgrims of New England

3. that half of the states have Native American names

4. because he taught the Pilgrims

5. about living and surviving in the wilderness

6. to devise a written alphabet

7. since Sequoyah was adept with language

8. a written alphabet of eighty-six characters

9. because they had an alphabet

10. one of the greatest athletes in history

Review set 24   Choose the best word or prefix to complete sentences 1–4.

1. Please (lie, lay) down if you're tired.
   (23)

2. Clouds gathered; the storm was (imminent, immanent,
   (20) eminent).

3. Calvary is a (common, proper) noun.
   (5, 18)

4. Gerunds, infinitives, and participles are also called
   (19, 23) (gerbils, verbals, pesticides).

5. Tell whether this sentence is declarative, interrogative,
   (1, 3) imperative, or exclamatory:

   King Elfin decorated the great hall splendidly.

6. Tell whether this group of words is a fragment, run-on, or
   (1, 3) complete sentence:

   The Night-raven delivered the invitations to the party
   for King Elfin.

7. Write each noun from this sentence and label it concrete
   (7) or abstract: The king seated his guests around the table
   according to their importance.

For 8–10, write the plural of each noun.

8. avocado   9. caddy   10. elk
   (12, 13)   (12, 13)   (12, 13)

11. Rewrite this sentence using correct capitalization:
(11, 20)
concerning slavery, william faulkner said, "to live anywhere in the world of a.d. 1955 and be against equality because of race or color is like living in alaska and being against snow."

12. Replace each blank with the missing prepositions from
(16) the fourth column in Lesson 16.

_____,   through,   _____,   till, _____, toward, under, underneath, until, unto, _____, upon, _____, within, without

13. Write the word from this list that is *not* a linking verb.
(4, 22)
is, am, are, was, were, be, being, been, look, feel, taste, smell, sound, seem, appear, grow, become, breathe, remain, stay

Choose the correct verb form for sentences 14–16.

14. The maidens (twirl, twirled) and entertained the guests.
(6, 15)

15. The mountain elf of Norway (has, have) brought his two
(14, 18) sons.

16. They (has, have) all come to the party.
(8, 14)

17. Write the present participle, past tense, and past
(6, 15) participle of the verb *diminish*.

For 18 and 19, write the verb phrase and name its tense.

18. Two little Norwegian mountain elves had placed their
(8, 18) feet on the table.

19. King Elfin was planning the marriage of his two
(8, 21) daughters to the sons of the old Norwegian elf.

20. Write each preposition in this sentence: After the meal,
(16, 17) the king stood in front of the assembly and presented each daughter along with her special talent.

For 21 and 22, write the verb and label it action or linking.

21. The Elfins tasted salads of mushroom seeds and wet
(4, 22) mice's snouts.

22. The adders' skins tasted delicious to the Elfins.
(4, 22)

23. Write the infinitive in this sentence and label it present
(18, 23) or perfect tense: To have chosen a bride from so many daughters must have been difficult for the Norwegian boys.

24. Write the gerund in this sentence and label it present or
(19) perfect tense: Telling the truth was the special gift of the sixth daughter.

For 25–28, write whether each expression is a phrase or a clause.

25. to disappoint the King Elfin
(2, 24)

26. after the boys fell asleep
(2, 24)

27. if explaining will prevent a misunderstanding
(2, 24)

28. exchanging their fancy little boots
(2, 24)

Diagram the simple subject and simple predicate of sentences 29 and 30.

29. Bowing may indicate respect for someone.
(19)

30. To giggle would be insensitive.
(23)

LESSON
25

The Direct Object • Diagramming the Direct Object

Dictation or Journal Entry

Vocabulary: The Greek prefix *peri-* means around, about, surrounding, or near.

The *pericardium* is the membranous sack enclosing the heart. Inflammation of the *pericardium* causes chest pain.

The *perimeter* is the border of a two-dimensional figure, like a square or a rectangle. We find the *perimeter* of a square by adding the lengths of each side.

Periodontics is a branch of dentistry that studies and treats our gums, which surround our teeth. The dentist's interest in gum disease led to graduate study in *periodontics*.

Finding the Direct Object

A **direct object** follows an *action verb* and tells who or what receives the action.

Ancient Egyptians built the pyramids.

action verb   direct object

We can answer these three questions to find the direct object of a sentence:

1. What is the verb in the sentence?

2. Is it an *action verb*?

3. Who or what receives the action? (direct object)

We will follow the steps above to find the direct object of this sentence:

The sphinx guards the pyramids.

QUESTION 1: What is the verb?
   ANSWER: The verb is "guards."

QUESTION 2: Is it an *action verb*?
   ANSWER: Yes.

QUESTION 3: Who or what receives the action?
   ANSWER: The *pyramids* are "guarded."

Therefore, "pyramids" is the direct object.

Example 1 Follow the procedure above to find the direct object of this sentence:

The reporter photographed the sphinx.

Solution We answer the questions as follows:

> QUESTION 1: What is the verb?
> ANSWER: The verb is "photographed."
>
> QUESTION 2: Is it an *action verb*?
> ANSWER: Yes.
>
> QUESTION 3: Who or what receives the action?
> ANSWER: The *sphinx* is "photographed."

Therefore, **sphinx** is the direct object.

Example 2 Answer the three questions above to find the direct object of this sentence:

> The sphinx has been the guard at Giza.

Solution We answer the questions as follows:

> QUESTION 1: What is the verb?
> ANSWER: The verb is "has been."
>
> QUESTION 2: Is it an *action verb*?
> ANSWER: No. "Has been" is a linking verb.

Therefore, this sentence has **no direct object.**

Diagramming the Direct Object Below is a diagram of the simple subject, simple predicate, and direct object of this sentence:

> Egyptians built the sphinx.

Egyptians	built	sphinx
(subject)	(verb)	(direct object)

Notice that a vertical line after the action verb indicates a direct object.

We remember that a gerund functions as a noun. The direct object in the sentence below is a gerund.

> Egyptians enjoyed building.

Egyptians	enjoyed	building
(subject)	(verb)	(direct object)

An infinitive can function as a noun as well. The direct object in the following sentence is an infinitive.

Do you want to sing?

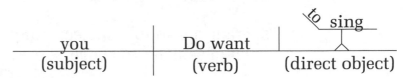

you	Do want	*to* sing
(subject)	(verb)	(direct object)

Example 3 Diagram the simple subject, simple predicate, and direct object of each sentence:

(a) The sphinx guards the pyramids.

(b) Does Karen like to travel?

(c) Have you tried skiing?

Solution (a) The vertical line after the verb, guards, indicates the direct object, pyramids.

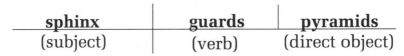

sphinx	**guards**	**pyramids**
(subject)	(verb)	(direct object)

(b) We see that the direct object in this sentence is an infinitive.

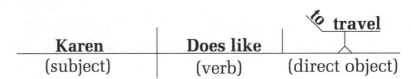

Karen	**Does like**	*to* **travel**
(subject)	(verb)	(direct object)

(c) The direct object is a gerund.

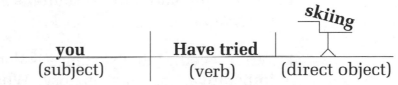

you	**Have tried**	**skiing**
(subject)	(verb)	(direct object)

Practice For a–d, write the direct object, if there is one, in each sentence.

a. The Egyptians worshipped many gods.

b. The pyramids of Giza are one of the wonders of the world.

c. Peasant farmers constructed these pyramids.

√ **d.** For their services, the farmers received food.

e. Diagram the simple subject, simple predicate, and direct object of sentence *a* above.

f. Diagram the simple subject, simple predicate, and direct object of sentence *d* above.

Diagram the simple subject, simple predicate, and direct object of sentences g and h.

g. They began to swim against the current.

h. Do you appreciate my cooking?

For i–l, replace each blank with the correct vocabulary word.

i. In geometry, we learn to find the _____, or distance around, two-dimensional figures.

j. The prefix meaning boundary, surrounding, or encircling is _____.

k. An inflamed _____ concerned the cardiologist.

l. The dentist referred his patient with swollen gums to a specialist in _____.

Review set 25   Choose the best word to complete sentences 1–3.

1. My great-uncle rode in the (cavalry, Calvary).
(18)

2. They left (there, they're, their) car at the airport.
(19)

3. A pleasant, harmonious sound is a (euphony, cacophony, cacography).
(11, 13)

4. Write whether this sentence is declarative, interrogative, imperative, or exclamatory: What treasure does the soldier find in "The Tinder-Box"?
(1, 3)

5. Write whether this expression is a complete sentence, sentence fragment, or run-on sentence: An old woman gave the soldier instructions he will find money.
(1, 3)

6. Write each noun in this sentence and circle the two that are collective: A pack of dogs protected the collection of coins.
(7, 9)

For 7–10, write the plural for each singular noun.

7. ax
(12. 13)

8. ploy
(12, 13)

9. mouse
(12, 13)

10. cuff
(12, 13)

11. Write each word that should be capitalized in this
(5, 11) sentence: william faulkner, born in new albany in 1897, admitted, "i hung around school just to play baseball...."

12. Write each preposition from this sentence: The soldier
(16, 17) kept the tinder-box away from the witch by means of his shrewdness.

For sentences 13–15, write the correct verb form.

13. The audience sang and (past of *clap*) to the music.
(6, 15)

14. The soldier (future of *enter*) the secret chamber.
(8, 10)

15. He (present of *do*) his homework daily.
(8, 14)

16. Write the present participle, past tense, and past
(8, 15) participle of the verb *climb*.

For sentences 17–19, write the verb phrase and name its tense.

17. By the end of the fairy tale, the princess will have
(8, 18) married a soldier.

18. Soon, the dogs will be rescuing the soldier.
(8, 21)

19. The soldier has been meeting with the princess.
(8, 18)

20. For a and b, write the verb and label it action or linking.
(4, 22) (a) The soldier feels brave.

(b) His princess feels a cold breeze.

For 21 and 22, write whether the expression is a phrase or a clause.

21. because the soldier preferred the gold coins
(2, 24)

22. except for an exceedingly clever woman
(2, 24)

For 23 and 24, write the gerund and label its tense present or perfect.

23. Sharing his wealth brought the soldier satisfaction.
(18, 19)

24. Having succeeded encouraged him.
(18, 19)

For 25 and 26, write the infinitive and label its tense present or perfect.

25. To escape the King's judgment proved difficult for the
(23)   soldier.

26. To have fulfilled every request would have been
(23)   impossible.

Diagram the simple subject, simple predicate, and direct object of sentences 27–30.

27. Rescue the princess!
(4, 25)

28. The princess wants to marry.
(4, 25)

29. Does marching tire soldiers?
(4, 25)

30. One soldier enjoys giving.
(4, 25)

LESSON 26

Capitalization: People Titles, Family Words, and School Subjects

> **Dictation or Journal Entry**
>
> **Vocabulary:**
> The Greek word *morphē* means form or structure and commonly appears in English words as *morph*. Knowing this helps us to analyze words like *endomorph, ectomorph,* and *mesomorph,* which refer to body types or structures. An *endomorph* is a person with a short, broad skeleton. An *ectomorph* is characterized by a tall and slender skeleton. A *mesomorph* falls between the two extremes.

We have learned that proper nouns require capital letters and that common nouns are capitalized when they are a part of a proper noun. We also capitalize parts of an outline, the first word of a sentence, the first word of every line of poetry, the pronoun *I*, the first word in a direct quotation, and the important words in titles. Now we will review additional capitalization rules.

Titles Used with Names of People

Titles used with names of people require a capital letter. Often, these are abbreviations. We capitalize initials when they stand for a proper name.

> T. S. Eliot
> Dr. Stanley Livingston
> Mr. and Mrs. Ralph Martinez
> General Ulysses S. Grant
> Reverend Billy Graham
> Grandma Ishida
> Uncle Charles
> Aunt Sukey

Family Words

When **family words** such as *father, mother, grandmother,* or *grandfather* are used instead of a person's name, these words are capitalized. However, they are not capitalized when words such as *my, your, his, our,* or *their* are used before them.

> Hey, *Mom*, thanks for the delicious meal.
> I thanked *my mom* for the spaghetti dinner.
>
> Fred asked *Uncle* to celebrate Christmas with him.
> Fred asked *his uncle* to celebrate Christmas with him.

School Subjects   When the name of a school subject comes from a proper noun, it is capitalized. Otherwise it is not. See the examples below.

Portuguese	industrial arts
Chinese	chemistry
Russian	language arts

Example   Correct the following sentences by adding capital letters where they are needed.

(a) We credit inventor thomas a. edison with the invention of electrical devices.

(b) I'm going to ask auntie to take me to the library.

(c) The student needs one more spanish class in order to graduate.

Solution   (a) We capitalize **Thomas A. Edison** because it is a proper noun, and the letter *A* is an initial.

(b) **Auntie** requires a capital because it is used instead of a person's name.

(c) **Spanish** comes from a proper noun, so we capitalize it.

Practice   Write each word that should be capitalized in a–d.

a. For your foreign language, will you take spanish, french, or latin?

b. Oh no, dad, our phone service has been discontinued!

c. barbara bush is the wife of president george h. w. bush.

d. my dad refuses to install cable television.

For e–h, replace each blank with the correct vocabulary word.

e. Some people wish they were a(n) _____ because that body shape is between the two extremes.

f. Ernest Hopkins has a(n) _____ body type because he has a tall and slender skeleton.

g. The Greek root meaning structure or form is _____.

h. A shorter, heavier body frame is labeled _____ .

More Practice   See Master Worksheets.

Review set 26   Choose the best word to compete sentences 1–3.

1. Removing a rainforest will change a region's (climactic,
(6)   climate).

2. A (statue, stature, statute) prohibits cutting trees in the
(10)   local forest.

3. How long can he (allude, elude) his pursuers?
(14)

4. Tell whether this sentence is declarative, interrogative,
(1, 3)   imperative, or exclamatory:

According to the story, a little fir tree despises its
smallness.

5. Tell whether this word group is a sentence fragment,
(1, 3)   run-on sentence, or complete sentence:

To be as tall and mature as the others in the forest.

6. From this sentence, write each noun and label it concrete
(7)   or abstract: This little tree displayed impatience and
discontentment.

7. Write each neuter gender noun from this list: sisters,
(9)   father, cattle, pasture, sparrow, forest,

For 8 and 9, write the plural of each noun.

8. piccolo   **9.** branch
(12, 13)   (12, 13)

Write each word that should be capitalized in sentences 10
and 11.

10. the fitzgerald family were distant relatives of francis scott
(20)   key, who wrote the words to "the star spangled banner."

11. yes, i believe uncle bob and his friend judge hegarty
(20)   studied latin and greek in school.

12. Write each preposition from this sentence: The little fir
(16, 17) tree had taken the shining sun and the singing birds for
granted prior to his experience in the attic.

13. Write the word from this list that is *not* a helping verb.
$_{(4, 8)}$ is, am, are, was, were, want, be, being, been, has, have, had, do, does, did, shall, will, should, would, can, could, may, might, must

For 14 and 15, write the verb and label it action or linking.

14. Mom sounded the bell for dinner.
$_{(4, 22)}$

15. Life at sea sounded appealing to the little fir tree.
$_{(4, 22)}$

For 16 and 17, write whether the word group is a phrase or a clause.

16. for he was sorrowful and homesick
$_{(2, 24)}$

17. into a large and splendid drawing room
$_{(2, 24)}$

Write the correct verb form for sentences 18–20.

18. Sylvester (present of *crush*) dry leaves under his feet.
$_{(6, 15)}$

19. Three men (present progressive of *cut*) down some of the
$_{(8, 21)}$ largest trees.

20. The little fir tree (past perfect of *wish*) to be something
$_{(8, 18)}$ taller and grander.

Write the direct object of sentences 21 and 22.

21. Children decorate the tree with gilded apples and sugar
$_{(4, 25)}$ plums.

22. The little tree has learned to rejoice.
$_{(18, 23)}$

For sentences 23–25, write the verb phrase and name its tense.

23. A group of mice were listening to tales about the little fir
$_{(8, 21)}$ tree.

24. Professor Snyder had explained the mystery.
$_{(8, 18)}$

25. Klumpy Dumpy will be marrying a princess.
$_{(8, 21)}$

Diagram the simple subject, simple predicate, and direct object of sentences 26–30.

26. Shall we decorate the tree?
$_{(4, 25)}$

27. Decorating takes time.
(19, 25)

28. Javier loves to draw.
(23, 25)

29. Gerard enjoys singing.
(19, 25)

30. On the happiest evening of its life, the tree wore a gold
(4, 25) star.

LESSON
27

Descriptive Adjectives
• Proper Adjectives

Dictation or Journal Entry

Vocabulary:

Let us examine the homophones *canon* and *cannon*.

A *canon* is an ecclesiastical law enacted by a church or council. The Presbyterian *canon* condemns polygamy.

A *cannon* is a mounted gun designed to fire large balls. The boom of the *cannon* was heard for miles.

An adjective is a word that describes a person, place, or thing. There are many different kinds of adjectives. There are **limiting adjectives** such as *a, an*, and *the*; **demonstrative adjectives** such as *this, that, those*, and *these*; and **possessive adjectives** such as *his, her, their, our, its, your*, and *my*.

Descriptive Adjectives   In this lesson we will concentrate on **descriptive adjectives** that describe a person, place, or thing. Sometimes they answer the question, "What kind?" Descriptive adjectives are italicized below.

sea nymph

lengthy siege

courageous, invincible warrior

Often descriptive adjectives come before the person, place, or thing, as in this sentence:

> The *powerful, cordlike* band of *connective* tissue behind the heel is known as the Achilles tendon.

Sometimes descriptive adjectives come after the noun or pronoun, as in this example:

> Achilles, *valiant* and *handsome*, was dipped into the River Styx by the heel.

Some descriptive adjectives end in suffixes like these:

—able	*adaptable, breakable, teachable, believable*
—al	*final, gradual, casual, natural*
—ful	*wishful, fanciful, thankful, helpful*
—ible	*forcible, credible, sensible, visible*
—ic	*anemic, emphatic, sarcastic, strategic*
—ive	*elusive, submissive, sportive, extensive*
—less	*defenseless, useless, fearless, careless*

| —ous | *gorgeous, notorious, enormous, dangerous* |
| —y | *tasty, funny, witty, nosy* |

Example 1 Write each descriptive adjective in sentences a–c.

    (a) We must protect defenseless children.

    (b) Tiresome people demand attention.

    (c) Spectators enjoyed the sportive monkeys.

Solution (a) **Defenseless** describes "children".

    (b) **Tiresome** describes "people".

    (c) **Sportive** describes "monkeys."

Improving Our Writing Descriptive adjectives help us to draw pictures using words. They make our writing more precise and more interesting. For example, eyes can be *protruding, slanted, squinting, glazed, hazel, swollen, clear, sparkling, healthy, sunken, round,* or *almond-shaped.* When we write, we can use descriptive adjectives to create more detailed pictures.

Example 2 Replace each blank with a descriptive adjective to add more detail to the word "voice" in this sentence:

> The villainous Uriah Heep answered David Copperfield in a _____, _____ voice.

Solution Our answers will vary. Here are some possibilities: ***cackling, wicked, hoarse, screeching, phony, deceitful, piercing, gloating, gleeful, sarcastic, ominous, vengeful, arrogant, condescending,*** and ***obnoxious.***

Proper Adjectives An adjective can be common or proper. Common adjectives are formed from common nouns and are not capitalized:

COMMON NOUN	COMMON ADJECTIVE
truth	truthful
analysis	analytical
year	yearly
valor	valiant

Proper adjectives are formed from proper nouns and are always capitalized:

PROPER NOUN	PROPER ADJECTIVE
Achilles	Achilles (tendon)

San Diego	San Diego (freeway)
Thanksgiving	Thanksgiving (meal)
Ford	Ford (sedan)

Sometimes the form of the proper adjective changes as in the examples below.

PROPER NOUN	PROPER ADJECTIVE
Greece	Greek
Italy	Italian
China	Chinese
Wales	Welsh

Example 3   For sentences a–d, write and capitalize each proper adjective. Then write the noun it describes.

(a) The athlete strained his achilles tendon.

(b) That mongolian restaurant allows its patrons to create their own dishes.

(c) Uncle Bill did a scottish dance.

(d) The american flag was still waving in the breeze.

Solution   (a) **Achilles tendon**   (b) **Mongolian restaurant**

(c) **Scottish dance**   (d) **American flag**

Practice   Write each descriptive and proper adjective in sentences a–d.

a. Scot and Archie, sweaty and exhausted, trudged back up the trail.

b. The ingenious veterinarian vaccinated the nervous horse.

c. The Irish, Scottish, and Welsh musicians gathered backstage before the concert.

d. The Columbus Day celebration included a parade and a picnic.

For e and f, write two descriptive adjectives to describe each noun. Answers will vary.

e. dog   **f.** noise

For g and h, write a noun that might be described by the proper adjective.

g. Asian   **h.** Easter

For i–k, replace each blank with the correct vocabulary word.

i. A Jewish _____ requires observance of the Sabbath.

j. On July Fourth, a _____ boomed loudly.

k. One circus act featured a human projectile shot from a _____.

More Practice   See "Slapstick Story #2" in Master Worksheets.

Review set 27   Choose the best word to complete sentences 1–5.

1. (Heresy, Hypocrisy) is an unacceptable doctrine or
(15) belief.

2. (There, Their, They're) are four quarts in a gallon.
(19)

3. The past tense of sit is (sat, set).
(24)

4. To make the (perfect, progressive) tense, we use some
(21) form of the verb *to be* plus the present participle, which ends in *ing.*

5. The (perfect, progressive) tense shows action that has
(18, 21) been completed.

6. Tell whether this sentence is declarative, interrogative,
(1, 3) imperative, or exclamatory:

Could one-legged Tin Soldier possibly win Dancing Lady's heart?

7. Tell whether this expression is a sentence fragment, run-
(1, 3) on sentence, or complete sentence:

Tin Soldier has only one leg there was not enough tin to finish him.

8. Write each noun from this sentence and label it concrete
(7) or abstract: Tin Soldier demonstrates courage, loyalty, and perseverance.

For 9–11, write the plural of each noun.

9. lunch
(12, 13)

10. Thursday
(12, 13)

11. attorney-at-law
(12, 13)

Write each word that should be capitalized in sentences 12 and 13.

12. dr. bryce darden, the family dentist, belongs to the
(11, 20) american dental association.

13. yesterday, i munched on danish cookies as grandpa read
(11, 26) me a story called "the constant tin soldier."

14. Write two helping verbs that rhyme with *could*.
(8)

15. Write the past tense of the verb *plop*.
(4, 15)

For sentences 16 and 17, write the verb phrase and name its tense.

16. The loyal, lone soldier has persevered through calamity
(8, 18) and disaster.

17. Children will be playing with the other twenty-four tin
(8, 21) soldiers.

For sentences 18 and 19, write the verb phrase and label it action or linking.

18. Tin Soldier has felt the heat of the stove.
(4, 22)

19. Dancing Lady has felt loved and appreciated.
(4, 22)

For 20 and 21, write whether the expression is a phrase or a clause.

20. a shining tinsel rose, as big as her whole face
(2, 24)

21. but she had a dress of the finest velvet
(2, 24)

22. Write each preposition from this sentence: Beneath the
(16, 17) moon, and across from Tin Soldier, stood Dancing Lady with both arms in the air.

Diagram the simple subject and simple predicate of sentences 23 and 24.

23. To dance came naturally to the little lady.
(4, 23)

(4, 19) **24.** Her dancing appealed to the tin soldiers.

Diagram the simple subject, simple predicate, and direct object of sentences 25–27.

25. Has Bea begun to read?
(23, 25)

26. This afternoon, Beatriz will start reading.
(19, 25)

27. Honor Tin Soldier for his bravery.
(4, 25)

Write each descriptive adjective from sentences 28–30.

28. Faithful ladies usually wait for valiant soldiers.
(27)

29. However, Goblin, mean and vicious, throws lonely, one-
(27) legged soldiers out.

30. At last, Tin Soldier finds that Dancing Lady, graceful and
(27) compassionate, has joined him.

LESSON 28

The Limiting Adjectives •
Diagramming Adjectives

Limiting adjectives help to define, or "limit," a noun or pronoun. They tell "which one," "what kind," "how many," or "whose." There are six categories of limiting adjectives. They include articles, demonstrative adjectives, numbers, possessive adjectives (both pronouns and nouns), and indefinites.

Articles   Articles are the most commonly used adjectives, and they are also the shortest—*a, an, the.*

a cannon	*the* hypocrisy
a statute	*the* heresy
an alley	*the* macrocosm
an antidote	*the* ectomorph

We use *a* before words beginning with a consonant sound, and *an* before words beginning with a vowel sound. It is the sound and not the spelling that determines whether we use *a* or *an*:

an honor	*a* hunt
an urchin	*a* unicycle
an R-rating	*a* rooster
an x-ray	*a* xylophone

Demonstrative   WHICH ONE?

this noise	*that* song
those allies	*these* maniacs

Numbers   HOW MANY?

three megaphones   *four* telephones   *one* microscope

Possessive Adjectives   Both pronouns and nouns commonly function as adjectives. They answer the question, WHOSE?

Pronouns   WHOSE?

his television	*her* telescope	*their* orthotics
our bibliomania	*its* perimeter	*your* monopoly
my advice		

Nouns   WHOSE?

Pandora's box	*Jacob's* ladder	*Adam's* apple
Ralph's medicine	*Joseph's* coat	*Dad's* opinion

Indefinites   HOW MANY?

some ingredients	*few* supporters	*many* soldiers
several campaigns	*no* participants	*any* leftovers

Example 1   Write each limiting adjective that you find in these sentences.

(a) Those mountains are the Adirondacks!

(b) One peak in this range is Mount Marcy.

(c) Many people visit these mountains.

(d) Our family enjoys the Appalachians.

(e) Dexter's son realized that the Adirondacks are part of the Appalachians.

(f) Those hikers carried few supplies.

Solution

(a) **Those, the**	(b) **One, this**
(c) **Many, these**	(d) **Our, the**
(e) **Dexter's, the, the**	(e) **Those, few**

Diagramming Adjectives   We diagram adjectives by placing them on a slanted line beneath the noun or pronoun they describe, limit, or "modify."

> *Tiffany's* (possessive adjective) *favorite American* (descriptive adjectives) author wrote *many* (indefinite adjective) books.

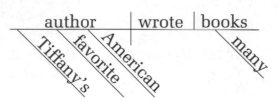

In the sentence above, *Tiffany's* tells "whose," and *favorite* and *American* tell "what kind" of author. *Many* is an indefinite adjective describing "books." We say that the adjective *many* "modifies" the noun *books.*

Example 2   Diagram this sentence:

> Aesop's popular fables give a moral lesson.

Solution   We see that the adjectives *Aesop's* and *popular* modify "fables," and *a* and *moral* modify "lesson," so we diagram the sentence like this:

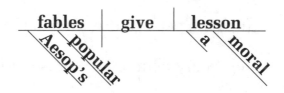

Practice   For a–d, replace each blank with the correct vocabulary word.

a. The transmission of data via telegraph, telephone, or television by electromagnetic signals is called _____.

b. The Greek prefix _____ means far or distant.

c. One has only to pick up the _____ to hear the voice of a distant friend.

d. Originally, _____ operators used Morse code to send and receive messages.

Write each limiting adjective that you find in sentences e–h.

e. Aesop's fable tells about a goose and its eggs.

f. His stories include many animals.

g. Several generations have passed down these fables.

h. That tortoise made some progress while this hare napped for a few minutes.

i. Diagram this sentence: Their literature class read Mark Twain's novels.

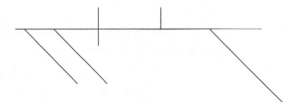

More Practice   See Master Worksheets

Review set 28

1. Write whether this sentence is declarative, interrogative,
(1, 3) imperative, or exclamatory:

For tomorrow, please read "The Swineherd," by Hans Christian Andersen.

2. Write whether this word group is a sentence fragment,
(1, 3) run-on sentence, or complete sentence:

There once was a prince with a very small kingdom.

3. Write the collective noun from this sentence: The
(7) swineherd cared for a litter of pigs.

4. Write the plural form of a–c.
(12, 13) (a) puff   (b) candy   (c) cupful

Write each word that should be capitalized in sentences 5 and 6.

5. the princess, i realize, learned a very hard lesson.
(11, 20)

6. my trustworthy knight, sir lancelot declared, "have no
(11, 20) fear, for i am here!"

(16) **7.** Write four prepositions that begin with the letter *o*.

8. Write each preposition from this sentence: From among
(16, 17)a hundred princesses, the prince chose one princess who
did not appreciate his gifts of love.

9. Write the word from this list that is *not* a linking verb: is,
(16, 22)am, are, was, were, be, being, been, with, look, feel, taste,
smell, sound, seem, appear, grow, become, remain, stay

For 10–12, choose the correct form of the irregular verb *have.*
10. you (has, have)   **11.** They (has, have)   **12.** It (has, have)
(6, 14)   (6, 14)   (6, 14)

For sentences 13 and 14, write the verb phrase and name its
tense.

13. The princess and her ladies have behaved shamefully
(8, 18) toward the swineherd.

14. The prince has been searching for a special princess.
(8, 21)

For 15 and 16, write the verb phrase and label it action or
linking.

15. The princess was looking dissatisfied with the rose and
(4, 22) the nightingale.

16. The prince was looking all over the castle grounds for the
(4, 22) princess.

For 17 and 18, tell whether the word group is a phrase or a
clause.

17. with sweet melodies in her little throat
(2, 24)

18. although the rose smelled sweet
(2, 24)

19. Write the infinitive in this sentence and label its tense
(18, 23)present or perfect: To please the princess became the
desire of the prince.

20. Write the present participle, past tense, and past
(6, 15) participle of the verb *reign.*

21. Write each article in this sentence: The prince brought a
(28) useful little saucepan and an assortment of other gifts for
the princess.

22. Write the indefinite adjective in this sentence: Some
(28) people do not understand the importance of gratitude.

Choose the correct word to complete sentences 23–26.

23. The progressive verb tense shows (completed, continuing) action.
(21)

24. Please (sit, set) in this comfortable chair.
(24)

25. Please (sit, set) your baggage by the door.
(24)

26. A prefix meaning "not" or "without" is (*a-*, *re-*, *eu-*).
(13, 22)

Diagram each word of sentences 27–30.

27. Studying will raise your scores.
(4, 19)

28. Flee fickle princesses.
(4, 25)

29. The prince desired to marry.
(23, 25)

30. Had the prince's gifts pleased the ungrateful princess?
(25, 28)

LESSON 29   Capitalization: Areas, Religions, Greetings

> **Dictation or Journal Entry**
>
> **Vocabulary:**
> *Perspective* and *prospective* are spelled similarly, yet they have very different meanings.
>
> A *perspective* is a "point of view"—the ability to evaluate all relevant data. From the teacher's *perspective*, an extra day of vacation is well deserved.
>
> *Prospective* means "of or in the future." The mayor's *prospective* budget provided for two additional middle schools.

There is an old saying, "Practice makes perfect." So it is with capitalization. Proper capitalization becomes easier with practice.

We have reviewed capitalizing proper nouns, parts of an outline, the first word of a sentence, the first word in a line of poetry, the pronoun *I,* the first word in a direct quotation, important words in titles, people titles, family words when used as names, and the names of school subjects that come from a proper noun. Now we will review more capitalization rules.

Areas of the Country

We capitalize North, South, East, West, Midwest, Northeast, etc. when they refer to **certain areas of the country.**

Alligators roam free in certain parts of the South.

The West often draws people from the East during winter months.

In 2001, the Middle East struggled with terrorists.

However, we do not capitalize these words when they indicate a direction.

The state of California lies south of Oregon.

The Mississippi River flows from north to south.

Roger lives south of Colorado Boulevard and north of Duarte Road.

Religious References   We capitalize **religions and their members, works regarded as sacred,** and **references to a supreme being.**

The Jewish and Christian religions share the Old Testament of the Bible.

Ancient Egyptians prayed to Isis.

Local Methodists support the project.

Many Buddhist homes have statues of Buddha.

Greeting and Closing of a Letter   We capitalize the first words in the **greeting and closing of a letter.**

Dear Francisco,

My generous guardian,

Love,

Sincerely,

Gratefully,

Example   Write each word that should be capitalized in these sentences.

(a) The Rivases live in the east.

(b) According to the map, the destination was northeast of the travelers.

(c) My mother attended a catholic school in the midwest until she was twelve years old.

(d) The gentleman wrote, "dear Kari," and ended his letter with, "gratefully, Tony."

Solution   (a) We capitalize **East** because it refers to a specific section of the United States.

(b) No correction is needed.

(c) We capitalize **Catholic** because it is a religion. We also capitalize **Midwest** because it is a specific part of the country.

(d) We capitalize **Dear** because it is the first word of a letter's greeting. **Gratefully** needs a capital because it is the first word of the closing.

Practice   For a–d, write each word that should be capitalized.

a. many people in the south enjoy catfish, grits, and okra.

    b. the episcopal priest cared for his people and asked for god's help.

    c. celia's hair salon is located five blocks north of huntington drive.

    d. dear father tim,
       thank you for your help.
       gratefully,
       cynthia

For e–h, replace each blank with the correct vocabulary word.

    e. From the defendant's _____, she is not guilty.

    f. The forecast of the nation's _____ economy is dismal.

    g. The _____ weather report is for cloudy days and some rainfall.

    h. Being much older, Mr. O'Rourke has a different _____ from his son.

More Practice   See Master Worksheets

Review set 29   Choose the best word to complete sentences 1–4.

    1. A (progressive, perfect) tense verb shows completed $^{(18,\,21)}$action.

    2. To (lie, lay) means to recline.
    $^{(23)}$

    3. A (consul, council, counsel) is one who represents his or $^{(21)}$ her fellow citizens in a foreign country.

    4. The prefix *an-* means (large, without, passion).
    $^{(17,\,22)}$

    5. Tell whether this sentence is declarative, interrogative, $^{(1,\,3)}$ imperative, or exclamatory:

    Have you read Hans Christian Andersen's "The Nightingale"?

6. Tell whether this word group is a sentence fragment,
(1, 3) run-on sentence, or complete sentence:

The Chinese emperor has a palace it is made entirely
of porcelain.

7. Write each noun from this sentence and label it concrete
(7) or abstract: People with discretion will not touch the
delicate, brittle palace.

8. For a and b, write the plural of each noun.
(12, 13)(a) studio   (b) stimulus

Write each word that should be capitalized in sentences
9–14.

9. cary's academic program included greek, hebrew,
(11, 26)keyboarding, history, and latin.

10. the granddaughter asked her grandmother if they could
(5, 11) go to the smithsonian institute.

11. hey, grandpa, may i go to the store with you?
(11, 26)

12. does the east or the west set fashion trends in our
country?

13. turn north on rosemead boulevard and go two miles
(26, 29)before veering east near the greek cathedral.

14. the company's president began his letter, "to all our loyal
(11, 20)patrons," and ended with "regretfully, mr. babikian."

15. Write each preposition from this sentence: According to
(16, 17)the narrator, the garden of the palace contained flowers
with silver bells tied to them.

16. For a–c, choose the correct form of the irregular verb *to be.*
(6, 14)(a) You (was, were) (b) I (am, are, is) (c) We (am, are, is)

For sentences 17 and 18, write the verb phrase and name its
tense.

17. The gardener had arranged the flowers admirably.
(8, 18)

18. The nightingale had been singing for all those who
(8, 21) chanced by.

For 19 and 20, write the verb phrase and label it action or linking.

19. A traveler might smell the wonderful flowers.

(4, 22)

20. In the garden, the air might smell fragrant.

(4, 22)

For 21 and 22, tell whether the expression is a phrase or a clause.

21. when they heard the nightingale

(2, 24)

22. a magnificent poem about a nightingale in a wood near a

(2, 24) deep lake

23. Write the present participle, past tense, and past

(6, 15) participle of the verb *answer*.

Write each adjective in sentences 24 and 25.

24. Of the many people in the court, one person had heard

(27, 28) the magnificent singing of the little nightingale.

25. That servant placed the king's chalice on its proper shelf

(27, 28) in the royal kitchen.

Diagram sentences 26 and 27.

26. Sprinting will improve Caesar's overall performance.

(19, 25)

27. His ten sons chose to listen.

(23, 25)

Write the correct verb form to complete sentences 28–30.

28. The king (past progressive of *listen*) to the nightingale's

(8, 21) sweet song.

29. Hart Crane (present perfect of *create*) a poem called "The

(8, 18) Black Tambourine."

30. We (future of *write*) poems next week.

(8, 10)

LESSON 30

No Capital Letter

Dictation or Journal Entry

Vocabulary:
The Greek prefix *pro-* means "before."

A *program* lists the schedule of activities or upcoming events. The *program* for Back-to-School Night includes the introduction of the school's teaching staff.

When used as a verb, *project* means to present a plan of action and its results before it happens. The school district *projects* greatly improved test scores for next year.

A *proponent* advocates something or supports a cause. Mr. Hake is a *proponent* of the traditional grammar program.

Most grammar books teach us when to capitalize words, but this lesson reminds us when **not** to capitalize words.

Common Nouns

Common nouns such as animals, plants, diseases, foods, trees, musical instruments, and games are not capitalized. If a proper adjective (descriptive word) appears with the noun, we only capitalize the proper adjective, not the common noun. Below are some examples.

COMMON NOUN	COMMON NOUN WITH PROPER ADJECTIVE
dachshund	Russian wolfhound
cabbage	Brussels sprouts
almond	Brazil nut
lettuce	Caesar salad
hibiscus	California poppy
tetanus	Hodgkins disease

Example 1 Add capital letters where needed.

(a) Currently, australian willow trees are a favorite among landscapers.

(b) Is there a thai restaurant in this town?

(c) Our neighbors borrowed our checkers and chess games.

(d) An orchestra consists of violins, flutes, tubas, percussion instruments, and french horns.

(e) Doctors advise us to be immunized against tuberculosis, hepatitis, and influenza.

Solution (a) We capitalize **Australian,** a proper adjective. However, willow is not capitalized because trees are common nouns.

(b) We capitalize **Thai,** a proper adjective. However, restaurant is not capitalized because it is a common nouns.

(c) We do not add capital letters because games are common nouns.

(d) Musical instruments are not capitalized unless part of their name is a proper noun. We capitalize **French** horn because France is a country.

(e) Diseases are common nouns; they require no capital letters.

Seasons of the Year   We do not capitalize **seasons of the year**—fall, winter, spring, and summer.

People in the East enjoy the changing colors of tree leaves in the fall.

Hyphenated Words   We treat a **hyphenated word** as if it were a single word. If it is a proper noun or the first word of a sentence, we capitalize only the first word, and not all the parts of the hyphenated word. See the examples below.

Twenty-nine years ago, my parents were married.

At the end of the year, Father-in-law Ernest paid a large amount in income taxes.

Example 2   Add capital letters where needed in this sentence:

Yes, brother-in-law robert will help us move in the summer.

Solution   **Yes, Brother-in-law Robert will help us move in the summer.**

We capitalize **Brother** because it is a proper noun (a family name as part of a person's name). However, we do not capitalize the other parts of the hyphenated word (in-law). We capitalize **Robert** because it is a person's name. However, we do not capitalize summer because it is a season of the year.

Practice   For a–d, replace each blank with the correct vocabulary word.

   a. The respected student was a _____ of a drug-free life-style.

b. My financial planner will _____ the cost of living for the next ten years.

c. The Greek prefix meaning "before" is _____.

d. The title of each song was listed in the _____ for the musical performance.

Write each word that should be capitalized in sentences e–i.

e. Last autumn, mother-in-law joyce turned seventy-one years of age.

f. The violin, viola, cello, and bass fiddle are classified as string instruments.

g. The spanish omelet had onions, green peppers, red peppers, greek olives, california avocados, and sour cream.

h. beau and belle played exquisitely in the chess tournament.

i. The gardener prided himself on his beautiful trees: california oak, chinese elm, liquid amber, crepe myrtle, and australian willow.

More Practice   See Master Worksheets.

Review set 30

1. Tell whether this sentence is declarative, interrogative,
(1, 3) imperative, or exclamatory:

How beautiful that is!

2. Tell whether this word group is a sentence fragment, run-
(1, 3) on sentence, or complete sentence: A brilliantly ornamented artificial nightingale singing to the emperor.

3. Write each noun from this sentence and label it abstract
(7) or concrete: The nightingale gave the emperor much pleasure.

4. Write each noun from this sentence and circle the one
(9) that is compound: A fisherman offered his honest opinion about the artificial bird.

5. For a–c, write the plural of each noun.
(12, 13) (a) child   (b) sketch   (c) Larry

6. Write each word that should be capitalized in this
(20, 30) sentence: yesterday, uncle eric said, "meet me at huntington beach on wednesday, and please bring your chinese checkers."

7. Write each preposition in this sentence: Because of the
(16, 17) nightingale's singing at the window of the dying emperor, the emperor regained his health.

Write the correct verb form to complete sentences 8 and 9.

8. A sparrow (past tense of *hop*) onto the window sill.
(6, 15)

9. It (present progressive tense of *harmonize*) with the
(8, 21) nightingale.

10. For a–c, choose the correct form of the irregular verb *do*.
(6, 14) (a) She (do, does) (b) You (do, does) (c) We (did, done)

For 11 and 12, write the verb phrase and name its tense.

11. We shall have earned a hundred dollars by Friday.
(8, 18)

12. By the end of the story, the bird will have been singing
(8, 21) for six months.

For 13 and 14, write the verb phrase and label it action or linking.

13. A nightingale appears at the window of the dying
(4, 22) emperor.

14. The emperor appears ill.
(4, 22)

For 15 and 16, write whether the word group is a phrase or a clause.

15. after the artificial nightingale was declared useless
(2, 24)

16. grieving for the dying emperor
(2, 24)

17. Write the present participle, past tense, and past
(4, 15) participle of the verb *smile*.

Write each adjective from sentences 18 and 19.

18. The arrogant, pedantic play-master bragged about his
(27, 28) jewel-studded nightingale.

19. Didn't any neighbors miss that real nightingale?
(27, 28)

For 20 and 21, write each proper adjective followed by the noun it describes.

20. The German ruler addressed the Japanese assembly.
(5, 28)

21. American youth have appreciated the fairy tales of Hans
(5, 28) Christian Andersen.

22. From this sentence, write the gerund and label its tense
(8, 18) present or perfect: Having pleased the emperor assured
him great favor in the kingdom.

Choose the best word to complete sentences 23–26.

23. A perfect tense verb shows (completed, continuing)
(18, 21) action.

24. A megalopolis is a large (city, heart, book).
(17)

25. The (Calvary, cavalry) arrived just in time to rescue their
(18) allies from the enemy.

26. (There, Their, They're) team won the game.
(19)

Diagram each word of sentences 27–30.

27. This restaurant features Italian food.
(25, 28)

28. The little bird loved the Chinese ruler.
(25, 28)

29. Her aunt relishes gardening.
(19, 25)

30. To sing can lift your spirits.
(23, 25)

LESSON 31

Transitive and Intransitive Verbs

Dictation or Journal Entry

Vocabulary:
The Latin prefix *ante-* means "before."

Antebellum means "before the war." The *antebellum* attitude of Americans was somewhat ambivalent.

To *antedate* means to be older than something or to precede in time. The radio *antedates* the television.

The *anteroom* refers to a smaller room that leads into a larger room. People waited in the *anteroom* until the banquet room doors opened.

Transitive Verbs   A **transitive verb** is an action verb that has a direct object. The sentences below have transitive verbs.

Aladdin <u>possessed</u> a magic lamp.

Aladdin <u>summoned</u> the genie from the lamp.

Intransitive Verbs   An **intransitive verb** has no direct object. The sentences below have intransitive verbs.

Moby Dick <u>is</u> a long novel.

linking verb — no direct object

The whale <u>was floating</u> lazily.

action verb — no direct object

The same verb can be transitive in one sentence and intransitive in another.

Herman Melville <u>wrote</u> *Moby Dick*. (transitive)

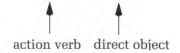

Herman Melville <u>wrote</u> creatively. (intransitive)

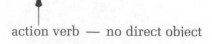
action verb — no direct object

Some action verbs are *always* intransitive. See examples below.

Martin <u>apologized</u> to Becky.

The diamond <u>sparkled</u> in the moonlight.

The sun <u>rose</u>.

Example Rewrite the following sentences. Underline the verb and star the direct object if there is one. Tell whether the verb is transitive or intransitive.

(a) Aladdin was the hero of the story.

(b) Have you read *Arabian Nights*?

Solution (a) **Aladdin <u>was</u> the hero of the story.** The verb "was" is **intransitive.** It has no direct object.

(b) **<u>Have</u> you <u>read</u> *Arabian Nights?** The verb "read" is **transitive.** It has a direct object, *Arabian Nights*.

Practice Rewrite sentences a–d. Underline the verb and star the direct object if there is one. Tell whether the verb is transitive or intransitive.

a. The genie fulfills Aladdin's extravagant demands.

b. The magic lamp glows magnificently.

c. The genie procures a princess for Aladdin.

d. Eventually, the magician is slain.

For e–h, replace each blank with the correct vocabulary word.

e. The prefix meaning "before" is _____.

f. Herbs and penicillin _____ many of our current antibiotics.

g. That clothing style was popular before the American Civil War, so we call it _____.

h. Patients usually wait in an _____ before being admitted to the hospital.

More Practice Tell whether each underlined verb is transitive or intransitive. Then write the direct object if there is one.

1. A cunning African magician <u>steals</u> the magic lamp.

2. This folklore <u>was passed</u> from one generation to another.

3. The sultan <u>replies</u> without hesitation.

4. <u>Has</u> the Princess Badroulboudour <u>arrived</u> at the palace?

5. The sultan's porters <u>open</u> the gates.

6. Wax candles <u>illuminate</u> a noble feast.

7. The gold plates, vases, and goblets <u>are</u> of exquisite workmanship.

8. Aladdin <u>hurries</u> to the mosque for prayers.

9. Aladdin eagerly <u>rubs</u> the lamp.

10. The sultan <u>returns</u> to the khan.

Review set 31

1. Write whether this sentence is declarative, interrogative,
(1, 3) imperative, or exclamatory:

No, I simply won't accept this!

2. Write whether the following is a sentence fragment,
(1, 3) run-on sentence, or complete sentence:

"Living in W'ales," by Richard Hughes, is an entertaining but silly short story it is about a man who built a model village in a strange location.

3. Write each common, concrete noun from this sentence
(7, 9) and name its gender:

A little girl, a grumpy old lady, a pleasant husband, and an Alsatian dog journey together.

4. Write each noun from this sentence and circle the one
(7, 9) that is possessive:

The author's group of characters eventually meets a whale.

5. For a–c, write the plural of each noun.
(12, 13) (a) leaf   (b) reef   (c) finch

Write each word that should be capitalized in sentences 6 and 7.

6. does this story take place in the fall, winter, spring, or
(11, 30) summer?

7. does the whale live in the bering sea or the indian ocean?
(5, 11)

8. Write whether this word group is a phrase or a clause: to
(2, 24) whisper into its blowhole

9. Replace each blank with the missing helping verb.
(8) is, _____, are, was, _____, be,
_____, been, may, might, _____, can,
could, should, would, shall, _____, do, does,
did, has, have, had

10. Write five simple prepositions that begin with the letter *t*.
(16) (Refer to Lesson 16 if necessary.)

11. Write each preposition in this sentence: Sitting on top of
(16, 17) the whale, the cross old lady of Liverpool whispers to the
huge mammal.

For sentences 12–14, write the verb phrase and label it action
or linking.

12. Actually, the old lady seems quite ignorant.
(4, 22)

13. She is looking rather silly to me.
(4, 22)

14. The whale will soon be blowing water out of its hole.
(4, 22)

Write the correct verb form to complete sentences 15 and 16.

15. Out at sea, Presley, Ariana, and Raudel (past progressive
(8, 21) tense of *watch*) for whales all day today.

16. In the distance, water (present tense of *fizz*) from the
(6, 15) blowhole of a whale.

17. For a–c, choose the correct form of the irregular verb
(8, 14) *have.*

(a) I (has, have) (b) They (has, have)(c)He (has, have)

18. Write the four principal parts (present tense, present
(6, 15) participle, past tense, past participle) of the verb *block.*

19. Write each descriptive adjective from this sentence: The
(27) enormous sneeze of the whale blows the grouchy lady
away.

20. Write each article from this sentence: The whale allows a
(28) little girl and an Alsatian dog to enter its mouth.

21. From this sentence, write the proper adjective followed
(28, 30) by the noun it describes: While inside the whale, the
Alsatian dog tries to dig holes.

22. Write the gerund from this sentence and label its tense
(18, 19) present or perfect: Having settled in the belly of a whale
creates some problems for the girl and her dog.

Diagram sentences 23 and 24.

23. The little girl will need to eat.
(23, 25)

24. The considerate whale provides Armenian food.
(25, 28)

Choose the correct word to complete sentences 25–30.

25. The progressive tense shows action that is (continuing,
(18, 21) completed).

26. To make the progressive tense, we use some form of the
(14, 21) verb *to be* plus the (present, past) participle.

27. The (present, past) participle ends in *ing.*
(15)

28. Can the Alsatian dog (adapt, adept, adopt) to its new
(1) environment?

29. The orthodontist's job is to (clean, straighten, whiten)
(9) teeth.

30. My aunt gave me wise (consul, council, counsel)
(21) concerning my social life.

LESSON 32

Object of the Preposition • The Prepositional Phrase

Dictation or Journal Entry

Vocabulary:

Note the difference between *forceful* and *forcible.*

Forceful means full of force, or powerful, vigorous, effective. The poverty-stricken nation made a *forceful* plea to Congress for assistance.

Forcible means "done by force." The burglar made a *forcible* entry into the building.

Object of the Preposition

We have learned to recognize common prepositions—connecting words that link a noun or pronoun to the rest of the sentence. In this lesson, we will identify the **object of the preposition,** which is the noun or pronoun that follows the preposition. Every preposition must have an object. Otherwise, it is not a preposition. We italicize prepositions and star their objects in the phrases below.

aboard the *ship	*according to* the *article
beneath a *crag	*except for* her *tuition
concerning this *issue	*in addition to* *Molly
despite the *frustration	*in regard to* a *complaint
within the *country	*on behalf of* the *team
except *Polly	*round about* *me
via *email	*owing to* some *delays

Prepositions may have compound objects:

He drove *in spite of* *snow and *ice.

They forged *through* *rivers and *streams.

Example 1 Star the object or objects of each preposition in these sentences.

(a) *In addition to* the beauty, we appreciate the meaning *of* paintings and sculptures.

(b) *Despite* the mess, don't cry *over* spilled milk.

Solution (a) *In addition to* the ***beauty**, we appreciate the meaning *of* ***paintings** and ***sculptures.**

(b) *Despite* the ***mess,** don't cry *over* spilled ***milk.**

Prepositional Phrase   A prepositional phrase begins with a preposition and contains a noun and its modifiers (the words that describe the noun). We italicize prepositional phrases below.

> Louisa May Alcott wrote classics *for children.*

> She learned much *from Ralph Emerson and Henry Thoreau.*

> *During the Civil War,* she worked in the hospital.

Notice that there can be more than one prepositional phrase in a sentence:

> Alexander the Great was one *of the greatest generals* (1) *of all time* (2).

> Lady trotted *out the gate* (1) and *through the lush green meadow* (2).

> *After our meeting* (1), let's walk *along the levee* (2) *to the park* (3).

Example 2   For each sentence, write each prepositional phrase and star the object(s) of each preposition.

(a) We see Aristotle on the list of famous philosophers.

(b) Aristotle stimulated Alexander's interest in rhetoric, literature, science, medicine, and philosophy.

(c) By means of symbolism, an allegory presents both literal and symbolic meaning.

Solution   (a) **on the *list, of famous *philosophers**

(b) **in *rhetoric, *literature, *science, *medicine, and *philosophy**

(c) **By means of *symbolism**

Practice   For sentences a–d, write each prepositional phrase and star the object of the preposition.

a. In a group of words, when two or more words begin with the same letter or sound, we call it alliteration.

b. According to this definition, the phrase "through thick and thin" is an example of alliteration.

    c. We find this literary device used in poetry, prose, and oratory.

    d. The phrase "alpha and omega" means from beginning to end.

For e–g, replace each blank with *forceful* or *forcible*.

    e. Because he forgot his key, he made a _____ entry into his house.

    f. A _____ jerk on the cord started the lawn mower.

    g. The President delivered a _____ speech in response to the nation's crisis.

More Practice   Write each prepositional phrase and star the object(s) of each preposition in these sentences.

1. Israel is the narrow strip of land between the Mediterranean Sea and the Jordan River.

2. In spite of its small size, Israel became the center of the ancient world.

3. Trade goods passed over Israel from the world's two oldest cultures, Mesopotamia and Egypt.

4. Ancient armies traveled through Israel to their battles.

5. Because of its location, Israel was often invaded by enemies.

6. We saw the Mediterranean Sea along Israel's coast.

7. The land closest to the sea is coolest; the land farthest from it is desert.

8. Across from the Sea of Galilee, on the map, we find the town of Nazareth.

9. According to historians, Jesus lived in Nazareth during his childhood.

10. The Jordan River runs through the middle of the deepest fault in the world.

11. This fault runs beyond Israel into the continent of Africa.

12. The Sea of Galilee is 688 feet below sea level.

Review set 32

1. Tell whether this sentence is declarative, interrogative, imperative, or exclamatory: Edward Lear wrote a short story called "The Story of the Four Little Children Who Went Around the World."
   [1, 3]

2. Tell whether the following is a sentence fragment, run-on sentence, or complete sentence: Violet, Slingsby, Guy, and Lionel are the four children in the story.
   [1, 3]

Choose the correct word to complete sentences 3–9.

3. The perfect verb tense shows action that is (completed, continuing).
   [18]

4. To form the perfect tense, we add a form of the helping verb (have, must) to the past participle.
   [18]

5. A(n) (transitive, intransitive) verb has no direct object.
   [25, 31]

6. A(n) (transitive, intransitive) verb is an action verb with a direct object.
   [25, 31]

7. Obviously, the crowd appreciated the (imminent, immanent, eminent) astrophysicist's comments.
   [20]

8. Aphonic means (with, without, loud) sound.
   [22]

9. Do you allow your dog to (lie, lay) on your sofa?
   [23]

10. Write the abstract, common noun from this sentence: The four children suffered from wanderlust.
    [7]

11. Write the plural noun from this sentence: The quangle-wangle's boat was painted blue with green spots.
    [9]

12. For a–c, write the plural for each noun.
    [12, 13] (a) barracuda   (b) contralto   (c) trench

Write each word that should be capitalized in sentences 13 and 14.

13. yes, i believe aunt della said, "my train will arrive in san diego on tuesday."
    [20, 26]

14. in "the story of the four little children who went around the world," violet puts parrot feathers in her hat and knits woolen frocks for fishes.
    [11, 20]

15. Tell whether the following is a phrase or a clause: while
(2, 24) they were collecting oranges

16. Write five simple prepositions that begin with the letter
(16) *b.* Refer to Lesson 16 if necessary.

17. Write each preposition from this sentence: Prior to their
(16, 17) visit with the blue-bottle flies, the children had docked
on land inhabited by white mice with red eyes.

18. Write three helping verbs that begin with the letter *m.*
(8)

19. Write five linking verbs that are related to our five senses.
(22)

20. Write the correct verb form to complete this
(6, 15) sentence: The children (past tense of *pry*) off the claws of
the willing crabs.

21. Write the four principal parts (present tense, present
(6, 15) participle, past tense, and past participle) of the verb
demolish.

For 22 and 23, write the verb phrase and label it action or
linking.

22. Yellow-nosed apes remain in places with pits full of
(4, 22) mulberry jam.

23. One ape remains fast asleep.
(4, 22)

For sentences 24 and 25, write the verb phrase and label it
transitive or intransitive.

24. A seeze pyder has bitten the children's boat into "fifty-
(25, 31) five thousand million hundred billion bits."

25. Now, the children are continuing by land.
(25, 31)

26. Write each adjective from this sentence: These curious
(27, 28) children enjoy eventful adventures in foreign lands.

Diagram sentences 27–30.

27. That San Francisco team plays baseball.
(25, 28)

28. Does traveling tire you?
(19, 25)

29. That rhinoceros wants to survive.
(23, 25)

30. To have traveled pleased the children.
(23, 25)

LESSON 33

The Prepositional Phrase as an Adjective • Diagramming

Dictation or Journal Entry

Vocabulary:
The Greek suffix *-phobia* means "irrational fear," as in *hydrophobia, agoraphobia,* and *claustrophobia.*

Hydrophobia is an unnatural dread of water. The kitten's *hydrophobia* was innate.

Agoraphobia is a fear of crowds and public places. The woman's *agoraphobia* made it impossible for her to shop in large malls.

Claustrophobia is the fear of narrow or enclosed places. Some people develop *claustrophobia* in elevators.

Adjective Phrases

We remember that a phrase is a group of words that functions as a single word. Prepositional phrases function as a single word, and some modify a noun or pronoun, so we call them **adjective phrases.** This type of prepositional phrase answers an adjective question such as "Which one?" "What kind?" or "How many?" Here are some examples:

This class *of vertebrates* is amphibia. (modifies the noun "class," and tells "what kind")

Amphibia is the class *between fishes and reptiles.* (modifies the noun "class," and tells "which one")

The skin *of amphibians* is smooth and sticky. (modifies the noun "skin," and tells "what kind")

The laboratory has cubicles *for twenty students.* (modifies the noun "cubicles," and tells "how many")

Example 1 Write the adjective phrase and tell which noun or pronoun it modifies.

(a) Susan B. Anthony was an American reformer on behalf of women's suffrage.

(b) She wrote that magazine article about women's suffrage.

(c) Lucretia bought tickets for twelve.

Solution (a) The phrase **on behalf of women's suffrage** modifies **reformer.** It tells "what kind" of reformer.

(b) The phrase **about women's suffrage** modifies **article.** It tells "which one."

(c) The phrase **for twelve** modifies **tickets.** It tells "how many."

Diagramming the Prepositional Phrase

To diagram a prepositional phrase, we place the preposition on a slanted line attached to the word that the phrase modifies. We place the object of the preposition on a horizontal line at the bottom of the slanted preposition line:

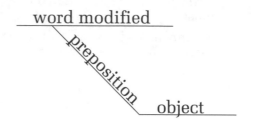

Let us diagram this sentence:

Sir Marcus Kent earned a doctorate in philosophy.

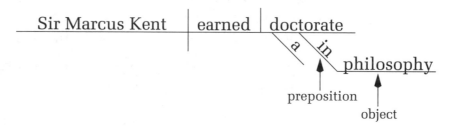

Example 2   Diagram this sentence:

The back of the book has an epilogue.

Solution   The prepositional phrase *of the book* modifies the subject of the sentence, *back*. We diagram the phrase as shown below, remembering to include the second *the*, which modifies *book*:

The back of the book has an epilogue.

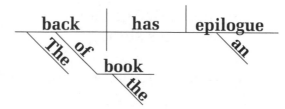

Two Prepositional Phrases

Sometimes a prepositional phrase immediately follows another one and modifies its object, as in the sentence below.

Some *of the people from Taiwan* shared their food.

In the sentence above, the first prepositional phrase, *of the people,* modifies the subject, *some*. The second prepositional phrase, *from Taiwan*, modifies the noun *people*. We show this by diagramming the sentence as follows:

Some of the people from Taiwan shared their food

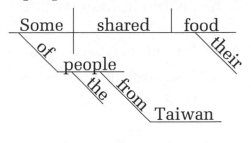

Example 3 Diagram this sentence:

He drove a minivan with a flag on its antenna.

Solution We place each preposition on a slanted line underneath the word it modifies. Then we place each object on a horizontal line attached to its preposition.

He drove a minivan with a flag on its antenna.

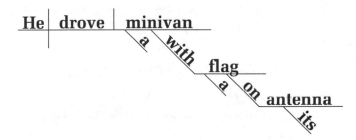

Practice For a–c, tell which noun or pronoun is modified by each italicized prepositional phrase.

a. My Aunt Cecilia writes articles *concerning the care of young children.*

b. People call her an expert *in her field.*

c. She has valuable tips *for mothers and fathers.*

Write each prepositional phrase in sentences d–f, and tell which noun or pronoun it describes.

d. Elizabeth II is the current queen of England.

e. A trip to England is a dream of mine.

f. The people in London must tolerate rain.

Diagram sentences g and h.

g. Do you know another name for "northern lights"?

h. People in high latitudes can see the aurora borealis.

For i–l, replace each blank with the correct vocabulary word.

i. Because he nearly drowned as a puppy, Rover suffered from _____.

j. The suffix meaning irrational fear is _____.

k. A vendor selling hot dogs and peanuts at a baseball game could not have _____.

l. People with _____ feel uncomfortable in caves or mines.

Review set 33

1. Tell whether the following sentence is declarative, interrogative, exclamatory, or imperative: A rabbit can't be heir to the throne!
(1, 3)

2. Tell whether the following is a sentence fragment, run-on sentence, or complete sentence: A competition to choose the successor to the throne.
(1, 3)

3. Write each noun in this sentence and circle the one that is collective: A crowd gathered to watch the competition for the next king.
(7, 9)

4. Write each possessive noun from this list: kings, kings', crown's, crowns, James's, Jameses
(9)

5. For a–c, write the plural for each noun.
(12, 13)
(a) serviceman   (b) torpedo   (c) wrench

Write each word that should be capitalized in sentences 6 and 7.

6. a lady declared, "twenty-one years is too old for a man competing for kingship."
(11, 20)

7. lord calomel swam from the pacific ocean to the gulf of california.
(5, 11)

8. Tell whether the following is a phrase or a clause: to
(2, 24) fight with Lord Calomel for the kingdom

9. Write each preposition in this sentence: The rabbit won
(16, 17) the sword fight by means of entangling himself between
the legs of Lord Calomel.

For sentences 10–12, write each prepositional phrase, and
star each object of the preposition.

10. In addition to tests of physical strength, the king imposed
(17, 32) tests of intelligence.

11. Prior to the math problem was the riddle of the kings.
(17, 32)

12. Owing to a tie between first and second place, the king
(17, 32) made the final test of kingship standing on two legs.

For sentences 13 and 14, write the verb phrase and name its
tense.

13. The enchanter has discovered Prince Silvio.
(8, 18)

14. Next semester, we shall be reading A.A. Milne's "Prince
(8, 21) Rabbit."

15. Write the gerund from this sentence and label its tense
(18, 19) present or perfect: Competing delights the rabbit and
Lord Calomel.

16. Write the infinitive from this sentence and label its tense
(19, 23) present or perfect: To have beaten Lord Calomel has
fulfilled the rabbit's dream.

For sentences 17 and 18, write the verb phrase and label it
action or linking.

17. At the beginning of the competition, someone sounded a
(4, 22) bugle.

18. The rabbit's answer to the math question sounded
(4, 22) convincing.

For 19 and 20, write the verb phrase and label it transitive or
intransitive.

19. The enchanter has revealed the secret.
(25, 31)

20. Both contestants have been transformed into rabbits.
(25, 31)

Write each adjective in sentences 21 and 22.

21. The forgetful enchanter transforms the resourceful rabbit
(27, 28) into the missing Prince Silvio.

22. Nine nobles and one rabbit are competing for kingship.
(27, 28)

23. Write the proper adjective from the following sentence,
(5, 28) followed by the noun it describes: This particular
kingdom does not have a Tudor castle.

Choose the correct word to complete sentences 24–28.

24. Last night, I (lay, laid) awake for hours.
(23)

25. Yesterday, my hen (lay, laid) a golden egg.
(23)

26. The prefix (*a-*, *eu-*, *peri-*) means around, about,
(25) surrounding, or near.

27. Pericardium refers to the membrane (around, inside,
(25) beneath) the heart.

28. The Greek root (*mania*, *morph*) means form or structure.
(26)

Diagram sentences 29 and 30.

29. To have won surprised the rabbit.
(25)

30. Has the enchanter in this story caused suffering?
(25)

The Indirect Object

LESSON
34

Indirect Object

We have learned that a transitive verb is an action verb with a direct object. A transitive verb may have two kinds of objects. A direct object receives the action. An **indirect object** receives the action indirectly. It tells *to whom* or *for whom* the action was done. In the sentences below, we have starred the direct objects and placed parentheses around the indirect objects.

The *actor* <u>told</u> (us) the *story of his life.

Jane's *sisters* <u>built</u> (her) a tree *house.

The *skipper* <u>threw</u> (Barbara) the *rope.

Swanson <u>brought</u> (everyone) *happiness.

In order to have an indirect object, a sentence must have a direct object. The indirect object usually follows the verb and precedes the direct object. One test of an indirect object is that it can be expressed alternately by a prepositional phrase introduced by *to* or *for:*

The actor told the story of his life *to us.*

Jane's sisters built a tree house *for her.*

The skipper threw the rope *to Barbara.*

Swanson brought happiness *to everyone.*

Indirect objects can be compound:

The horrible *performance* <u>caused</u> (the actors) and (the audience) *grief.

Example 1   Identify the indirect object(s), if any, in each sentence.

(a) The *professor* <u>told</u> the audience his views on recent discoveries.

(b) My *friend* <u>gave</u> me an account of the lecture.

(c) These hard *workers* <u>swept</u> the stadium.

(d) Our *club* <u>gave</u> Juan and Marnie special awards for their help throughout the year.

Solution (a) The professor told his views *to the audience.* Therefore, **audience** is the indirect object.

(b) My friend gave an account *to me.* Therefore, **me** is the indirect object.

(c) This sentence has **no indirect object.**

(d) Our club gave special awards *to Juan and Marnie.* **Juan** and **Marnie** are the two indirect objects.

Diagramming Below is a diagram showing the simple subject, simple predicate, direct object, and indirect object of this sentence:

The *conductor* <u>gave</u> (the organist) a *piece by Johann Sebastian Bach.

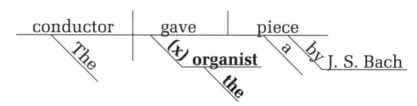

Notice that the indirect object (organist) is attached beneath the verb by a slanted line as though it were a prepositional phrase with the preposition (x) understood, not stated.

Example 2 Diagram sentences a and b.

(a) *Bach* <u>showed</u> (us) the *beauty of counterpoint.

(b) *Bach* <u>gave</u> (the baroque era) well-structured *music.

Solution (a) We think, "Bach showed the beauty of counterpoint *to us.*" So, we diagram the sentence like this:

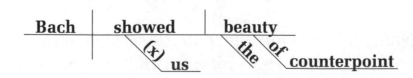

(b) We think, "Bach gave well-structured music *to the baroque era.*" We diagram it like this:

Practice   For a–d, replace each blank with the correct vocabulary word.

a. Please be _____ if you leave the seminar early.

b. Two words that sound the same but differ in meaning are called _____.

c. The essay was divided into four _____ sections.

d. A _____ silence followed the passionate outburst.

Write the indirect object, if any, in sentences e–h.

e. The muffin man presented (me) a baker's dozen.

f. A baker's dozen consists [verb] of [prep] thirteen items. n/a

g. He told (us) the reason.

h. Bakers paid the (government) high fines for short weights and measures.

For i and j, diagram each sentence.

i. Fido brought me the newspaper.

j. Dad made us sandwiches.

More Practice   Write the indirect object, if any, in each sentence.

1. Please tell (me) your secret. n/a

2. Have you told (him) the truth?

3. They offered (us) a ride to the park.

4. Scott Joplin composed ragtime music for piano. n/a

5. Mr. Olafsson gave them a tour of Iceland, his homeland.

6. I will write Mr. Habib a long letter.

7. The police should issue that speeding driver a ticket. n/a

Review set 34

1. Tell whether the following sentence is declarative,
   (1, 3) interrogative, imperative, or exclamatory: Shall we
   discuss Mary E. Wilkins's short story "The Pumpkin
   Giant"?

2. Tell whether this word group is a sentence fragment,
   (1, 3) run-on sentence, or complete sentence: A long, long
   time ago, there lived a gigantic pumpkin called Pumpkin
   Giant.

3. Write the proper, collective noun from this sentence:
   (5, 7) Many flavorful coffee beans come from South America.

4. Write the compound, common noun from this sentence:
   (5, 9) The Pumpkin Giant greatly outweighs the giant who lives
   on Jack's beanstalk.

5. For a–c, write the plural of each noun.
   (12, 13) (a) porch   (b) matron of honor   (c) Henry

Write each word that should be capitalized in sentences 6
and 7.

6. in the fall, pumpkins decorate porches and tables.
   (11, 30)

7. shall i read "the pumpkin giant" to my nephew next
   (11, 20) monday?

8. Tell whether the following is a phrase or a clause: if I tell
   (2, 24) you a great many details of this story

9. Write the indirect object in this sentence: Did you bake
   (25, 34) me a pumpkin cream pie with a delicate, flaky crust?

10. Write each preposition in this sentence: In front of
    (16, 17) Pumpkin Giant's castle lies a moat full of bones.

11. Write each prepositional phrase and star each object of
    (17, 32) the preposition in this sentence: Round about the
    country, Pumpkin Giant, king of the castle with the
    courtyard, stirred fear in children.

12. Write three helping verbs that begin with the letter *h*.
(8)

13. For a–c, choose the correct past tense form of the
(6, 14) irregular verb *to be.*

(a) we (was, were) (b) they (was, were) (c) you (was, were)

For sentences 14 and 15, write the verb phrase and name its tense.

14. In June, this book will have been circulating among
(8, 21) readers for fifty-four years.

15. Since its beginning, the Salvation Army has provided
(8, 18) food for the homeless.

For sentences 16 and 17, write the verb phrase and label it action or linking.

16. The king has offered to knight the Great Pumpkin's
(4, 22) eliminator.

17. Patroclus is feeling anxious about his son's welfare.
(4, 22)

For sentences 18 and 19, write the verb phrase and label it transitive or intransitive.

18. Patroclus has been throwing enormous potatoes at
(25, 31) Pumpkin Giant.

19. Aha, Pumpkin Giant will perish!
(25, 31)

20. Write each descriptive adjective from this sentence: The
(27) scattered seeds from the smashed Pumpkin Giant might sprout into little yellow pumpkins on long green vines.

21. Write the possessive adjective from this sentence: Will
(28) his son consume these little pumpkins?

22. From this sentence, write the proper adjective followed
(28) by the noun it modifies: Does the Pumpkin Giant's castle remain standing today?

Choose the correct word to complete sentences 23–25.

23. The Greek root *morph* means (form, around, passion).
(26)

24. I think (there, their, they're) coming with us.
(19)

25. The Greek prefix *megalo-* means (madness, small, large).
(17)

Diagram sentences 26–30.

26. The king of this country fears the giant.
(25, 28)

27. Hire the industrious mother of Aeneas.
(25, 28)

28. Give the king a bite of pie.
(25, 34)

29. The king enjoys eating.
(19, 25)

30. To bake takes a special knack.
(19, 23)

LESSON 35

The Period • Abbreviations

> **Dictation or Journal Entry**
>
> **Vocabulary:**
>
> The Greek prefix *syn-* means "with" or "together."
>
> To *synchronize* is to cause to work at the same rate or happen at the same time with something else. The jeweler *synchronized* the watches.
>
> A *syndicate* is a group of individuals or organizations that join together to accomplish a single purpose. The American Council of Exercise is part of an exercise *syndicate*.
>
> A *synonym* is a word that means the same as another word in the same language. "Fatigued" and "tired" are *synonyms*.

The Period   **Punctuation marks** help the reader to understand the meaning of what is written. **A period** helps the reader to know where a sentence begins and ends, but there are other uses for the period as well.

Declarative Sentence   A **declarative sentence** (statement) needs a period at the end.

Alexander Graham Bell invented the telephone.

Imperative Sentence   An **imperative sentence** (command) needs a period at the end.

Watch how the lips, tongue, and throat move as a person speaks.

Initials   We place periods after the **initials** in a person's name.

Alexander G. Bell

J. J. Curtis

Outline   In an **outline**, letters and numbers require a period after them.

I. Types of flowers
  A. Annuals
  B. Perennials

Example 1   Add periods where they are needed in each expression.

(a) I Alexander Graham Bell
    A Professor of vocal physiology
    B Inventor of the telephone

(b) Come here

(c) Bell invented the photophone to transmit speech by light rays

(d) G H Curtiss and Bell developed the aileron to control airplane roll

Solution   (a) We place periods after the numbers and letters in an **outline.**

     I. Alexander Graham Bell
       A. Professor of vocal physiology
       B. Inventor of the telephone

(b) We place a period at the end of an **imperative sentence.**
Come here.

(c) We place a period at the end of a **declarative sentence.**

Bell invented the photophone to transmit speech by light rays.

(d) We place periods after **initials** in a person's name. This is also a **declarative sentence.**

G. H. Curtiss and Bell developed the aileron to control airplane roll.

Abbreviations   Sometimes we shorten words by abbreviating them. **Abbreviations** often require periods, but not always. Because there are so many abbreviations, and because some abbreviations are used for more than one word, we check our dictionaries. Below are some common abbreviations that require periods. While it is important to become familiar with these, we do not generally use abbreviations in formal writing. **When in doubt, spell it out.**

Time of Day   a.m. (Latin *ante meridiem*, "before noon")

p.m. (Latin *post meridiem*, "after noon")

Days of the Week

Sun. (Sunday)	Thurs. (Thursday)
Mon. (Monday)	Fri. (Friday)
Tues. (Tuesday)	Sat. (Saturday)
Wed. (Wednesday)	

Months of the Year

Jan. (January)	July (no abbreviation)
Feb. (February)	Aug. (August)
Mar. (March)	Sept. (September)
Apr. (April)	Oct. (October)
May (no abbreviation)	Nov. (November)
June (no abbreviation)	Dec. (December)

Proper Place Names	Dr. (Drive)	Rd. (Road)
	St. (Street)	Ave. (Avenue)
	Pl. (Place)	Blvd. (Boulevard)
	Mt. (Mount, Mountain)	Bldg. (Building)

Personal Titles

Mr. (Mister)   Miss (no abbreviation)

Mrs. (Mistress; a married woman)

Ms. (any woman, especially one whose marital status is unknown)

Jr. (Junior)	Sr. (Senior)
Dr. (Doctor)	Rev. (Reverend)
Prof. (Professor)	Pres. (President)
Gen. (General)	Capt. (Captain)
Sen. (Senator)	Rep. (Representative)

Compass Directions	N. (north)	N.E. (northeast)
	S. (south))	N.W. (northwest)
	E. (east)	S.E. (southeast)
	W. (west)	S.W. (southwest)

Others	Co. (company)	etc. (Latin *et cetera*, "and so forth")
	Ltd. (Limited)	est. (estimated)
	Inc. (Incorporated)	cont. (continued)
	govt. (government)	anon. (anonymous)
	dept. (department)	misc. (miscellaneous)
	lb. (pound)	oz. (ounce)
	tsp. (teaspoon)	tbs. or tbsp. (tablespoon)
	ft. (foot)	mo. (month)

Example 2   Write the abbreviation for each expression.

(a) Mister   (b) February

(c) August   (d) Street

Solution   (a) **Mr.**   (b) **Feb.**

(c) **Aug.**   (d) **St.**

In most of our writing, we spell out entire words and do not abbreviate. However, we use the following abbreviations even in formal writing:

Personal titles such as Mr., Mrs., Jr., Ph.D., etc.

Abbreviations that are part of a organization's legal name such as Inc., Co., Ltd., etc.

Abbreviations used in expressions of time such as a.m., p.m., EST (eastern standard time), and B.C. and A.D.

Example 3 Rewrite the following sentences using whole words instead of abbreviations that are not appropriate in formal writing.

(a) Mrs. Curtis paid fifty cents per lb. for bananas.

(b) Richard Curtis, Ph.D., has worked for Skyquest Inc. since Feb.

(c) In A.D. 868, the Chinese printed a book in the form of a scroll nearly twenty ft long.

Solution (a) Mrs. Curtis paid fifty cents per **pound** for bananas. (We keep the abbreviation **Mrs.** because it precedes a personal name and is used in formal writing, but we write out the entire word **pound.**)

(b) Richard Curtis, Ph.D., has worked for Skyquest Inc. since **February.** (We keep the abbreviations **Ph.D.** and **Inc.** because they are acceptable in formal writing, but we write out the word **February.**)

(c) In A.D. 868, the Chinese printed a book in the form of a scroll nearly twenty **feet** long. (We keep the abbreviation **A.D.** because it is acceptable in formal writing, but we write out the word **feet.**

Practice Rewrite and add periods as needed in a–f.

a. I Berlin Wall
     A Constructed in 1961
     B Dismantled in 1989

b. East Germany constructed the Berlin Wall in 1961 to keep East Germans from escaping to West Germany

c. Study the reasons for escaping

d. P T Barnum was a famous American showman

e. V I P is the abbreviation for "very important person."

f. Taggart's curfew was 11:00 p m

For g–k, rewrite each sentence, adding periods and making the necessary changes to abbreviations for formal writing.

g. Dr Chin is over six ft tall.

h. Mrs Goody's recipe calls for two tsp of baking powder.

i. The staff meets the third Tues of each mo. to discuss upcoming school events.

j. Venezuela occupies the NE portion of the S American continent.

k. Eduardo Perez, Ph D, described the location of Mt Everest.

l. Write the abbreviation for each expression.
   a. Friday   b. January   c. Doctor   d. Avenue

For m–p, replace each blank with the correct vocabulary word.

m. The group of swimmers must _____ their strokes to make their dance uniform and impressive.

n. The Greek prefix meaning "with" or "together" is _____.

o. *The San Francisco Chronicle* cooperates with a large newspaper _____.

p. The word "little" is a _____ of the word "small."

Review set 35

1. (1, 3) Tell whether this sentence is declarative, interrogative, imperative, or exclamatory: Carl Sandburg wrote a short story called "How They Broke Away to Go to the Rootabaga Country."

2. (1, 3) Tell whether this word group is a sentence fragment, run-on sentence, or complete sentence: The name of the father was Gimme the Ax, the names of the children were Please Gimme and Ax Me No Questions.

For sentences 3 and 4, write the verb phrase and name its tense.

3. The animated, wild-eyed storyteller was winking at the
(8, 21) captivated listeners.

4. Gimme the Ax had been complaining about life for a long
(8, 21) time.

5. From this sentence, write each noun and circle the one
(5, 7) that is abstract: Most citizens of Rootabaga Country do not practice Judaism.

6. From this sentence, write each concrete noun labeling its
(7, 9) gender masculine, feminine, neuter, or indefinite: What mother would give her children such crazy names?

7. For a–c, write the plural of each noun.
(12, 13) (a) earful   (b) way   (c) watch

Write each word that should be capitalized in sentences 8 and 9.

8. the alaskan husky, the polar bear, and the samoyed have
(11, 28) white coats.

9. in her story "the pumpkin giant," mary e. wilkins says,
(11, 20) "he's dead, the nation doth rejoice...."

10. Tell whether the following is a phrase or a
(2, 24) clause: shadows of valleys by night in their eyes

For 11 and 12, write each prepositional phrase and star each object of the preposition.

11. Next to the country of Balloon Pickers lies the Over and
(17. 32) Under Country.

12. The engineer of the train hooted and tooted the whistle
(16, 32) on account of a cow on the tracks.

13. Rewrite this sentence, adding periods and making
(5, 35) necessary changes to abbreviations for formal writing: Last Aug, Dr Snipe moved into a home on Azusa St

14. Write two helping verbs that begin with the letter *c.*
(8)

15. For a–c, choose the correct form of the irregular verb *do.*
(6, 14)

    (a) he (do, does) (b) you (do, does) (c) they (do, does)

For sentences 16 and 17, write the verb phrase and label it action or linking.

16. Patroclus tasted the little pumpkin heads first.
(4, 22)

17. Daphne's pumpkin pies tasted delicious to everyone.
(4, 22)

For sentences 18 and 19, write the verb phrase and label it transitive or intransitive.

18. In Rootabaga Country, the pigs are wearing bibs.
(25, 31)

19. A train is chugging down the tracks toward the Village of
(25, 31) Liver-and-Onions.

Write the indirect object in sentences 20 and 21.

20. Gimme the Ax gave the conductor his train ticket.
(25, 34)

21. Did the family sell you their belongings?
(25, 34)

22. Write the indefinite adjective from this sentence: Some
(27, 28) pigs wore bibs with stripes and polka dots.

Diagram sentences 23–27.

23. We will ride the train.
(4, 25)

24. Have you seen a pig with a bib?
(25, 32)

25. Clowns presented us a show of somersaults.
(32, 34)

26. Traveling requires stamina.
(19, 25)

27. One of the balloon pickers began to sing.
(23, 25)

Choose the correct word to complete sentences 28–30.

28. (Imminent, Immanent, Eminent) means distinguished or
(20) prominent.

29. Please (lie, lay) the papers on my desk.
(23)

(25) **30.** The prefix peri- means (across, around, under).

LESSON
36

Coordinating Conjunctions

Conjunctions are connecting words. They connect words, phrases, and clauses. There are three kinds of conjunctions: coordinating, correlative, and subordinating. In this lesson, we will learn to recognize coordinating conjunctions.

Coordinating Conjunctions   We use a **coordinating conjunction** to join parts of a sentence that are equal in form, or parallel. Parts of sentences, such as words, phrases, and clauses, are called **elements**. A coordinating conjunction connects a word to a word, a phrase to a phrase, or a clause to a clause. When joined by a conjunction, they are called **compound elements**.

Here are the common coordinating conjunctions:

and   but   or   nor   for   yet   so

They may join a word to another word.

stars *and* stripes   butter *or* margarine

chocolate *and* vanilla   quickly *but* carefully

fast *yet* accurate   ingenuous *or* ingenious

They may join a phrase to another phrase.

to study the material *and* to take the exam

in the river *or* on the bank

languishing in the dark *but* thriving in the light

They may connect a clause to another clause.

Clara Barton established the American Red Cross, *and* she served as its first president in 1881.

She was called a philanthropist, *for* she helped wounded soldiers.

Example   Underline each coordinating conjunction that you find in these sentences.

(a) Clara Barton was honored with the Iron Cross of Germany, for she assisted in establishing hospitals in the Franco-German War.

(b) The American Red Cross helps victims in war, but it also serves victims of peacetime disaster.

(c) The travelers remembered their tickets and luggage, yet they forgot their passports.

(d) Please bring your birth certificate and your passport.

(e) That candidate is ingenuous, so we can trust him.

Solution   (a) Clara Barton was honored with the Iron Cross of Germany, **for** she assisted in establishing hospitals in the Franco-German War.

(b) The American Red Cross helps victims in war, **but** it also serves victims of peacetime disaster.

(c) The travelers remembered their tickets **and** luggage, **yet** they forgot their passports.

(d) Please bring your birth certificate **and** your passport.

(e) That candidate is ingenuous, **so** we can trust him.

Practice   a. Replace each blank to complete the list of coordinating conjunctions:

_____, but, _____, nor, _____, yet, _____

b. Replace each blank to complete the list of coordinating conjunctions.

and, _____, or, _____, for, _____, so

c. Memorize the seven coordinating conjunctions, and say them to a friend or teacher.

Write each coordinating conjunction, if any, that you find in sentences d–j.

d. The circus exhibited a man who was reputedly one hundred sixty-one years old and still active.

e. The circus clowns made me laugh, but the tight-rope walkers gave me a fright.

f. People know Barnum as a showman, yet he also served as a Connecticut State legislator.

g. Barnum began "The Greatest Show on Earth" in New York, but the circus became internationally famous when Bailey joined him, for they launched the Barnum and Bailey Circus.

i. Do you enjoy the animal performers, or do you prefer the acrobats?

j. I had some extra circus tickets, so I invited my sister and brother to go with me.

For k–n, replace each blank with *ingenuous* or *ingenious*.

k. The man's _____ responses to the prosecutor's questions convinced the jury that he was innocent.

l. The word _____ means straightforward and candid.

m. What an _____ solution to a complicated problem!

n. The word _____ means clever or inventive.

Review set 36 Rewrite sentences 1 and 2, adding periods and making necessary changes to abbreviations for formal writing:

1. Mrs Conseco will meet you on Fri at three p m
(5, 35)

2. At birth, Robert A Hake weighed nine lbs, two oz
(5, 35)

3. Write the seven common coordinating conjunctions.
(36)

4. Write each coordinating conjunction from this sentence: John and James have red hair, but they look different, for John's hair is straight, yet James's hair is curly.
(36)

5. Tell whether the following is a sentence fragment, run-on
(1, 3) sentence, or complete sentence: Time and time again,
Brer Rabbit has outsmarted Brer Fox.

6. Write the verb phrase from this sentence and label it
(25, 31) transitive or intransitive: Brer Rabbit's ingenious plan
may save his life.

7. For a–c, write the plural of each noun.
(12, 13) (a) mouse   (b) louse   (c) turkey

Write each word that should be capitalized in sentences
8–10.

8. we shall fish for trout at lake mary in the sierra nevada
(5, 11) mountains.

9. did uncle herbert read you a story called "prince rabbit"?
(11, 20)

10. sometimes, people from the northeast come to the
(11, 30) southwest for milder winters.

11. Write the prepositional phrase and star the object of the
(17, 32) preposition in this sentence: Across from Brer Fox's fire
lies a briar patch.

12. Write the four principal parts (present tense, present
(6, 15) participle, past tense, and past participle) of the verb
study.

For sentences 14 and 15, write the entire verb phrase and
name its tense.

13. Brer Fox had assumed his victory over Brer Rabbit.
(8, 18)

14. Brer Rabbit has been making a fool out of Brer Fox for a
(8, 21) long, long time.

15. Write each adjective from this sentence: That Brer Rabbit
(27, 28) is one smart rabbit!

Replace each blank with the correct word to complete
sentences 16–22.

16. The _____ helps the reader to know where a
(35) sentence ends, but there are other uses for it as well.

17. A declarative sentence ends with a _____ .
(35)

18. We place a _____ after an initial in a person's
(35) name.

19. In an outline, each letter and number requires a
(35) _____ after it.

20. Abbreviations often require _____, but not always.
(35)

21. A verb form that ends in *ing* and functions as a noun is
(19) called a _____ .

22. The _____ participle of a verb ends with *ing*.
(6, 15)

Diagram each word of sentences 23 and 24.

23. That dog with the red collar loves digging.
(23, 25)

24. She gave her dog a bath.
(25, 33)

For 25 and 26, tell whether the word group is a phrase or a clause.

25. with a reputation for fickleness and treachery
(2, 24)

26. as marauders vaulted the wall
(2, 24)

Choose the correct word to complete sentences 27–30.

27. An (ectomorph, infinitive, allusion) is the basic form of
(23, 26) the verb, usually preceded by the preposition "to."

28. Endomorph refers to one's body (color, form, strength).
(26)

29. The church's (canon, cannon) condemns lying and
(27) stealing.

30. The Greek prefix *tele-* means (near, around, distant).
(28)

**LESSON
37**

Compound Subjects and Predicates
• Diagramming Compounds

Dictation or Journal Entry

Vocabulary:

The common Greek word *graphein* (to write) gives us the common English suffix *-graphy*, meaning "drawing, writing, or recording."

Choreography is the art of creating dance movements. The musical displayed brilliant *choreography*.

A *biography* is a written account of a person's life. I read an interesting *biography* of Abraham Lincoln.

Photography is the art of recording images with a camera. Students in the *photography* class learned to use light in order to create the best photographs.

Orthography is the proper spelling of words. The editor checked the *orthography* of the document.

**Compound
Subjects**

The predicate or verb of a sentence may have more than one subject, as in the sentence below.

> The *Magna Carta,* the *Petition of Rights*, and the *Declaration of Rights* <u>influenced</u> the formation of the Bill of Rights.

The verb, influenced, has three subjects: "the Magna Carta," "the Petition of Rights," and "the Declaration of Rights." We call this a **compound subject.**

**Compound
Predicates**

Likewise, a subject may have more than one predicate, as in the sentence below.

> The *Bill of Rights* <u>defines</u> and <u>safeguards</u> fundamental individual rights.

The subject, the Bill of Rights, has two predicates: "defines" and "safeguards." We call this a **compound predicate.**

**Diagramming
Compounds**

To diagram a compound subject, predicate, direct object, or indirect object, we place each part of the compound on a separate, horizontal line. We write the conjunction on a vertical dotted line that joins the horizontal lines.

COMPOUND SUBJECT DIAGRAM:

> *Timothy* and *Patrick* <u>saw</u> the Blarney Castle.

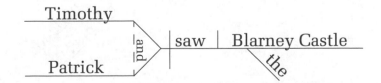

COMPOUND PREDICATE DIAGRAM:

Many *tourists* <u>visit</u> and <u>kiss</u> the Blarney Stone.

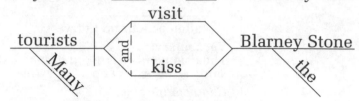

COMPOUND SUBJECT AND COMPOUND PREDICATE DIAGRAM:

Timothy and *Patrick* <u>visited</u> and <u>kissed</u> the Blarney Stone.

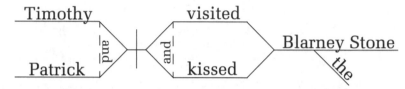

COMPOUND DIRECT OBJECT DIAGRAM:

Brahms <u>played</u> the *violin and the *cello.

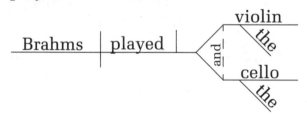

COMPOUND INDIRECT OBJECT DIAGRAM:

He <u>gave</u> (Robert) and (Clara) his lifelong friendship.

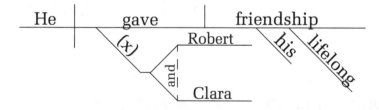

COMPOUND ADJECTIVES DIAGRAM:

Brahms, talented and perfectionistic, <u>burned</u> his early works.

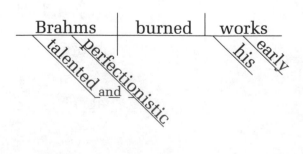

Example   Diagram each sentence.

(a) Brahms and Bach wrote amazing organ music.

(b) Johannes Brahms composed and played his music.

(c) Brahms, Bach, and Handel wrote and presented musical masterpieces.

Solution   (a) This sentence contains a compound subject.

Brahms and *Bach* wrote amazing organ music.

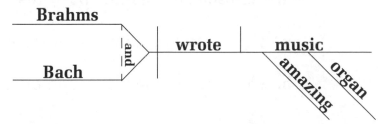

(b) This sentence has a compound predicate. The subject, *Johannes Brahms,* did two things. He <u>composed</u>, and he <u>played</u>.

Johannes Brahms <u>composed</u> and <u>played</u> his music.

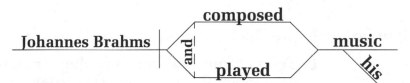

(c) This sentence has a compound subject (*Brahms, Bach, Handel*) and a compound predicate (<u>wrote</u>, <u>presented</u>).

Brahms, Bach, and *Handel* <u>wrote</u> and <u>presented</u> musical masterpieces.

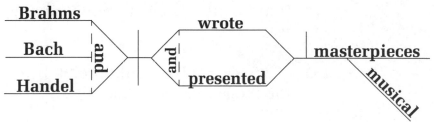

Practice   For a–e, replace each blank with the correct vocabulary word.

a. The careless _____ of the paper made it difficult to read.

b. The Greek root meaning drawing, writing, or recording is _____ .

   c. The life story, or _____, of Johannes Brahms reveals his merciless self-criticism.

   d. One's interest in _____ often leads to acquiring better cameras and developing techniques.

   e. The _____ of the ballet reflected the mood of the music.

Diagram sentences f–i.

   f. Children enjoy "Little Boy Blue" and "Jack Sprat."

   g. The librarian read the boys and girls nursery rhymes.

   h. The butcher, the baker, and the candlestick maker sailed a bucket.

   i. The silly and adventuresome knaves rocked and rolled.

More Practice See Master Worksheets.

Review set 37 Choose the best word to complete sentences 1–6.

1. Telecommunication is the transmission of words, sounds, and images over (long, short) distances.
(28)

2. A (perspective, prospective) is a point of view.
(29)

3. The prefixes *pro-* and *ante-* mean (before, after, distant).
(30, 31)

4. (Imminent, Antebellum, Euphony) means "before the war."
(20, 31)

5. Harry gave a (forceful, forcible) speech, which convinced the judge to change her mind.
(32)

6. A(n) (transitive, intransitive) verb has a direct object.
(25, 31)

7. Tell whether the following is a phrase or a clause: because she thinks beyond tomorrow
(2, 24)

8. Write the verb phrase in this sentence and label it action or linking: Molly had tasted each cookie on the plate.
(4, 22)

9. Tell whether this word group is a complete sentence,
(1, 3) sentence fragment, or run-on sentence: Telling the fox a
tale about fishing.

10. Write the collective noun from this sentence: A sloth of
(7, 9) bears was clearing the forest.

11. Write each noun from this sentence and label its gender
(7, 9) masculine, feminine, neuter, or indefinite: Has the rabbit
jumped into a well?

12. For a–c, write the plural of each noun.
(13, 14) (a) elk   (b) brother-in-law   (c) box

Write each word that should be capitalized in sentences 13
and 14.

13. the house of representatives and the senate balance the
(5, 11) power of the president of the united states.

14. a little boy asked uncle remus, "wasn't the rabbit
(11, 20) scared?"

15. Write two simple prepositions that begin with the letter *c*.
(16, 17)

16. Write the prepositional phrase and star the object of the
(17, 32) preposition in this sentence: Brer Rabbit successfully
slipped away from the others.

17. From this sentence, write the adjective phrase and the
(9, 33) noun it modifies: Brer Rabbit remains the victor of this
contest.

For sentences 18 and 19, write the verb phrase and name its
tense.

18. By the end of the semester, we shall have learned about
(8, 18) several silly stories.

19. For years, Brer Rabbit had been running from Brer Fox.
(8, 21)

Write the correct verb form to complete sentences 20 and 21.

20. The little boy (future tense of *discover*) how Brer Rabbit
(8, 10) escapes from the well.

21. The brilliant rabbit (present tense of *convince*) the
(6, 15) gullible fox to jump into the water bucket at the other end
of the rope.

Rewrite 22–24, adding periods and making necessary
corrections to abbreviations for formal writing.

22. Mr Remus reports that the ten-lb fox sinks into the well,
(35) lifting the two-lb rabbit to the surface

23. Harry P Broomhead Jr has worked for the Western
(35) Codliver Co since Jan of 1955

24. I Uncle Remus's stories
(35)   A "Briar Patch"
     B "Down the Well"
     C "Dinner with Brer Rabbit"

25. Write the seven common coordinating conjunctions.
(36)

26. Write the coordinating conjunction from this sentence:
(36) Have you ever fallen down a well or into a deep hole?

Diagram each word of sentences 27–30.

27. To escape will require cleverness.
(4, 23)

28. The foolish fox gave the rabbit an avenue of escape from
(25, 33) the well.

29. Have you seen the fox?
(2, 25)

30. Bring me that bucket and a rope.
(25, 34)

LESSON
38

Correlative Conjunctions

Dictation or Journal Entry

Vocabulary:

Let us examine the words *audacity, treason,* and *dissension.*

Audacity is a bold recklessness or disregard for normal restraints. Renee displayed *audacity* when she demanded to be served before anyone else.

Treason is a betrayal of trust, especially the betrayal of one's country, such as helping the enemy during wartime. Benedict Arnold committed *treason* against America during the Revolutionary War.

Dissension is strong disagreement or strife. Sometimes, there is *dissension* between the Senate and the House of Representatives.

Correlative Conjunctions

Correlative conjunctions are similar to coordinating conjunctions. They connect elements of a sentence that are equal in form, or parallel. Correlative conjunctions are always used in pairs. Here we list the most common ones:

both—and   either—or

neither—nor   not only—but also

The parts they join must be equal in form, or parallel. In the sentences below, the parallel elements are italicized.

Successful gardening requires both *hard work* and *planning.*

Either *the gymnasium* or *the stadium* will be the site of the graduation ceremony.

Neither *Ms. Grantsky* nor *Mr. Minnick* can chaperone the dance.

Not only *jeans* but also *sweatshirts* are on sale at the mall.

Example 1   Underline the correlative conjunctions in each sentence.

(a) Both "Peasant Brueghel" and "The Droll" are names for Pieter the Elder, the famous Flemish painter.

(b) Not only Pieter the Younger but also Jan the Elder were artistic sons of Pieter the Elder.

(c) Neither Pieter the Younger nor Jan the Elder are as well known as their father, Pieter the Elder.

Solution   (a) **Both** "Peasant Brueghel" **and** "The Droll" are names for Pieter the Elder, the famous Flemish painter.

(b) <u>**Not only**</u> Pieter the Younger <u>**but also**</u> Jan the Elder were artistic sons of Pieter the Elder.

(c) <u>**Neither**</u> Pieter the Younger <u>**nor**</u> Jan the Elder are as well known as their father, Pieter the Elder.

Diagramming   We diagram correlative conjunctions this way:

Pieter the Elder painted not only landscapes but also peasant rural life.

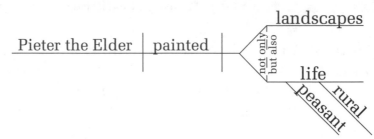

Example 2   Diagram this sentence:

Either   museums   or   art   galleries   will   exhibit   Brueghel's paintings.

Solution   We diagram the sentence as follows.

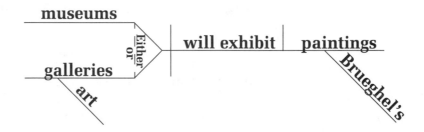

Practice   Write the correlative conjunctions from sentences a–d.

a. Paul Bunyan comes from either French-Canadian or European folklore.

b. Neither Jason nor Jacqui remembered the directions to the library.

c. Both prodigious strength and cunning are characteristics of Paul Bunyan.

d. Not only rugged loggers but also imaginative children enjoy the "tall stories" of Paul Bunyan.

e. Diagram this sentence:

I want neither sympathy nor pity.

Replace each blank with the correct vocabulary word.

    f. Unfortunately, _____ over rules divided the team members.

    g. Marian was shocked by her neighbor's _____ when his loud party lasted until dawn.

    h. Because it threatens national security, _____ is among the most serious of crimes.

Review set 38

1. Tell whether this sentence is declarative, exclamatory, imperative, or interrogative:
(1, 3)

    Do not boast about your physical prowess.

2. Write each word that should be capitalized in this sentence: last may, i read *the lion, the witch and the wardrobe* by c. s. lewis.
(11, 20)

3. Write the abstract, common noun from this sentence: Was Puddleglum's pessimism contagious?
(7, 9)

4. For a–c, write the plural of each noun.
(12, 13) (a) lady   (b) man   (c) handful

5. Write five simple prepositions that begin with the letter *a*.
(16)

6. Write the prepositional phrase and star the object of the preposition in this sentence: Brer Terrapin accepts Brer Rabbit's challenge in spite of the rabbit's boasting.
(17, 32)

7. For a–c, choose the correct form of the irregular verb *to be.*
(6, 14) (a) he (was, were) (b) you (was, were) (c) we (was, were)

For sentences 8 and 9, write the verb phrase and label it action or linking.

8. Does Brer Rabbit smell the fire?
(4, 22)

9. The smoky air smells pungent.
(4, 22)

For sentences 11 and 12, write the verb phrase and label it transitive or intransitive.

11. Brer Rabbit has been hopping through the briar patch.
(25, 31)

(25, 31) **12.** Can Brer Fox trap the rabbit?

13. Write each adjective in this sentence: The ingenious
$^{(27, 28)}$ rabbit has been outsmarted by the clever Brer Terrapin.

Rewrite sentences 14 and 15, adding periods and making necessary changes to abbreviations for formal writing.

14. On the first Tues in Sept, Ms Weezle will move to a new
$^{(35)}$ house on Fox Pl in the Frazier Mts

15. Mr Hoogle drove N E on Canyon Blvd to see Dr Rudy P
$^{(35)}$ Cruz

16. Write the seven common coordinating conjunctions.
$^{(36)}$

17. Write the coordinating conjunction in this sentence: Will
$^{(36)}$ Brer Turkey Buzzard or Jedge Buzzard monitor the race?

18. In this sentence, write the verb phrase and name its tense:
$^{(8, 18)}$ Have you synchronized your watches?

For sentences 19 and 20, write the gerund and label its tense present or perfect.

19. Having finished the race was a big accomplishment for
$^{(18, 19)}$ Brer Terrapin.

20. The observers of the race began laughing at Brer Rabbit.
$^{(6, 15)}$

21. Write the infinitive in this sentence and label its tense
$^{(6, 23)}$ present or perfect: To boast may cause disaster.

22. Tell whether the following is a phrase or a clause: to have
$^{(2, 24)}$ lost to a worthy opponent

Choose the correct word to complete sentences 23–27.

23. The Greek suffix *-phobia* means irrational (thought, fear,
$^{(33)}$ behavior).

24. Antebellum means (after, before, during) the war.
$^{(31)}$

25. Granny gave the intruder a (prospective, forcible) shove
$^{(29, 32)}$ that sent him tumbling down the stairs.

26. A syndicate is a group that works (together, apart,
$^{(35)}$ happily).

$^{(36)}$ **27.** My (ingenuous, ingenious) friend tells the truth.

Diagram sentences 28–30.

28. Both Moe and Cloe hope to grow.
(23, 38)

29. Painting will improve the room's appearance.
(19, 25)

30. Old folks watch the race between Brer Terrapin and Brer
(25, 33) Rabbit.

LESSON
39

Diagramming Predicate Nominatives

Dictation or Journal Entry

Vocabulary:

The Greek word *chronos*, meaning time, gives us the common prefix *chrono-*.

A *chronology* is an arrangement according to the order of time or occurrence. Do you know the *chronology* of events that led to the American Revolution?

Chronobiology studies the effect of time on living organisms. The *chronobiology* students observed the effects of aging.

A *chronometer* is a sophisticated timepiece for accurately telling time. The *chronometer* indicated the exact moment the new century began.

More than one name can identify people, animals, or things.

Lewis Carroll <u>is</u> a famous British *author*.

"Author" is another name for "Lewis Carroll."

Renames the Subject A **predicate nominative** is a noun that follows the verb and renames the subject person, animal, or thing. It explains or defines the subject and is identical with it. The subject and the predicate nominative are joined by a linking verb such as *am, is, are, was, were, be, being, been, become,* or *seem*. We remember that a linking verb does not show action, nor does it "help" the action verb. Its purpose is to connect the person, animal, or thing (the subject) to its new name (the predicate nominative).

Predicate nominatives are circled in the sentences below.

Lewis Carroll <u>is</u> Mr. Dodgson's (pen name).

"pen name" renames "Lewis Carroll"

Mr. Dodgson <u>was</u> a well-known (mathematician)

"mathematician" renames "Mr. Dodgson"

If we reverse the subject and the predicate nominative, as in the sentences below, the meaning of the sentence is not affected.

A pen *name* for Mr. Dodgson <u>is</u> (Lewis Carroll)

A well-known *mathematician* <u>was</u> (Mr. Dodgson)

Identifying the Predicate Nominative

Reversing the subject and predicate in this manner helps us to identify the predicate nominative. If the linking verb is not a "to be" verb, we can replace it with a "to be" verb to determine whether there is a predicate nominative that renames the subject:

> *Alice in Wonderland* <u>became</u> a popular (story) for children.

> *Alice in Wonderland* <u>was</u> a popular (story) for children.
>
> ↑
> "to be" linking verb

Now we can reverse the subject and predicate, and we see that the predicate does indeed rename the subject. The meaning is the same, so we have identified a predicate nominative.

> A popular *story* for children <u>was</u> (*Alice in Wonderland.*)

Predicate nominatives are more difficult to identify in interrogative sentences. Turning the question into a statement will help us.

> Question: Is Lewis Carroll the author of *Alice in Wonderland*?

> Statement: Lewis Carroll is the author of *Alice in Wonderland.*

In the statement above, we see that "author" renames "Lewis Carroll." Therefore, "author" is a predicate nominative.

Compound Predicate Nominatives

Predicate nominatives may be compound, as in the sentence below.

> Favorite characters <u>from</u> *Alice in Wonderland* are the (March Hare,) the (Mad Hatter,) and the (Cheshire Cat.)

Diagramming

In a diagram, the predicate nominative is indicated by a line that slants toward the right. Here we diagram the sentence above:

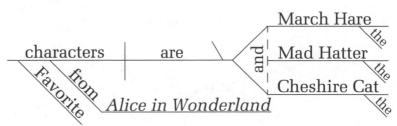

Below are more diagrams showing predicate nominatives.

James has been a diligent student.

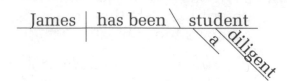

Lincoln was our sixteenth president.

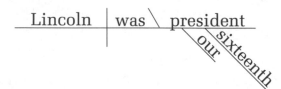

Example   Diagram the following sentences.

(a) Mr. Clemens was a printer, steamboat pilot, Confederate soldier, and silver miner.

(b) Samuel Clemens's pen name is Mark Twain.

(c) Bret Harte and Mark Twain were good friends.

Solution   (a)

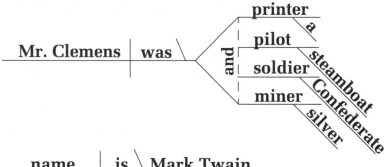

(b)

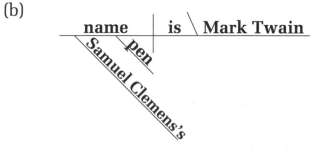

(c)

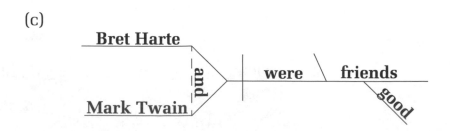

We remember that gerunds and infinitives can function as nouns. Therefore, a predicate nominative may be a gerund or an infinitive, as in these sentences:

GERUND

Anton's favorite sport is *skiing*.

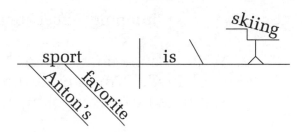

INFINITIVE

His goal was *to float*.

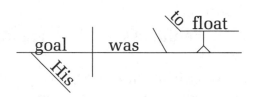

Practice Vocabulary: For a–e, replace each blank with the correct word.

a. A word part that forms the base of other words is a _____ word.

b. Many of our root words come from the _____ language.

c. The two ships used a _____ to meet at a specified time and place.

d. I'd like to hear the _____ of events that led to the invention of the wheel.

e. The _____ project showed the growth of infants from crawling to walking.

For f–i, diagram each sentence.

f. His reward for hard work will be to pass.

g. King James was a monarch.

h. His joy has been his cooking.

i. He became an expert.

**Review set
39**

1. Tell whether this sentence is declarative, interrogative,
(1, 3) exclamatory, or imperative:

Jumping Jehoshaphat, it's an ouphe!

2. Write each noun from this sentence: Mr. Webster
(5, 7) explained, "An ouphe, pronounced *oofee*, is an old-
fashioned word for goblin or elf."

3. For a–c, write the plural of each noun.
(12, 13) (a) hanky   (b) key   (c) pitch

Write each word that should be capitalized in sentences 4
and 5.

4. benito asked, "hey, grandpa, do you believe in ouphes?"
(11, 26)

5. goldie mae sharp, your great grandmother, claims to have
(11, 26) seen an ouphe in the woods.

6. Write the four principal parts (present tense, present
(6, 15) participle, past tense, past participle) of the verb *tap*.

7. Tell whether the following is a phrase or a clause: since
(2, 24) the ouphe was disguised as an old man

8. Write each prepositional phrase from this sentence and
(17, 32) star the object of each preposition: Outside of the house,
an old man tapped quietly on the door.

9. Write the verb phrase from this sentence and label it
(25, 31) transitive or intransitive: Kitty invited the old man into
the house.

10. For a and b, choose the correct form of the verb.
(6, 14) (a) (Has, Have) you heard of an ouphe?

(b) (Do, Does) it seem like a true story?

11. Write the verb phrase from this sentence and name its
(8, 21) tense: Kitty was waiting for her husband, Will, to come
home.

12. Write each adjective in this sentence: Kitty served her
(27, 28) old, weak guest some crispy bacon, brown bread, and
seasoned potatoes.

Rewrite 13–15, adding periods and making necessary
changes to abbreviations for formal writing.

13. I Ouphes
(35) A Rich
      B Hermits
      C Disguised as old men

14. Please meet me at the library on Huntington Dr at two
(35) p m this Tues

15. Mr and Mrs Salazar have been happily married since Aug
(35)

16. Write the seven common coordinating conjunctions.
(36)

17. Write the coordinating conjunction from this sentence:
(36) Does Kitty choose poverty or wealth?

18. List the four most common pairs of correlative
(38) conjunctions.

Write each pair of correlative conjunctions from sentences 19
and 20.

19. Neither Kitty nor the baby recognized the ouphe.
(38)

20. The old man was not only grateful but also generous.
(38)

21. Write the verb phrase from this sentence and label it
(4, 22) action or linking: From her perspective, the man seemed
ancient.

22. Write the gerund from this sentence and label its tense
(8, 18) present or perfect: Having dreamed about the effects of
wealth changed Kitty's attitude toward poverty.

23. Write the infinitive from this sentence and label its tense
(18, 23) present or perfect: To think about consequences might
save you from disaster.

Choose the correct word to complete sentences 24–28.

24. Hydrophobia is the unnatural (love, fear, amount) of
(33) water.

25. (Discrete, Discreet) means separate and distinct.
(34)

26. Words that mean the same are (synonyms, antonyms,
(35) homophones).

27. The witness seemed (ingenuous, ingenious), so the jury
(36) believed him.

28. The prefix meaning around, about, surrounding is (*miso-*,
(13, 25) *eu-*, *peri-*).

Diagram sentences 29 and 30.

29. Both Kitty and Will gave the old man their gracious
(25, 38) hospitality.

30. Winning was Jo's dream.
(19, 39)

LESSON
40

Noun Case

> **Dictation or Journal Entry**
>
> **Vocabulary:**
> Notice the difference between *costume* and *custom*.
>
> *Costume* is a style of dress that might be peculiar to a country, era, holiday, or group. On Thanksgiving Day, some people wear Pilgrim or Native American *costumes*.
>
> A *custom* is a habit, practice or usual way of doing something. It was the doctor's *custom* to visit his patients in the hospital before going to his office.

We can group nouns into three **cases:** *nominative, possessive, and objective.* The case of the noun explains how the noun is used in the sentence.

Nominative Case

SUBJECT OF A SENTENCE

A noun is in the **nominative case** when it is the subject of a sentence. In the sentence below, the noun *countries* is in the nominative case because it is the subject of the sentence.

> The *countries* coexisted peacefully despite their religious and political differences.

PREDICATE NOMINATIVE

A noun is also in the **nominative case** when it is used as a predicate nominative. A predicate nominative follows a linking verb ("to be" verbs—is, am, are, was, were, etc.) and renames the subject. In the sentence below, *friends* renames the compound subject, Margaret and Sheryl. *Friends* is in the nominative case because it is a predicate nominative.

> Margaret and Sheryl were *friends.*

Below, we see verbals used as predicate nominatives:

> His hope was *to cook.* (infinitive)

> Your ideal exercise might be *cycling.* (gerund)

Possessive Case

We are familiar with nouns that show possession or ownership. These nouns are in the **possessive case.** In the sentence below, the possessive noun *professor's* is in the possessive case.

> The *professor's* map showed the Continental Divide.

Example 1   Tell whether the italicized noun in each sentence is in the nominative case or the possessive case. If it is in the nominative case, tell whether it is the subject of the sentence or a predicate nominative.

(a) This *divide* separates west-flowing from east-flowing rivers.

(b) Davy Crockett was an American *pioneer.*

(c) Was *Davy Crockett's* hat made from fur?

(d) His decision was *to obey.*

Solution   (a) The word *divide* is in the **nominative case.** It is the **subject of the sentence.**

(b) The word *pioneer* is in the **nominative case.** It is a **predicate nominative**; it follows the linking verb *was,* and it renames the subject.

(c) *Davy Crockett's* is in the **possessive case.** It shows possession; it tells whose hat.

(d) *To obey* is in the **nominative case.** It functions as a **predicate nominative**.

Objective Case   A noun is in the **objective case** when it is used as a direct object, an indirect object, or an object of a preposition.

Direct Object   A noun or pronoun is called a **direct object** when it is the direct receiver of the action of the verb. Direct objects are starred in the sentences below.

Davy Crockett helped *Andrew Jackson. (Davy helped who or what?)

Defending the Alamo cost Davy's *life.

The Crockett Almanacs contained tall *tales about Davy.

He liked *to hunt. (Infinitive as a direct object)

Do you enjoy *skydiving? (Gerund as a direct object)

Indirect Object   An **indirect object** is the noun or pronoun that tells "to whom" or "for whom" the action was done. In the following examples, the indirect objects are starred.

Have you told *me everything?
(Have you told everything to *me*?)

Politicians gave *Davy recognition.
(Politicians gave recognition to *Davy*.)

Please pass *Robert the broccoli.
(Please pass the broccoli to *Robert*.)

Object of a Preposition   A noun or pronoun that follows a preposition is called the **object of a preposition.** Objects of the prepositions are starred in the examples below.

on account of *illness	on top of the *hill
outside of the *country	except for *swimming
beside *him	within two *months

Example 2   For sentences, a–c, tell whether each italicized noun is a direct object, an indirect object, or the object of a preposition.

(a) The restaurant offers *customers* a choice of green beans or buttered squash.

(b) Our cousin painted his *house* bright green.

(c) The title of her essay refers to her *experiences* in Colombia.

Solution   (a) *Customers* is an **indirect object.** It tells "to whom" the choice was offered.

(b) *House* is a **direct object.** It is the receiver of the action verb "painted."

(c) *Experiences* is the **object of the preposition** "to."

Example 3   Tell whether the italicized noun is in the nominative, possessive, or objective case.

(a) Please describe a cumulus *cloud*.

(b) The *artist's* cumulus clouds looked like cauliflower.

(c) Mr. Ng became a *meteorologist*.

(d) We flew above the *clouds.*

Solution (a) *Cloud* is a direct object. Therefore, it is in the **objective case.**

(b) *Artist's* is a possessive noun. Therefore, it is in the **possessive case.**

(c) *Meteorologist* is a predicate nominative. It renames the subject. Therefore, it is in the **nominative case.**

(d) *Clouds* is the object of the preposition "above." Therefore, it is in the **objective case.**

Practice For sentences a–e, tell whether the italicized noun is in the nominative case or the possessive case. If it is in the nominative case, tell whether it is the subject of the sentence or a predicate nominative.

a. *To interrupt* would be insensitive.

b. My favorite pastime is *writing.*

c. *Investors'* greed caused a stock market crash in 1929.

d. Did the *market* crash in 1929?

e. Davy Crockett was a *member* of the Tennessee State Legislature.

For sentences f–h, tell whether the italicized noun is a direct object (D.O.), an indirect object (I.O.), or the object of a preposition (O.P.).

f. Pierre and Marie Curie were educated at the *University of Paris.*

g. Physicists give *Marie Curie* credit for isolating radium.

h. Pierre and Marie Curie received the *Nobel Peace Prize* in 1903 for their investigation of radioactivity of uranium.

For i–l, tell whether the italicized noun is in the nominative, possessive, or objective case.

i. *Studying* takes discipline.

j. Lindsay's cousin crafted the *bowl.*

k. *George Custer's* army met disaster.

l. Professor Plum told his *students* the story of Custer's Last Stand.

For m–p, replace each blank with *costume* or *custom.*

m. The pirate's _____ consisted of an eye patch and a black felt hat with crossbones on the front.

n. Vacationing in the summer is a _____ for many American families.

o. Scottish _____ includes bagpipe music.

p. Santa wears a red and white _____.

Review set 40

1. Tell whether the following is a complete sentence, sentence fragment, or run-on sentence: Stealing food from the kitchen during the night.
(1, 3)

2. Tell whether the following is a phrase or a clause: because of dissension among the world leaders
(2, 24)

3. Write the verb phrase in this sentence and label it transitive or intransitive: Has he been sneaking around the house?
(25, 31)

4. Tell whether this sentence is declarative, interrogative, imperative, or exclamatory: Brownies are little elves that live in coal cellars and only come out after dark when nobody is about.
(1, 3)

5. Write each noun in this sentence and circle the one that is abstract: Another name for a brownie is Mr. Nobody.
(7, 9)

6. For a–c, write the plural for each noun.
(12, 13)
    (a) calf   (b) roof   (c) child

7. For this sentence, write the verb phrase and label it action or linking: After his midnight snack, he felt ill.
(4, 22)

Write each word that should be capitalized in sentences 8 and 9.

8. at some american universities, college students must
(5, 11) complete four years of either french, spanish, latin, or another foreign language.

9. in the southwest, a greater amount of rainfall occurs in
(29, 30) the spring than in the summer.

10. Write the four principal parts (present tense, present
(6, 15) participle, past tense, and past participle) of the verb *jog*.

11. Write each prepositional phrase in this sentence and star
(17, 32) the object of each preposition: Apart from his appearance, a brownie may be a pleasant fellow and the nicest companion in the whole world.

Write the correct verb form to complete sentences 12–14.

12. A brownie (present of *squelch*) its enemies with tricks
(6, 15) and mischief.

13. Cats (past progressive of *hiss*) at the brownies.
(8, 21)

14. The new cook (past perfect of *trap*) the cats in the cellar.
(8, 18)

15. Write each adjective from this sentence and underline
(27, 28) those that are articles: The old cook provided an adequate supper for a famished brownie each evening.

Rewrite sentences 16 and 17, adding periods and making necessary changes to abbreviations for formal writing.

16. Upon arrival at eight a m on Wed, the young cook finds
(35) huge quantities of food missing

17. It doesn't take a PhD to determine that a brownie had
(35) been in the kitchen Tues night

Write each pair of correlative conjunctions in sentences 18 and 19.

18. Neither the old cook nor the young cook ever saw the
(38) brownie.

19. The young cook was both careless and lazy.
(38)

20. Write the infinitive from this sentence and label its tense
(18, 23) present or perfect: To have frustrated the cook was the
brownie's intent.

21. Write the gerund from this sentence and label its tense
(6, 19) present or perfect: The brownie had enjoyed teasing to
his heart's content.

Choose the correct word to complete sentences 22–26.

22. The past tense of set is (sat, set, setted).
(24)

23. Don't (lie, lay) in the sun too long.
(23)

24. The words endomorph, ectomorph, and mesomorph refer
(26) to body (height, structure, color).

25. From Mom's (perspective, prospective), forty years of age
(29) is young.

26. The prefix *ante-* means (after, before, during).
(31)

27. Tell whether the italicized noun in this sentence is
(7, 40) nominative, possessive, or objective case: The program
for the talent *show* listed twenty performers.

Diagram sentences 28–30.

28. Tiny brought the brownie a bone.
(25, 34)

29. Jonah not only frowns but also complains.
(37, 38)

30. Teasing is the brownie's favorite pastime.
(19, 39)

LESSON 41

Diagramming Predicate Adjectives

Dictation or Journal Entry

Vocabulary:
The Greek prefix *hyper-* means "over, excessive, or exaggerated."

A *hyperbole* is a figure of speech consisting of an extreme exaggeration not meant to be taken literally. The statement "I've told you a million times..." is an example of *hyperbole.*

Hyperactivity is excessive activity. Does sugar cause *hyperactivity* in children?

Hyperglycemia is a condition of too much glucose in the blood. The doctor tested the patient's blood for *hyperglycemia.*

Describes the Subject

We have learned that a predicate nominative follows a linking verb and *renames* the subject. A **predicate adjective** follows a linking verb and *describes* or gives more detail about the subject.

An appaloosa <u>is</u> nimble.

In the sentence above, the word "nimble" is a predicate adjective. It describes "appaloosa"— nimble appaloosa.

The linking verb that connects the subject to the predicate adjective may be a "to be" verb (*is, am, are, was, were, be, been*), but other linking verbs such as *become, seem, feel, appear, look, taste,* and *smell* also can link the predicate adjective to the subject.

That appaloosa <u>looks</u> lively.

Identifying Predicate Adjectives

To help us identify the predicate adjective, we can replace a possible linking verb with a "to be" verb.

That appaloosa <u>is</u> lively.

"to be" verb

In the sentence above, we see that "lively" describes the subject "appaloosa"— lively appaloosa. Therefore, "lively" is a predicate adjective.

Compound Predicate Adjectives

A predicate adjective may be compound, as in the sentence below. Predicate adjectives are circled.

Jonathan Edwards <u>was</u> (brilliant) and (fiery.)

Diagramming

We diagram a predicate adjective in the same way we diagram a predicate nominative. Here is a diagram of the simple subject, linking verb, and predicate adjectives of the sentence above:

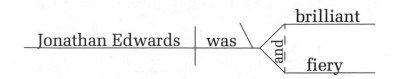

brilliant and fiery Jonathan Edwards

Example Diagram the simple subject, linking verb, and predicate adjectives in sentences a–c.

(a) His religious writings are famous.

(b) Jonathan Edwards seemed sincere.

(c) Was he devout and unbending?

Solution (a)

| writings | are | \ famous |

(b)

Jonathan Edwards | **seemed** \ **sincere**

(c)

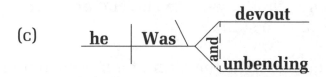

Practice For sentences a–d, diagram the simple subjects, linking verbs, and predicate adjectives.

a. The view from the Eiffel tower is spectacular.

b. The Eiffel tower appears tall, majestic, and beautiful.

c. That talented athlete seems very intelligent.

d. Petunia's pink lemonade tasted sour.

For e–h, replace each blank with the correct vocabulary word.

e. The Greek prefix meaning excessive or exaggerated is _____.

f. The child's _____ prevented her from sitting still.

g. A disease associated with _____ is diabetes.

h. "I am so tired, I could sleep for a month," is an example of _____.

Review set 41

1. *(4, 15)* Write the four principal parts (present tense, present participle, past tense, and past participle) of the verb *try*.

2. *(4, 22)* In this sentence, write the verb phrase and label it action or linking: The king has remained in the castle throughout the entire battle.

3. *(2, 24)* Tell whether the following is a phrase or a clause: with a superb orchestra and beautiful choreography

4. *(1, 3)* Tell whether the following sentence is declarative, interrogative, exclamatory, or imperative: Be careful whom you forget to invite to a party.

5. *(1, 3)* Tell whether this word group is a sentence fragment, run-on sentence, or complete sentence: *Hyper-*, *chron-*, *syn-*, *ante-*, *pro-*, *tele-*, *peri-*, *a-*, and *an-* are all prefixes, *phobia* is often a suffix.

6. *(12, 13)* For a–c, write the plural form of each noun. (a) bibliography   (b) justice of the peace (c) wife

7. *(5, 20)* Write each word that should be capitalized in this sentence: the president of the united states might have read george macDonald's "the light princess" when he was a boy.

8. *(32, 33)* Write the adjective phrase from this sentence followed by the noun it modifies: A king with no children has no heir.

Write the correct verb form to complete sentences 9 and 10.

9. *(8, 21)* The king and the queen (past progressive tense of *chat*) about this frustrating issue.

10. The queen's solution (past tense of *to be*) patience.
(6, 14)

For sentences 11 and 12, write the verb phrase and name its tense.

11. The queen has delivered a little princess.
(8, 18)

12. The king has been learning about patience.
(8, 21)

For sentences 13 and 14, write the verb phrase and label it transitive or intransitive.

13. The little princess was christened immediately.
(25, 31)

14. The king's father had forgotten the baby's aunt, Princess
(25, 31) Makemnoit, in his will.

15. Write each adjective in this sentence: Sour, spiteful
(27, 28) Princess Makemnoit had many peevish and contemptuous wrinkles across her face.

16. Rewrite this outline, adding periods as needed:
(35)
I Daughters of the American Revolution
   A Mrs Adeline Curtis's comments
   B Research by Miss Virginia Otto, Ph D

17. Write seven common coordinating conjunctions.
(36)

Write the predicate nominative in sentences 18 and 19.

18. Princess Makemnoit was a wicked fairy.
(39, 40)

19. The baby princess became a victim of her atrocious aunt.
(39, 40)

Choose the correct word to complete sentences 20–26.

20. A (common, concrete, predicate) nominative follows the
(7, 39) verb and renames the subject.

21. The (subject, verb, object) and the predicate nominative
(22, 39) may be joined by linking verbs such as *am, is, are, was, were, be, being, been, become,* or *seem.*

22. (Imminent, Immanent, Eminent) means innate or inborn.
(20)

23. Crowds gathered to hear the (imminent, immanent,
(20) eminent) scholar's lecture.

24. The silent movie was (phonic, aphonic).
(22)

25. Please (sit, set) your luggage by the door.
(24)

26. Please (lie, lay) your plates on the kitchen counter.
(23)

Diagram sentences 27–30.

27. Bea likes jumping and bouncing.
(19, 25)

28. Her aunt became treacherous.
(28, 39)

29. Have you experienced the loss of gravity?
(25, 33)

30. To float seems fun.
(23, 39)

LESSON 42

Comparison Adjectives

> **Dictation or Journal Entry**
>
> **Vocabulary:**
>
> The Greek prefix *hypo-* means "under," the opposite of *hyper-*.
>
> *Hypoglycemia* means too little glucose in the blood. People with *hypoglycemia* raise their blood sugar by eating.
>
> *Hypocalcemia* means not enough calcium in the blood. Calcium-rich dairy products may prevent *hypocalcemia*.
>
> *Hypothyroidism* refers to deficient activity of the thyroid gland. The young woman lacked energy due to *hypothyroidism*.

Adjectives are often used to compare nouns or pronouns. These **comparison adjectives** have three forms that show greater or lesser degrees of quality, quantity, or manner: positive, comparative, and superlative. Below are examples of the positive, comparative, and superlative forms of some adjectives.

POSITIVE	COMPARATIVE	SUPERLATIVE
short	shorter	shortest
small	smaller	smallest
bright	brighter	brightest
fine	finer	finest
brave	braver	bravest

Positive The positive degree, or basic form, describes a noun or pronoun without comparing it to any other. (Do not confuse *positive* with *good.* In this context, positive simply means "possessing the quality." The quality itself may be good, bad, or neutral.)

James is *silly.*

The soldier is *brave.*

Lydia is *tall.*

Comparative The comparative form compares **two** persons, places, or things.

James is *sillier* than John.

The soldier is *braver* than I am.

Is Lydia *taller* than Josie?

Superlative   The superlative form compares **three or more** persons, places, or things.

>James is the *silliest* of the four brothers.

>That soldier is the *bravest* in the army.

>Of the three ladies, Lydia is the *tallest*.

Example 1   Choose the correct adjective for each sentence.
(a) My house is (old, older, oldest) than yours.

(b) Of the three trees, which is (tall, taller, tallest)?

(c) Scamp, the Siamese cat, is (spunky, spunkier, spunkiest) than Kit Kat, the Himalayan.

Solution   (a) My house is **older** than yours. We use the comparative form because we are comparing two houses.

(b) Of the three trees, which is **tallest?** We use the superlative form because we are comparing more than two.

(c) Scamp, the Siamese cat, is **spunkier** than Kit Kat, the Himalayan. We use the comparative form because we are comparing only two cats.

Forming Comparison Adjectives   How we create the comparative and superlative forms of an adjective depends on how the adjective appears in its positive form. There are three main categories to remember.

One-Syllable Adjectives   Most one-syllable adjectives become comparative by adding *er* to the ending; they become superlative by adding *est* to the ending.

>light   lighter   lightest

Two-Syllable Adjectives that end in y   When a two-syllable adjective ends in *y,* we create the comparative and superlative forms by changing the *y* to *i* and adding *er* or *est*.

POSITIVE	COMPARATIVE	SUPERLATIVE
friendly	friendlier	friendliest
happy	happier	happiest
noisy	noisier	noisiest

Two or More Syllables Most adjectives with two or more syllables do not have comparative or superlative forms. Instead, we use the word "more" (or "less") before the adjective to form the comparative, and the word "most" (or "least") to form the superlative.

POSITIVE	COMPARATIVE	SUPERLATIVE
trustworthy	more trustworthy less trustworthy	most trustworthy least trustworthy
diligent	more diligent less diligent	most diligent least diligent
responsible	more responsible less responsible	most responsible least responsible

There are exceptions to these guidelines. Below are a few examples of two-syllable adjectives whose comparative and superlative forms are created by adding *er* or *est*.

POSITIVE	COMPARATIVE	SUPERLATIVE
little (size, not amount)	littler	littlest
clever	cleverer	cleverest
quiet	quieter	quietest
simple	simpler	simplest
narrow	narrower	narrowest

We check the dictionary if we are unsure how to form the comparative or superlative of a two-syllable adjective.

Spelling Reminders Remember that when adding *er* or *est* to the positive form of an adjective, we often must alter the word's original spelling. We apply the same rules we use when adding *ed* to form a past tense verb.

When an adjective ends with **two or more consonants,** *er* or *est* is simply added to the positive form of the adjective.

old	older	oldest
long	longer	longest

When an adjective ends with **a single consonant following one vowel,** we double the final consonant before adding *er* or *est*.

flat	flatter	flattest
big	bigger	biggest

When an adjective ends with **a single consonant following two vowels,** we do not double the final consonant.

| proud | prouder | proudest |
| cool | cooler | coolest |

When a one-syllable adjective ends in **w, x, or y preceded by a vowel,** we do not double the final consonant.

| new | newer | newest |
| gray | grayer | grayest |

When a two-syllable adjective ends with **y,** we change the *y* to *i* before adding the *er* or *est.*

| nosy | nosier | nosiest |
| curly | curlier | curliest |

When an adjective ends with a **silent e,** we drop the *e* and add *er* or *est.*

| rude | ruder | rudest |
| true | truer | truest |

Example 2 Complete the comparison chart by adding the comparative and superlative forms of each adjective.

POSITIVE	COMPARATIVE	SUPERLATIVE
(a) wet	_____	_____
(b) smart	_____	_____
(c) windy	_____	_____
(d) fantastic	_____	_____
(e) pure	_____	_____

Solution

POSITIVE	COMPARATIVE	SUPERLATIVE
(a) wet	**wetter**	**wettest**
(b) smart	**smarter**	**smartest**
(c) windy	**windier**	**windiest**
(d) fantastic	**more fantastic**	**most fantastic**
(e) pure	**purer**	**purest**

Practice For a–f, choose the correct adjective for each sentence and tell whether it is positive, comparative, or superlative.

    a. That employee is (healthy, healthier, healthiest) than the employer.

    b. Of all the grandfathers, he was the (trim, trimmer, trimmest).

    c. Portia's kittens are (old, older, oldest) than Cornflower's.

    d. Isn't this the (fabulous, more fabulous, most fabulous) day ever?

    e. This tomato is (ripe, riper, ripest) than that one.

    f. In a contest between chocolate and vanilla, chocolate was the (more, most) popular.

For g and h, write the comparative and superlative form of each positive adjective.

    g. wide   **h.** generous

For i–l, replace each blank with the correct vocabulary word.

    i. The Greek prefix meaning "under" is _____.

    j. _____ exists in patients with osteoporosis, a disorder caused by too little calcium.

    k. _____ is a deficiency in thyroid secretion, which causes fatigue and other problems.

    l. Dizziness, disorientation, and tingling are symptoms of too little blood sugar, or _____.

Review set 42

    1. *(32, 40)* Tell whether the italicized noun in this sentence is in the nominative, possessive, or objective case: The king and queen worry about the *princess.*

    2. *(6, 15)* Write the four principal parts (present tense, present participle, past tense, and past participle) of the verb *trim.*

    3. *(1, 3)* Tell whether this sentence is declarative, interrogative, exclamatory, or imperative: What will the king and the queen do about their daughter's uncontrollable laughing?

4. Tell whether the following is a phrase or a clause: if they
(3, 24) send for the metaphysicians

5. Write the verb phrase from this sentence and label it
(4, 22) action or linking: The people of the kingdom have
remained distraught.

6. Write the verb phrase from this sentence and label it
(25, 31) transitive or intransitive: Hum-Drum and Kipy-Keck will
volunteer their services.

7. For a–c, write the plural of each noun.
(12, 13) (a) bunch   (b) tablespoonful   (c) Debby

8. Write each word that should be capitalized in this
(11, 20) sentence: on monday, quan and james drank tea and
played checkers at a chinese restaurant.

9. Write the five words from this list that are *not*
(16, 17) prepositions: beside, besides, treason, between, beyond,
but, by, climactic, concerning, considering, anteroom,
despite, down, during, eminent, except, excepting, fewer,
for, from

Choose the correct verb form for sentences 10 and 11.

10. Hum-Drum and Kipy-Keck (was, were) philosophers
(6, 14) from the College of Metaphysicians in the country of
Hocuspocus.

11. Did they (has, have) solutions to the princess's lack of
(6, 14) gravity?

For sentences 12 and 13, write the verb phrase and name its
tense.

12. The weightlessness of the little princess has troubled the
(8, 18) king and queen.

13. Metaphysicians have been discussing the weightlessness
(8, 21) of the princess for a long, long time.

For sentences 14 and 15, write each direct object.

14. Each philosopher offers his own solution to the
(4, 25) princess's dilemma.

15. Neither solution pleases the king or queen.
(4, 25)

16. Rewrite this sentence, adding periods and making
(35) necessary changes to abbreviations for formal writing:
This morning at six a m, from the top of Mt Palomar, Mr
Chang watched the sun rise

17. Write the predicate nominative from this sentence:
(22, 39) Submersion in water was one effective solution to the
problem.

18. Write the predicate adjective from this sentence: On
(22, 41) occasion, the king became tyrannical.

For sentences 19–21, replace each blank with the correct
word.

19. We group nouns into three cases: _____,
(40) possessive, and objective.

20. The _____ of a noun explains how the noun is
(40) used in the sentence.

21. When a noun is a sentence subject or predicate
(40) nominative, it is in the _____ case.

Choose the correct word to complete sentences 22–25.

22. Agoraphobia is the (love, fear, enjoyment) of crowds and
(33) public places.

23. (Discrete, Discreet) means careful and prudent.
(34)

24. The Greek root (*eu-*, *ortho-*, *graphy*) means drawing,
(13, 37) writing, or recording.

25. (Audacity, Treason, Dissension) is strong disagreement or
(38) strife.

26. Write the gerund from this sentence and label its tense
(18, 19) present or perfect: Having tried many possible solutions
only frustrated the king.

27. Write the infinitive from this sentence and label its tense
(18, 23) present or perfect: One form of relief for the princess was
to swim.

Diagram sentences 28–30.

28. A human tear might be a solution.
(28, 30)

29. Will water offer the little princess freedom from her
(25, 33) weightlessness?

30. Swimming is the princess's salvation.
(19, 39)

LESSON
43

Irregular Comparison Adjectives

> **Dictation or Journal Entry**
>
> **Vocabulary:**
> The adjectives *luxuriant* and *luxurious* have similar spellings but different meanings.
>
> *Luxuriant* means abundant or lush in growth. The *luxuriant* valley is famous for its agriculture.
>
> *Luxurious* means rich, sumptuous, or given to pleasure. Many famous celebrities frequented the *luxurious* hotel.

Some adjectives have irregular comparative and superlative forms. We must learn these if we haven't already.

POSITIVE	COMPARATIVE	SUPERLATIVE
little (amount, not size)	less	least
good, well	better	best
bad, ill	worse	worst
far	farther	farthest
many, much	more	most

Little or Few? We use *little*, *less*, and *least* with things that cannot be counted. We use *few*, *fewer*, and *fewest* for things that can be counted.

> CANNOT BE COUNTED:
> I have *less* time today than I had yesterday.

> CAN BE COUNTED:
> Will *fewer* spectators come to the parade this year?

Much or Many? We use *much* with things that cannot be counted, and we use *many* for things that can be counted.

> CANNOT BE COUNTED:
> I don't need *much* help.

> CAN BE COUNTED:
> *Many* people offered to help me.

Example 1 Choose the correct adjective for each sentence.

(a) I have (little, less, least) interest in skydiving than in scuba diving.

(b) Hurricane Andrew was the (baddest, worst) hurricane I have ever experienced.

(c) Teachers have (less, fewer) pupil-free days this year than last year.

(d) In the past, (less, fewer) stores remained open on Sundays.

(e) (Many, Much) of our previous presidents earned high marks from world historians for their performances.

Solution   (a) I have **less** interest in skydiving than in scuba diving. (The sentence is comparing two sports, so we use the comparative form of "little.")

(b) Hurricane Andrew was the **worst** hurricane I have ever experienced. ("Baddest" is not a word.)

(c) Teachers have **fewer** pupil-free days this year than last year. ("Days" can be counted.)

(d) In the past, **fewer** stores remained open on Sundays. ("Stores" can be counted.)

(e) **Many** of our previous presidents earned high marks from world historians for their performances. ("Presidents" can be counted.)

Avoid Double Comparisons   We do not use double comparisons. In other words, we do not use *more* with *er,* or *most* with *est.*

NO: Julio was *more better* than Jonah at football.
YES: Julio was *better* than Jonah at football.

NO: Is your garage the *most messiest* on the block?
YES: Is your garage the *messiest* on the block?

Example 2   Choose the correct adjective for each sentence.

(a) The Knave of Hearts was (hungrier, more hungrier) than the King of Hearts.

(b) Stealing the tarts was the (worst, most worst) thing the Knave had ever done.

Solution   (a) The Knave of Hearts was **hungrier** than the King of Hearts. ("More hungrier" is a double comparison. We do not use *more* with *er.*)

(b) Stealing the tarts was the **worst** thing the Knave had ever done. ("Most worst" is a double comparison. We do not use *most* with *est.*)

Practice For a–f, choose the correct adjective for each sentence.

    a. We find (much, many) written criticism of literary classics.

    b. Children all over the world enjoy (much, many) nursery rhymes.

    c. One of the (better, best) nursery rhymes is "Jack Sprat."

    d. "Hickety, Pickety, my black hen," laid (more, most) eggs today than yesterday.

    e. The scholar made (few, little) effort to arrive at school on time.

    f. Little Miss Muffet felt (better, more better) after the spider left.

For g–j, replace each blank with *luxuriant* or *luxurious.*

    g. The _____ jungles along the Amazon River provide homes for many tropical animals.

    h. Miss Pringle's _____ bathtub cost thousands of dollars.

    i. Their _____ limousine featured a red leather interior with polished wood paneling.

    j. A latticed patio was covered with _____ foliage for added coolness.

More Practice Choose the correct adjective for each sentence.

    1. My yard has (little, less) grass than hers.

    2. Quan is a (gooder, better) tennis player than Bo.

    3. That brush fire was the (worse, worst) we've ever had.

    4. Sidney feels (better, weller) today than he felt yesterday.

    5. My new telephone is (reliabler, more reliable) than my old one.

    6. She ate (more, most) pizza than I did.

7. Which impostor is the (more conniving, most conniving) of the three?

8. Are you the (smarter, smartest) of the two?

9. Of the two students, Danielle lives (farther, farthest) from town.

10. Kyle missed (fewer, less) days of school than I did.

11. Olga has (fewer, less) absences than Kyle.

12. We have (fewer, less) homework tonight.

Review set 43

1. *(1, 3)* Tell whether the following is a run-on sentence, complete sentence, or sentence fragment: Frances Browne wrote "The Little Princess" it is a fairy tale.

2. *(3, 24)* Tell whether this word group is a phrase or a clause: down by the creek bank in an old hollow log

3. *(12, 13)* For a–c, write the plural of each noun.
    (a) stripe   (b) cliff   (c) pony

4. *(5, 11)* Write each word that should be capitalized in this sentence: christina is studying microbiology in heidelberg, germany.

5. *(16, 32)* From this sentence, write each prepositional phrase and star the object of each preposition: Amid fanfare and applause, the politician stepped down from the platform and circulated among the people.

6. *(25, 31)* From this sentence, write the verb phrase and label it transitive or intransitive: Did they rescue the injured iguana?

7. *(4, 22)* Write the verb phrase from this sentence and label it action or linking: Does this question seem complicated?

For sentences 8–10, write the verb phrase and name its tense.

8. *(8, 18)* A prince has made an embarrassing mistake.

9. *(18, 21)* Before evening falls, the princess will have been swimming in the lake for several hours.

10. By the end of this school year, we shall have discussed
(8, 18) many silly stories.

11. Write the indirect object from this sentence: Finally, the
(25, 34) prince offered the princess his assistance.

12. Write each adjective from this sentence, and circle those
(27, 28) that are articles: An exasperated student tossed the
difficult test into a wastebasket.

13. Write the four principal parts (present tense, present
(6, 15) participle, past tense, and past participle) of the verb
rescue.

14. Tell whether the italicized noun in this sentence is
(32, 40) nominative, objective, or possessive case: Please write
your name on this *line.*

15. Rewrite the following sentence, adding periods and
(35) making necessary changes to abbreviations for formal
writing: Thurs morning, Dr Cabrera took giant steps to
avoid the cracks in the sidewalk on W Hope St

16. Write the predicate nominative in this sentence: A cave
(22, 39) in a rock became the prince's home.

For sentences 17–19, write whether the italicized noun is a
direct object, an indirect object, or the object of a preposition.

17. He gave the *princess* his undying love.
(25, 34)

18. The prince sang a *song* to attract her attention.
(4, 25)

19. They enjoyed jumping into the water off of big *rocks.*
(16, 32)

Diagram sentences 20 and 21.

20. Nam eats neither beans nor rice.
(25, 38)

21. Have you tried to explain?
(23, 25)

22. Write the gerund in this sentence and label its tense
(8, 19) present or perfect: Having ruined the young girl's day
delighted the old hag.

23. Write the infinitive in this sentence and label its tense
(18, 23) present or perfect: The king's cruel sister purposed to
empty the lake.

24. Write the comparative and superlative forms of the
(42, 43) adjective *silly*.

Choose the correct word to complete sentences 25–30.

25. Of the two dogs, mine is the (larger, largest).
(42, 43)

26. Homer revealed his (treason, audacity, dissension) when
(38) he told his neighbors that their newly painted house was
ugly.

27. The Greek root (*graphy*, *morph*, *chrono*) means time.
(37, 39)

28. Can the kangaroo (adopt, adapt, adept) to cold weather?
(1)

29. A bad, discordant sound is a (symphony, euphony,
(11, 13) cacophony).

30. A phobia is a (program, fear, strength).
(33)

LESSON
44

The Comma, Part 1: Dates, Addresses, Series

Dictation or Journal Entry

Vocabulary:

The Greek prefix *hetero-* (opposite of *homo-*) means "not the same; different."

Heterogeneous means having unrelated or dissimilar parts. Many different races comprised the *heterogeneous* group of people.

Heterophony is the sound made by two or more different performers playing the same melodic line with slight variations. The listener appreciated the identifiable *heterophony* of the musical composition.

Heteronyms are words with the same spelling but different pronunciations and meanings. "Lead" (to guide) and "lead" (the metal) are *heteronyms*.

Commas are another form of punctuation we use to clarify the meaning of a phrase or a sentence. We use commas to group words that belong together and to separate those that do not.

Parts of a Date We use commas to separate the **parts of a date.** When we write a complete date, we always place a comma between the day and the year.

May 3, 1947

If a complete date appears in the middle of a sentence, we place a comma after the year.

On December 17, 1903, the Wright Brothers made the first powered airplane flight in history.

If the day of the week appears as part of the date, we place a comma after the day.

We remember Tuesday, September 11, 2001.

Note: When just the month and the year appear in a sentence, no comma is required.

People all over the world remember September 2001 as a time of loss and pain.

Example 1 Place commas wherever they are needed in the parts of the date in this sentence:

Tommy's birth occurred on Thursday March 23 1978 three days before Easter Sunday.

Solution   We place a comma after the day of the week (Thursday). We also place a comma after the day (March 23). Lastly, we place a comma after the year, because the date appears in the middle of a sentence.

> Tommy's birth occurred on Thursday, March 23, 1978, three days before Easter Sunday.

Parts of an Address   We use commas to separate the **parts of an address** and the names of geographical places or political divisions.

The parts of a street address are separated by commas according to the following pattern:

> house number and street, city, state and zip code

> 10662 Lora Street, Monrovia, California 91016

> 117 North Pine Street, Roseburg, OR 97470

Note: We use the state abbreviation when addressing a letter or package.

We also use commas to separate the names of geographical places or political divisions.

> Seattle, Washington   San Salvador, El Salvador
> London, England, UK   Bejing, Zhangjiakou, China

If the city and state or country appear in the middle of the sentence, we place a comma after the state or country.

> Carol Williams lived in Oxnard, California, when her daughter was born.

Example 2   Place commas wherever they are needed in the parts of the address in these sentences.

(a) The package was delivered to 327 Magnolia Avenue Redlands CA 91338 U.S.A.

(b) The Ware Family has lived in Heidelberg Germany for the last two months.

Solution   (a) We separate the parts of the address with commas. One comma goes after the house number and street, another goes between the city and the state, and another goes between the zip code and the country.

> The package was delivered to 327 Magnolia Avenue, Redlands, CA 91338, U.S.A.

(b) We place a comma between the city and the country, and another between the country and the rest of the sentence.

The Ware Family has lived in Heidelberg, Germany, for the last two months.

Words in a Series   We use a comma to separate three or more **words or phrases in a series**, as in the sentence below.

Eisenhower directed the invasions of Sicily, Italy, Normandy, and Germany.

Amazing self-discipline, strong courage, and impeccable integrity made him a good president.

Example 3   Place commas as needed in this sentence:

Eisenhower convinced Congress to cut taxes lower credit rates expand the space program and extend aid to foreign countries.

Solution   We separate the items in the series with commas.

Eisenhower convinced Congress to cut taxes, lower credit rates, expand the space program, and extend aid to foreign countries.

Practice   For a–d, replace each blank with the correct vocabulary word.

a. The Greek prefix *homo-* means "same"; the prefix _____ means "different."

b. The bibliophile had a large collection of _____ writings.

c. The words "desert" (a hot, dry place) and "desert" (to abandon or leave) are not homonyms; they are _____.

d. The conductor requested two violin players and two cello players to create the _____.

Rewrite sentences e–g, inserting commas as needed to separate parts of a date.

e. The Emancipation Proclamation of January 1 1863 was issued by President Abraham Lincoln.

f. On March 13 1862 President Lincoln forbade the Union army officers to return fugitive slaves.

g. Christmas fell on Tuesday December 25 in the year 2001.

Rewrite sentences h–j, inserting commas as needed to separate parts of an address.

h. The Statue of Liberty is located on Liberty Island New York New York 10004.

i. San José Costa Rica attracts many tourists each year.

j. Will you visit Madrid Spain this spring?

Rewrite sentences k–m, inserting commas as needed to separate words in a series.

k. We will enjoy seeing the Coliseum the Eiffel Tower and Michelangelo's *David* in Europe.

l. Italy Germany France Austria and England are countries on our tour's itinerary.

m. Some favorite American holidays are New Year's Day Valentine's Day Martin Luther King Day President's Day St. Patrick's Day and Independence Day.

More Practice   See Master Worksheets.

Review set 44   Choose the correct word to complete sentences 1–10.

1. Bill has (less, fewer) cavities than I.
(42, 43)

2. A(n) (concrete, abstract) noun names something that
(7, 9) cannot be seen or touched.

3. Meg is the (taller, tallest) of the two sisters.
(42, 43)

4. Debby doesn't eat (much, many) bananas.
(42, 43)

5. The chimpanzee has some (human, humane) physical
(3) traits.

6. Somehow, Mom managed to (allude, elude) her annoying
(14) neighbor.

7. (Perspective, Prospective) means "of or in the future."
(29)

8. (Ingenuous, Ingenious) means clever, inventive, and
(36) resourceful.

9. A predicate adjective describes the sentence (subject,
(22, 41) verb, object).

10. The predicate adjective follows a (linking, action) verb
(22, 41) and gives more detail about the subject.

11. Rewrite this sentence adding periods and making
(35) necessary changes to abbreviations for formal writing:
Miss Vong glanced up at the San Gabriel Mts as she
hurried to her nine a m interview at the Varoom
Appliance Co

12. For a–c, write the plural of each noun.
(12, 13) (a) deer   (b) video   (c) match

Write each word that should be capitalized in sentences 13
and 14.

13. the king declared, "if the nation can not provide a hero, it
(11, 20) is time for it to perish."

14. please, father, come with us to the beach.
(11, 20)

15. Write each prepositional phrase in this sentence, starring
(16, 32) the object of each preposition: The drummer on the bus
placed her lunch underneath the seat with the rest of her
stuff.

Write the correct form of the verb to complete sentences 16
and 17.

16. The obnoxious aunt's snake (present tense of *hiss*).
(6, 15)

17. The prince (present progressive tense of *offer*) his
(8, 21) services to the king.

Write each adjective in sentences 18 and 19.

18. Will the king accept the prince's brave offer?
(27, 28)

19. His courage may save many lives.
(28)

20. Write the predicate adjective in this sentence: Is his royal
(41) highness agreeable?

21. Write the verb phrase in this sentence and label it
(21, 31) transitive or intransitive: My border collie has been lying on the sofa all day.

22. Write the four principal parts (present tense, present
(6, 15) participle, past tense, and past participle) of the verb *sneeze.*

23. Tell whether the italicized noun in this sentence is
(40, 41) nominative, objective, or possessive case: The prince is the *hero* of the story.

For 24 and 25, write whether the word group is a phrase or a clause.

24. hoping to complete the project before midnight
(3, 24)

25. if he completes it
(3, 24)

26. Tell whether the following is a complete sentence, run-on
(1, 3) sentence, or sentence fragment: A luxurious palace dining hall with elegant silver goblets and glittering, crystal chandeliers.

Diagram sentences 27–30.

27. The fruits on the king's table smell delicious.
(33, 41)

28. The princess grew listless and weak.
(22, 41)

29. Both watering and fertilizing encourage new growth.
(19, 38)

30. I need to sleep.
(23, 25)

LESSON
45

Appositives

Dictation or Journal Entry

Vocabulary:
Sometimes people confuse the similar words *epoch* and *epic.*

An *epoch* is a particular period of time marked by distinctive activities or events. The Victorian *epoch* was characterized by rigid social conventions.

An *epic* is a long narrative poem centered upon a specific hero. *Beowulf* is an example of an *epic* poem.

Appositives   A word or group of words that immediately follows a noun to identify or give more information about the noun is called an **appositive.** In the sentences below, the appositives are underlined.

> *Romeo and Juliet*, <u>a play by William Shakespeare</u>, is being performed at the community college.

> Mrs. Sheker, <u>Sam's chemistry teacher</u>, encouraged him to repeat the experiment.

> My friend <u>Shirley</u> has read the Constitution.

Example 1   Identify the appositives from each sentence.

(a) Winter, the coldest season, is when animals' coats are the thickest.

(b) One amendment of the United States Constitution, the Fifth, states that a person cannot be forced to testify against himself.

Solution   (a) The appositive **the coldest season** gives more information about the subject "winter."

(b) The appositive **the Fifth** gives more information about "amendment."

Improving Our Writing   Using appositives skillfully can improve our writing. With an appositive, we can combine two choppy sentences to make one good one.

> Two Choppy Sentences:
> The First Amendment guarantees freedom of religion. The First Amendment is part of the United States Constitution.

ONE GOOD SENTENCE:

The First Amendment, part of the United States Constitution, guarantees freedom of religion.

Example 2   Combine this pair of choppy sentences to make one good sentence by using an appositive.

Benjamin Franklin was born in Boston, Massachusetts. Benjamin Franklin was an American printer, author, diplomat, philosopher, and scientist.

Solution   We can make an appositive from the first sentence and combine it with the second sentence:

Benjamin Franklin, born in Boston, Massachusetts, was an American printer, author, diplomat, philosopher, and scientist.

Or, we can make an appositive from the second sentence and combine it with the first sentence:

Benjamin Franklin, an American printer, author, diplomat, philosopher, and scientist, was born in Boston, Massachusetts.

Diagramming the Appositive   We diagram an appositive by placing it in parentheses beside the noun it identifies or describes. We place modifiers of the appositive directly beneath the appositive.

The first public library, the Philadelphia Library, was one of Benjamin Franklin's first projects.

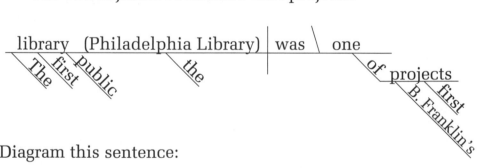

Example 3   Diagram this sentence:

My sister, a gourmet cook, prepared escargot.

Solution   We place the appositive **cook** in parentheses beside the subject "sister." We place the appositive's modifiers directly beneath it.

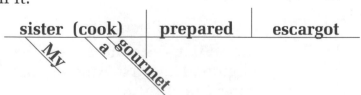

Practice For a–d, replace each blank with *epoch* or *epic.*

a. The *Iliad*, an _____ poem, is a long account of the Trojan War and the Greeks' attempts to rescue Helen.

b. Perhaps the twenty-first century will be an _____ of peace and goodwill.

c. An _____ of kings began with the anointing of Saul by Samuel.

d. _____ poems have been written about heroes like King Arthur and Robin Hood.

For e and f, write the appositive from each sentence.

e. The author, Benjamin Franklin, wrote *Poor Richard's Almanac* under the pen name of Richard Saunders.

f. One of Benjamin Franklin's inventions, the Franklin stove, furnished heat more efficiently.

g. Diagram this sentence: Benjamin Franklin, an inventor, made the lightning rod.

For h and i, use an appositive to combine each pair of sentences to make one sentence.

h. The American Philosophical Society was a discussion group. It was organized by Ben Franklin.

i. Ben Franklin signed the Declaration of Independence. The Declaration of Independence is a document that declares the Colonies independent of England.

More Practice See "Slapstick Story #3 in Master Worksheets.

Review set 45 1. Write the verb phrase from this sentence and label it (25, 31) transitive or intransitive: The university might waive the foreign language requirement.

2. Write each noun from this sentence and circle the one (7, 9) that is collective: Each football team brought a mascot to the game.

3. Write each possessive noun from this list: teams, team's, (7, 9) teams', mascots, mascot's

4. Tell whether the following is a complete sentence, run-on
(1, 3) sentence, or sentence fragment: The light princess realized that the prince would drown if she did not rescue him.

5. For a–c, write the plural of each noun.
(12, 13) (a) radius   (b) torpedo   (c) crutch

6. Write each word that should be capitalized in this
(11, 20) sentence: aunt clara and uncle meredith want to know how "the light princess" ends.

7. Rewrite the following, adding commas as needed: Let's
(44) wash the dishes fold the laundry and mow the lawn.

8. Write the verb phrase from this sentence and label it
(4, 22) action or linking: The princess appears panicky over the prince's welfare.

Write the correct verb form to complete sentences 9 and 10.

9. The prince (past progressive tense of *drown*) in the lake.
(15, 21)

10. An old nurse (present tense of *save*) him.
(6, 15)

11. Write each prepositional phrase from this sentence and
(17, 32) star the object of each preposition: From under the water, the princess frees the legs of the prince from the snare.

12. Write each adjective from this sentence: To revive the
(27, 28) gallant prince was her first concern.

Replace each blank with the correct word to complete sentences 13 and 14.

13. A predicate adjective follows a _____ verb and
(22, 41) gives more detail about the subject.

14. The three forms of adjectives showing greater or lesser
(42, 43) degrees are the positive, the _____, and the superlative.

Choose the correct adjective for 15 and 16.

15. The (big, bigger, biggest) surprise of all was that gravity
(42, 43) returned to the princess as a result of her tears.

16. The amount of water from the princess's tears was (great,
^(42, 43) greater, greatest) than the amount of rainfall in a storm.

17. Rewrite this sentence, adding periods and making
⁽³⁵⁾ necessary changes to abbreviations for formal writing: On
the first Mon in Aug, Mr Moses A Zamora will be here at
two p m to discuss the benefits of Healthquest, Inc

18. List the four most common pairs of correlative
⁽³⁸⁾ conjunctions.

19. Write the predicate nominative in this sentence: The
^(22, 39) princess became a happy bride.

For 20 and 21, tell whether the italicized noun is nominative,
objective, or possessive case.

20. Human beings are orthograde *walkers.*
^(39, 40)

21. Learning to walk was not easy for the *princess.*
^(32, 40)

Diagram sentences 22 and 23.

22. She began smiling and giggling.
^(23, 25)

23. The people of the kingdom were ecstatic.
^(33, 41)

24. Tell whether the following is a phrase or a clause: along
^(3, 24) with the strange customs and unusual costumes

25. Write the infinitive from this sentence and label its tense
^(18, 23) present or perfect: To have punished the princess's aunt
would have been pointless.

Choose the correct word to complete 26–30.

26. Jayne's (costume, custom) was finished only moments
⁽⁴⁰⁾ before curtain time.

27. The Greek prefix *hyper-* means (under, angry, excessive).
^(41, 42)

28. Ingenuous means (clever, sincere).
⁽³⁶⁾

29. The past participle of *smile* is (smiling, smiled).
⁽¹⁵⁾

30. The prince and the princess (was, were) gregarious and
⁽¹⁴⁾ courageous.

LESSON
46

The Comma, Part 2: Direct Address, Appositives, Academic Degrees

---

Dictation or Journal Entry

Vocabulary:

The Greek word *theos-* meaning god, is seen in the common prefix *theo-*.

Theocracy is the government of a state by a god or by officials thought to be divinely guided. Was ancient Egypt a *theocracy*?

Theology is the study of religious faith and practice. The seminary student took classes in *theology* as well as Greek and Hebrew.

A *theologian* is a person who specializes in religious knowledge. Some *theologians* are professors; others are rabbis, pastors, or priests.

In this lesson, we will discuss more uses for commas.

Nouns of Direct Address

A **noun of direct address** names the person who is being spoken to (the person who is receiving the information in the sentence). The noun can be the person's name or a "name" you are using for him or her. Nouns of direct address can appear anywhere in a sentence. We offset them with commas.

> Miss Garby, are we going to read any poems by Robert Frost?

> Please, Abby, recite the poem for us.

> How many times did Robert Frost win the Pulitzer Prize for poetry, Mr. Yan?

There may be more than one noun of direct address in a sentence. Also, like any noun, a noun of direct address can be modified by adjectives. We offset the entire noun phrase with commas, as in the sentences below.

> Don't eat those cookies, James and Robbie!

> Please save them, my dear sons, for our guests.

Example 1 Insert commas to separate the noun of direct address in the sentence below.

> I have heard Mr. and Mrs. Yan that Robert Frost worked as a farmer, a bobbin boy, a shoemaker, a country schoolteacher, and an editor of a rural newspaper.

Solution We insert commas before and after "Mr. and Mrs. Yan" because Mr. and Mrs. Yan are being spoken to. They are nouns of direct address.

> **I have heard, Mr. and Mrs. Yan, that Robert Frost worked as a farmer, a bobbin boy, a shoemaker, a country schoolteacher, and an editor of a rural newspaper.**

Appositives We have learned that an **appositive** is a word or group of words that immediately follows a noun to identify or give more information about the noun. In the sentence below, "an American poet" is an appositive. Notice how commas offset it from the rest of the sentence.

> Robert L. Frost, <u>an American poet</u>, won the Pulitzer Prize four times for his poetry.

In the sentence below, "Edward Thomas" is also an appositive. But it is not offset by a comma. Why?

> Robert Frost was supported early in his career by the British poet <u>Edward Thomas</u>.

Essential and Nonessential Appositives Whether or not an appositive is offset with commas depends on how essential it is to the meaning of the sentence.

Let's look at the first sentence, above. If we remove the appositive, the sentence still makes sense:

> Robert L. Frost won the Pulitzer Prize four times for his poetry.

The phrase "Robert L. Frost" has already identified the person the sentence is about. The appositive "an American poet" is informative but **nonessential** to the meaning of the sentence. **Nonessential appositives are offset with commas.**

Now let's remove the appositive from the second sentence:

> Robert Frost was supported early in his career by the British poet.

The British poet? Which British poet? This sentence no longer makes sense. The appositive "Edward Thomas" is **essential** to the meaning of the sentence. **Essential appositives are not offset by commas.**

Example 2 Insert commas where necessary in the sentence below.

> Mark Twain the author of *Life on the Mississippi* wrote about his adventures as captain of a steamboat.

Solution If we remove the appositive, "author of *Life on the Mississippi*," the meaning of the sentence is still clear. (Mark Twain wrote about his adventures as captain of a steam boat.) Therefore, it is a nonessential appositive and we offset it with commas.

> **Mark Twain, the author of *Life on the Mississippi*, wrote about his adventures as captain of a steamboat.**

Example 3 Insert commas where necessary in the sentence below.

> In 1807, the American steamboat the *Clermont* was launched on the Hudson River.

Solution If we remove the appositive, "the *Clermont*," the reader is left to wonder *which* American steamboat and the meaning of the sentence is lost. Therefore, it is an essential appositive so we do not offset it with commas.

> **In 1807, the American steamboat the *Clermont* was launched on the Hudson River.**

Academic Degrees When an **academic degree** or similar title follows a person's name, it is usually abbreviated. Here are some abbreviations you're likely to see:

> M.D. (Doctor of Medicine)
> D.D.S. (Doctor of Dental Surgery)
> D.V.M. (Doctor of Veterinary Medicine)
> Ph.D. (Doctor of Philosophy)
> Ed.D. (Doctor of Education)
> D.D. (Doctor of Divinity)
> LL.D. (Doctor of Law)
> R.N. (Registered Nurse)
> L.P.N. (Licensed Practical Nurse)
> M.B.A. (Master of Business Administration)

We use commas to offset academic degrees or other titles that follow a person's name.

> Elizabeth Brown, Ph.D., analyzed Edmund Spenser's *Faerie Queene* for her doctoral thesis.

Example 4 Insert commas to offset the academic degree in this sentence.

> Marc Tyrell M.D. specializes in orthopedic surgery.

Solution   Since "M.D." is an academic degree, it is offset with commas.

Marc Tyrell, M.D., specializes in orthopedic surgery.

Practice   Rewrite sentences a and b, using commas to offset nouns of direct address.

  a. Students Robert Fulton began his career as an American painter.

  b. Did you know Raffi that Robert Fulton invented machines for cutting marble, for spinning flax, and for twisting hemp into rope?

Rewrite sentences c and d, using commas to offset appositives.

  c. *Fulton the First* the first steam-propelled warship was developed by Robert Fulton.

  d. Jack London author of *To Build a Fire* battled the elements of nature in many of his stories.

Rewrite sentences e and f, using commas to offset academic degrees.

  e. Sara Brown D.V.M. informed us that our dog needed to lose weight.

  f. Polly Wafer R.N. collapsed into bed after working a twelve-hour shift at the hospital.

For g–j, replace each blank with the correct vocabulary word.

  g. The Greek prefix meaning god is _____.

  h. Mr. Shyster, a _____, ruled his cult followers as though he were God.

  i. The _____ spent several years in seminary learning about doctrinal issues.

  j. Freddy read several books of the Old Testament for his _____ class.

More Practice   See Master Worksheets.

Review set   Choose the best word to complete sentences 1–10.
46
1. Hyperactivity is (suspicious, excessive, confidential)
(41, 42) activity.

2. The Greek prefix (ante-, hyper-, hypo-) means under.
(41, 42)

3. Synonyms mean the (same, opposite).
(22, 35)

4. Adapt and adjust are (antonyms, synonyms, homonyms).
(1, 35)

5. The past tense of the verb *plot* is (ploted, plotted).
(6, 15)

6. Stories about dreams and enchantments (am, is, are)
(6, 14) entertaining.

7. A (positive, comparative, superlative) adjective compares
(42, 43) three or more persons, places, or things.

8. A (positive, comparative, superlative) adjective compares
(42, 43) two or more persons, places, or things.

9. A (positive, comparative, superlative) adjective describes
(42, 43) a noun or pronoun without comparing it to any other.

10. Tell whether the following is a sentence fragment, run-on
(1, 3) sentence, or complete sentence: Bobo, the youngest son
of an old widow.

11. Tell whether this word group is a phrase or a clause:
(3, 24) since he was as bald as a kneecap

12. Write each noun from this sentence and circle those that
(7, 9) are feminine: Princess Zena took Bobo away from his
mother.

13. For a–c, write the plural of each noun.
(12, 13) (a) stitch   (b) simpleton   (c) portfolio

14. Write each word that should be capitalized in this
(11, 20) sentence: the princess asked, "shall we send bobo in
search of the lost half-hour?"

For 15 and 16, write each prepositional phrase and star the object of each preposition.

15. The wise folk at the castle send Bobo on ridiculous
(16, 32) errands.

16. Outside of Tilda, Bobo can trust no one in the
(16, 32) community.

17. Write the verb phrase from this sentence and name its
(8, 18) tense: Wise folk have sent Bobo for a white crow's feather, a spray of yellow bluebells, a square wheel, and a glass of dry water.

18. Write the verb phrase from this sentence and label it
(25, 31) transitive or intransitive: Bobo will be searching for a lost half-hour.

19. Write the verb phrase from this sentence and label it
(4, 22) action or linking: Does Tilda remain faithful?

20. For a–c, write the comparative and superlative forms of
(42, 43) each positive adjective.

(a) slow   (b) enthusiastic   (c) subtle

21. Write the four principal parts (present tense, present
(6, 15) participle, past tense, and past participle) of the verb *drop.*

22. Use an appositive to combine this pair of sentences to
(45, 46) make one sentence: Bobo relies on Tilda. Tilda is the kitchen maid.

23. Write the seven common coordinating conjunctions.
(36)

24. Rewrite this sentence, adding periods and making
(35) necessary changes to abbreviations for formal writing: H Bestron wrote a story about the Kingdom of the E and the Kingdom of the W

25. Tell whether the italicized noun in this sentence is
(39, 40) nominative, objective, or possessive case: Tilda is actually the *daughter* of a king.

26. Write the gerund from this sentence and label its tense
(18, 19) present or perfect: Having received the lost half-hour from Father Time pleased Bobo.

27. Rewrite this sentence, adding commas as needed: My
(44, 46) mother Isabel Curtis works at a library in Arcadia California.

Diagram sentences 28–30.

28. Bobo desires to return.
(23, 25)

29. The courageous Tilda gives the dragon his request.
(25, 34)

30. The rescue of Tilda requires ingenuity and
(25, 33) resourcefulness.

LESSON 47

Overused Adjectives • Unnecessary Articles

Dictation or Journal Entry

Vocabulary:

Let us not confuse the words *anecdote* and *antidote*.

An *anecdote* is a short story or an account of an amusing or interesting incident. Historians tell the *anecdote* of Benjamin Franklin's kite flying near lightning.

An *antidote* is a medicine or other remedy to counteract the effects of a poison. The hospital stocks an *antidote* for rattlesnake bites.

Overused Adjectives

Do you find yourself using the same adjective over and over again? In this lesson we will learn to choose more vivid adjectives. Some of the adjectives that people use too often are as follows:

great	bad	rotten
nice	terrible	wonderful
good	awful	super

While there is nothing wrong with the adjectives above, we should try to use more specific or interesting ones if we can. We can always consult the dictionary or thesaurus for more choices.

WEAK: The Bowl Championship Game was *good*!
BETTER: The Bowl Championship Game was *stupendous* (or *breath-taking, magnificent, thrilling, intense, splendid*).

WEAK: Benjamin Franklin was *great.*
BETTER: Benjamin Franklin was *brilliant* (or *accomplished, clever, wise, inventive, intelligent, knowledgeable, expert*).

WEAK: I feel *bad* today.
BETTER: I feel *poorly* (or *ill, depressed, guilty, disappointed, despondent, miserable, sad, unhappy, wretched*) today.

Example 1

Rewrite each sentence, replacing each overused adjective with a more vivid one.

(a) The hurricane was *terrible*.

(b) Our principal is a *good* speaker.

(c) Scary movies can be *bad* for young children.

(d) That bulldog is *nice.*

Solution   Our answers will vary. Here are some possibilities:

(a) The hurricane was (**brutal, atrocious, wild, devastating**).

(b) Our principal is a (**charismatic, powerful, informative, entertaining**) speaker.

(c) Scary movies can be (**frightening, terrifying, alarming, disturbing, unsettling**) for young children.

(d) That bulldog is (**pleasant, agreeable, enjoyable, friendly, well-behaved**).

Unnecessary Articles   We have learned that the articles *a*, *an*, and *the* are adjectives. Sometimes they are used unnecessarily. Avoid these errors:

We do not use *the* before "both."

NO: *The both* of them need a vacation.
YES: *Both* of them need a vacation.

NO: Show *the both* of them to their seats.
YES: Show *both* of them to their seats.

We do not use *a* or *an* after the phrases "kind of," "sort of," or "type of."

NO: Grandma was that *kind of a* person.
YES: Grandma was that *kind of* person.

NO: Do you like that *type of a* cat?
YES: Do you like that *type of* cat?

Example 2   Rewrite each sentence correctly.

(a) I gave the both of them some advice.

(b) What kind of a climate do you like best?

Solution   (a) **I gave both of them some advice.** (We remove the word *the*. It is not used before "both.")

(b) **What kind of climate do you like best?** (We remove the word *a*. We do not use it after "kind of.")

Practice Rewrite sentences a–d, replacing each overused adjective with a more interesting one.

    a. I read an *awful* biography.

    b. Maggie looked *good.*

    c. Kristopher had a *nice* time.

    d. This bread tastes *bad.*

Rewrite sentences e and f correctly.

    e. That sort of an assignment is difficult for most people.

    f. Harriet brought the both of them to the wedding.

For g–j, replace each blank with *anecdote* or *antidote.*

    g. The grandparents enjoyed hearing any _____ about their grandchild.

    h. A bee sting kit contains an _____ for a bee sting.

    i. Ipecac syrup is an _____ for some types of poison.

    j. Have you heard the _____ about George Washington and the apple tree?

Review set Choose the best word to complete sentences 1–5.
47
    1. John has (less, fewer) cattle today than yesterday.
    (12, 13)

    2. (Human, Humane) means characteristic of man.
    (3)

    3. The American flag (waives, waves) from many homes.
    (5)

    4. The prefix (pro-, ante-, syn-) means together.
    (30, 35)

    5. Emelina's (costume, custom) was to make a hundred tamales every Christmas.
    (40)

    6. Tell whether this word group is a phrase or a clause: "The Dutch Cheese," by Walter De La Mare, although a short story
    (3, 24)

7. A transitive verb has a direct object. Write the verb in this
(25, 31) sentence and label it transitive or intransitive: John, a young farmer, lives in a cottage with his sister, Griselda.

8. Write each noun in this sentence and circle the one that
(7, 9) is abstract: John was full of frustration concerning the fairies in the forest.

9. For a–c, write the plural of each noun.
(12, 13) (a) tomato   (b) fairy   (c) lady-in-waiting

10. Rewrite this outline, adding capital letters as needed:
(20)
      i. "the dutch cheese"
         a. results of obstinacy
         b. effects of a loving nature

11. Write each prepositional phrase from this sentence and
(16, 32) star the object of each preposition: Inside the forest live countless birds and fairies with mischievous ideas.

12. Tell whether the following is a complete sentence, run-on
(1, 3) sentence, or sentence fragment: These sly, mischievous fairies torment John however they love Griselda dearly.

13. For a–c, choose the correct form of the irregular verb
(14) *have.*
      (a) John (has, have) an unfounded grudge against the fairies.
      (b) The fairies (has, have) fun tormenting John.
      (c) (Have, Has) the fairies really done anything bad?

For 14 and 15, write the verb phrase and name its tense.

14. The fairies have been harassing John in a variety of ways.
(15, 21)

15. The sheep have fled John's wrath.
(15, 18)

16. Write the verb phrase in this sentence and label it action
(4, 22) or linking: John must have felt angry at the fairies' slightest provocation.

Write each adjective in sentences 17 and 18.

17. The mischievous fairies have hidden the sheep.
(27, 28)

18. John hurls one great, round cheese at an impish fairy.
(27, 28)

19. Write the four common pairs of correlative conjunctions.
(38)

20. Write the unnecessary article in this sentence: I hope the both of you will be here on time.
(47)

21. Rewrite the following, adding periods and making necessary changes to abbreviations for formal writing: On Tues, Jan 14, 2002, Clifton Junior High School presented Mr De La Mare's "The Dutch Cheese" as a play
(35)

22. Rewrite the following, adding commas as needed: Please send all mail to 80 Easing Way Oghh City Fairyland.
(44)

For sentences 23 and 24, write whether the italicized noun is nominative, objective, or possessive case.

23. Playful *fairies* respond to the genuine care and concern of a loving person.
(2, 40)

24. Griselda makes a *bargain* with the fairies.
(25, 40)

25. Use an appositive to combine this pair of sentences to make one sentence: Armando is a college student. He plays the piano, guitar, and bass.
(45, 46)

Diagram sentences 26–30.

26. Stubborn John is foolish and unreasonable.
(4, 41)

27. Wise Griselda saves John and his dog.
(4, 25)

28. To reason with stubborn people can be difficult.
(23, 41)

29. Do you hear whistling?
(25, 34)

30. She gave me her word.
(19, 25)

LESSON
48

Verbals as Adjectives: Infinitives and Participles

Dictation or Journal Entry

Vocabulary:

The words *historic* and *historical* appear similar but have different meanings.

Historic means famous or noteworthy in history. The city decided that the *historic* building should be preserved.

Historical means "related to the facts or events of history." *Historical* records show that the San Gabriel tribe of Native Americans lived in the local mountains.

Infinitives   We have learned that an infinitive can function as a noun and so can be the subject or an object in a sentence. In this lesson, we will see that infinitives can function as adjectives as well.

INFINITIVE AS A NOUN (SUBJECT):

> *To celebrate* would be appropriate.

INFINITIVE AS AN ADJECTIVE:

> This is the day *to celebrate*.

In the sentence above, "to celebrate" modifies the noun, "day." Below, we italicize other infinitives that function as adjectives. The arrows point to the nouns that these adjectives modify.

> She found the strength *to finish*.

> Her desire *to win* helped her.

> I saw her determination *to succeed*.

Diagramming   Notice how we diagram an infinitive that is used as an adjective. We place the infinitive on stilts underneath the word it modifies, as shown below:

> She is the player *to watch*.

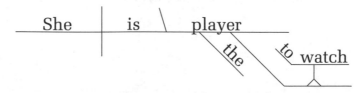

Example 1   Write the infinitive in each sentence and tell whether it is a noun or an adjective. If it is an adjective, tell which word it modifies.

(a) Do you need to prepare?

(b) This is the time to prepare.

Solution   (a) **To prepare** is the infinitive. It is the direct object. Therefore, it is a **noun.**

(b) **To prepare** is the infinitive. It is an **adjective modifying the word "time."**

Participles   We remember that a **participle** is a verb form that usually ends in *ing* or *ed* but sometimes ends in *en, d,* or *t.* When a participle stands alone (without a helping verb), it usually functions as an adjective.

Our *barking* dog irritated the neighbors.

Joey took responsibility for the *broken* window.

The carpenter could not use the *bent* nail.

Example 2   Write the participle in each sentence and tell which noun it modifies.

(a) The fallen gate allowed the pony to escape.

(b) The blaring horn hurt the pedestrian's ears.

(c) The lost child was returned to his baby-sitter.

Solution   (a) The participle **fallen** modifies the noun **gate.**

(b) The participle **blaring** modifies the noun **horn.**

(c) The participle **lost** modifies the noun **child.**

The participle has three tense forms: present, past, and perfect.

PRESENT PARTICIPLE: *hiding, speaking*

PAST PARTICIPLE: *hidden, spoken*

PERFECT PARTICIPLE: *having hidden, having spoken*

Present participles are italicized in the sentences below:

The baby *crawling* is Karla's cousin.

The *crowing* rooster woke us each morning.

Past participles are italicized in these sentences:

Spoilt milk smells rancid.

The *frightened* child hid under a bed.

Perfect participles are italicized in these sentences:

Having talked for hours on the phone, I did not finish my homework.

Having spent two dollars for a soda, the sports fan felt cheated.

Example 3   Write the participle in each sentence. Tell whether it is present, past, or perfect tense.

(a) Fried eggs are delicious.

(b) Having thrown himself into his work, he forgot about life's problems.

(c) The laughing hyena attracted my attention.

Solution   (a) The participle **fried** is **past tense.**

(b) The participle **having thrown** is **perfect tense.**

(c) The participle **laughing** is **present tense.**

Diagramming   The diagrams below show participles that function as adjectives. We place the participle on a pair of angled lines below the noun it modifies.

That man *running* is my dad.

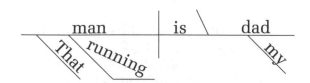

The police retrieved the *stolen* purse.

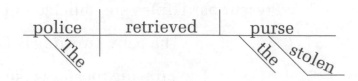

Having eaten, I left the party.

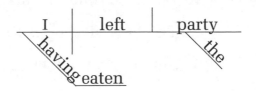

Practice   For a–d, replace each blank with *historic* or *historical*.

    a. The _____ train station was built during the Civil War.

    b. Preservationists wanted to save the _____ site.

    c. The guest speaker gave a brief_____ account of the Lewis and Clark Expedition.

    d. We will learn about the Boston Tea Party and other _____ events.

For e and f, write the infinitive and tell whether it is a noun or an adjective. If it is an adjective, write the noun it modifies.

    e. The convict wanted to flee.

    f. Make a list of important tasks to do.

For g–i, write the participle and the noun it modifies. Then label it is present, past, or perfect tense.

    g. Having followed the line, the runner did not stray from the course.

    h. The leaping teenager showed his excitement after winning the soccer championship.

    i. Avoid the frightened animal.

Diagram sentences j and k.

    j. Important ingredients to have are flour and sugar.

    k. The working husky pulled the sled.

More Practice   Diagram each sentence.

1. We have time to walk.

2. The lady singing is Russian.

3. She found the lost coin.

4. Having slept, she felt better.

5. I need a book to read.

6. The man to see is Mr. Ngo.

Review set 48   Choose the best word to complete sentences 1–8.

1. An (interrogative, exclamatory) sentence shows
(1, 3) excitement or strong feeling and ends with an
exclamation point.

2. A(n) (transitive, intransitive) verb has no direct object.
(25, 31)

3. A(n) (appositive, preposition, conjunction) is a word or
(3, 45) group of words that immediately follows a noun to
identify or give more information about the noun.

4. Bagpipe music is a Scottish (custom, costume).
(40)

5. A hyperbole is an (anteroom, exaggeration, example).
(41, 42)

6. An (epoch, epic) is a period of time.
(45)

7. The Greek prefix (*homo-*, *hetero-*, *theo-*) means god.
(44, 46)

8. Molly is the (taller, tallest) of the two cousins.
(42, 43)

9. Rewrite this run-on sentence, making two complete
(3, 6) sentences: People in the town of Pueblo De Chamelecon
enjoy storytelling a grandmother of the town tells about a
rat with a tail like a horse.

10. For a–c, write the plural of each noun.
(12, 13) (a) Saturday   (b) theology   (c) calf

11. Write the verb phrase from this sentence and label it
(25, 31) transitive or intransitive: In the days of Hunbatz, people
lived on beetles and spiders.

12. Write each word that should be capitalized in this
(11, 20) sentence: "a tale of three tails," i realize, is an imaginary
story by charles j. finger.

13. Tell whether the following is a phrase or a clause: if they
(3, 24) sing and play for half the day

For 14 and 15, write each prepositional phrase and star the
object of each preposition.

14. Next to the old lady with the cigar between her teeth sits
(16, 32) a little girl.

15. A long time ago, the rat had a beautiful tail with long
(16, 32) sweeping hairs like a horse.

16. For a–c, choose the correct form of the irregular verb *to be.*
(14) (a) We (was, were) surprised at the fear in old Hunbatz.

(b) He (was, were) determined to ruin the two brothers.

(c) The brothers (was, were) acting according to their
father's instructions.

17. Write the verb phrase from this sentence and label it
(4, 22) action or linking: Does Hunbatz smell trouble?

18. Write the verb phrase in this sentence and name its tense:
(18, 21) The boys had been clearing part of the dense forest.

19. Write the four principal parts (present tense, present
(6, 15) participle, past tense, and past participle) of the verb
dwindle.

20. Write the proper adjective from this sentence: The
(26, 28) narrator of "A Tale of Three Tails" brings a French
instrument to Pueblo De Chamelecon.

21. Write each predicate adjective from this sentence: The
(22, 41) iguana in this tale is wise, old, and caring.

22. Write the correlative conjunctions in this sentence: On
(38) both the first day and the second day, the brothers
cleared as much land as they were instructed.

23. Rewrite this sentence adding periods and commas as
(35, 44) needed: On Saturday June 2 Mrs Vong will inspect the

plumbing roofing and painting on the house at 87 Thicket Road Jungle City Africa

24. Write each predicate nominative from this sentence: The
(22, 39) evil characters in this tale are the wizard and the owl.

25. Write whether the italicized noun in this sentence is
(9, 40) nominative, objective, or possessive case: The owl suggests using some forest animals to destroy the *brothers'* work.

26. Write the appositive in this sentence: Old Hunbatz, an
(45, 46) angry wizard, almost succeeds in defeating the brothers.

Diagram sentences 27–30.

27. Singing birds might wake her.
(25, 48)

28. Was Gideon, a mighty man of valor, hiding?
(32, 45)

29. Diagramming gives her a headache.
(19, 25)

30. Ms. Williams is the woman to hire.
(23, 39)

LESSON 49

Pronouns and Antecedents

Dictation or Journal Entry

Vocabulary:
The Greek word *philos,* meaning "loving," gives us the common prefixes *phil-* and *philo-*.

A *philatelist* is one who enjoys collecting, arranging, and studying postage stamps. The *philatelist* searched the catalog to find the value of a stamp.

A *philanthropist* is one who loves mankind. A generous *philanthropist* donated funds for a new city auditorium.

A *philologist* is one who loves literature and other written records. My friend, a *philologist*, can hardly wait to study the Dead Sea Scrolls.

Pronouns

A **pronoun** is a word that takes the place of a noun or a noun phrase. Rather than using the same noun over and over again, we use pronouns.

Without pronouns, our language would be tiresome:

Mr. Grumblesnort demands that no one trespass on Mr. Grumblesnort's property. Mr. Grumblesnort's dog protects Mr. Grumblesnort's yard so that no trespassers can enter Mr. Grumblesnort's house. Some lost travelers once yelled for Mr. Grumblesnort, but Mr. Grumblesnort ignored the people asking for Mr. Grumblesnort. Then, Mrs. Grumblesnort called out to Mr. Grumblesnort's trespassers and said, "Get off of Mr. Grumblesnort's property. Mr. Grumblesnort isn't friendly." So Mrs. Grumblesnort convinced Mr. Grumblesnort's unwanted guests to leave Mr. Grumblesnort's yard.

Pronouns (italicized) simplify the passage:

Mr. Grumblesnort demands that no one trespass on *his* property. *His* dog protects *his* yard so that no trespassers can enter *his* house. Some lost travelers once yelled for *him*, but *he* ignored *them*. Then, Mrs. Grumblesnort called out to *his* trespassers and said, "Get off of *his* property. *He* isn't friendly." So *she* convinced *them* to leave *his* yard.

Pronouns are the words (such as *he, she, it, we, they*) we use to refer to people, places, and things that have already been mentioned. Pronouns are italicized in the examples below.

Salvador launched a rocket, and *he* watched *it* disappear into the clouds.

In the sentence above, the pronoun *he* replaces "Salvador," and the pronoun *it* replaces "rocket."

Antecedents   The noun or noun phrase to which the pronoun refers is called the **antecedent.** The prefix *ante-* means "before" and the root *ced* means "go." The antecedent usually "goes before" the pronoun. In the example above, "Salvador" and "rocket" are antecedents for the pronouns *he* and *it.*

Notice the antecedents for the pronouns *them* and *it* in this sentence:

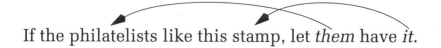

If the philatelists like this stamp, let *them* have *it.*

The antecedent of the pronoun *them* is "philatelists," and the antecedent of the pronoun *it* is "stamp."

Often we find the antecedent in an earlier sentence:

Alexander Hamilton (antecedent) was a famous American statesman. *He* began *his* fight for the American cause by delivering a speech calling for a general congress for the colonies.

Sometimes the antecedent comes after the pronoun:

Although *he* wrote some pamphlets, Alexander Hamilton did not receive credit at first.

An antecedent might be another pronoun:

Have *you* (antecedent) completed all *your* chores?

She (antecedent) lost *her* keys in the ocean!

A pronoun can also have more than one antecedent:

After General Nathanael Greene (antecedent) and George Washington (antecedent) saw the brilliance of Alexander Hamilton (antecedent), *they* made *him* confidential secretary.

Likewise, a noun can serve as the antecedent for more than one pronoun.

Alexander Hamilton (antecedent) was one of the most eminent lawyers in New York City when *he* delivered *his* plan of a strongly federalized government.

Example 1 List the pronouns in a–d. Beside each pronoun, write its antecedent. (Example: her/Annette)

(a) Although he was unable to obtain his desired type of government, Alexander Hamilton still worked to ratify the Constitution.

(b) Alexander Hamilton's reports on a wide range of subjects show his versatility.

(c) Aaron Burr resented Alexander Hamilton, so he challenged him to a duel.

(d) Although Alexander strongly disliked dueling, he felt an obligation do to it.

Solution (a) **he/Alexander Hamilton, his/Alexander Hamilton**

(b) **his/Alexander Hamilton's**

(c) **He/Aaron Burr, him/Alexander Hamilton**

(d) **he/Alexander, it/dueling**

Each pronoun needs a clear antecedent. The meaning of the sentence below is unclear because the antecedent is unclear:

Mom said that *her* cholesterol is too high.
Whose cholesterol is too high?
What is the antecedent of *her*?

The following sentences are unclear because they have more than one possible antecedent.

Gordito told Joe that *he* eats too much fat.
Which is the antecedent of *he*?
Is it Gordito, or is it Joe?

Dottie and Beth hiked to *her* cabin.
Whose cabin?
Dottie's? Beth's?

Dustin swam with Dominic after *he* ate.
Does *he* refer to Dustin or to Dominic?

To make our meaning clear, we can use nouns instead of pronouns, we can rearrange a few words, or we can rewrite the whole sentence:

Gordito said Joe eats too much fat.

Dottie and Beth hiked to Beth's cabin.

After Dustin ate, he swam with Dominic.

Example 2 Write the clearer sentence of each pair.
(a) He flew to Heidelberg, Germany.

Bob flew to Heidelberg, Germany.

(b) Delaney played jacks with Deanne and lost her ball.

Delaney lost her ball while playing jacks with Deanne.

Solution (a) We choose the second sentence because it clearly tells *who* flew to Germany.

Bob flew to Heidelberg, Germany.

(b) We choose the second sentence because it clearly tells *whose* ball was lost.

Delaney lost her ball while playing jacks with Deanne.

Practice List the pronouns in a–d. Beside each pronoun, write its antecedent.

a. Cory read the popular novel, and he liked it.

b. Dirk slid down the slope, but he climbed back up again.

c. Hanfu wants to remember all he can.

d. Although the boots look ancient, they will still keep Sunny's feet dry.

For e and f, write the clearer sentence of each pair.

e. While Georgiana and Marissa were shopping, she bought a new suede jacket.

While Georgiana and Marissa were shopping, Marissa bought a new suede jacket.

f. It cost five hundred dollars.

The jacket cost five hundred dollars.

For g–j, replace each blank with the correct vocabulary word.

g. Wanda, a _____, delivers food and clothing to the needy and donates large sums of money to improve people's lives.

h. Peter, a _____, remains a student in his old age and enjoys studying literature and historical records.

i. Stephen, a _____, collects postage stamps from Scandinavia and Iceland.

j. The Greek root meaning "loving" is _____.

Review set 49

Choose the correct word to complete sentences 1–9.

1. An action verb that has a direct object is called a
(25, 31) (transitive, intransitive) verb.

2. *This, that, those,* and *these* are called (descriptive,
(28) demonstrative, possessive) adjectives.

3. *His, our, my, her, its, their,* and *your* are called
(28) (descriptive, demonstrative, possessive) adjectives.

4. The California gold rush started an (epic, epoch) of
(45) mobility and westward movement in our country.

5. The Greek prefix *theo-* means (god, man, woman).
(46)

6. Heavy rainfall made the forest (luxuriant, luxurious).
(43)

7. "My backpack weighs a ton!" is an example of
(41) (hyperactivity, hyperbole, hyperglycemia).

8. The Greek root *graphy* means (god, recording, excessive).
(37)

9. The Greek prefix *hypo-* means (over, under, around).
(42)

Write the correct verb form to complete sentences 10 and 11.

10. The identity of their father (present tense of *mystify*)
(6, 15) them.

11. We (future tense of *learn*) his identity.
(10, 15)

12. Write the four principal parts (present tense, present
(8, 15) participle, past tense, and past participle) of the verb
flip.

13. Write each noun in this sentence and circle the one that
(9) is compound: The twins see a running hare in the
moonlight.

Write each word that should be capitalized in sentences 14
and 15.

14. the story "the two youths whose father was under the
(11, 20) sea" is full of adventure.

15. during their english class, jack whispered, "hey, john, i
(20, 26) am going to search for dad."

16. For a–c, write the plural of each noun.
(12, 13) (a) person   (b) safe   (c) fox

17. Tell whether the following is a phrase or a clause:
(3, 24) searching for their father throughout the north, the south,
the east, and the west

18. Write each prepositional phrase in this sentence and star
(16, 32) the object of each preposition: John Sea shares his basket
of provisions with the red fox along with the fox's wife
and children.

19. Write the verb phrase from this sentence and name its
(10, 18) tense: In the end, John will have searched for many
weeks.

20. Write the comparative form of the adjective *smooth.*
(42, 43)

21. Write the superlative form of the adjective *appreciative.*
(42, 43)

Rewrite sentences 22 and 23, adding commas and periods
and making necessary changes to abbreviations for formal
writing.

22. On Mar 31 2002 fifty needy families received five-lb
(35, 44) hams from Deborah Schneider PhD

23. The Hag of Hollows an old lady spoke with John
(45, 46)

24. Tell whether the following is a complete sentence,
(1, 3) sentence fragment, or run-on sentence: We stayed in a
luxurious hotel the garden was luxuriant.

25. Tell whether the italicized noun in this sentence is
(32, 40) nominative, objective, or possessive case: John's payment
for working at the *castle* is a hawk, a hound, and a horse.

26. Write the verb phrase from this sentence and label it
(4, 22) action or linking: Does the castle smell musty?

27. Use an appositive to combine these sentences into one
(45, 46) sentence: Mr. Angles is a plumber. He fixed our leaky
faucet.

28. Write the unnecessary adjective from this sentence: What
(47) kind of a car does he drive?

Diagram sentences 29 and 30.

29. Having spoken, she refused to listen.
(23, 48)

30. Can John and Jack locate their lost father?
(25, 37)

LESSON
50

The Comma, Part 3: Greetings and Closings, Last Name First, Introductory and Interrupting Elements, Afterthoughts, Clarity

---

Dictation or Journal Entry

Vocabulary:

Antagonist, protagonist, melodrama, and *foreshadowing* are common literary terms.

The *antagonist* is the person or thing fighting against the hero of a story. The *antagonist* in a melodrama is often called a villain.

The *protagonist* is the hero of the story. In *The Adventures of Tom Sawyer,* the *protagonist* is Tom Sawyer.

A *melodrama* is an exaggerated drama intended to evoke strong feeling in the reader or viewer. A modern-day *melodrama* is the TV soap opera.

Foreshadowing is a hint of what is going to happen in a story. Little Nell's preoccupation with death was Charles Dickens' *foreshadowing* of her upcoming demise.

Greeting   We use a comma after the opening or **greeting** of a friendly letter.

Dear Mr. Handel,

My vivacious cousin,

Closing   We use a comma after the **closing** of a letter.

Warmly,

Sincerely,

Example 1   Place commas where they are needed in the letter below.

Dear Handel

Thank you for creating the English oratorio. My favorite is the *Messiah.*

Your fan
Chrissy

Solution   We place commas after the greeting and closing of the letter.

Dear Handel,

Thank you for creating the English oratorio. My favorite is the *Messiah.*

Your fan,
Chrissy

Last Name First   When we alphabetize a list of names, we usually alphabetize by the person's last name. We place the last name first and the first name (followed by middle names, if any) last. They are separated by a comma, as shown:

> Anthony, Susan B.
>
> Carver, George Washington
>
> Poe, Edgar Allen
>
> Smith, Kate
>
> Zenger, John Peter

Other than in lists, we don't often write names this way. When we do, we are usually referring to a list. Quotation marks may indicate this:

> "Handel, George Fredrick" can be located under famous musical composers.

> Because "Zorilla, Britnii" is always last on the class list, Britnii complained to the administration.

Example 2   Insert a comma where it is needed in the sentence below.

> For information on the composer of *The Star-Spangled Banner*, look under "Key Francis Scott."

Solution   We place a comma when we use a last name first.

> For information on the composer of *The Star-Spangled Banner*, look under **"Key, Francis Scott."**

Comma = Pause   When we speak, we often pause between words. If we wrote down exactly what we were saying, most of those pauses would be indicated by commas. Pauses usually occur when we insert words or phrases that interrupt the natural flow of the sentence. Notice how commas are used to offset the italicized words, phrases, and clauses in the sentences below.

> Handel wrote Italian operas, *I think*, before writing English oratorios.

> Handel's approach to choral writing set the standard for later British composers, *of course.*

> *Yes,* I enjoy his music very much.

Introductory Elements   An **introductory element** begins a sentence. It may refer to a previous sentence or express the writer's attitude about what is being said. An introductory element can also be a request or command. We place a comma after an introductory element.

> *Well*, Handel was actually born in Germany in 1685.

> *However*, Handel became a British subject in 1726.

> *Please remember*, not all great composers are German.

> *Therefore,* we shall study composers from other countries as well.

A comma is not needed after an introductory adverb or short phrase that answers the question when, where, or how often.

> *Now* let us sing the second verse.

> *In this room* we shall practice with the bell choir.

> *Tomorrow* the piano tuner is coming.

> *Occasionally* some of the notes sound odd.

Interrupting Elements

An **interrupting element** appears in the middle of a sentence, interrupting the flow from subject to verb to object. An interrupting element can be removed without changing the meaning of the sentence.

> Composers, *it would seem,* are born with musical talent.

> I, *on the other hand,* cannot carry a tune!

Afterthoughts

Afterthoughts are similar to introductory and interrupting elements except that they are added to the ends of sentences.

> Bob wrote the music and the lyrics, *by the way.*

> He composed a love song, *if I remember correctly.*

Some afterthoughts turn the sentence into a question:

> He is very talented, *isn't he?*

Example 3

Rewrite these sentences and use commas to offset introductory or interrupting elements and afterthoughts.

(a) Sir Thomas Mallory I believe wrote stories of King Arthur.

(b) Unfortunately the stories were not based on historical facts.

(c) People still enjoy the stories don't they?

Solution (a) The words "I believe," are not essential to the meaning of the sentence. They interrupt the flow of the sentence, so we offset them with commas.

Sir Thomas Mallory, **I believe,** wrote stories of King Arthur.

(b) The word "unfortunately" is an introductory element, so we place a comma after it.

Unfortunately, the stories were not based on historical facts.

(c) The words "don't they" are an afterthought, so we offset them with a comma.

People still enjoy the stories, **don't they?**

Clarity We use commas to **clarify the meaning** of sentences.

UNCLEAR: Without Laura Marshall felt helpless.
CLEAR: Without Laura, Marshall felt helpless.

UNCLEAR: As she read the story unfolded.
CLEAR: As she read, the story unfolded.

Example 4 Rewrite each sentence, using a comma to make the meaning clear.

(a) To Henry James seemed tired.

(b) Shortly after James fell asleep.

Solution (a) If we are talking about a man named Henry James, then the sentence is incomplete. However, if Henry and James are two different people, the sentence is complete. We use a comma to clarify the meaning:

To Henry, James seemed tired.

(b) Without a comma, this sentence seems incomplete. Shortly after James fell asleep...*what?* The phone rang? He began snoring? To avoid confusion, we insert a comma to clarify the meaning:

Shortly after, James fell asleep.

Practice   Rewrite a and b, inserting commas as needed.

   a. Dear Alana

          Have you heard the expression "The handwriting is on the wall?" What does it mean?

                       Love

                       Clara

   b. Use the card catalog to find the writings of "Jefferson Thomas."

Rewrite sentences c–f, inserting commas to offset introductory or interrupting elements and afterthoughts.

   c. "The handwriting is on the wall " I believe refers to an imminent occurrence.

   d. The Hippocratic Oath they say is taken by all physicians before they begin practicing medicine.

   e. No I am not familiar with the words in the Hippocratic Oath.

   f. It includes the duties and responsibilities of the physician I think.

Rewrite sentences g and h, inserting commas to clarify the meaning.

   g. With Molly Curtis acts silly.

   h. Ever since she has eaten more nutritious foods.

For i–l, replace each blank with the correct vocabulary word.

   i. King Arthur is an example of a _____.

   j. Mordred fights against the hero, King Arthur. Therefore, Mordred is the _____.

   k. The mystery writer uses _____ to hint about "who did it."

   l. We picture the villain standing over the "damsel in distress" in a _____.

More Practice   See Master Worksheets.

Review set   Choose the best word to complete sentences 1–7.
50

1. Dominic is the (less, least) recalcitrant of the three
(42, 43) brothers.

2. (Do, Does) some people believe in duendes?
(6, 14)

3. The cruel man's treatment of his mule was not (human,
(3) humane).

4. The Greek root *mania* means (large, hatred, passion) or
(16) madness.

5. Hitler believed he was the greatest man on earth. He
(11, 17) suffered from (megalomania, cacophony, euphony).

6. Did (there, their, they're) dog bark all night?
(19)

7. The speaker told an (anecdote, antidote) about his fishing
(47) trip.

8. Tell whether the following is a complete sentence, run-on
(1, 3) sentence, or sentence fragment: Duendes are the Mexican
equivalent of Irish leprechauns and English
elves.

9. Rewrite this sentence, adding capital letters and commas
(11, 50) as needed: in cuautla mexico so the story goes duendes
let out chickens tease dogs and turn on lights.

10. Write each prepositional phrase in this sentence and star
(16, 32) the object of each preposition: On behalf of Lorenzo, the
duendes will teach Sarita a lesson about hard work.

11. Write each adjective in this sentence: No other mother
(27, 28) would allow her little sons to wear torn pants.

For sentences 12 and 13, write each verb phrase and label it
transitive or intransitive.

12. Donato spies Lorenzo crying in the woods.
(4, 31)

13. Is Lorenzo crying over his home situation?
(4, 31)

(36) **14.** Write seven common coordinating conjunctions.

15. Write the correlative conjunction pair in this sentence:
(38) Neither Lorenzo nor his father knows how to help Sarita.

For sentences 16 and 17, tell whether the italicized noun is nominative, objective, or possessive case.

16. "Sarita and the Duendes" is the *name* of this tale by
(39, 40) Patricia Fent Ross.

17. Lorenzo's family dislikes their messy *house.*
(25, 40)

18. Rewrite this sentence, adding periods and commas and
(35, 46) making necessary changes to abbreviations for formal writing: Mr B Smart our new principal arrived on Tues Sept 3 2002

19. Write the appositive in this sentence: Sarita, Lorenzo's
(45, 46) mother, takes pride in her housework now.

20. Write the four principal parts of the verb *try.*
(6, 15)

21. Tell whether the following is a phrase or a clause: among
(3, 24) three discrete categories of literature

Write the correct verb form to complete sentences 22 and 23.

22. Sarita (present tense of *wash*) the dishes without thinking
(4, 15) about it.

23. She (present perfect of *learn*) the value of hard work.
(8, 18)

24. For a–c, write the plural of each noun.
(12, 13) (a) index   (b) penny   (c) knife

25. Write the comparative and superlative forms of the
(42, 43) adjective *low.*

26. Rewrite this sentence correctly: She surprises the both of
(47) them with a clean house.

27. Write each pronoun in this sentence and indicate its
(49) antecedent: Sarita beams with delight when she receives praise from her family.

28. In this sentence, write the verb phrase and name its tense:
(8, 21) The duendes are showing Sarita a better way of life.

Diagram sentences 29 and 30.
29. Amigo, my stuffed bear, plays games like dominoes and
(25, 45) chess.

30. Sweeping is a helpful thing to do.
(19, 23)

LESSON 51

Personal Pronouns

Dictation or Journal Entry

Vocabulary:

The Greek noun *gōnia,* meaning "angle," gives us the common suffix -gon.

A *pentagon* is a closed plane figure with five sides and five angles. A *hexagon* is a closed figure with six sides and six angles. An *octagon* has eight sides and eight angles, while a *heptagon* has seven sides and seven angles. *Pentagons,* squares, triangles, quadrilaterals, *hexagons, heptagons,* and *octagons* are all *polygons* (closed plane figures with three or more sides).

Remember the five categories of pronouns: personal, relative, indefinite, interrogative, and demonstrative. This lesson reviews personal pronouns.

Like nouns, **personal pronouns** refer to people and things (and also places, if you think of a place as an "it"). Personal pronouns are italicized in these sentences.

I acknowledged *them.*

Have *you* seen *my* bibliography?

He claims that *it* will help *us.*

There are three forms of personal pronouns: person, number and case.

Person   *First person* is the speaker: *I, me, mine, we, us, ours.*

I shall plan a trip.

We shall travel together.

That airline ticket is *mine.*

Second person is the person being spoken to: *you, yours.*

Will *you* come too?

All of *you* are important.

That train ticket is *yours.*

Third person is the person being spoken about: *he, she, it, him, her, his, hers, they, them, theirs.*

He and *she* will visit Jerusalem.

They will leave on Tuesday.

That bus ticket is *hers.*

Give *it* to *them.*

Example 1   For each sentence below, write the pronoun and tell whether it is first person, second person, or third person.

(a) They say roses represent love.

(b) I don't understand why roses are so expensive.

(c) Do you know where to plant rose bushes?

Solution   (a) *They* is **third person,** the person being spoken about.

(b) *I* is **first person,** the speaker.

(c) *You* is **second person,** the person being spoken to.

Number   Some personal pronouns are singular:

I, me, mine, you, yours, he, him, his, she, her, hers, it

Others are plural:

we, us, ours, you, yours, they, them, theirs

Example 2   For a–d, write each personal pronoun and tell whether it is singular or plural.

(a) They set their watches.   (b) Mine was slow.

(c) Tom synchronized his.   (d) Give them the time.

Solution   (a) *They* is **plural.**   (b) *Mine* is **singular.**

(c) *His* is **singular.**   (d) *Them* is **plural.**

Case   Case shows the job the pronoun is performing in the sentence.

Some pronouns are used as *subjects*:

She loved snowboarding. *They* snowboarded too. *I* have not snowboarded yet. Have *you* attempted to snowboard?

Others are used as *objects*:

Jalana brought *them* too. (direct object)

Walt gave *her* a lesson. (indirect object)

Unhappy Bob paid for all of *us.* (object of a preposition)

Some pronouns show *possession*:

Where is *yours*?

Ryan took *his*.

Dan hid *mine*.

Theirs was broken.

Example 3 Tell whether each italicized pronoun shows possession or whether it is used as a subject or an object. If it is an object, tell what kind (direct object, indirect object, object of a preposition).

(a) Joy loaned *him* a snowboard.

(b) Today, *they* will go to the local mountains.

(c) Bryan raced *her* down the slope.

(d) Sorry, Joel lost *yours*.

Solution (a) The pronoun *him* is an **indirect object.**

(b) The pronoun *they* is the **subject** of the sentence.

(c) The pronoun *her* is a **direct object.**

(d) The pronoun *yours* shows **possession.**

Practice For a–f, replace each blank with the correct vocabulary word.

a. A closed figure with at least three sides is called a _____.

b. The Greek suffix meaning "angled" is _____.

c. A(n) _____ is a closed figure with eight sides and eight angles.

d. A five-sided polygon is a _____.

e. A figure with seven sides and seven angles is a _____.

f. A six-sided polygon is a _____.

For sentences g–i, write the personal pronoun and tell whether it is first, second, or third person.

   g. Holly argued with me.

   h. She created dissension.

   i. Did you agree with Holly?

For j and k, write the personal pronoun and tell whether it is singular or plural.

   j. Dad bought us tickets to the football game.

   k. Please bring me a hotdog.

For l–o, tell whether the italicized personal pronoun is used as a subject, direct object, indirect object, object of a preposition, or whether it shows possession.

   l. Brad loaned *him* a shirt.

   m. Matt surprised *her* with roses.

   n. That burrito is *mine*.

   o. *They* traveled to Guadalajara today.

More Practice Write each personal pronoun from sentences 1–10, and tell whether it is first, second, or third person. Also tell whether it is singular or plural. (Example: we, first person plural; you, second person singular)

   1. May we help you?

   2. Were they discreet?

   3. Please loan him a costume.

   4. They're over there working on their choreography.

   5. Are you familiar with Japanese customs?

   6. Everyone sat in the anteroom except her.

   7. Please sit down and set your shopping bags on the floor.

   8. I advised them to seek counsel.

   9. They took my advice and sought help.

   10. She spoke confidentially to us.

11–20. Tell how each pronoun is used in sentences 1–10 above. Write "subject," "object," or "possession." (Example: 1. we, subject; you, object)

Review set 51

1. *(1, 3)* Tell whether the following is a complete sentence, run-on sentence, or sentence fragment: A philanthropist making a large donation to charity.

2. *(3, 24)* Tell whether the following is a phrase or a clause: because the philologist had read so many books

3. *(25, 31)* Write the verb phrase from this sentence and label it transitive or intransitive: The philatelist is guarding his priceless stamp collection.

4. *(4, 22)* From sentences a and b, write the verb phrase and label it action or linking.
   (a) The antagonist appears heinous.
   (b) The antagonist appears in the first scene of the play.

5. *(12, 13)* For a–c, write the plural of each noun.
   (a) candy   (b) beach   (c) sky

6. *(1, 3)* Tell whether this sentence is declarative, interrogative, exclamatory, or imperative: Did you know that "Aladdin" is from the *Arabian Nights*?

7. *(5, 11)* Write each word that should be capitalized in this sentence: in a large, rich city of china lived a man named mustapha.

8. *(20, 35)* Rewrite this outline, adding periods and capital letters as needed:
   i   "aladdin"
      a   childhood
      b   african magician
      c   genies

9. *(17, 32)* Write each prepositional phrase in this sentence and star the object(s) of each preposition: Except for his mother, no one else knew of Aladdin's lamp and ring.

10. *(6, 15)* Write the four principal parts of the verb *grin*.

11. Write each adjective in this sentence: The African
(27, 28) magician travels to a large Chinese city.

12. Replace the underlined, overused adjective in this
(27, 47) sentence with one that might be more descriptive: The
African magician was <u>mean</u> to Aladdin.

13. Rewrite this sentence, adding periods and commas as
(35, 50) needed: Yes the genie provided Aladdin and his mother
with food clothing and riches

14. Replace the blanks with the missing pair of common
(38) correlative conjunctions: both/and; either/or; not
only/but also; _____/_____

15. Write the appositive from this sentence: Aladdin's father,
(45, 46) Mustapha, died when Aladdin was very young.

16. Use an appositive to combine these two choppy
(45, 46) sentences into one longer sentence: The sorcerer arrived
from his native country. Africa was the sorcerer's native
country.

Replace each blank with the correct word to complete
sentences 17–21.

17. A _____ is a word that takes the place of a noun.
(49)

18. The word to which the pronoun refers is called the
(49) _____.

19. The prefix *ante-* means _____.
(31, 49)

20. The root *ced* means _____.
(49)

21. The antecedent usually goes _____ the pronoun.
(49)

22. In this sentence, write each pronoun and its antecedent:
(49) When Jenny returned, she asked her brother to help her
with her chores.

Choose the correct word to complete sentences 23–26.

23. Theology is the study of (life, earth, religion).
(46)

24. The pastor's sermon contained several (anecdotes,
(47) antidotes), which made people laugh.

25. The first moon landing was a(n) (antebellum, historic, (31, 48) prospective) event.

26. The Greek root *phil-* means (laughing, crying, loving). (49)

Diagram sentences 27–30.

27. Aladdin and his mother trust and appreciate the African (25, 37) magician.

28. Aladdin, trapped, discovers a way to escape. (23, 48)

29. The magic lamp of the palace was the object of the (33, 39) magician's desire.

30. He loves winning. (19, 23)

LESSON 52

Irregular Verbs, Part 2

> **Dictation or Journal Entry**
>
> **Vocabulary:**
> Additional literary terms include *caricature*, *allegory*, *cliché*, and *denouement*.
>
> A *caricature* is a description or drawing that ridiculously exaggerates the characteristics or striking features of a person or thing. *Caricatures* of public figures can be unflattering.
>
> An *allegory* is a story in which the characters and events represent an underlying truth about life. *Pilgrim's Progress* is an *allegory* with deeper meaning beyond the mere travels of a pilgrim.
>
> A *cliché* is a trite expression that has been used so much that it is no longer an effective way to say something. The *cliché* "sharp as a tack" was used to describe the bright student.
>
> *Denouement* refers to the resolution of a story or plot. Readers of *The Old Curiosity Shop* begged Charles Dickens to provide a happy *denouement*.

Regular verbs form the past tense by adding *d* or *ed* to the present tense of the verb. Irregular verbs form the past tense in different ways. There are no rules for forming their past tense and past participles. Fortunately, we recognize the principal parts of most irregular verbs just by hearing them. We must memorize the irregular verb parts that we do not know already.

Irregular verbs can cause people trouble because it is easy to confuse the past tense and past participle.

> Helen Keller began (NOT begun) to hear by feeling the vibration of Anne Sullivan's lips.

> Helen Keller had chosen (NOT chose) to overcome her auditory and visual disabilities.

We can group some irregular verbs because they follow similar patterns. Here we list four groups of irregular verbs:

VERB	PAST TENSE	PAST PARTICIPLE
1. blow	blew	(has) blown
know	knew	(has) known
throw	threw	(has) thrown
grow	grew	(has) grown
2. bear	bore	(has) borne
tear	tore	(has) torn
wear	wore	(has) worn
swear	swore	(has) sworn

3. begin	began	(has) begun
ring	rang	(has) rung
shrink	shrank	(has) shrunk
sing	sang	(has) sung
drink	drank	(has) drunk
4. choose	chose	(has) chosen
freeze	froze	(has) frozen
speak	spoke	(has) spoken
break	broke	(has) broken
steal	stole	(has) stolen

Example   Write the correct verb form for sentences a–d.

(a) No one (knowed, knew, known) how to help Helen Keller until she was seven years old.

(b) Anne Sullivan did not (shrink, shrank, shrunk) from helping Helen Keller.

(c) Helen (growed, grew, grown) competent in reading by using the Braille system.

(d) Finally, she has (speaked, spoke, spoken).

Solution   (a) No one **knew** how to help Helen Keller until she was seven years old.

(b) Anne Sullivan did not **shrink** from helping Helen Keller.

(c) Helen **grew** competent in reading by using the Braille system.

(d) Finally, she has **spoken**.

Practice   For a–d, replace each blank with the correct vocabulary word.

a. C. S. Lewis's *The Lion, the Witch, and the Wardrobe*, an adventure story with an underlying meaning, is a(n) _____.

b. Read the _____ of Uncle Pumblechook from *Great Expectations*: He was "a large hard breathing middle-aged slow man, with a mouth like a fish, dull staring eyes, and sandy hair standing upright on his head, so that he looked as if he had just been all but choked..."

   c. The saying "fresh as a daisy" is a _____.

   d. The death of Nell was an unhappy _____ for *The Old Curiosity Shop.*

For e–p, write the correct verb form for each sentence.

   e. The knave has (stealed, stole, stolen) the tarts.

   f. Has Little Boy Blue (blow, blew, blown) his horn?

   g. Humpty Dumpty (teared, tore, torn) his jacket when he fell off the wall.

   h. Do you think the cow that jumped over the moon has (froze, frozed, frozen)?

   i. Yesterday, I (bear, bore, borne) good news!

   j. Jack (break, broke, breaked) his crown.

   k. Have you (throwed, thrown, threw) the softball yet?

   l. The fans should have (wear, weared, worn) raincoats in the rain.

   m. The scholar (sweared, swore, sworn) that he'd be on time for school the next day.

   n. The bell (ringed, rang, rung) loudly when the kitty fell in the well.

   o. After saying the flag salute, the class (sing, sang, sung) "God Bless America."

   p. Little Miss Muffet has (drinked, drank, drunk) her curds and whey.

More Practice Write the past tense and past participle of each verb.

1. blow	**2.** know	**3.** throw	**4.** grow
5. bear	**6.** tear	**7.** wear	**8.** swear
9. begin	**10.** ring	**11.** sing	**12.** drink
13. choose	**14.** speak	**15.** freeze	**16.** steal

Review set   Choose the best word(s) to complete sentences 1–10.

52

1. We form the perfect verb tense by adding a form of the
(8, 18) helping verb (to be, have, do) to the past participle.

2. The (positive, comparative, superlative) form compares
(42, 43) three or more persons, places, or things.

3. A (verb, conjunction, predicate nominative) follows a
(22, 39) linking verb and renames the subject.

4. A(n) (direct, indirect) object is the noun or pronoun that
(25, 34) tells "to whom" or "for whom" the action was done.

5. The pronoun *you* is (first, second, third) person.
(49, 51)

6. The pronoun *they* is (singular, plural).
(49, 51)

7. The pronoun *he* is (first, second, third) person, (singular,
(49, 51) plural).

8. With practice, Dale became (adapt, adept, adopt) at
(1) roofing houses.

9. The megalomaniacs thought they were extremely (lucky,
(17) great, unfortunate).

10. The (antagonist, protagonist) is the hero of the story.
(50)

11. A melodrama evokes (happy, sad, strong) feelings in the
(50) reader or viewer.

12. Write the verb phrase in this sentence and label it
(25, 31) transitive or intransitive: Aladdin loves Princess
Badroulboudour, daughter of the sultan.

13. Write each noun in this sentence and circle the one that
(7, 9) is collective: Does the sultan keep a harem in his palace?

14. Write each word that should be capitalized in this
(20, 26) sentence: aladdin declares, "mother, i love the princess
more than i can express."

15. Write the adjective phrase in this sentence and then write
(27, 33) the noun it modifies: The sultan has received Aladdin's
gift of fine jewels.

16. Write each adjective from this sentence: In three months,
(27, 28) the beautiful princess may marry the courageous Aladdin.

17. Write the predicate adjective from this sentence: Does the
(27, 44) grand visier's son feel embarrassed?

18. Tell whether the following is a complete sentence, run-on
(1, 3) sentence, or sentence fragment: An ingenious engineer has designed a new ski lift.

19. Tell whether the following is a phrase or a clause: a
(3, 24) candid, ingenuous soul full of sincerity and compassion

20. For a–c, write the plural of each noun.
(12, 13) (a) turkey   (b) charity   (c) city

21. Write the four principal parts of the irregular verb *know*.
(6, 15)

22. Write the past tense and past participle of the irregular
(15, 52) verb *tear.*

23. Rewrite this letter, adding commas as needed.
(50)
> Dear Majesty
>
>   You gave me your word that the princess could be my bride. What happened?
>
>   Yours truly
>   Aladdin

24. Use an appositive to combine these two sentences into
(45, 46) one sentence: Princess Badroulboudour is Aladdin's fiancée. She accepts his gifts of jewels, servants, and gold.

25. Write the gerund in this sentence: Foreshadowing hints
(19, 50) at future events.

26. Rewrite this sentence, adding commas and periods and
(35, 44) making necessary changes to abbreviations for formal writing: On Jan 2 1992 Mr and Mrs Soop welcomed an eight-lb son and named him Brock Lee.

27. Write each personal pronoun and its antecedent in this
(49, 51) sentence: Aladdin's kind treatment of the people wins
him their affection.

28. Write the participle from this sentence and indicate the
(27, 48) noun it modifies: The thwarted African magician
discovers the whereabouts of Aladdin.

Diagram sentences 29 and 30.

29. Is Aladdin's palace the wonder of the kingdom?
(33, 39)

30. Does Aladdin give the princess many riches?
(25, 34)

LESSON 53

Nominative Pronoun Case

Nominative Case

We remember that nouns can be grouped into three cases: nominative, objective, and possessive. We also remember that the same is true of pronouns. In this lesson we will concentrate on the **nominative case.** A pronoun used as a subject or predicate nominative is nominative case.

He was a U.S. President. (subject)

The thirty-fifth President was *he.* (predicate nominative)

Robert Kennedy and *he* were brothers. (subject)

They dug all the postholes. (subject)

The posthole diggers were *they.* (predicate nominative)

The gardeners and *they* have sore arms. (subject)

Example 1 Complete this chart by replacing each blank with the correct nominative case pronoun.

NUMBER	PERSON		NOMINATIVE CASE (subject or predicate nominative)
Singular	First		_____
	Second		_____
	Third	(masc.)	_____
		(fem.)	_____
		(neuter)	_____
Plural	First		_____
	Second		_____
	Third		_____

Solution   We complete the chart as follows:

NUMBER	PERSON		NOMINATIVE CASE (subject or predicate nominative)
Singular	First		I
	Second		you
	Third	(masc.)	he
		(fem.)	she
		(neuter)	it
Plural	First		we
	Second		you
	Third		they

Subjects   These sentences use nominative case personal pronouns as subjects:

> *I* remember John F. Kennedy.
> *He* served in our military during World War II.

When we use the pronoun *I* as part of a compound subject, it is polite to refer to ourselves last.

> Ester and *I* presented an oral report on JFK.
> Joe and *I* work for the same law firm.

Example 2   Which sentence is more polite?

> We and Abby share the household chores.
> Abby and we share the household chores.

Solution   It is more polite to refer to ourselves (we) last.

> **Abby and we share the household chores.**

Example 3   Write a sentence using a nominative case personal pronoun as a subject.

Solution   Your answer will be unique. Here are some correct examples:

> ***It* frightens the dog.**

> ***They* rode a gondola in Italy.**

> ***You* and *she* perform well together.**

Predicate Nominatives   These sentences use nominative case personal pronouns as predicate nominatives:

The author is *he* on the stage.

Jacqueline is *she* in the picture.

Predicate nominatives can also be compound:

The soloists are Jo and *she.*

The violinists are *she* and *he.*

Example 4   Write a sentence using a nominative case pronoun as a predicate nominative.

Solution   Your answer will be unique. Here are some correct examples:

The winners were *they.*

The most qualified applicant is *he.*

The last in the race was *I.*

Practice   **a.** Study the nominative case pronoun chart from Example 1. Then try to reproduce it from memory. You may abbreviate. (Example: 1st, 2nd, 3rd, sing. pl.)

b. Unscramble these words to make a sentence with a personal pronoun as a subject:

defeated   election   Nixon   in   he   the

c. Unscramble these words to make a sentence with a personal pronoun as a predicate nominative:

was   door   at   the   the   he   man

d. Write the sentence that is more polite:

I and he will run for the Presidency.

He and I will run for the Presidency.

e. Write each nominative case pronoun from this list:

me	him	I	she	them
they	he	her	we	us

Choose the nominative case pronoun for sentences f–i.
f. The lady beside the President is (she, her).

g. The diplomats were (them, they) on the bench.

h. The man in the photo was (him, he).

i. It is (I, me) who must decide.

For j–m, replace each blank with the correct vocabulary word.

j. _____ proved that the tallest man in the tribe had been under five feet.

k. The Greek root meaning "human" is _____.

l. The scientist completed his paper on _____ dealing with human bones found in archeological digs in the Middle East.

m. The animals in the fairy tale were _____; they looked somewhat human.

Review set 53   Choose the correct word to complete sentences 1–9.

1. The (perspective, prospective) presidential candidates
(29) attempted to garner support for their parties.

2. (There, They're, Their) running a few minutes late.
(19)

3. James drew a flower from an ant's (prospective,
(29) perspective).

4. To *project* is to present a plan of action and its results
(30) (before, after, while) it happens.

5. Of my ten cousins, Kim is the (more, most) ingenuous.
(42, 43)

6. The personal pronouns *I, me, mine, we, us,* and *ours* are
(51, 53) (first, second, third) person.

7. The personal pronouns *you* and *yours* are (first, second,
(51, 53) third) person.

8. Yesterday, Judson (wear, wore, worn) his superhero
(52) costume.

9. The African magician has (steal, stole, stolen) the magic
(52) lamp from Aladdin.

10. For a–c, write the plural of each noun.
(12, 13)(a) lunch   (b) deer   (c) life

11. In this sentence, write the verb phrase and name its tense:
(18, 21) The choreographer has been synchronizing the dance movements.

12. Tell whether the following is a phrase or a clause:
(3, 24) because the Mud Valley News belongs to a greater news syndicate

13. Tell whether the following is a complete sentence, run-on
(1, 3) sentence, or sentence fragment: The African magician wants to steal Aladdin's lamp he offers the princess a new, shiny lamp in exchange.

14. Write the verb phrase in this sentence and label it action
(4, 22) or linking: Does that anecdote sound familiar?

15. Write each word that should be capitalized in this
(28, 29) sentence: in the far east, belief in african magic was common.

16. Write the correct verb form to complete this sentence:
(15, 52) Last night, Miss Pecksbeak (past tense of *sing*) a lullaby.

17. Write the comparative and superlative forms of the
(42, 43) adjective *lucky*.

Rewrite 18 and 19, adding periods, commas, and capital letters as needed.

18. look under "pape eric" to find other works by this artist
(35, 50)

19. dear genie
(29, 50)   i am in trouble please help me
                    gratefully
                    aladdin

20. Write each prepositional phrase in this sentence and star
(16, 32) the object of each preposition: Chronobiology studies the effect of time on living organisms.

21. Write the participle used as an adjective in this sentence:
(27, 48) A disguised magician is seeking revenge for the African magician's death.

22. Write the verb phrase in this sentence and label it
(25, 31) transitive or intransitive: The lamp's genie exposes an
impostor.

23. Tell whether the italicized noun is nominative, objective,
(25, 40) or possessive case: The counterfeit intends to assassinate
Aladdin with his *dagger.*

24. Write the appositive from this sentence: Aladdin's wife,
(45, 46) Princess Badroulboudour, has known nothing.

25. Write each pronoun in this sentence and indicate its
(49) antecedent: Molly and Kurt will take their dog on
vacation with them.

26. Write the four principal parts of the irregular verb *drink.*
(15, 52)

27. For a and b, write the past tense and past participle of
(52) each verb.

(a) grow   (b) bear

28. Write the gerund from this sentence and label its tense
(18, 19) present or perfect: Having witnessed the accident gave
him a better perspective concerning the victim.

Diagram sentences 29 and 30.

29. She hopes to have finished.
(23, 25)

30. Moe gave me a broken lamp to repair.
(23, 25)

LESSON 54

Objective Pronoun Case

> **Dictation or Journal Entry**
>
> **Vocabulary:**
> Let us become familiar with these literary terms: *motif, pathos, narrator,* and *figure of speech.*
>
> A *motif* is a recurring subject or theme in a work of literature. A common melodrama *motif* features the hero rescuing a "damsel in distress" from a villain.
>
> *Pathos* is the part of the story that makes the reader feel sorry for the characters. *Pathos* occurs in *The Old Curiosity Shop* when Nell is robbed by her own grandfather.
>
> The *narrator* is the person telling the story. Esther Summerson, the *narrator*, tells the story in *Bleak House.*
>
> *Figures of speech* are word pictures using comparisons—for example, "His head was as bald as an egg." Metaphors, similes, and personification are *figures of speech.*

Pronouns are in the **objective case** when they are used as direct objects, indirect objects, or objects of a preposition.

> Johannes Kepler confounded *them.* (direct object)
>
> Kepler gave *us* three laws on planetary motion. (indirect object)
>
> The scientist shared his research with *me.* (object of a preposition)

Objective case pronouns can be compound. We politely mention ourselves last.

> Bao sent *her* and *me* a postcard.
>
> Xana presented Anna Maria and *us* an invitation.
>
> Trina laughed with *him* and *me.*

Example 1 Choose the sentence that is more polite.

> Dad fried potatoes for me and her.
>
> Dad fried potatoes for her and me.

Solution It is more polite to mention ourselves last.

> **Dad fried potatoes for her and me.**

Example 2   Complete this chart by replacing each blank with the correct objective case pronoun.

NUMBER	PERSON		OBJECTIVE CASE (direct object, indirect object, or object of a preposition)
Singular	First		_____
	Second		_____
	Third	(masc.)	_____
		(fem.)	_____
		(neuter)	_____
Plural	First		_____
	Second		_____
	Third		_____

Solution   We complete the chart as follows:

NUMBER	PERSON		OBJECTIVE CASE (direct object, indirect object, or object of a preposition)
Singular	First		me
	Second		you
	Third	(masc.)	him
		(fem.)	her
		(neuter)	it
Plural	First		us
	Second		you
	Third		them

Direct Objects   The following sentences have personal pronouns as direct objects. Notice that they are objective case pronouns.

The geese chased *them.

One caught *me.

I calmed *him.

Example 3   Write a sentence using a pronoun as a direct object.

Solution   Your answer will be unique. Here are some correct examples:

Annie Mae doesn't remember *him*.

Winona will invite Esther and *her*.

Boomer buried *it*.

Indirect Objects   These sentences have personal pronouns as indirect objects. They are objective case.

Jack Sprat ordered *her* some fat.

The Knave of Hearts denied *her* and *me* the tarts.

Grandpa fixed *us* a banana split.

Example 4   Write a sentence using an objective case personal pronoun as an indirect object.

Solution   Our answers will vary. Here are some possibilities:

The Red Cross offered *us* hot food.

The cook baked *them* a blackbird pie.

Sergeant Stern read *her* and *me* the law.

Objects of a Preposition   The sentences below have personal pronouns used as objects of a preposition. Of course they are objective case.

Al's plane swooped over *them*.

Velma sets dainty dishes before *him* and *me*.

The ground was trembling under *us*.

Example 5   Write a sentence using a personal pronoun as an object of a preposition.

Solution   Here are some possible answers:

The queen will parade near *them*.

The king is gathering ideas from *them* and *us*.

Some rhymes seem ridiculous to *me*.

Practice   **a.** Study the objective case pronoun chart from Example 1. Then try to reproduce it from memory.

b. Unscramble these words to make a sentence with a personal pronoun as a direct object:

> basket   a   her   carries   moon   the   to

c. Unscramble these words to make a sentence with a personal pronoun as an indirect object:

> told   narrator   us   a   a   story

d. Unscramble these words to make a sentence with a personal pronoun as an object of a preposition:

> cobwebs   Wilda   with   swept   me   and   him

e. Write the sentence that is more polite.

Mom used to sing "Rock-a-Bye, Baby" to my brother and me.

Mom used to sing "Rock-a-Bye, Baby" to me and my brother.

f. Write each objective case pronoun from this list:

me	him	I	she	them
they	he	her	we	us

Choose an objective case pronoun for sentences g–i.

g. Will the cradle fall with my brother and (I, me) in it?

h. The clock gave the mouse and (she, her) a scare.

i. Contrary Mary left Larry and (they, them) out in the rain.

For j–m, replace each blank with the correct vocabulary word.

j. The character's grave illness created _____ in the story.

k. In a western novel, the _____ is often the cowboy in white beating the rustler in black.

l. As _____, Pip told the story of *Great Expectations* from his point of view.

m. The poem was full of word pictures, or _____ of _____.

**Review set
54**   Choose the best word to complete sentences 1–11.

1. *He, him, his, she, her, hers,* and *it* are (first, second, third)
(53, 54) person pronouns.

2. Pronoun (gender, case) shows the job the pronoun
(53, 54) perform in the sentence.

3. Tiki-Pu (know, knew, known) by heart the names of all
(52) the painters and their schools.

4. The light of dawn has (grow, grew, grown) brighter with
(52) each passing moment.

5. The students had (tear, tore, torn) their rice paper.
(52)

6. Has the bell (ring, rang, rung) yet for class?
(52)

7. Of the two artists, Jaime has the (good, better, best) idea.
(42, 43)

8. The Greek root (*phil-*, *-morph*, *chrono-*) means loving.
(39, 49)

9. Some people use ipecac syrup as an (anecdote, antidote)
(47) for poison.

10. A protagonist is a (villain, hero, melodrama).
(50)

11. Pentagons, hexagons, octagons, and polygons all have
(51) (eyes, angles, feet).

12. Tell whether the following is a phrase or a clause: as
(3, 24) scarce as feathers on a fish

13. For a–c, write the plural of each noun.
(12, 13)

    (a) battery   (b) key   (c) result

For 14 and 15, write the verb phrase and label it action or
linking.

14. Lan has grown three inches since school started.
(4, 22)

15. The pile of discarded art supplies has grown larger and
(4, 22) larger.

16. Rewrite this letter, adding capital letters, periods, and
(29, 50) commas as needed:

dear counselor hegarty

   twenty-four years ago today your son and my son were born at huntington memorial hospital are they still friends?

warmly

judge brooke

17. For a and b, write the past tense and past participle of
(52) each irregular verb.

(a) choose   (b) take

18. Write the comparative and superlative form of the
(42, 43) adjective *trustworthy*.

Replace each blank with the correct word to complete sentences 19 and 20.

19. We can group nouns into three cases: _____
(40) case, objective case, and possessive case.

20. A noun is in the nominative case when it is the subject of
(39, 40) a sentence or when it is used as a _____ nominative.

21. Write the appositive in this sentence: Wio-Wani, an
(45, 46) accomplished painter, offers to help Tiki-Pu learn to paint.

22. Use an appositive to combine these two choppy
(45, 46) sentences to make one longer sentence: Stephanie makes puppets. Stephanie is my sister-in-law.

23. Tell whether the italicized pronoun in this sentence is
(51, 53) nominative, objective, or possessive case: Wio-Wani gives *him* instruction in painting.

24. Write each pronoun in this sentence and indicate its
(49) antecedent: After his experience with Wio-Wani, Tiki-Pu changes his manner.

25. Write the participle used as an adjective in this sentence:
(27, 48) The scheming master seeks to ruin Tiki-Pu's dream.

26. Write each adjective from this sentence and circle the one
(47) that is sometimes overused: The bad master paints bricks
over Tiki-Pu's access to Wio-Wani's palace.

27. Write the correlative conjunction pair from this sentence:
(38) Surprisingly, both Wio-Wani and Tiki-Pu burst out of the
painting.

Diagram sentences 28–30.

28. Having started, she had the confidence to continue.
(19, 23)

29. Do both Fong and Fred like painting?
(19, 25)

30. The lady on stage is she.
(32, 39)

LESSON 55

Personal Pronoun Case Forms

Dictation or Journal Entry

Vocabulary:

The Greek word *gnosis* means knowledge.

A *prognosis* is the prediction of the probable course and outcome of a disease. The doctor's *prognosis* concerning my illness was "complete recovery."

A *diagnosis* is the labeling of a disease after tests and examination. The nurse practitioner's *diagnosis* of the child's eye problem was "pink eye."

Agnosia is the loss of ability to interpret sensory stimuli, such as sounds or images. After his automobile accident, he suffered from mild agnosia.

An *agnostic* believes that the existence of God is unknowable.

Case Forms   The following chart helps us to sort out the three personal pronoun **case forms:** (1) If a pronoun is a subject or predicate nominative, it is *nominative case*. (2) A pronoun used as a direct object, indirect object, or object of a preposition is *objective case*. (3) If a pronoun shows possession, it is *possessive case*.

NUMBER	PERSON		CASE	
		NOMINATIVE	OBJECTIVE	POSSESSIVE
Singular	First	I	me	mine
	Second	you	you	yours
	Third (masc.)	he	him	his
	(fem.)	she	her	hers
	(neuter)	it	it	its
Plural	First	we	us	ours
	Second	you	you	yours
	Third	they	them	theirs

Example 1   Tell whether each italicized pronoun is nominative, objective, or possessive case.

(a) Larry, Gary, and *he* built the doghouse.

(b) Mary put *him* in the doghouse.

(c) *His* is the biggest dog dish.

Solution   (a) **nominative case**

(b) **objective case**

(c) **possessive case**

The pronoun case form depends on how the pronoun is used in the sentence. We refer to the chart to decide which pronoun is correct for this sentence:

(We, Us) men built the doghouse.

The pronoun renames "men," which is the subject of the sentence. We use the nominative case pronoun *we* (NOT *us*) as a subject. Therefore, we write

We men built the doghouse.

Example 2 Tell how the pronoun is used in each sentence (subject, direct object, indirect object, object of a preposition, possession).

(a) Boomer likes *him* for building a doghouse.

(b) That doghouse is *hers*.

(c) *They* found themselves "in the doghouse" because they were late to dinner.

(d) Boomer growled at *them* for trying to crawl into his house.

(e) He gave *her* a lick for filling his dish with meat.

Solution (a) *Him* is a **direct object.**

(b) *Hers* shows **possession.**

(c) *They* is the **subject.**

(d) *Them* is an **object of a preposition.**

(e) *Her* is an **indirect object.**

Example 3 Determine how the pronoun is used in each sentence. Then refer to the chart to help you choose the correct pronoun. Rewrite each sentence correctly.

(a) Both Mr. Tangelo and (she, her) attended the fair.

(b) Mr. Mango won stuffed animals for Miss Grape and (she, her).

(c) The fair bored Miss Prune and (he, him).

Solution (a) The pronoun is a **subject of the sentence,** so we choose the nominative case pronoun *she.*

Both Mr. Tangelo and *she* attended the fair.

(b) The pronoun is the **object of the preposition** "for," so we choose the objective case pronoun *her.*

Mr. Mango won stuffed animals for Miss Grape and *her.*

(c) The pronoun is a **direct object,** so we choose the objective case pronoun *him.*

The fair bored Miss Prune and *him.*

Practice For a–c, tell whether the pronoun is nominative, objective, or possessive case.

  a. Mr. Gala noticed *them.*

  b. *You* sighed.

  c. The art exhibit was *hers.*

For d–i, tell how the pronoun is used in each sentence (subject, predicate nominative, direct object, indirect object, object of a preposition, possession).

  d. The roller coaster frightened *me.*

  e. That giant slide ticket is *yours.*

  f. *We* enjoyed the classic car exhibit.

  g. Mr. Berry tossed *her* a tangerine.

  h. Ants crawled over *them* at the picnic.

  i. It was *I* who enjoyed the fair the most.

For j and k, choose the correct pronoun.

  j. (We, Us) students voted for a field trip to the fair.

  k. Old Dead Eye stared at Homer and (*I, me*).

For l–p, replace each blank with the correct vocabulary word.

l. An _____ doesn't know if there is a God.

m. A temporary case of _____ left him unable to interpret the sounds.

n. The doctor's _____ was that the growth was a benign tumor.

o. The _____ for skin cancer is excellent, but why not prevent it in the first place?

p. The Greek root meaning knowledge is _____.

Review set 55   Choose the best word to complete sentences 1–6.

1. A (clause, phrase) is a group of words with a subject and
(3, 24) a predicate.

2. The Greek root *gon* means (foot, angle, eye).
(51)

3. An overused expression is a(n) (caricature, allegory,
(52) cliché).

4. The denouement is the (beginning, middle, end) of the
(52) story.

5. Anthropometry measures (animals, humans, mountains).
(53)

6. The (motif, pathos, narrator) tells the story.
(54)

7. For a–c, write the plural of each noun.
(12, 13) (a) foot   (b) inch   (c) yard

8. Write the verb phrase in this sentence and label it
(25, 31) transitive or intransitive: Molly and she might be exploring the Amazon River in Brazil.

9. Write each prepositional phrase from this sentence and
(16, 32) star the object of each preposition: At the age of eighteen, Ernest Hemingway became a reporter for the *Kansas City Star.*

10. Write the four principal parts of the irregular verb *swear.*
(6, 15)

11. Write the comparative and superlative forms of the adjective *little*, meaning "amount."
(42, 43)

Rewrite sentences 12 and 13, adding capital letters, periods, and commas, and making necessary changes to abbreviations for formal writing.

12. mr hemingway died on sun july 2 1961 a few days before his sixty-second birthday
(11, 44)

13. ernest hemingway said "courage is grace under pressure"
(20, 46)

14. Write the seven common coordinating conjunctions.
(36)

15. Write the verb phrase from this sentence and label it action or linking: Benito and I were feeling nervous about the test.
(4, 22)

For 16–18, refer to this sentence: Dr. Clarence Hemingway, Ernest's father, had taught his boys the sports of fishing and hunting.

16. Write the verb phrase and name its tense.
(8, 18)

17. Write the appositive.
(45, 46)

18. Write the pronoun and its antecedent.
(49)

19. Tell whether the following is a phrase or a clause: the knights jousting in the arena
(3, 24)

20. Reproduce the nominative case pronoun chart. You may abbreviate "1st, 2nd, 3rd, sing., pl., etc."
(53)

21. Write the three *articles,* which function as adjectives in a sentence.
(27)

22. Unscramble these words to make a sentence with a personal pronoun as a predicate nominative:
(51, 53)

was   winner   the   he

23. For a and b, write the past tense and past participle of each irregular verb.
(52)

(a) blow   (b) shrink

24. Which sentence below is more polite? Write A or B.
(51, 53) A. He and I will mop the floor.

B. I and he will mop the floor.

25. Write the participle used as an adjective in this sentence:
(27, 48) Having deteriorated in health, Ernest Hemingway returned to Idaho for his last days.

26. Write each gerund in this sentence: Hemingway's favorite
(19) pastimes were hunting and fishing.

Diagram sentences 27–30.

27. Do you need to practice?
(23, 25)

28. Bake them some bread.
(4, 25)

29. Knitting, she began humming.
(19, 48)

30. The guests of Earl and Lea are she and I.
(33, 39)

LESSON
56

Possessive Pronouns and Possessive Adjectives • Diagramming Pronouns

---

Dictation or Journal Entry
Vocabulary:
Let's examine the literary terms *action, comedy, dialogue,* and *paradox.*

The *action* of a story is everything that happens in it. The story's fast *action* kept me on the edge of my seat.

Comedy refers to the humor in a story. The author used *comedy* to make readers laugh.

Dialogue is the conversation among the characters. The characters' *dialogue* revealed the plot of the story.

A *paradox* is a statement that seems to go against common sense, yet it is true. To hate to wake up to an alarm clock, yet to be thankful to wake up, is an example of *paradox.*

Possessive Pronouns

We have learned that a pronoun takes the place of a noun. The possessive pronouns *mine, yours, his, hers, ours,* and *theirs* replace nouns to tell "whose."

That's *yours,* not *mine.*

His has hand brakes, but *hers* has coaster brakes.

The Hopewells will sell *theirs* if Bo and I sell *ours.*

Notice that in each of the sentences above, the possessive pronoun **replaces a noun** and stands alone.

Possessive Adjectives

There is another group of words that is very similar to possessive pronouns except that they **come before a noun** rather than replace it. These words are the possessive adjectives *my, your, his, her, its, our,* and *their.*

Did *my* pig frighten *your* hen?

Her aunt married *his* uncle.

Their goat nibbled *our* petunias.

In each of the sentences above, the possessive adjective comes before a noun to tell "whose."

Many people consider these words pronouns. Others see them as adjectives because they always come before nouns to modify them. What is important is using them correctly.

POSSESSIVE ADJECTIVE (IN FRONT OF A NOUN)	POSSESSIVE PRONOUN (STANDING ALONE)
my	mine

your	yours
his	his
her	hers
its	its *(very seldom used)*
our	ours
their	theirs

Errors to Avoid Possessive pronouns do not have apostrophes. The words *yours, hers, its,* and *ours* are already possessive.

> INCORRECT: I found Al's lost wallet but not **your's**.
> CORRECT: I found Al's lost wallet but not **yours**.

> INCORRECT: That ten-dollar bill is **her's**, I think.
> CORRECT: That ten-dollar bill is **hers**, I think.

Also, we must not confuse contractions and possessive adjectives.

POSSESSIVE ADJECTIVE	CONTRACTION	
your	you're	(you are)
their	they're	(they are)
its	it's	(it is)

Example 1 Choose the correct word to complete each sentence.

(a) Is that horse (yours, your's)?

(b) (It's, Its) corral is on the east side of the ranch.

(c) Do you think (it's, its) injured?

(d) The saddle is (theirs, their's).

Solution (a) Is that horse **yours?**

(b) **Its** corral is on the east side of the ranch.

(c) Do you think **it's** injured?

(d) The saddle is **theirs.**

Diagramming Pronouns We diagram pronouns in the same way we diagram nouns.

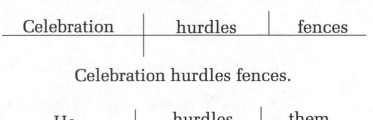

Celebration hurdles fences.

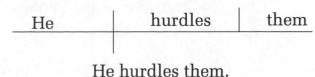

He hurdles them.

Diagramming a sentence helps us determine which pronoun to use, because it clearly shows *how* the pronoun is used in the sentence. We diagram the main parts of the sentence below to help us choose the correct pronoun:

Cattle stampeded toward Sal and (*I, me*).

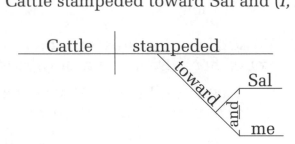

We see from the diagram that the pronoun is an object of the preposition *toward*, so we choose the objective case pronoun *me*.

Cattle stampeded toward Sal and *me*.

Example 2   Diagram the following sentence in order to choose the correct pronoun. Then rewrite the sentence correctly.

Zane and (I, me) galloped our horses.

Solution   We diagram the sentence this way:

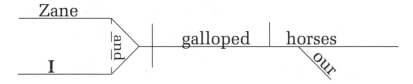

We see from our diagram that the pronoun is part of the subject of the sentence, so we choose the nominative case pronoun *I*.

Zane and *I* galloped our horses.

Practice   Diagram sentences a–c, choosing the correct pronoun.
  a. Grandma and (we, us) string popcorn.

  b. Send Ayeesha and (*me, I*) pictures.

  c. Charlie called Lucy and (*she, her*).

Choose the correct word to complete sentences d–h.
  d. The hockey stick is useless; (it's, its) handle is cracked.

  e. Those goalie sticks are (theirs, their's).

f. Please hand me (your, you're) hockey puck.

g. (They're, Their) the most talented hockey team in the league.

h. (Its, It's) a challenge to score against that team.

For i–l, replace each blank with the correct vocabulary word.
   i. A lion laying down with a lamb is a _____.

   j. The _____ between Huck Finn and Jim revealed their plans of escape.

   k. Funny descriptions or silly behavior of characters add _____ to a novel.

   l. The car chase provided exciting _____ in the story.

More Practice Choose the correct word(s) to complete each sentence.

   1. Insect-eating birds make (their, there) nests in deciduous forests.

   2. Those woodchucks are fat; (they're, there, their) ready to hibernate for the winter.

   3. Although the bird has migrated south, it will find (it's, its) way back here in the spring.

   4. Greenland's winter is longer and colder than (ours, our's).

   5. My yard has deciduous trees, but (hers, her's) has only conifers.

   6. Is this forest (yours, your's)?

   7. Did you bring (you're, your) binoculars for bird watching?

   8. (They're, Their) in my backpack over (there, they're, their) under the tree.

   9. A deciduous tree loses (it's, its) leaves in the fall.

   10. (You're, Your) not likely to see alligators in a cold climate.

   11. Perhaps (they're, there, their) lying near a swamp in the Everglades.

12. I believe (their, there, they're) home is in Florida.

Review set 56

1. Tell whether the following is a complete sentence, run-on
(1, 3) sentence, or sentence fragment: Ali Baba hears the secret words they open and close the cave.

Choose the correct word to complete sentences 2–8.

2. Cassim is the (bad, worse, worst) of the two brothers.
(42, 43)

3. (Do Does) the band of robbers find riches in the cave?
(6, 14)

4. The forty thieves believe that this treasure is (there's,
(51, 56) their's, theirs).

5. The expression "busy as a bee" is overused; it is a
(52) (caricature, cliché, denouement).

6. The Greek root (*phil-*, *-morph*, *anthropos*) means human.
(49, 53)

7. Ingenious means (clever, sincere).
(36)

8. Discreet means (separate, careful).
(34)

For 9 and 10, refer to this sentence: No other people besides Ali Baba and his wife know about the abundant treasure in the hidden cave.

9. Write each adjective in the sentence.
(27, 28)

10. Write each prepositional phrase and star the object(s) of
(16, 32) each preposition.

For 11 and 12, write the verb phrase and label it transitive or intransitive.

11. Gold pours out of Ali Baba's bags and onto the floor.
(22, 31)

12. Ali Baba's wife pours the gold onto a measure.
(4, 31)

13. Write the seven common coordinating conjunctions.
(36)

14. Write the pair of correlative conjunctions from this
(38) sentence: Neither Ali Baba nor his wife can believe their good fortune.

Rewrite 15 and 16, adding periods, commas and capital letters and making necessary changes to abbreviations for formal writing.

15. long ago dr habib lived at 1000 e oasis ave cavetown
(35, 44) persia

16. dear ali baba family
(29, 35)   the captain and his forty thieves are seeking revenge please be on your guard against any strangers

with concern

morgiana

17. Use an appositive to make one sentence from these two
(45, 46) sentences: Morgiana is a clever and intelligent slave. Morgiana saves Ali Baba's life four times.

18. Write the verb phrase from this sentence and label it
(4, 22) linking or action: Does Cassim seem greedy?

19. For a–c, write the plural of each noun.
(12, 13) (a) thief   (b) alley   (c) ally

20. Reproduce the objective case pronoun chart. You may
(54) abbreviate.

21. Tell whether the following is a phrase or a clause: with
(3, 24) robbers chasing after them.

For sentences 22 and 23, write the pronoun and label it nominative, objective, or possessive case.

22. He marks Ali Baba's door with chalk to identify the house
(51, 53) for the robbers.

23. Morgiana foils them by marking several houses with
(51, 54) chalk.

24. For a and b, write the past tense and past participle of
(15, 52) each irregular verb.

(a) freeze   (b) speak

25. Write the four principal parts of the verb *sing*.
(15, 52)

26. Write each participle used as an adjective in this
(27, 48) sentence: The burning oil surprises the hiding thieves.

27. Write the verb phrase from this sentence and name its
(8, 21) tense: The philatelists are organizing their valuable
stamp albums.

Diagram sentences 28–30.

28. Will Bob and he try surfing or sailing?
(19, 25)

29. Kim loves to swim.
(23, 25)

30. Take time to think.
(23, 31)

LESSON 57

Dependent and Independent Clauses • Subordinating Conjunctions

---

Dictation or Journal Entry

Vocabulary:

The Greek prefix *poly-* means "many."

A *polyglot* is one who speaks, understands, or writes several languages. The *polyglot* was hired as a translator at the international airport.

A *polygraph* is an instrument that simultaneously measures and records changes in heartbeat, blood pressure, respiration, etc., and is used as a lie detector. The police gave each suspect a *polygraph* test to determine whether or not they were telling the truth.

Polytechnic means devoted to many arts or sciences and their practical application. Henry plans to attend a local *polytechnic* school.

Independent Clauses

There are two types of clauses. One type is the **independent clause,** also called the main clause. An independent clause expresses a complete thought. It makes sense all by itself.

Polygons have more than two sides.

Millard Fillmore was America's thirteenth president.

Dependent Clauses

A **dependent clause** is the other type of clause. It cannot stand by itself and is sometimes called the subordinate clause. Alone, it does not make sense because it is incomplete.

If they practice all day

After the fog in the glen lifted

Although the clauses above each contain a subject and a predicate, they do not make a complete sentence. If we remove the introductory words, "if" and "after," they become independent clauses. They make sense and can stand alone:

They practice all day.

The fog in the glen lifted.

Example 1

For a–d, tell whether the clauses are dependent or independent.

(a) when Evelyn's boss promoted her to manager

(b) she received the good news in the morning

(c) as soon as Evelyn phoned home

(d) her husband began to plan a special dinner

Solution   (a) This is a **dependent** clause. It depends on another clause in order to make sense.

(b) This is an **independent** clause. It can stand by itself and does not require another clause in order to make sense.

(c) This is a **dependent** clause. Alone, it makes no sense.

(d) This is an **independent** clause. It makes sense and can stand alone.

Subordinating Conjunctions   A **subordinating conjunction** introduces a dependent clause. We can turn an independent clause into a dependent clause by adding a subordinating conjunction. In the dependent clauses below, *when* and *since* are subordinating conjunctions.

INDEPENDENT CLAUSE	DEPENDENT CLAUSE
He was successful.	*When* he was successful,...
The economy suffered.	*Since* the economy suffered,...

Here we list some common subordinating conjunctions:

after	*because*	*so that*	*when*
although	*before*	*than*	*whenever*
as	*even though*	*that*	*where*
as if	*if*	*though*	*wherever*
as soon as	*in order that*	*unless*	*while*
as though	*since*	*until*	

Many of these words also function as prepositions. Sometimes phrases begin with prepositions such as *after*, *before*, *since,* or *until*. In this case, these words are not subordinating conjunctions but prepositions. Remember that a clause has both a subject and a verb. Notice how the word *before* is used in the two sentences below.

SUBORDINATING CONJUNCTION:
We must bring in the ficus tree *before* the first frost occurs. ("before the first frost occurs" is a **clause**)

PREPOSITION:

We must bring in the ficus tree *before* the first frost. ("before the first frost" is a prepositional **phrase.**)

Example 2 Identify the subordinating conjunctions in the following sentences.

(a) Although he was a British writer, Rudyard Kipling is well known in the United States.

(b) He wrote about life in India even though he married an American girl and settled in England.

Solution (a) ***Although*** is the subordinating conjunction. It introduces the dependent clause "Although he was a British writer."

(b) ***Even though*** is the subordinating conjunction. It introduces the dependent clause "even though he married an American girl and settled in England."

Practice For a–d, tell whether the clauses are dependent or independent.

a. as soon as he received the Nobel Prize

b. the prolific Kipling wrote short stories, poems, and novels

c. the writings project intense patriotism

d. that we should lead active lives

Write each subordinating conjunction in sentences e–g.

e. After the small car stopped, six tall frowning people got out.

f. Scot ate the raspberry cobbler with gusto, even though blueberry was his favorite.

g. When you hear the bell, you have five minutes left to play.

For h–k, replace each blank with the correct vocabulary word.

h. A prefix meaning "many" is _____.

     i. The _____ spoke German, French, Spanish, Russian, Hebrew, Swahili, and Japanese.

     j. The _____ will indicate whether you are lying or telling the truth.

     k. The _____ school offered instruction and training in applied science.

More Practice See Master Worksheets.

Review set 57 **1.** Write the verb phrase from this sentence and name its tense: The king has tired of his daughter's annoying suitors.
(8, 18)

2. From memory, reproduce the objective case pronoun chart.
(54)

Choose the correct word(s) to complete sentences 3–12.

3. Is this parakeet (your's, yours)?
(56)

4. It has escaped from (its, it's) cage.
(56)

5. (Him, He) and Zeke live in New Jersey.
(51, 53)

6. (Your, You're) boots remind me of a story called "How Boots Befooled the King."
(56)

7. "I'm as frustrated as a bird without wings" is a (motif, figure of speech, epic).
(54)

8. The Greek word (*anthropos, gonia, gnosis*) means knowledge.
(53, 55)

9. Anthropogenesis studies the beginning of (humans, animals, insects).
(53)

10. A philanthropist (hates, distrusts, loves) mankind.
(49)

11. In the race between Duke and Sparky, Duke was (faster, fastest).
(42, 43)

12. John had never (sang, sung) that song before.
(15, 52)

13. From memory, reproduce the nominative case pronoun
(53) chart.

14. From this sentence, write each noun and circle the one
(7, 9) that is abstract: Great and precious promises lie within
those pages.

15. Rewrite this outline, adding periods and capital letters as
(20, 35) needed:

       i howard pyle's stories
         a "how boots befooled the king"
         b "king stork"
         c "the stool of fortune"

16. Tell whether the following is a phrase or a clause: if you
(3, 24) can pay me five shillings

17. Write the overused adjective from the sentence below.
(27, 47) Then write one that is more descriptive.

             It's a good story.

18. Write the four principal parts of the irregular verb *blow.*
(15, 52)

19. Write each adjective in this sentence and circle the one
(28) that is demonstrative: This lad wants to befool the king.

20. Write the infinitive from the sentence below. Then tell
(23, 25) how it functions in the sentence.

       Boots's brothers fail to outsmart the king.

21. Write the verb phrase from this sentence and label it
(4, 31) transitive or intransitive: With a bag of gold, the foolish
king may purchase an old tattered hat.

Replace each blank with the correct word to complete
sentences 22 through 24.

22. A noun or pronoun used as a direct object, an indirect
(54) object, or an object of a preposition is in the _____
case.

23. The word to which a pronoun refers is called the
(49) _____.

24. A noun or pronoun used as a subject or predicate
(40, 53) nominative is in the _____ case.

25. From this sentence, write the verb phrase and label it
(4, 22) linking or action: Does that tattered hat appear valuable?

26. For a and b, write the plural of each noun.
(12, 13) (a) daughter-in-law   (b) mouthful

27. From this sentence, write each prepositional phrase,
(16, 32) starring the object of each preposition: According to my
mother, cleanliness is next to godliness.

28. Use an appositive to make one sentence from these two
(45, 46) sentences: The high councilor is the wisest man in the
world. He is Boots's next victim.

Diagram sentences 29 and 30.

29. Having swum, Pat felt weak.
(39, 52)

30. Eating renewed his energy to continue.
(19, 25)

LESSON
58

Gerunds vs. Participles and Verbs • Gerund Phrases

Dictation or Journal Entry

Vocabulary:

Let us discuss the literary terms *autobiography, conflict, falling action, exaggeration,* and *description.*

An *autobiography* is the writer's story of his or her own life. *The Diary of Anne Frank* is considered an *autobiography.*

The *conflict* is the problems and complications of a story. The *conflict* in the novel involved the main character's rejection, remorse, and revenge.

Falling action occurs after the high point or climax in the story. Once the hero conquers the villain, the remaining part of the story is the *falling action.*

Exaggeration is stretching the truth. Writers use it for effectiveness. The author used *exaggeration* when describing his memorable characters.

Description is the use of words to draw a clear picture of a person, place, or thing. Charles Dickens is famous for his character *descriptions.*

Gerunds vs. Participles and Verbs

We remember that a gerund may be the present participle of a verb (the *-ing* form) functioning as a noun. The gerund can be a sentence subject, a direct object, an object of a preposition, or a predicate nominative. We also recall that not every word ending in *ing* is a gerund. Some are verbs or participles. To determine if the *-ing* word is a gerund, we must examine how it is used in the sentence.

Gerunds:

> *Vacuuming* is John's chore. (sentence subject)
>
> A carpenter enjoys *building.* (direct object)
>
> Sven's favorite job is *sweeping.* (predicate noun)
>
> Good health is crucial for *singing.* (object of preposition)

Participles:

> Otar held a *smiling* baby. (adjective)
>
> The *laughing* grandfather adjusted his glasses.

Verbs:

> He *had been laughing* all morning.
>
> The baby *is smiling* in the picture.

Example 1 Tell whether the *-ing* word in each sentence is a verb, participle, or gerund.

(a) The filly is racing for the first time.

(b) The racing jackrabbit escaped its predator.

(c) Auto racing entertains many spectators.

Solution   (a) **Is racing** is a present progressive tense **verb.**

(b) **Racing** is a **participle.** It is used as an adjective and modifies "jackrabbit."

(c) **Racing** is a **gerund.** It is the subject of the sentence.

Gerund Phrases   A **gerund phrase** contains a gerund and its objects and modifiers. It is always used as a noun. The gerund phrase may have adjectives, adverbs, direct objects, or prepositional phrases within it. We will learn about adverbs in a later lesson. Gerund phrases are italicized below.

Baking delicious cookies takes practice.
(gerund + direct object)

Efficient studying produces good results.
(adjective + gerund)

They prefer *skiing on fresh snow.*
(gerund + prepositional phrase)

Below, we show how gerund phrases function in sentences:

SENTENCE SUBJECT:
Our *having blown the whistles* prevented further crime.

DIRECT OBJECT:
He dislikes *dumping the kitchen trash.*

OBJECT OF A PREPOSITION:
Joyce purchased new pans for *baking tall cakes.*

PREDICATE NOMINATIVE:
Your job is *washing the windows in the dining room.*

Example 2   Write the gerund phrase in each sentence. Then write whether the phrase functions as a subject of a sentence, direct object, object of a preposition, or a predicate nominative.

(a) The cafeteria manager's goal is providing a nutritious lunch for students.

(b) Requesting assistance was difficult for him.

(c) Many support the mayor's plan of adding a new wing to the museum.

(d) Mom regrets having shoveled the snow.

Solution (a) **Providing a nutritious lunch for students** functions as a predicate nominative.

(b) **Requesting assistance** is the subject of the sentence.

(c) **Adding a new wing to the museum** is the object of the preposition "of."

(d) **Having shoveled snow** is the direct object of the sentence.

When a noun or pronoun modifies a gerund or gerund phrase, it is possessive.

I enjoyed *their* coming by.
(NOT: I enjoyed *them* coming by.)

Because of *Moe's* panicking over spiders, we all left.
(NOT: Because of *Moe* panicking over spiders, we all left.)

Is there any point to *our* staying?
(NOT: Is there any point to *us* staying?)

Example 3 Choose the possessive noun or pronoun to precede each gerund phrase.

(a) The physician appreciated (me, my) asking questions.

(b) (Bryon, Bryon's) reading stories at night pleases Kurt.

(c) Molly laughs at (them, their) dancing to ragtime music.

Solution (a) The physician appreciated **my** asking questions.

(b) **Bryon's** reading stories at night pleases Kurt.

(c) Molly laughs at **their** dancing to ragtime music.

Practice For a–e, replace each blank with the correct vocabulary word(s).

a. The action that follows the climactic capture of Injun Joe in *The Adventures of Tom Sawyer* is called the _____.

b. Paul Bunyan's size is an example of _____.

c. John F. Kennedy's written record of his life is his _____.

d. The following is Charles Dickens's character
_____: "...whom I now saw to be a brown
corrugated old woman, with a small face that might have
been made of walnut shells, and a large mouth like a cat's
without the whiskers...."

e. Tom Sawyer's negative response to Aunt Polly's
upbringing is an example of _____.

For f–i, write the gerund phrase and tell how it functions in
the sentence (subject, predicate nominative, direct object, or
object of a preposition).

f. People in Pasadena enjoy hearing the church bells.

g. Collecting unusual stamps excited the philatelist.

h. Before revealing the solution, the mathematician
presented the problem.

i. Gerald's favorite form of exercise is biking to the beach.

Choose the correct word to precede the gerund phrase in j–l.

j. I appreciate (you, your) hammering my tent stakes.

k. (Him, His) sitting on a rock proved dangerous.

l. He is tired of (me, my) crocheting hats and scarves.

For m–o, tell whether the *-ing* word is a gerund (noun),
participle (adjective), or verb.

m. Exercising is Jeannie's commitment.

n. Juan has been swimming for hours.

o. A honking horn woke me before dawn.

**More
Practice**   Write each gerund phrase and tell whether it functions as a
subject of a sentence, direct object, object of a preposition, or
predicate nominative.

1. Sid tried a different tool for painting the eaves of his
house.

2. His limping deceived us.

3. They accused her of cheating on the test.

4. She denied cheating on the test.

5. Cheating on the test would be shameful.

6. Thoreau placed great value on living simply.

7. Her favorite pastime is clipping coupons.

8. He applauds her clipping coupons.

Review set 58

Choose the best word(s) to complete sentences 1–10.

1. A philologist (destroys, loves, despises) literature.
(7, 49)

2. We thought that something tragic was about to happen in the story because of the author's (melodrama, protagonist, foreshadowing).
(50)

3. The Greek root (*phil-*, *chrono-*, *-gon*) means angled or angular.
(49, 51)

4. The Greek word *gnosis* means (man, angled, knowledge).
(55)

5. "She has a memory like a steel trap" is a (figure of speech, pathos, motif).
(54)

6. The (direct, indirect) object tells to whom or for whom the action was done.
(25, 34)

7. Our beagle is friskier than (theirs, their's).
(56)

8. My tree has as (much, many) apricots as yours does.
(42, 43)

9. Yesterday, she (steal, steals, stole) my favorite pencil.
(15, 52)

10. The lady climbing the tree is (her, she).
(51, 53)

11. Tell whether the following is a complete sentence, sentence fragment, or run-on sentence: The drummer, a good-natured lad with plenty of talent.
(1, 3)

12. Tell whether the following is a phrase or a clause: stripping the faded wallpaper from the dining room walls
(3, 24)

13. Rewrite this sentence, adding periods, commas, and capital letters and making necessary changes to abbreviations for formal writing: mrs sanchez said "on sat aug 3 2002 i played chinese checkers read a french novel and cleaned my refrigerator"
(35, 44)

Replace each blank with the correct word to complete sentences 14–16.

14. Clauses may be either independent or _____.
(57)

15. The _____ of a noun explains how the noun is
(40) used in a sentence.

16. Nouns and pronouns are in the _____ case when
(40, 54) they are used as direct objects, indirect objects, or objects of a preposition.

17. Write the proper adjective in this sentence: "King Stork"
(28) is an English tale from long ago.

18. Write the verb phrase from this sentence and label it
(4, 31) transitive or intransitive: Has the stork flown away from its enemy?

19. Write the verb phrase from this sentence and name its
(8, 21) tense: Has she been expecting you?

20. Write the seven common coordinating conjunctions.
(36)

21. Write the verb phrase from this sentence and label it
(4, 22) linking or action: Does your damp basement smell musty?

22. For a–c, write the plural of each noun.
(12, 13) (a) woman   (b) baby   (c) day

23. Write the four principal parts of the irregular verb *throw*.
(15, 52)

24. Write the dependent clause from this sentence and circle
(24, 57) the subordinating conjunction: I am working hard today so that I can play tomorrow.

25. Which sentence is more polite? Write A or B.
(51, 54) A. Please call me and Bob.   B. Please call Bob and me.

26. Unscramble these words to make an interrogative
(25, 54) sentence with a personal pronoun as a direct object:

him can I help Daisy and

For 27 and 28, refer to this sentence: Having failed two tests, Meg decided to study.

27. Write the participle and name its tense.
(27, 48)

28. Write the direct object.
(23, 25)

Diagram sentences 29 and 30.

29. Sinclair Lewis sold Jack London some interesting ideas.
(25, 34)

30. Lewis's *Arrowsmith* was a prize-winning novel.
(28, 39)

LESSON 59 Participial Phrases • Diagramming Participial and Gerund Phrases

We remember that participles are verbals that function as adjectives. Most participles end in *ing* or *ed* but some end in *en*, *d*, or *t*. They have three tenses:

PRESENT:	sketching, scrutinizing
PAST:	sketched, scrutinized
PERFECT:	having sketched, having scrutinized

Participial Phrases A **participial phrase** contains a participle and its objects and modifiers. It is used an as adjective to modify a noun or pronoun. Participial phrases are italicized in the sentences below.

Sealed in plastic bags, the fruit will keep for months.
(modifies "fruit")

Having met the competition, the team determined to perform well.
(modifies "team")

Painting with different media in their studio, the artists produced some original pieces.
(modifies "artists")

Watching the animal, the zookeeper cleaned the cage.
(modifies "zookeeper")

Before trying to identify a participial phrase, we first find the simple subject and simple predicate of the sentence. Then we look for the participial phrase.

simple subject   simple predicate

The *spectators* were supporting the team playing in red jerseys.

In the sentence above, "playing in red jerseys" is a participial phrase and modifies "team."

We may find a participial phrase either before or after the word it modifies. A sentence becomes confusing if there are too many words between the participial phrase and the word it modifies.

> Wanda wanted pizza *lying on her bed.* (Who or what is lying on her bed, Wanda or pizza?)

To make the sentence easier to understand, we try to place the participial phrase as close as possible to the noun it modifies:

> *Lying on her bed,* Wanda wanted pizza.

Example 1   For each sentence, write the participial phrase and the noun or pronoun that it modifies.

(a) Hiring an expert, the executive submitted the company's financial reports for evaluation.

(b) Using creativity and determination, the writer submitted the manuscript on time.

(c) Children, seated on the curb, awaited the parade.

Solution   (a) **Hiring an expert** modifies **executive.**

(b) **Using creativity and determination** modifies **writer.**

(c) **Seated on the curb** modifies **children.**

Diagramming Participial and Gerund Phrases

THE PARTICIPLE PHRASE

We diagram the participial phrase under the word it modifies.

> *Leading the spectators,* the cheerleaders performed their routine.

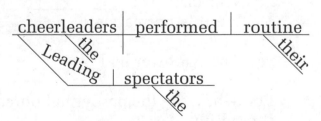

THE GERUND PHRASE

We diagram the gerund phrase to show how the gerund functions in the sentence.

Rehearsing for a show requires much time.

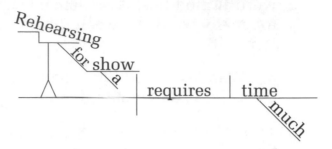

Example 2 Diagram each sentence.

    (a) Her gift was cleaning the bedroom.

    (b) Challenging the climbers, the slope was steep and slippery.

Solution (a)

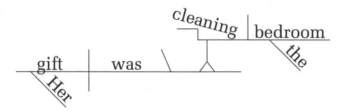

    (b)

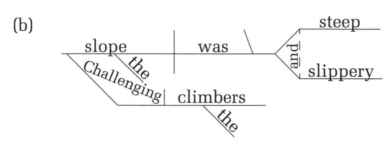

Practice For a–d, replace each blank with *borne* or *born*.

    a. Some diseases are labeled air-_____ because they are transmitted through the air.

    b. Do you know when the litter of kittens was _____?

    c. The baby was _____ with a funny-shaped head, but it is normal now.

    d. The widower had _____ his grief well.

For e–h, write the participial phrase and the noun or pronoun it modifies.

    e. The snake, hiding under the rock, watched the hiker.

    f. Exiting the theater, the crowd headed toward the ice-cream parlor.

g. Joyce spied a lighthouse painted by her favorite artist.

h. Gilbert bought one drawn in pencil.

Diagram sentences i and j.

i. Adopting a pet requires forethought.

j. The waiter washing tables is ours.

More Practice   See Master Worksheets.

Review set 59   Choose the best word to complete sentences 1–9.

1. An (anecdote, antidote) is a short story or an account of
(47) an amusing or interesting incident.

2. Joe has (wore, worn) his cowboy hat every day this week.
(15, 52)

3. A theologian studies (science, religion, stars).
(46)

4. I read the *Aeneid*, an (epoch, epic) poem of great length.
(45)

5. This three-legged stool is his; (your's, yours) is under the
(55, 56) table over there.

6. Even though it's a (cliché, plot, melodrama), my brother
(52) really does "sleep like a log."

7. The present participle of a verb functioning as a noun is
(15, 19) a(n) (infinitive, gerund, preposition).

8. I am depending on you and (he, him) to help me.
(51, 54)

9. Which is the (purer, purest) of the two gold nuggets?
(42, 43)

10. For a–c, write the plural of each noun.
(12, 13) (a) Freddy   (b) daddy   (c) son-in-law

11. Write each predicate adjective in this sentence: The
(27, 41) obnoxious antagonist in this story remains stubborn,
greedy, and rude.

12. Write the verb phrase in this sentence and name its tense:
(8, 21) The young soldier has been trying to escape from the old
man's ancient, ramshackle house.

Write the correct verb form for sentences 13 and 14.

13. I (present perfect tense of *break*) my toe twice this year.
(18, 52)

14. Carolyn (present perfect progressive tense of *spin*) wool
(21, 52) all morning.

Replace each blank with the correct word to complete sentences 15 and 16.

15. _____ conjunctions connect parts of a sentence
(38) and always come in pairs.

16. When used as the subject of a sentence, a noun or
(40, 53) pronoun is in the _____ case.

17. Tell whether the following is a phrase or a clause:
(3, 24) grimacing, shrieking, and smashing gigantic cockroaches

18. Write the verb phrase from this sentence and label it
(4, 31) transitive or intransitive: Nine fine pines line my
driveway.

19. Write the verb phrase from this sentence and label it
(8, 22) action or linking: Can the jubilant graduates remain quiet
during the ceremony?

20. Write the four principal parts of the irregular verb *break*.
(15, 52)

21. Rewrite the following, adding periods, commas, and
(35, 50) capital letters and making necessary changes to
abbreviations for formal writing:

dear dr paine

    on mon oct 8 2001 you filled a cavity in my tooth it
still hurts

            regretfully

            miss sniffle

22. Use an appositive to make one sentence from these two
(45, 46) sentences: Howard Pyle wrote a story called "The Stool
of Fortune." Howard Pyle was an American illustrator
and writer.

(51, 54) **23.** Write the objective case, third person plural pronoun.

For 24 and 25, refer to this sentence: After rescuing the princess, the soldier gave her a beautiful palace of white marble.

24. Write the pronoun and its antecedent.
(49)

25. Write the indirect object.
(25, 34)

26. Tell whether this sentence is true or false: Possessive
(56) pronouns always have apostrophes.

27. Write the dependent clause from this sentence and circle
(57) the subordinating conjunction: After he found the princess, the soldier came up with a plan to foil the magician.

Diagram sentences 28–30.

28. Recovering the princess became the reason for the
(39, 59) soldier's existence.

29. Tipping his hat, Clyde gave me a cheerful greeting.
(25, 59)

30. Flapping its wings, the duckling tried to fly.
(34, 59)

LESSON 60

Reflexive and Intensive Pronouns

Reflexive Pronouns

Reflexive pronouns end in "-self" or "-selves." A reflexive pronoun throws the action back upon the subject of the sentence. **The antecedent of a reflexive pronoun is always the subject of the sentence.** It is a necessary part of the sentence and cannot be omitted. The singular reflexive pronouns are *myself, yourself, himself, herself,* and *itself.*

> The proud contestant congratulated *himself.*

> You'll disappoint *yourself* if you don't try again.

The plural reflexive pronouns are *ourselves, yourselves,* and *themselves.*

> Can Bob and Larry protect *themselves?*

> We shielded *ourselves* from the wind.

Like all pronouns, the reflexive pronouns match their antecedents in person, number, and gender; are used as direct objects, indirect objects, and objects of a preposition; and are diagrammed like this:

INDIRECT OBJECT:

> Walt cooked *himself* breakfast.

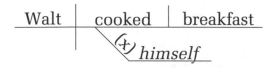

DIRECT OBJECT:

> He burned *himself.*

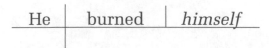

OBJECT OF A PREPOSITION:

They were chattering among *themselves.*

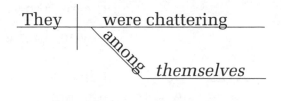

Errors to Avoid   We do not use *hisself* and *theirselves.* They are not words.

> NO: Howard criticized *hisself.*
> YES: Howard criticized *himself.*

> NO: They quizzed *theirselves* on state capitals.
> YES: They quizzed *themselves* on state capitals.

We do not use reflexive pronouns in place of the simple personal pronoun.

> NO: Celeste and *myself* won the mile relay.
> YES: Celeste and *I* won the mile relay.

Example 1   Choose the correct personal pronoun for each sentence.

(a) Hannah and (myself, I) visited Mount Parnassus in Greece.

(b) Abel and Tom prided (theirselves, themselves) on growing the sweetest tomatoes in the country.

Solution   (a) **Hannah and *I* visited Mount Parnassus in Greece.** We do not use a reflexive pronoun in place of a simple personal pronoun.

(b) We do not use *theirselves.* It is not a word. **Abel and Tom prided *themselves* on growing the sweetest tomatoes in the country.**

Intensive Pronouns   **Intensive pronouns** have the same form as reflexive personal pronouns. However, they are used to emphasize or intensify another noun or pronoun. We can leave the intensive pronoun out of a sentence without changing the meaning of the sentence. The antecedent is whatever word the intensive pronoun emphasizes; it need not be the subject of the sentence. Notice that the following sentences make sense without the intensive pronoun.

The explorer *himself* blazed the trail.

Karina and Kristina *themselves* built a fort.

I'll repair the damage *myself*.

Can you do the work *yourself*?

Again, we do not use *hisself* and *theirselves*. They are not words. Also, we do not replace simple personal pronouns with intensive pronouns.

We diagram intensive pronouns like this:

You must wash the dog *yourselves*.

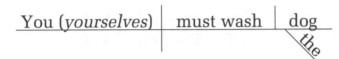

They made the pizza *themselves*.

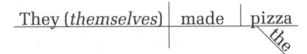

Example 2   Choose the correct pronoun for each sentence.

(a) Eliza and I will address the invitations (ourself, ourselves).

(b) Jose (hisself, himself) coached the basketball team to victory.

(c) Perhaps they will discover a cure for influenza (*theirselves, themselves*).

Solution   (a) The intensive pronoun must be plural because its antecedent is plural. **Eliza and I will address the invitations *ourselves*.**

(b) *Hisself* is not a word. **Jose *himself* coached the basketball team to victory.**

(c) *Theirselves* is not a word. **Perhaps they will discover a cure for influenza *themselves*.**

Practice   Choose the correct personal pronoun for sentences a–d.

a. Neither Briana nor (myself, I) will visit Mount Saint Helens, an active volcano.

b. Mitch wrote the script (hisself, himself).

c. (You, Yourself) may photograph Mount Vernon, the home and tomb of George Washington.

d. While in Italy, they injured (theirselves, themselves) on the volcanic rock of Mount Vesuvius.

e. Diagram this sentence:

We ourselves rocked the babies.

For f–i, replace each blank with the correct vocabulary word.

f. The _____ unfairly obtained a handicapped parking permit.

g. The Greek word _____ means *false* or *pretend*.

h. Alexander Hamilton wrote using "Westchester Farmer" as his _____ .

i. Although the literary work bore similarities to classic Greek literature, the modern novel was labeled a _____ .

More Practice   Choose the correct personal pronoun for each sentence.

1. Dad fixed the television (himself, hisself).

2. My friends tried to repair the car (theirselves, themselves) since they could not afford a mechanic.

3. They helped (theirself, themselves) to cake.

4. Cecilia and (I, myself) drove to Princeton.

5. Julio taught Flora and (me, myself) to play chess.

6. I believe Jon and Julie wrote the song (theirselves, themselves).

7. Since the other choir members were late, Mike sang the harmony (hisself, himself).

8. They don't use pseudonyms (theirselves, themselves), but others do.

9. He learned to repair computers (hisself, himself).

10. Tom and (he, himself) visited the invalid.

Review set   Choose the best word to complete sentences 1–9.

60
   1. A (motif, pathos, narrator) is a recurring theme in
   (54) literature.

   2. An (allegory, anthropogenesis, autobiography) is the
   (52, 58) writer's story of his or her own life.

   3. A (comedy, dialogue, paradox) is a true statement that
   (56) goes against common sense.

   4. The prefix (*geo-, caco-, poly-*) means many.
   (11, 57)

   5. A polyglot speaks (primitive, obsolete, many) languages.
   (57)

   6. A (first, second, third) person pronoun indicates the
   (51, 55) speaker.

   7. *You* and *yours* are (first, second, third) person
   (51, 55) pronouns.

   8. Both Selma and (him, he) were anxious to find the
   (51, 53) answer.

   9. That responsibility will be (her's, hers).
   (56)

   10. For a–c, write the plural of each noun.
   (12, 13) (a) louse   (b) Amy   (c) coach

   11. Rewrite the following sentence, adding periods, commas,
   (11, 35) and capital letters and making necessary changes to
   abbreviations for formal writing.

   your uncle and i attended a lecture about mars at the
   observatory in griffith park last tues the eleventh of june

   12. Write each prepositional phrase in this sentence and star
   (32, 33) the object of each preposition: A great black bear with a
   deep voice carried Selma to the queen.

   13. Write the seven common coordinating conjunctions.
   (36)

   14. Write the verb phrase in this sentence and label it action
   (4, 22) or linking: Do most border collies stay loyal to their
   masters?

15. From this list, write the two sentence types that end with
(1, 3) a period: interrogative, exclamatory, imperative, declarative

16. Write the four pairs of common correlative conjunctions.
(38)

17. Write the personal pronoun from this sentence and name
(51, 53) its case: That lady rowing frantically in piranha-infested waters is she.

18. Write the verb phrase in this sentence and label it
(25, 31) transitive or intransitive: Does Jules's jealousy cloud his good sense?

19. Tell whether the following is a phrase or a clause: as
(3, 24) aardvarks march through the dark

20. Write the dependent clause in this sentence, circling the
(24, 57) subordinating conjunction: Paul watered his lawn even though it was raining.

21. Which sentence is more polite? Write A or B.
(51, 54) A. Jules was relieved to see me and him.
B. Jules was relieved to see him and me.

22. Tell whether the following is a complete sentence,
(1, 3) sentence fragment, or run-on sentence: The generous gifts of many benevolent philanthropists.

23. Write each possessive pronoun from this list: your,
(55, 56) they're, his, her's, it's, its, their, you're

24. Choose the possessive noun or pronoun to precede the
(55, 56) gerund phrase in this sentence: Jules regrets (us, our) knowing about his greediness.

25. Write the superlative form of the adjective *bright*.
(42, 43)

26. Write the four principal parts of the irregular verb *know*.
(15, 52)

27. Use an appositive to make one sentence from these two
(45, 46) sentences: Sylvester is a guitarist. Sylvester played for our music festival last Sunday.

Diagram sentences 28–30.

28. Doodle, my poodle, brings me the neighbors' newspaper.
(25, 44)

29. Vaulting the fence, Fido attempts to escape.
(23, 25)

30. Exploring the streets is his plan.
(19, 39)

**LESSON
61**

The Comma, Part 4: Descriptive Adjectives, Dependent Clauses

Dictation or Journal Entry
Vocabulary:
Let us examine the literary terms *allusion, connotation, denotation,* and *didactic.*

An *allusion* is a reference to a well-known place, person, thing, or event. The English professor made an *allusion* to the plays of William Shakespeare.

Connotation is an implied meaning of a word in addition to its literal meaning. *Connotations* of the word "fireplace" include warmth, coziness, and affection.

Denotation is the dictionary or literal meaning of a word. The *denotation* of the word "fireplace" is the section of the chimney that opens into a room.

The *didactic* meaning of literature is its message or moral. Fables are considered *didactic* because they contain a moral.

We remember that commas indicate the natural pauses of speech. In this lesson we will discuss more uses for commas.

Descriptive Adjectives We use a comma to separate two or more **descriptive adjectives.**

> The *volatile, destructive* Mount Vesuvius wiped out the ancient city of Pompeii in Italy.

However, if one adjective is a color, we do not use a comma to separate it from another adjective.

> The red fiery lava slithered down Mount Vesuvius and engulfed the ancient city of Herculaneum as well.

One way to decide whether a comma is needed is to insert the word "and" between the adjectives.

> IF YOU COULD SAY: It was a *cold and windy* night.
> YOU DO NEED A COMMA: It was a *cold, windy* night.

> YOU WOULDN'T SAY: I saw a *shaggy and white* dog.
> SO YOU DON'T NEED A COMMA: I saw a *shaggy white* dog.

Example 1 Insert commas where they are needed in the sentences below.
(a) Would a cold wet dog like an old red bedspread?

(b) The famous facetious Murphy's Law means that if anything can go wrong, it will.

Solution (a) We place a comma between the two adjectives "cold" and "wet," but we do not place a comma before the color adjective "red."

Would a **cold, wet** dog like an **old red** bedspread?

(b) We separate the adjectives "famous" and "facetious" with a comma.

The ***famous, facetious*** Murphy's Law means that if anything can go wrong, it will.

Dependent Clauses We remember that a **dependent clause** cannot stand alone, while an independent clause, or main clause, makes sense without the dependent clause. We use a comma after a **dependent clause** when it comes before the main clause.

Because he was handsome, Narcissus attracted women.
       (DEPENDENT CLAUSE)   (INDEPENDENT/MAIN CLAUSE)

However, we do not use a comma when the dependent clause follows the main clause.

Narcissus attracted women because he was handsome.
       (INDEPENDENT/MAIN CLAUSE)   (DEPENDENT CLAUSE)

Example 2 Insert commas if needed in the sentences below.

(a) Since Narcissus cruelly rejected Echo the avenging goddess caused Narcissus to fall in love with his own reflection.

(b) Narcissus died staring at his own image since he had been unkind to others.

Solution (a) We place a comma after the dependent clause "Since Narcissus cruelly rejected Echo" because it comes before the main clause.

Since Narcissus cruelly rejected Echo, the avenging goddess caused Narcissus to fall in love with his own reflection.

(b) No comma is needed in this sentence because the dependent clause follows the main clause.

Practice Rewrite sentences a–c, inserting commas to separate descriptive adjectives.

a. The brilliant ingenious Sir Isaac Newton was an English mathematician and scientist.

b. The young motivated scientist conceived the idea of universal gravitation at the age of twenty-five.

c. Common white light is really a mixture of all other colors.

Rewrite sentences d–f, inserting a comma after each dependent clause.

d. Because he formulated our theories of physics Sir Isaac Newton is recognized as one of the greatest geniuses of all time.

e. Even though Newton explained rainbows they remain a mystery to me.

f. While he is most famous for the law of universal gravitation he also built the first reflecting telescope.

For g–j, replace each blank with the correct literary term.

g. The _____ message of *Beauty and the Beast* is that inner beauty is more powerful than outer beauty.

h. Some _____ of an overcast day are depression, gloominess, and listlessness.

i. The _____ of an overcast day is cloud cover with little sunshine.

j. The historian made an _____ to the Confederate Army when discussing the American Civil War.

More Practice See Master Worksheets.

Review set 61 Choose the best word(s) to complete sentences 1–9.

1. A philatelist (loves, hates, sells) postage stamps.
(49)

2. That forest fires encourage new plant growth is a
(53, 56) (prognosis, anthropometry, paradox) of nature.

3. Hartwig is a polyglot, for he speaks (ancient, unknown,
(57) many) languages.

4. The camel had (borne, born) hundreds of pounds on its
(59) back across the hot desert.

5. Please accompany Silvia and (myself, me) to the
(51, 54) museum.

6. Can Mr. Ortiz repair the flat tire (hisself, himself)?
(60)

7. *She, her,* and *hers* are (first, second, third) person
(51, 55) pronouns.

8. I mailed an invitation to Zack and (he, him).
(51, 54)

9. This mailbox is (their's, theirs), not (our's, ours).
(51, 56)

10. For a–c, write the plural of each noun.
(12, 13) (a) battery (b) attorney-at-law (c) dish

Rewrite sentences 11 and 12, adding periods, commas, and capital letters and making necessary changes to abbreviations for formal writing.

11. mr cod's seafood recipe i believe calls for one lb of
(11, 50) shrimp three lbs of halibut and three oz of wisconsin cheese

12. on sept 21 1902 mrs shade planted a peach tree at 2091
(5, 44) spruce st oak city west virginia

13. Write each prepositional phrase in this sentence and star
(32, 33) the object of each preposition: According to the newspaper, the rain will continue throughout the week.

14. Write the reflexive pronoun in this sentence: The Dryad
(60) thought to herself that perhaps she ought to return Old Pipes's money.

15. Tell whether this sentence is declarative, imperative,
(1, 3) interrogative, or exclamatory: Please help me bring home the cows, goats, and sheep.

16. Rewrite this sentence correctly: Old Pipes was the kind of
(47) a person whom everyone respected.

17. Write the personal pronoun from this sentence and name
(51, 54) its case: Rocky told his story to Andrew and me.

18. Write the verb phrase in this sentence and label it
(25, 31) transitive or intransitive: Is Miss Trinh walking on thin ice?

19. Write the seven common coordinating conjunctions.
(36)

20. Write the dependent clause in the sentence below and
(57) circle the subordinating conjunction:

Although David is wearing a raincoat, he is still getting quite wet.

21. Write the verb phrase in this sentence and name its tense:
(0, 21) Are Dryads living in trees on the hillsides?

22. Tell whether the following is a complete sentence,
(1, 3) sentence fragment, or run-on sentence:

His fish story wasn't true it was an exaggeration.

23. Write the gerund phrase in this sentence: He invents a
(19, 32) plan for recapturing the beautiful Dryad.

24. Choose the correct word to precede the gerund phrase in
(56, 58) this sentence:

I appreciate (Sal, Sal's) driving me home each day.

25. Write the comparative form of the adjective *happy*.
(42, 43)

26. Write the four principal parts of the irregular verb *blow*.
(6, 15)

27. Use an appositive to make one sentence from these two
(45, 46) sentences:

Stephen collects Scandinavian postage stamps. Stephen is an avid philatelist.

Diagram sentences 28–30.

28. Kerry must paint the entire fence herself.
(25, 60)

29. Having roamed the streets, Fido returned.
(25, 48)

30. Growing large zucchinis proved simple.
(19, 39)

LESSON 62

Compound Sentences • Coordinating Conjunctions

> **Dictation or Journal Entry**
>
> **Vocabulary:**
> The Greek noun *pathos,* meaning "feeling, suffering" gives us our common suffix *-pathy*.
>
> To have *sympathy* means to share the feeling of another person. When Mel's cat died, his friends expressed their *sympathy*.
>
> *Antipathy* is an aversion or hatred of someone or something. The student's *antipathy* toward physical education class was unwarranted.
>
> *Apathy* is a state of indifference or the absence of feeling. The *apathy* of some Americans towards endangered animals frustrates activists.
>
> *Empathy* is the ability to imagine oneself in a condition or situation like that of another person. The priest had *empathy* for those who had been
humbled by circumstances in their lives.

Compound Sentences

Two or more simple sentences (independent clauses) joined by a connecting word like *and*, *or*, or *but* form a **compound sentence.** Only sentences closely related in thought should be joined to form a compound sentence. Below, we connect two simple sentences to form a compound sentence.

TWO SIMPLE SENTENCES:
The nurse <u>showed</u> sympathy for the patient.
The doctor <u>was</u> apathetic.

ONE COMPOUND SENTENCE:
The nurse <u>showed</u> sympathy for the patient, but the doctor <u>was</u> apathetic.

Here we diagram the simple subjects and simple predicates of the compound sentence above:

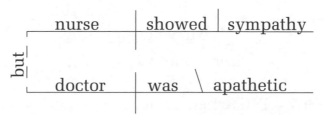

Notice that the compound sentence is made up of two independent clauses that can each stand alone and make sense. Remember that any number of independent clauses can be joined to form a compound sentence. For example, here we join four independent clauses (simple sentences) to form one compound sentence:

> Dan cooked dinner, and Milly washed the dishes, but I just watched, and the captain fell asleep.

Coordinating Conjunctions   A **coordinating conjunction** can join two simple sentences to form a compound sentence. We have learned that the following are coordinating conjunctions:

> and   but   or   nor   for   yet   so

Notice how coordinating conjunctions are used in the compound sentences below.

> *AND* INDICATES ADDITIONAL INFORMATION:
> Long ago, *Poor Richard's Almanac* was popular, **and** its proverbs have endured until now.

> *BUT* SHOWS CONTRAST:
> Readers believed Richard Sanders wrote *Poor Richard's Almanac*, **but** this was the pen name of Benjamin Franklin.

> *OR* SHOWS A CHOICE:
> Writers could use their own names, **or** they could choose a pseudonym.

Conjunctions may also connect the parts of a compound subject or predicate. Do not confuse a compound subject or a compound predicate with a compound sentence. Remember that a compound sentence has both a subject and a predicate on each side of the conjunction. A compound sentence follows this pattern:

> *subject* <u>predicate</u>, (conjunction) *subject* <u>predicate</u>

> *Words* <u>can injure</u>,   (or)   *words* <u>can heal</u>.
> *We* <u>have been eating</u>,   (but)   *they* <u>have been starving</u>.
> *Kurt* <u>composes</u> music,   (and)   *Molly* <u>writes</u> lyrics.

Example 1   Tell whether each sentence is simple or compound. If it is compound, write the coordinating conjunction that joins the two independent clauses.

(a) The Pulitzer Prize is awarded for outstanding achievement in literature, but not every outstanding writer receives it.

(b) The value of the Pulitzer Prize is $1000 for journalism, but it is only $500 for music.

(c) William Faulkner wrote remarkable fiction and received two Pulitzer Prizes.

(d) John Steinbeck won the Pulitzer Prize for *The Grapes of Wrath*, and Ernest Hemingway won it for *The Old Man and the Sea.*

Solution   (a) We find a subject and a predicate on each side of the conjunction: *Pulitzer Prize* is awarded (conjunction), *writer* receives. Therefore, the sentence is **compound.** The coordinating conjunction **but** joins the two independent clauses.

(b) This sentence is **compound.** It consists of two independent clauses joined by the coordinating conjunction **but.**

(c) This is a **simple** sentence. It is a single, independent clause with one subject (*William Faulkner)* and a compound predicate (wrote, received).

(d) This is a **compound** sentence. Two independent clauses are joined by the coordinating conjunction **and.**

Diagramming   To diagram the simple subjects and simple predicates of a compound sentence, we follow these steps:

1. Diagram each simple sentence, one below the other.

2. Join the two sentences with a dotted line on the left side.

3. Write the conjunction on the dotted line.

Below, we diagram the simple subjects and simple predicates of this compound sentence:

Leroy is sanding, and Julia is painting.

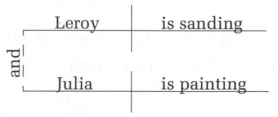

Example 2   Diagram this compound sentence:

> Elinor Wylie wrote a poem about velvet shoes, but Joyce Kilmer wrote a poem about trees.

Solution   We diagram the simple subject and simple predicate of each simple sentence and place them one below the other. Then we join them with a dotted line on which we write the coordinating conjunction "but."

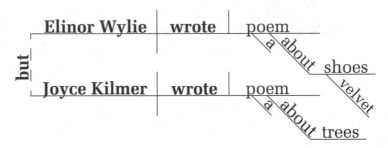

Practice   For a–e, tell whether each sentence is simple or compound. If it is compound, write the coordinating conjunctions which join the two or more independent clauses.

a. Pygmalion and Galatea bore a son named Paphos.

b. Venus endowed Galatea with life, and she returned Pygmalion's love.

c. Moses parted the Red Sea, so the Israelites escaped from the bondage of Egypt.

d. Rapunzel endures many trials, but readers remember her long, golden hair.

e. The term "red herring" refers to a diversion from the real problem.

f. Diagram this compound sentence:

> John has arrived, so we may begin.

For g–k, replace each blank with the correct vocabulary word.

g The Greek word meaning feeling or suffering is _____.

h. Citizens sometimes show their _____ by failing to vote during elections.

i. The tender-hearted veterinarian showed _____ for the sick horse by speaking softly to it and caressing its nose.

j. Randolf understood his friend's situation, for he had _____.

k. Zilla had poor nutrition; she had great _____ toward vegetables and whole-grain breads.

Review set 62

Choose the best word(s) to complete sentences 1–10.

1. The (exaggeration, comedy, conflict) is the problems and
(56, 58) complications of a story.

2. The Greek word meaning *false* or *pretend* is (logos, zoe,
(60) pseudo).

3. (Connotation, Denotation) is an implied meaning.
(61)

4. (Allusion, Didactic, Pseudo) means having a moral or
(60, 61) message.

5. Maggie and (me, myself, I) will meet at the library on
(51, 53) Saturday.

6. Did the Ngo Family build their house (theirselves,
(51, 60) themselves)?

7. Robin Hood gave (he, him) and (I, me) green clothing to
(51, 54) wear in the forest.

8. The bowman with the feather in his hat was (he, him).
(51, 53)

9. Is this border collie (your's, yours)?
(51, 56)

10. The *Robin Hood Ballads* were (sing, sang, sung) and
(15, 52) passed on from generation to generation.

11. For a–c, write the plural of each noun.
(12, 13) (a) trench   (b) territory   (c) property

12. Rewrite the following, adding periods, commas, and
(35, 62) capital letters as needed: the green shaggy merry
followers of robin hood enjoyed life to the fullest they

sang songs ate venison and played games in the forests of england

13. Write each prepositional phrase in this sentence and star
$^{(32, 33)}$ the object of each preposition: Several bowmen appeared from between the trees in the grove.

14. For sentences a and b, write the verb phrase and label it
$^{(4, 22)}$ action or linking.

   (a) Little John could smell the roasting venison.

   (b) Roasting venison may have smelled delicious to the bowmen.

15. Tell whether the following is a phrase or a clause:
$^{(24, 57)}$ refusing to allow Robin Hood to pass over the narrow bridge

16. Rewrite this sentence correctly: That type of a collie likes
$^{(47)}$ to herd.

17. Write the personal pronoun from this sentence and name
$^{(51, 53)}$ its case and its antecedent(s): Since Little John refused to let Robin Hood pass on a narrow bridge, they fought for the right of passage.

18. Write the verb phrase in this sentence and label it
$^{(25, 31)}$ transitive or intransitive: Did Little John defeat Robin Hood on the bridge?

19. Write the four common pairs of correlative conjunctions.
$^{(38)}$

For sentences 20 and 21, write the dependent clause and circle the subordinating conjunction.

20. Robin Hood could not cross the bridge unless he knocked
$^{(24, 57)}$ Little John off the bridge.

21. Robin Hood was twenty years old when he met Little
$^{(24, 57)}$ John.

22. Which sentence is more polite? Write A or B.
$^{(51, 54)}$ A. Little John can follow me and Robin Hood.

   B. Little John can follow Robin Hood and me.

23. Write the participial phrase in this sentence: Bowmen,
(48) hiding in the surrounding trees, emerged at the sound of
Robin Hood's horn.

24. Choose the correct pronoun to precede the gerund phrase
(19, 58) in this sentence: The authorities will honor (him, his)
telling the truth.

25. Write the superlative form of the adjective *delightful*.
(42, 44)

26. Write the four principal parts of the irregular verb *drink*.
(15, 52)

27. Write the indirect object in this sentence: F.J. Child has
(25, 34) provided us the *Robin Hood Ballads*.

Diagram sentences 28–30.

28. The old English ballad remains a popular genre of
(33, 39) literature.

29. Have they found a place to hide?
(23, 25)

30. Both Robin Hood and Little John are excellent athletes.
(37, 39)

LESSON
63

The Comma, Part 5: Compound Sentences, Direct Quotations

> **Dictation or Journal Entry**
> **Vocabulary:**
> *Diction* is a writer's choice of words. A writer may use archaic, colloquial, profane, slang, trite, or vulgar diction.
>
> *Archaic diction* is old-fashioned. Using the word "wrap" for a coat is *archaic.*
>
> *Colloquial diction* is used in ordinary, or familiar, conversation. "What's up?" is *colloquial.*
>
> *Profane diction* is irreverent or obscene. We avoid using *profane diction,* for it offends people.
>
> *Slang* is a language used by a certain group of people when talking to each other. To describe something as "bunk" or "rad" is to use *slang.*
>
> *Trite diction* is overused and therefore ineffective. Saying that her face was "red as a beet" is *trite.*
>
> *Vulgar diction* is crude and inappropriate, lacking good taste. The convict's *vulgar* language revealed his lack of refinement.

Compound Sentences

We remember that two sentences or independent clauses joined by a coordinating conjunction (*and, but, or, for, nor, yet, so*) is called a compound sentence. We place a comma after the first independent clause and before the coordinating conjunction in a compound sentence.

> Pablo Picasso was Spanish, but Norman Rockwell was American.
>
> Norman Rockwell painted scenes from everyday life, and he often added humor to the pictures.

We have memorized these *coordinating conjunctions*, which signal the need for a comma in a compound sentence:

> and   but   or   nor   for   yet   so

Example 1 Identify the coordinating conjunction in each compound sentence.

(a) Rockwell designed many posters, but he is especially famous for a series of murals entitled "The Four Freedoms."

(b) Rosh Hashanah is the Jewish New Year, for it begins the Ten Penitential Days.

(c) James is working on an art project, so he will be late for dinner.

Solution   (a) **but**   (b) **for**   (c) **so**

Example 2   Insert a comma before the coordinating conjunction to separate the two independent clauses in the sentences below.

    (a) Thoroughbred horses are bred for speed but Arabian horses are bred for endurance.

    (b) Cats sometimes develop hair balls for they groom their fur with their tongues.

Solution   We place a comma after the first independent clause and before the coordinating conjunction.

    (a) Thoroughbred horses are bred for speed, but Arabian horses are bred for endurance.

    (b) Cats sometimes develop hair balls, for they groom their fur with their tongues.

Direct Quotations   We use a comma or commas to offset the exact words or of a speaker, a **direct quotation**, from the rest of the sentence.

Miss Etiquette explained, "When you see RSVP on an invitation, it means that you need to tell the host or hostess whether or not you'll attend the function."

"Your response," Miss Etiquette continued, "will allow your host or hostess to plan adequately for the event."

"Please remember that a well-mannered person always responds to an invitation," finished Miss Etiquette.

Notice that the comma stays next to the word it follows. If a comma follows a direct quote, the comma goes inside the quotation marks.

YES: "Please come to my party," said Peter.

NO: "Please come to my party", said Peter.

Example 3   Rewrite sentences a and b, inserting commas as needed to offset direct quotations.

    (a) "One must include Charles Dickens" shared Miss Violet "when discussing the Victorian Age."

    (b) "Scrooge is the main character from the *Christmas Carol* by Charles Dickens" continued Miss Violet.

Solution   (a) We use commas to set off Miss Violet's words.

> **"One must include Charles Dickens," shared Miss Violet, "when discussing the Victorian Age."**

(b) We place a comma after Miss Violet's words.

> **"Scrooge is the main character from the *Christmas Carol* by Charles Dickens," continued Miss Violet.**

Practice   **a.** List the seven coordinating conjunctions.

For b–d, identify the coordinating conjunction in each sentence.

b. Scrooge was a hopeless curmudgeon, for he shared nothing with anyone.

c. There seemed to be no hope for Scrooge, yet the three ghosts changed his outlook on life.

d. Scrooge became one of the most generous men in town, and he was blessed with good friends and family as a result.

Rewrite sentences e and f, inserting a comma before a coordinating conjunction in a compound sentence.

e. The Hebrew word *shalom* means "peace but it is also used as a greeting or farewell.

f. Father took Mother on a vacation to Holland for he knew it was her fondest dream.

Rewrite sentences g and h, inserting commas to set off direct quotations.

g. The music teacher asked "Does anyone know the name of John Philip Sousa's first band?"

h. "At the age of thirteen " the teacher continued "John Philip Sousa played in the Marine Band, the official band of the President of the United States."

For i–o, replace each blank with the correct vocabulary word.

i. "Betrothed" (meaning "engaged") is an example of _____ diction.

j. Words like "cool," "rad," "fresh," and "bunk" are sometimes used as _____.

k. A writer's choice of words is called _____.

l. "I'm just veggin' out," is a _____ phrase.

m. Words that show disrespect for sacred things are _____.

n. To describe something as "cold as ice" is to use a _____ expression.

o. Crude, unrefined phrases are _____.

More Practice   See Master Worksheets.

Review set 63   Choose the best word to complete sentences 1–11.

1. A pseudonym is a (true, false, fancy) name adopted by an
(60)   author.

2. In what year were you (borne, born)?
(59)

3. The (connotation, denotation) of the word *steel* is "an
(61)   alloy; a commercial iron that contains carbon."

4. (Comedy, Dialogue, Paradox) is conversation among
(56)   characters.

5. A (philatelist, philanthropist, philologist) loves mankind.
(49)

6. Robin Hood and his bowmen conducted the wedding
(60)   (theirselves, themselves).

7. Green clothing would look ridiculous on my friends and
(51, 54)   (I, me, myself).

8. Bonnie and (she, her) seem ingenuous, so I trust them.
(51, 53)

9. The statement, "Possessive pronouns have apostrophes,"
(56)   is (true, false).

10. Robin Hood and his men (stealed, stole, stolen) from the
(15, 52) rich to feed the poor.

11. The plural form of *glass* is (glasses, glass's).
(12, 13)

12. Rewrite the following, adding periods, commas, and
(26, 63) capital letters as needed: uncle nigel and aunt catherine
are proud of their scottish ancestry they play bagpipes eat
mutton and roam the highlands every summer

13. Tell whether the following is a phrase or a clause:
(24, 57) because Robin Hood robbed the rich

14. Write the verb phrase from this sentence and label it
(4, 22) action or linking: Does Robin Hood's life sound exciting?

15. Write each prepositional phrase in this sentence and star
(17, 32) the object of each preposition: On behalf of Robin Hood,
Little John and Nick intercept Allen a Dale along the way.

16. Tell whether the following is a complete sentence,
(1, 3) sentence fragment, or run-on sentence: The narrator tells
the story of a bold outlaw who lives in Nottinghamshire.

17. Write the verb phrase from this sentence and label it
(25, 31) transitive or intransitive: The outlaw demands the
presence of Allen a Dale.

18. Write the personal pronoun from this sentence and name
(49, 53) its case and its antecedent: The young man clothed in
scarlet is he.

19. Write the seven common coordinating conjunctions.
(36)

20. Write the dependent clause from this sentence and circle
(24, 57) the subordinating conjunction: My dog, Petey, howls
whenever he hears a siren.

21. Use an appositive to make one sentence from these two
(44, 45) sentences: *Beowulf* is an epic poem. Last summer, Jenny
read *Beowulf.*

22. Write the gerund phrase in this sentence and label its
(18, 19) tense present or perfect: Having discovered the reason for

Allen a Dale's unhappiness gave Robin Hood new motivation.

23. Write the participial phrase in this sentence: The
(48, 59) photographer taking pictures of the sunset was using a tripod.

24. Choose the correct pronoun to precede the gerund phrase
(56,58) in this sentence: Do you admire (them, their) helping the poor?

25. Write the comparative form of the adjective *helpful.*
(42, 43)

26. Write the four principal parts of the irregular verb
(15) *choose.*

For 27 and 28, tell whether the sentence is simple or compound. If it is compound, write the coordinating conjunction that joins the two independent clauses.

27. David was having a hard time learning to ice skate, but he
(36, 62) was not alone.

28. This morning, Beth is frying bacon, scrambling eggs, and
(36, 62) toasting wheat bread for a nutritious breakfast.

Diagram sentences 29 and 30.

29. Cloe appreciates Jim's feeding the chickens.
(19, 25)

30. Allen a Dale, a worthy bridegroom, marries his true love,
(45, 62) but the haughty knight remains a single man.

LESSON 64   Relative Pronouns • Diagramming the Dependent Clause

Relative Pronouns

Relative pronouns play the part of subject or object in clauses:

> John Philip Sousa, *who* composed much American band music, invented the sousaphone. (subject)

> The sousaphone, with *which* he played a march, had an adjustable bell. (object)

Relative pronouns often refer to nouns that have preceded them, making the sentence more compact.

> WORDY:
> John Philip Sousa wrote distinctly American marches; these marches were brilliant and stirring.

> COMPACT:
> John Philip Sousa wrote distinctly American marches *that* were brilliant and stirring.

Simple Relative Pronouns

The following are simple relative pronouns:

> *who, whom, whose, what, which, that*

WHO REFERS TO PEOPLE (OR TO ANIMALS THAT ARE PERSONIFIED OR "NAMED"):

> John Philip Sousa, *who* is known as the "march king," wrote "The Stars and Stripes Forever."

> My finch Cheep, *who* lives in the kitchen, chirps at the beep of the microwave.

WHICH REFERS TO ANIMALS OR THINGS:

> Stalactites, *which* are accumulated carbon carbonate, can be enormous in size and beautiful in appearance.

> The possum, *which* had lost its way, wandered among the stalagmites and stalactites.

THAT REFERS TO PEOPLE, ANIMALS, OR THINGS:

> The most notable Russian *that* influenced world affairs after World War II was Joseph Stalin.

> There's the dog *that* won Best In Show.

> Games *that* are fun when you are six aren't always fun when you are eight.

Notice that **we do not use *which* for people.**

Example 1 Choose the correct relative pronoun for each sentence.

> (a) The popular congressman, (who, which) was running for re-election, began his speech with a joke.

> (b) The works of Gertrude Stein, (who, which) experiment with the different uses of language, make her a celebrated American writer.

> (c) The woman (which, that) influenced such writers as Ernest Hemingway, Sherwood Anderson, and Thronton Wilder was Gertrude Stein.

Solution (a) We choose **who** because it refers to "congressman," a person. We do not use *which* for people.

> (b) We choose **which** because it refers to "works," a thing. We do not use *who* for things.

> (c) We choose **that** because it refers to "woman," a person. We do not use *which* for people.

Errors to Avoid The relative pronoun *who* can cause problems, because it changes form depending on the part it plays in the clause:

SUBJECT	OBJECT	POSSESSIVE
NOMINATIVE CASE	OBJECTIVE CASE	POSSESSIVE CASE
who	*whom*	*whose*

In the following sentences, we diagram the dependent clause to show how the pronoun is used.

SUBJECT:
Harriet Beecher Stowe, who wrote *Uncle Tom's Cabin*, opposed slavery.

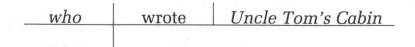

OBJECT:
Harriet Beecher Stowe, whom I mentioned, solidified antislavery sentiment in the North.

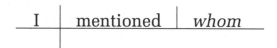

POSSESSIVE:
Harriet Beecher Stowe, whose contributions influenced the Civil War, wrote novels rich in pathos and drama.

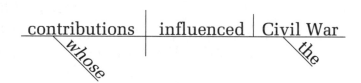

Diagramming the Dependent Clause

Now let us diagram an entire complex sentence, showing both the dependent and independent clauses. We attach the dependent clause to the independent clause by connecting the relative pronoun to its antecedent with a dotted line. We place the dependent clause below the independent clause.

Antonio Stradivari, *whom* I studied, made stringed instruments.

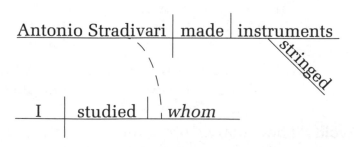

Example 2 Diagram the sentence to help you determine whether the relative pronoun is a subject or an object. Then choose the correct pronoun form.

(a) Those violinists, (who, whom) I recognize, are playing Stradivarius violins.

(b) Nicolo Amati, (who, whom) taught Stradivari, shared traditions of the Cremonese instrument makers.

Solution (a) Those violinists, **whom** I recognize, are playing Stradivarius violins. (object)

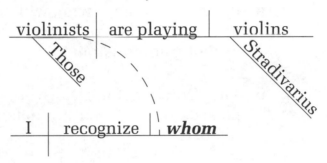

(b) Nicolo Amati, **who** taught Stradivari, shared traditions of the Cremonese instrument makers. (subject)

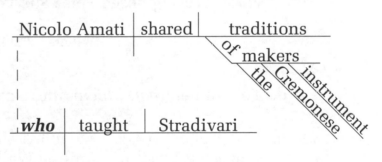

Compound Relative Pronouns The following are compound relative pronouns:

whoever	*whomever*	*whosoever*
whatever	*whatsoever*	*whichever*

The concert violinist may choose *whichever* violin he wants.

You may sing *whatever* you like.

Notice that we carefully choose *whoever* or *whomever* depending on the part the compound relative pronoun plays in the clause.

You may sing with *whomever* you want. (object)

Whoever is ill must go home. (subject)

Example 3 Choose the correct compound relative pronoun for this sentence:

> (*Whoever, Whomever*) wants to go hiking should wear comfortable shoes.

Solution **Whoever** wants to go hiking should wear comfortable shoes. The pronoun is the subject, so the proper form is *whoever*.

Practice Choose the correct relative or appositive pronoun for sentences a–e.

a. Peter Stuyvesant, (who, which) served as director general of New Netherland, became known as an able but despotic administrator.

b. The Dutch colonists, (who, whom) he overtaxed and persecuted, refused to defend their land against the English.

Think: ___he___ | ___overtaxed___ | ___?___

c. The Dutch settlers would have supported (whoever, whomever) opposed Peter Stuyvesant.

Think: ___settlers___ | ___would have supported___ | ___?___

d. The soldier (*that, which*) rides a motorcycle lives next door.

e. Mr. Cohen, (*who, whom*) I have known for years, suggested I visit the Wailing Wall.

Think: ___I___ | ___have known___ | ___?___

f. Diagram this sentence:

We can trust people who tell the truth.

For g–j, replace each blank with the correct vocabulary word.

g. The _____ viewed books as beautiful sources of literary expression.

h. That _____ must pay for damaging the books.

i. The Greek root meaning book is _____.

j. We will list the sources for our research paper in a
_____.

More Practice Choose the correct relative pronoun for each sentence.

1. Mr. Sims asked everyone (who, whom) signed up to meet after class.

Think: $\underline{\quad ? \quad}$ | $\underline{\text{signed}}$

2. Ms. Harper, (whom, who) was our director last year, is unavailable.

Think: $\underline{\quad ? \quad}$ | $\underline{\text{was}}$ \ $\underline{\text{director}}$

3. The auditioners, (who, whom) we welcomed, were nervous.

Think: $\underline{\text{we}}$ | $\underline{\text{welcomed}}$ | $\underline{\quad ? \quad}$

4. The lighting director, with (who, whom) I have consulted, has a lot to accomplish.

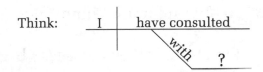

5. The cast members, (who, whom) you know, are doing their own makeup.

Think: $\underline{\text{you}}$ | $\underline{\text{know}}$ | $\underline{\quad ? \quad}$

6. Those (who, whom) attended the play were enthusiastic.

Think: $\underline{\quad ? \quad}$ | $\underline{\text{attended}}$ | $\underline{\text{play}}$

7. Mr. Ng, (who, which) sat in the front row, clapped the loudest.

8. We will always appreciate those (who, which) entertain us.

Review set   Choose the best word to complete sentences 1–13.
64

1. A (costume, custom) is a habit or usual way of doing
    (40) something.

2. A(n) (allegory, caricature, cliché) exaggerates the striking
    (52) features of a person or thing.

3. Polytechnic means devoted to (ancient, modern, many)
    (57) arts or sciences and their applications.

4. Didactic literature has a (connotation, denotation, moral),
    (61) or message.

5. The Greek word (*theos, graphein, pathos*) means feeling
    (62) or suffering.

6. Robin Hood fought the friar (hisself, himself).
    (60)

7. He and the friar (was, were) both dressed for battle.
    (37, 53)

8. Willy and (himself, he, him) wore camouflaged shirts.
    (51, 53)

9. The best ideas were (your's, yours).
    (51, 56)

10. By nightfall, Robin Hood had (grew, grown) fatigued.
    (15, 52)

11. He had (begin, began, begun) another skirmish with the
    (15, 52) friar.

12. Do you like (me, my) whistling ragtime tunes?
    (56, 58)

13. A (subordinating, coordinating) conjunction may join
    (36, 62) two simple sentences to form a compound sentence.

Rewrite 14 and 15, adding periods, commas, and capital
letters as needed.

14. nettie said "if you help me we can capture all these
    (20, 63) jerusalem crickets before colonel kleen arrives on friday"

15. dear robin hood
    (29, 50)   although you are an excellent archer the friar is even
    better you can visit him for he lives nearby
                                        sincerely
                                        will scadlock

16. Tell whether the following is a phrase or a clause: to test
(24, 57) his arching skills against the friar

17. Write a possessive case, second person, singular or plural
(55, 56) personal pronoun.

18. Write the verb phrase from this sentence and label it
(25, 31) transitive or intransitive: Have the fifty yeomen emerged
from the forest yet?

19. Write the objective case pronoun from this sentence and
(49, 54) name its antecedent: Robin Hood summoned the yeomen,
for he could not win the battle without them.

20. For a–c, write the plural of each noun.
(12, 13) (a) antenna   (b) knife   (c) theory

21. Write the dependent clause from this sentence and circle
(24, 57) the subordinating conjunction: As soon as the white flag
waves, the battle will cease.

22. Use an appositive to make one sentence from these two
(45, 46) sentences: Hester often uses clichés in her writing.
Clichés are overused phrases.

23. Write the participial phrase from this sentence, followed
(27, 48) by the word it modifies: Having invented a new type of
camera, my ingenious father became famous.

24. Write the intensive personal pronoun in this sentence: I
(60) think he invented the camera himself.

25. Write the superlative form of the adjective *smooth*.
(42, 43)

26. Write the four principal parts of the irregular verb *tear*.
(15, 52)

For 27 and 28, tell whether the sentence is simple or
compound. If it is compound, write the coordinating
conjunction that joins the two independent clauses.

27. Anna Louisa can serve as a United States consul in
(36, 62) Brazil, for she speaks Portuguese.

28. Shiela attended a meeting of the PTA council and gave a
(36, 62) long, complicated treasurer's report.

Diagram sentences 29 and 30.

29. Jason felt shy, so he refused to sing.
(23, 62)

30. Losing our passports slowed our progress, but we enjoyed
(19, 62) the rest of the trip.

LESSON
65

The Comma, Part 6: Nonessential Parts • *That* or *Which*

Dictation or Journal Entry

Vocabulary:
The Latin words *bene* and *bonus* mean "well" or "good."

Benevolent is an adjective meaning "good," "kind," and "generous." The *benevolent* veterinarian offered her services to any abandoned animal.

A *bonus* is something good given beyond what is due. The salesperson will receive a *bonus* for any sales beyond the quota.

A *benefactor* is a kindly helper. Mr. Jarndyce was Esther Summerfield's *benefactor* in *Bleak House*.

A *bonanza* is unexpected good luck or sudden wealth. The land proved to be a *bonanza* for its owner.

Nonessential Parts Parts of a sentence that modify other parts are sometimes essential to the meaning of the sentence and sometimes not. When a modifying word, phrase, or clause is not necessary for the meaning of a sentence, we call it **nonessential,** and we set it off with commas. (Appositives are an example of this.) **Nonessential parts** are underlined in the sentences below.

NONESSENTIAL WORD

My mother, <u>Isabel</u>, organized the library.

NONESSENTIAL PHRASE

Herman Melville idolized his father, <u>a successful merchant</u>.

NONESSENTIAL CLAUSE

Henry Melville obtained a job on the *Saint Lawrence*, <u>which was sailing for England</u>.

Essential and nonessential parts are underlined in the sentence pairs below. Notice that nonessential parts are set off by commas while essential parts are not. Compare each pair of sentences.

no commas = *essential*

commas = *nonessential*

The wonderful man <u>who repaired the car</u> is my father. (The essential clause tells *which* man.)

My dad, <u>who repaired the car</u>, is a mechanical genius. (The clause is not necessary to the meaning of the sentence; it is nonessential.)

When we write, we are careful to use commas to indicate exactly what we mean. As readers, we use the commas to understand the writer's meaning. Compare each pair of sentences.

Our dog <u>Jake</u> likes to swim. (The lack of commas makes the clause essential, and indicates that the writer has more than one dog.)

Our dog, <u>Jake</u>, likes to swim. (The commas make the clause nonessential, and indicate that the writer has only one dog, whose name is Jake.)

I envy my brother <u>who lives at the lake</u>. (The lack of a comma indicates that the writer has more than one brother. The clause provides essential information: *which brother.*)

He admires his father, <u>who picks up litter by the roadside every day</u>. (The comma is necessary because the clause is nonessential. We need not be told *which father.*)

Example 1 Tell whether each underlined expression is essential or nonessential.

(a) The letter <u>that is on the table</u> is addressed to me.

(b) The letter, <u>which I received today</u>, is addressed to me.

Solution (a) The lack of commas indicates that his clause is **essential.** It tells *which* letter. There may have been other letters.

(b) The commas indicate that this clause is **nonessential.** It adds information, but it is not necessary for the meaning of the sentence.

That or Which In adjective clauses, the use of *that* or *which* depends on whether the clause is essential or nonessential. We use *that* for essential clauses. We use *which* for nonessential clauses, and we set them off with commas.

ESSENTIAL CLAUSE

A book **that** I consider an American masterpiece is *Moby Dick*.

NONESSENTIAL CLAUSE

Moby Dick, **which** received negative reviews, was an economic failure for Melville.

ESSENTIAL CLAUSE

The bicycle **that** <u>I was riding</u> had a flat tire.

NONESSENTIAL CLAUSE

The bicycle, **which** <u>I was riding</u>, belonged to my brother.

Example 2   Choose *that* or *which* for each sentence.

(a) He wrote a book (that, which) was published after his death.

(b) *Billy Budd*, (that, which) is now a popular novel, tells about a naive young soldier on a warship.

Solution   (a) He wrote a book **that** was published after his death. (The clause is not set off by commas. Therefore, we know that it is an essential clause, so we choose *that*.)

(b) *Billy Budd*, **which** is now a popular novel, tells about a naive young soldier on a warship. (The clause is set off by commas, which indicate a nonessential clause. Therefore, we choose *which*.)

Practice   For a–e, replace each blank with the correct vocabulary word.

a. The well was a _____ with its gallons of oil rushing forth.

b. The Latin words _____ and _____ mean "well" or "good."

c. He received a _____ in addition to his salary.

d. The orphans had a _____ who provided clothing, shelter, and education.

e. The _____ boy picked up the frightened puppy and sheltered it from harm.

For f–h, tell whether the underlined expression is essential or nonessential.

f. "The Raven," <u>which is one of Poe's most familiar works</u>, is unforgettable.

g. The poet <u>who invented the detective story</u> was Edgar Allen Poe.

h. Poe, <u>who was a tormented genius</u>, wrote many melodic poems and imaginative tales.

For i–l, choose *that* or *which*.

i. The habit (that, which) destroyed his health was drinking.

j. I'll show you the picture (that, which) I painted today.

k. She showed me her house, (that, which) is seventy years old.

l. He plays the trumpet, (that, which) once belonged to his uncle.

Review set 65

Choose the correct word(s) to complete sentences 1–12.

1. In classical literature, we find many (denotations,
(61) connotations, allusions) to the Bible as well as to mythology.

2. Sympathy means sharing the (money, work, feelings) of
(62) another person.

3. (Antipathy, Apathy, Empathy) is hatred.
(62)

4. Diction is a writer's choice of (subject, characters, words).
(63)

5. (Profane, Vulgar, Colloquial) diction refers to ordinary, or
(63) familiar, conversation.

6. Mac and Moe have disguised (theirselves, themselves) by
(55, 60) wearing lobster costumes.

7. Kelly and (me, myself, I) recognized them immediately.
(51, 53)

8. Little John and (them, they) pray that Robin Hood will
(51, 53) survive.

9. Robin Hood, (who, whom, which) cares for the poor,
(64, 65) needs help.

10. Had Little John (know, knew, known) about the danger?
(15, 52)

11. The neighbors detest (him, his) tap dancing on the roof at
(28, 56) midnight.

12. This clause is (dependent, independent): although he
(24, 57) appeared invincible

Rewrite 13 and 14, adding periods, commas, and capital letters as needed.

13. molly pitcher who carried pitchers of water to thirsty
(5, 65) soldiers is a famous heroine of the american revolution

14. the pennsylvania legislature gave molly a pension for she
(5, 62) had bravely served her country

15. Tell whether the following is a complete sentence,
(1, 3) sentence fragment, or run-on sentence: Under the weeping willow tree beside the creek running through Mr. McGregor's farm.

16. Write the nominative case, first person, plural personal
(51, 53) pronoun.

17. For sentences a and b, write the verb phrase and label it
(4, 22) action or linking.
    (a) Robin Hood felt weak.
    (b) He felt raindrops pelting his face.

18. Write the pronoun from this sentence and name its case
(49, 53) and its antecedent: Young Augustina carried food to the Spanish soldiers every afternoon as they fought the French.

19. For a–c, write the plural of each noun.
(12, 13) (a) James   (b) Ortiz   (c) Jerry

20. Write the dependent clause from this sentence and circle
(24, 57) the subordinating conjunction: Since it had rained, the foliage on the hillside was luxuriant.

21. Write the correct verb form in this sentence: Luke
(18, 52) (present perfect of *throw*) out the moldy grapes and stale bread.

22. Use an appositive to make one sentence from these two
(45, 46) sentences: A cliché is a trite form of diction. The
expression "busy as a beaver" is a cliché.

23. Write the gerund phrase in this sentence and label its
(18, 19) tense present or perfect: The fun-loving bowmen enjoy
challenging each other.

24. Write the participial phrase in this sentence, followed by
(48, 59) the word it modifies: The lady carrying pitchers of water
has rallied the troops.

25. Write the comparative form of the adjective *unusual*.
(42, 43)

26. Write the four principal parts of the irregular verb *freeze*.
(15, 52)

For 27 and 28, tell whether the sentence is simple or
compound. If it is compound, write the coordinating
conjunction that joins the two independent clauses.

27. Augustina aided the Spanish soldiers, but Mary Ambree
(36, 62) helped the English troops.

28. On a hot afternoon in August, Eliza brought water and
(36, 62) fresh fruit to the marathon runners on their twenty-six
mile course.

Diagram sentences 29 and 30.

29. Each runner who finishes a marathon deserves praise.
(25, 62)

30. Andre cheered, for his wife completed the race.
(25, 62)

LESSON 66

Pronoun Usage: Appositions and Comparisons

Dictation or Journal Entry

Vocabulary:

Let us look at the literary terms *analogy, context, empathy, farce,* and *irony.*

An *analogy* is a comparison of two or more objects. If we compare a heart to a pump, we make an *analogy.*

The *context* of a word or phrase refers to the words around it. The Biblical *context* of the phrase "an eye for an eye" gives us a fuller understanding of its meaning.

In a literary sense, *empathy* is an author's ability to feel like a character in the story and to portray these feelings. Charles Dickens showed *empathy* for the children working in factories.

A *farce* is a play with a deliberately improbable and humorous plot. *A Connecticut Yankee in King Arthur's Court* is an example of a *farce.*

Irony uses a word or phrase to mean the exact opposite of its usual meaning. I detected *irony* in the student's statement, "I've never had so much fun in my life as I had doing this oral report on lettuce!" *Irony* is also an outcome of events opposite to what might naturally have been expected. The students saw an *irony* when their English teacher wrote, "These students missed two many words on there spelling test: ..."

Written vs. Spoken Language

The traditional rule for pronouns is that a pronoun following a form of "be" must be in the nominative case, as in the examples below:

It is *I.*

Was it *they* who called?

We knew it was *she.*

When we write, we should follow this rule. When we are speaking, however, we tend to be less formal. Our ear tells us that in casual conversation, "It is I" sounds stiff. Instead, we are more likely to say:

It is *me.*

Was it *them* who called?

We knew it was *her.*

Remember that this relaxed pronoun usage is acceptable in casual conversation, but would be unacceptable in formal speech or any form of writing.

Now we will discuss two more areas that often cause trouble in pronoun usage.

Appositions   We remember than an appositive renames a person or thing. An **apposition** can be a pronoun used to rename a noun for emphasis.

>   Only one driver, *you*, will be ticketed for illegal parking.

>   The two teams, *they* and *we*, will advance to the finals.

The apposition must be in the same case form as the noun it renames. Consider the examples below.

>   SUBJECT:
>   *We* (NOT *us*) patriotic Americans fly our flags.

>   OBJECT:
>   The train dropped *us* (NOT *we*) travelers off at the main depot.

>   SUBJECT:
>   Both voters, Edgar and *she* (NOT *her*), decided to change the current policy.

Example 1   Choose the correct apposition for this sentence:

>   The two flight attendants, Phyllis and (he, him), tried to serve the passengers despite the turbulence.

Solution   The apposition "Phyllis and he" renames "attendants," which is the sentence subject, so we use the nominative case pronoun:

>   The two flight attendants, Phyllis and **he**, tried to serve the passengers despite the turbulence.

Comparisons   In comparison sentences, a verb is sometimes omitted, often following the words *than* or *as*.

>   My friend works harder than *I*. ("do" is omitted)

>   We tap dance as well as *they*. ("do" is omitted)

Notice that the pronouns in the sentences above are in the nominative case because they are used as subjects of clauses whose verbs are understood (not stated).

The pronoun used in a comparison is important because it can change the meaning of the sentence:

>   José loves pizza as much as *she*. ("does" is omitted)
>   [MEANING: José loves pizza as much as she does.]

>   José loves pizza as much as *her*. ("he loves" is omitted)
>   [MEANING: José loves pizza as much as he loves her.]

Example 2 Choose the correct pronoun for the following sentences.

(a) This group writes better than (*they, them*).

(b) I speak Spanish as well as (*she, her*).

Solution (a) This group writes better than **they.** ("do" is omitted)

(b) I speak Spanish as well as **she.** ("does" is omitted)

Practice Choose the correct pronoun for sentences a–e.

a. (We, Us) students memorized Walt Whitman's poem "O Captain! My Captain!"

Think: ___?___ | ___memorized___

b. It is okay with (we, us) football fanatics if you bring your friends to the game.

Think: \with ?___

c. The coach gave (we, us) players the information we needed.

Think: ___teacher___ | ___gave___ | ___?___

d. Kyle is better at playing drums than (I, me). ["am" omitted]

e. They bake bread as often as (*we, us*). ["do" omitted]

For f–i, replace each blank with the correct vocabulary word.

f. Depicting in words the glistening tears and quivering lip of a disappointed child is an author's way of showing _____.

g. The author manufactured an unbelievable plot for his hilarious new _____.

h. The poet made an _____ between the lazy man and a dog.

i. Be certain to read the entire article so that you will not be accused of taking something out of _____.

j. A cold, hungry boy exclaiming, "I've never felt more comfortable in my life!" uses _____ to emphasize his condition.

More Practice   Choose the correct pronoun for each sentence.

1. Charlie had more patience than (she, her). ["did" omitted]

2. (We, Us) Americans enjoy democracy.

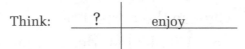

Think: ____?____ | ____enjoy____

3. The guide showed (we, us) travelers the ancient ruins.

Think: __guide__ | __showed__ | _?_

4. Isael and (her, she) will paint the pictures.

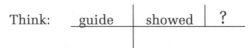

Think: ____?____ | __will paint__

5. We saw two old friends, Jaime and (he, him).

Think: __We__ | __saw__ | _?_

6. Rondo walked farther than (she, her). ["did" omitted]

7. Letha works later than (he, him). ["does" omitted]

8. I write letters as frequently as (they, them). ["do" omitted]

9. (We, Us) girls ate lunch together.

Think: ____?____ | __ate__

10. The teacher's new joke made (we, us) students laugh.

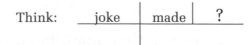

Think: __joke__ | __made__ | _?_

Review set 66   Choose the best word to complete sentences 1–14.

1. (Antipathy, Apathy, Empathy) is the ability to imagine
(62)   yourself in another person's situation.

2. The angry scowl on Mom's face showed her (antipathy,
(62)   apathy) toward soap operas.

3. (Formal, Slang, Trite) diction is used by a certain group of
(63) people when talking to each other.

4. The Greek word *biblion* means (passion, form,
(64) book).

5. An (allegory, allusion, exaggeration) is a reference to a
(58, 61) well-known person, place, or thing.

6. We use commas to set off (essential, nonessential) parts
(65) of a sentence.

7. Davy and (him, himself, he) roam the Texas prairies.
(51, 53)

8. The message is for Sam Houston, (who, whom) you
(64, 65) know.

9. Is Sam taller than (him, he)?
(53, 66)

10. (We, Us) Texans often endure hot weather.
(53, 66)

11. The man (who, which, whom) tells the *Davy Crockett*
(64, 65) *Legends* is an old hunter.

12. (Who, Whom) is an objective case pronoun.
(51, 54)

13. My parents appreciate (me, my) washing the car.
(58)

14. The pronoun *who* is in the (nominative, objective) case.
(53, 54)

Rewrite 15 and 16, adding periods, commas, and capital
letters and making necessary changes to abbreviations for
formal writing.

15. father serra a franciscan priest actively assisted the
(35, 45) indigenous population in the southwest

16. on mon aug fifth col brett jones will meet davy crockett at
(5, 35) the u s army base in saint louis missouri

17. Write the possessive case, third person, plural personal
(55, 56) pronoun.

18. Write the verb phrase in this sentence and label it
(25, 31) transitive or intransitive: Frightened by a thunderstorm,
the stallion galloped across the plain without stopping.

19. Write each prepositional phrase in this sentence and star
(32, 33) the object of each preposition: Because of his fame, twenty years after his death, people continued to tell stories about Davy.

20. For a–c, write the plural of each noun.
(12, 13) (a) leaf (b) branch (c) berry

21. Write the dependent clause from this sentence and circle
(24, 57) the subordinating conjunction: Although he sometimes rides wild horses, Davy usually rides Death Hug, a bear.

22. Write the correct verb form in this sentence: Davy (past
(18, 52) perfect of *speak*) to Sam before lunch.

23. Unscramble these words to make an interrogative
(1, 3) sentence: Davy does a buffalo tame

24. Write the participial phrase in this sentence, followed by
(48, 59) the word it modifies: The grizzly bear catching trout weighs over four hundred pounds.

25. Write the superlative form of the adjective *good*.
(42, 43)

26. Write the four principal parts of the verb *drop*.
(6, 15)

27. Tell whether the underlined expression in this sentence
(46, 65) is essential or nonessential: My cat <u>Muff</u> plays the piano.

Diagram sentences 28–30.

28. Chris likes to skate, but Tom prefers to hike.
(23, 25)

29. Flying kites is Dan's new hobby.
(19, 39)

30. The teacher reading Shakespeare is she.
(39, 48)

LESSON
67

Interrogative Pronouns

> **Dictation or Journal Entry**
>
> **Vocabulary:**
> The Greek word *metron* means "measure" and appears in English and other languages as *meter.*
>
> A *barometer* is a device that measures atmospheric pressure. The *barometer* indicated low atmospheric pressure and possible rain.
>
> An *altimeter* is a device that measures an aircraft's altitude above sea level. The altimeter indicated that the plane was flying at about 33,000 feet.
>
> A *thermometer* measures temperature. The hot, sunny day registered 100 degrees Fahrenheit on the *thermometer.*
>
> A *centimeter* is one-hundredth of a meter, a measurement of length. The huge insect was 10 *centimeters* long.

When a relative pronoun introduces a question, it is called an **interrogative pronoun.** *Who, whom, whose, what, that, which, whoever, whichever,* and *whatever* are interrogative pronouns.

> *Who* is Walt Whitman?
>
> *What* did he write?
>
> *Which* is your favorite?
>
> *Whom* are you meeting?
>
> *Whoever* would memorize that?

A sentence doesn't have to end with a question mark in order to contain an interrogative pronoun. Sometimes an interrogative pronoun introduces a question that is contained inside a declarative sentence:

> She asked *who* was on the phone.
>
> Clotilda wondered *what* they wanted.
>
> Zeke didn't know *which* would taste best.

Example 1   Write each interrogative pronoun that you find in each sentence.

(a) I couldn't imagine what had happened.

(b) Who is the suspect?

(c) The detective decided which was pertinent.

(d) Whose are these footprints?

Solution   (a) **what**   (b) **who**   (c) **which**   (d) **whose**

Who* or *Whom   In order to decide whether we should use *who* or *whom*, we must determine what part the interrogative pronoun plays in the sentence. If it functions as a subject or predicate nominative, we use *who*.

Who frightened Ebenezer Scrooge? (subject)

$$\underline{\quad\textit{Who}\mid\text{frightened}\quad}$$

Who gave the Cratchetts a turkey? (subject)

$$\underline{\quad\textit{Who}\mid\quad\text{gave}\quad}$$

The crippled boy is *who*? (predicate nominative)

$$\underline{\quad\text{boy}\mid\text{is}\setminus\textit{who}\quad}$$

If the interrogative pronoun is an object (direct object, indirect object, object of a preposition), we use *whom*.

Whom did Marley visit? (direct object)

$$\underline{\quad\text{Marley}\mid\text{did visit}\mid\textit{Whom}\quad}$$

To *whom* did Fanny return the engagement ring? (object of a preposition)

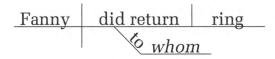

To check to see that we have used *who* or *whom* correctly, we can turn the questions above into statements and substitute *he/she* for *who*, and *him/her* for *whom*:

RIGHT: Marley visited *him/her*.
WRONG: Marley visited *he/she*.

RIGHT: Fanny returned the ring to *him*.
WRONG: Fanny returned the ring to *he*.

Errors to Avoid   Do not confuse *whose* and *who's*. *Whose* is a possessive or interrogative pronoun. *Who's* is a contraction for "who is." Remember, possessive pronouns do not have apostrophes.

Who's the poet? (Who is the poet?)

Whose ballad is that?

Example 2 Choose the correct interrogative pronoun for each sentence.

(a) (Who, Whom) stole Frosty the Snowman's hat?

(b) (Who, Whom) did you suspect?

(c) To (who, whom) was he singing?

(d) This hat belongs to Frosty, but (who's, whose) is that?

Solution (a) The pronoun is used as the subject, so we choose *who.*

Who stole Frosty the Snowman's hat?

(b) The pronoun is used as an object, so we choose *whom.*

Whom did you suspect?

$$\underline{\text{you}} \mid \text{did suspect} \mid \underline{\text{Whom}}$$

To check to see that we have used *who* or *whom* correctly, we change the question into a statement, substituting *he* or *she* for *who* and *him* or *her* for *whom.*

RIGHT: You <u>did suspect</u> *him.*
WRONG: You <u>did suspect</u> *he* or *she.*

(c) The pronoun is used as an object of a preposition, so we choose *whom.*

To **whom** was he singing?

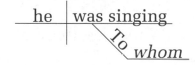

(d) *Who's* is a contraction for "who is." We choose *whose* because it is the interrogative pronoun.

This hat belongs to Frosty, but **whose** is that?

Adjective or Pronoun? When *which, whose,* and *what* come before nouns, they are adjectives. When *which, whose,* and *what* stand alone, they are interrogative pronouns.

ADJECTIVE: *Which* shoe goes on the right foot?
PRONOUN: *Which* goes on the right foot?

ADJECTIVE: *What* dish broke?
PRONOUN: *What* broke?

ADJECTIVE: *Whose* bicycle is this?
PRONOUN: *Whose* is this?

Example 3   Tell whether the italicized word in each sentence is an adjective or an interrogative pronoun.

(a) I wonder *whose* notebook this is.

(b) *What* made that loud noise?

(c) *What* kind of sandwich would you like?

(d) *Which* of the two is the better response?

Solution   (a) *Whose* comes before the noun *notebook*, so it is an **adjective.**

(b) *What* stands alone, so it is an **interrogative pronoun.**

(c) *What* precedes the abstract noun *kind*, so it is an **adjective.**

(d) *Which* stands alone. It is an **interrogative pronoun.**

Practice   For a–c, write the interrogative pronoun from each sentence.

a. Do you know what Walt Whitman did during the American Civil War?

b. Which of the duties did he perform?

c. Whose are those hiking boots?

For d–f, choose the correct interrogative pronoun for each sentence.

d. With (who, whom) will you share all this secret information?

e. (Who's, Whose) is that stunning black stallion?

f. (Who, Whom) nursed injured soldiers during the Civil War?

For g and h, tell whether the italicized word is an adjective or an interrogative pronoun.

g. *What* do you know about Walt Whitman?

    h. *Which* poet was the foremost spokesperson of the American way of life?

    For i–l, replace each blank with the correct vocabulary word.

    i. How many _____ are there on a meter stick?

    j. The Greek word for measure is _____.

    k. The nurse placed a _____ under Bob's tongue to determine if he had a fever.

    l. The pilot reads his _____ to be sure he is flying at the right altitude.

    m. The _____ indicated that the air pressure was rising and that warmer weather was approaching.

More Practice

Choose the correct word to complete each sentence.

  1. (Who's, Whose) singing that monotonous song?

  2. (Who's, Whose) voice do I hear?

  3. (Who, Whom) cleaned the house? $\underline{\quad ? \quad | \quad \text{cleaned}\quad}$

  4. To (who, whom) does that barking dog belong?

                    $\diagdown_{To}\ \underline{\ ?\ }$

  5. (Who, Whom) are you paging? $\underline{\ \text{you}\ } | \underline{\ \text{are paging}\ } | \underline{\ ?\ }$

  6. (Who's, Whose) the barefoot runner wearing red?

  7. (Who's, Whose) half-eaten sandwich is that?

  8. To (who, whom) would you like to give this valuable gift?

                    $\diagdown_{To}\ \underline{\ ?\ }$

  9. (Who, Whom) will wash the car? $\underline{\ \ ?\ \ } | \underline{\ \text{will wash}\ }$

10. (Who, Whom) have you chosen for your best friend?

         $\underline{\ \text{you}\ } | \underline{\ \text{have chosen}\ } | \underline{\ ?\ }$

Review set 67

Choose the best word to complete sentences 1–14.

  1. (Borne, Born) means given birth.
    (59)

  2. (Sympathy, Apathy, Empathy) is the absence of feeling; indifference.
    (62)

3. (Profane, Trite, Slang) diction is irreverent or obscene.
₍₆₃₎

4. A biblioclast destroys (bridges, people, books).
₍₆₄₎

5. The Latin words *bene* and *bonus* mean (alone, around, good).
₍₆₅₎

6. Quan swims faster than (I, me).
₍₆₆₎

7. Davy promised Ben and (me, myself, I) a bear steak.
₍₅₄₎

8. We will write about Davy Crockett, (who, whom) you know.
_(64, 67)

9. (We, Us) Californians are accustomed to sunshine.
_(53, 66)

10. (Who's, Whose) book is this?
₍₆₇₎

11. Miss Fit and (her, herself, she) wore matching exercise outfits.
_(51, 53)

12. The moose, (which, that) had appeared out of nowhere, stared into our headlights.
_(64, 65)

13. His friends are tired of (him, his) complaining.
_(56, 58)

14. The pronoun *whom* is in the (nominative, objective) case.
_(54, 64)

Rewrite 15 and 16, adding periods, commas, and capital letters and making necessary changes to abbreviations for formal writing.

15. dear mr crockett
_(29, 50)   unfortunately your bear growled tues morning so my hen refused to lay eggs

if this continues i will take you to court

your neighbor

mr grump

16. death hug davy crockett's pet bear weighs one hundred fifty lbs and stands six ft tall
_(11, 35)

17. Write the objective case, first person, singular personal pronoun.
_(51, 54)

18. Tell whether the underlined expression in this sentence is essential or nonessential: We've had our Saint Bernard, <u>Bach</u>, for ten years.
₍₆₅₎

19. Write the verb phrase from this sentence and label it
(4, 22) action or linking: Does Ben Hardin's story about the hurricane sound fictional to you?

20. For a and b, write the plural of each noun.
(12, 13) (a) Davy   (b) Commander in Chief

21. Write the dependent clause from this sentence and circle
(24, 57) the subordinating conjunction: Ben Hardin helped the frontiersmen since he was a congressman.

22. Write the correct verb form in this sentence: During the
(21, 52) storm, the wind (past progressive of *blow*) over two hundred miles per hour.

23. Tell whether the following is a phrase or a clause: when
(24, 57) he crossed the Cannon Ball River

24. Write the gerund phrase from this sentence: Ben Hardin
(19) and he enjoyed hunting buffalo, deer, and elk.

25. Write the comparative form of the adjective *bad*.
(42, 43)

26. Write the four principal parts of the irregular verb *shrink*.
(15, 52)

27. Write the participial phrase in this sentence, followed by
(27, 48) the word it modifies: Bragging about the hurricane, Ben Hardin captured everyone's attention.

Diagram sentences 28–30.

28. Davy built a boat out of an ancient gum tree.
(25, 32)

29. Hunting was strenuous.
(19, 39)

30. The teacher who taught me to read has retired.
(4, 64)

LESSON
68

Quotation Marks, Part 1

Direct Quotation

A **direct quotation** gives a speaker's exact words. To indicate a direct quotation, we enclose the speaker's words in quotation marks.

> The historian said, "Eli Whitney's cotton gin made cotton the most profitable crop in the South."

> "This machine separated the seeds from the fibers of the cotton plant," he continued.

Notice that in each of the examples above, the punctuation mark following the direct quotation appears **inside** the quotation marks.

Example 1

Place quotation marks where they are needed in the sentence below.

> Well, since inventors are copying my cotton gin, I'll invent something else! Eli Whitney declared.

Solution

We place quotation marks before and after Eli Whitney's words.

> **"Well, since inventors are copying my cotton gin, I'll invent something else!" Eli Whitney declared.**

Direct Quotation with Explanatory Note

Sometimes a direct quotation is interrupted by an **explanatory note** such as *he said, she replied, the teacher explained,* etc. We enclose in quotation marks only the direct quotation parts, not the explanatory note. Notice that both parts of the direct quotation are enclosed in quotation marks.

> "Let's go blaze a trail," suggested the pioneer, "so that others may follow us west."

> "You may walk," said the elderly farmer, "but I will ride in the wagon."

Example 2 Place quotation marks where they are needed in the sentence below.

> Although James Watt is often given credit for inventing the steam engine, Professor Snodgrass explained, Thomas Savery and Thomas Newcomen were the actual inventors.

Solution We place quotation marks around both parts of the direct quotation, but we do not enclose the explanatory note in quotation marks.

> **"Although James Watt is often given credit for inventing the steam engine," Professor Snodgrass explained, "Thomas Savery and Thomas Newcomen were the actual inventors."**

Indirect Quotations An **indirect quotation** tells about what someone said, but it does not give the speaker's exact words. We do not use quotation marks with indirect quotations.

> Daniel Boone told his family that he had made a trail through Cumberland Gap.

> He said the trail was not wide enough for a wagon.

Example 3 Add quotation marks as needed to the sentence below.

> Professor Snodgrass explained that Thomas Savery and Thomas Newcomen actually invented the steam engine.

Solution **No quotations marks** are necessary, because this is not a direct quotation. It is an **indirect quotation.**

Practice For a–d, rewrite correctly each sentence that needs quotation marks. If the sentence does not need quotation marks, write "none."

a. The docent shared that Daniel Webster was a notable American statesman, orator, and lawyer.

   b. One of the visitors asked if Daniel Webster belonged to the Federalist party.

   c. Yes, the docent replied, and Daniel Webster defended the Federalists' principles eloquently.

   d. In addition, said the guide, Daniel Webster delivered the famous Plymouth and Bunker Hill speeches.

For e–h, replace each blank with the correct computer term.

   e. Lillian bought new _____ for her computer in order to study foreign languages.

   f. Richard stores all his tax information on a computer _____.

   g. The school developed a computer lab consisting of a _____ of thirty-six computers and four printers.

   h. Unfortunately, the computer _____ was damaged when it fell out of the truck.

More Practice   See Master Worksheets.

Review set 68

Choose the best word to complete sentences 1–10.

1. A (connotation, denotation) of the word "steel" is
(61) strength and stability.

2. Yin understood her husband's grief, for she had
(62) (antipathy, apathy, empathy).

3. A benevolent person is (lonely, generous, selfish).
(65)

4. A bonanza is (good, bad) luck.
(65)

5. The secretary thought it was an (analogy, antipathy,
(62, 66) irony) that the math teacher frequently miscounted the number of students in class.

6. We have more homework than (them, they).
(53, 66)

7. Grandpa warned Alex and (me, myself, I) about Davy's
(54, 66) pet alligator.

8. The lady (who, whom) lives next door raises llamas.
(64)

9. (We, Us) students deserve a vacation.
(53, 66)

10. This address is not (their's, theirs).
(55, 56)

11. The book (which, that) I need is in my backpack.
(64, 66)

12. For (who, whom) are you waiting?
(54, 67)

13. Ms. Snit was annoyed with (me, my) giggling during her
(58) ludicrous lecture on beneficial eggplant enzymes.

14. We use the relative pronoun (which, that) for non-
*(64, 65)*essential clauses, and we set them off with commas.

Rewrite 15 and 16, adding periods, commas, and capital letters as needed.

15. dear mr grump
(35, 50)   bears growl and roosters crow
          if you will silence your rooster i will silence my bear
                  your neighbor
                  davy crockett

16. i davy crockett's pets
(20, 35)   a the bear
          b the alligator
          c the cougar

17. Write the personal pronoun that is second person.
(51, 55)

18. Write the four common pairs of correlative conjunctions.
(38)

19. Write the verb phrase from this sentence and label it
(4, 22) action or linking: Speaking in a loud voice, Professor Bullwink might prove his point.

20. Tell whether the underlined expression in this sentence
*(64, 65)*is essential or nonessential: The hound <u>that lives next door</u> howled all night.

21. Write the dependent clause from this sentence and circle
*(24, 57)*the subordinating conjunction: Although most of Davy Crockett's legends are wild exaggerations, some details might be true.

22. Write the correct verb form in this sentence:
[18, 52] Unfortunately, his baseball cap (past perfect of *shrink*) so
that he could no longer wear it.

23. Tell whether the following is a phrase or a clause: to
[24, 57] accurately predict changes in the weather

24. Rewrite the following direct quotation, adding periods,
[20, 68] commas, capital letters, and quotation marks as needed:
you can lead a horse to water said grandma but you can't
make it drink

25. Write the comparative form of the adjective *euphonic.*
[42, 43]

26. Write the four principal parts of the irregular verb *wear.*
[15, 52]

27. Write the participial phrase in this sentence, followed by
[27, 48] the word it modifies: Using his creativity, Davy taught all
his animals to dance the polka.

Diagram sentences 28–30.

28. I want to walk, but she prefers to drive.
[25, 62]

29. People in Kentucky and Tennessee spread stories about
[25, 33] Davy Crockett.

30. Whistling familiar tunes, he teaches animals to dance.
[23, 25]

LESSON 69

Quotation Marks, Part 2

Dictation or Journal Entry

Vocabulary: —
The Greek word *chroma,* which means "color," is seen in English as
-chrome and *chromo-*

A *chromosome* is a tiny cell part that carries the genetic material that
determines sex, size, color, and many other characteristics. One type of
chromosome carries the genes for blue eyes.

Monochrome means "having one color." The bleak gray sky was
monochrome.

Polychrome means "having many colors." A rainbow is *polychrome.*

Speaker Changes

A set of quotation marks can contain the words of only one speaker. When the speaker changes, we use a new set of quotation marks. Also, when writing conversation, we start a new paragraph every time the speaker changes.

Notice how quotation marks are used with changing speakers in this excerpt from "The Bull and the Bullfrog."

"Father, I saw the most gigantic animal in the world," said the young bullfrog.

"Now, son," his father replied, "everyone knows that I'm the biggest animal in this pond. Just watch me."

Example 1

Rewrite the following conversation from "The Bull and the Bullfrog," inserting quotation marks as needed.

Was that animal bigger than this? his father asked.
Much bigger than that, said his son.
How about now? asked the father, puffing himself even bigger.
I'm afraid he was much bigger still, said the son.

Solution

We know that a new paragraph means that the speaker has changed. We insert quotation marks around the actual words of each speaker.

"Was that animal bigger than this?" his father asked.
"Much bigger than that," said his son.
"How about now?" asked the father, puffing himself even bigger.
"I'm afraid he was much bigger still," said the son.

Titles   Titles of short literary words are enclosed in quotation marks. This includes short stories, parts of books (chapters, lessons, sections, etc.), essays and sermons, one-act plays, newspaper and magazine articles, and short poems. We also enclose in quotation marks the titles of songs.

> The book of *Aesop's Fables* includes short tales such as "The Fox and the Grapes," "The Gnat and the Bull," and the "Bull and the Bullfrog."
>
> Marge Piercy is the author of the poem "Barbie Doll."
>
> "How Does a Poet Put Bread on the Table" is the title of an essay from *What is Found There: Notebooks on Poetry and Politics.*

We do not use quotation marks for larger literary works such as books, plays, movies, or operas. Instead, these are italicized or underlined (<u>Aesop's Fables</u>, *Evita*).

Example 2   Rewrite the sentences below, inserting quotation marks where they are needed.

(a) We sing The Star-Spangled Banner at sporting events.

(b) The sermon this week was Stretch your Arm no Farther than your Sleeve Will Reach.

(c) Have you read the last chapter, Happily Ever After?

Solution   (a) We place quotation marks around "The Star-Spangled Banner" because it is a song title. We sing "The Star-Spangled Banner" at sporting events.

(b) We enclose "Stretch your Arm no Farther than your Sleeve Will Reach" in quotation marks because it is the title of a sermon. The sermon this week was "Stretch your Arm no Farther than your Sleeve Will Reach."

(c) We enclose the chapter title, "Literary Tradition as Context," in quotation marks. Have you read the last chapter, "Happily Ever After"?

Practice   For a–d, replace each blank with the correct vocabulary word.

a. The Greek word meaning color is _____.

b. The _____ sketch featured just the strokes of charcoal.

c. Many colors contributed to the _____ painting.

d. Biologists study the _____ to determine how genes combine to form different eye colors, hair colors, and skin colors.

e. Rewrite this dialog from "The Bull and the Bullfrog," inserting quotation marks where they are needed.

> Well, said the father bullfrog, as he sucked in as much air as he could, he couldn't have been much bigger than this.
> But he really was much bigger than that, replied the young bullfrog.
> Okay son, watch me now. He couldn't possibly have been bigger than this.

Rewrite sentences f–h, inserting quotation marks as needed.

f. In The Bull and the Bullfrog, the old bullfrog puffed himself up so big that he burst into tiny pieces!

g. Have you heard the song Climb Every Mountain ?

h. Mark Twain wrote an essay entitled Fennimore Cooper's Literary Offenses.

More Practice See Master Worksheets.

Review set 69 Choose the best word(s) to complete sentences 1–12.

1. It is an (allegory, irony, allusion) that someone stole the
(61, 66) bank robber's getaway car.

2. The Greek word (*biblion, mania, metron*) means measure.
(64, 67)

3. A bibliophile loves and collects (stamps, rocks, books).
(49, 64)

4. An (empathy, irony, analogy) compares two or more
(62, 66) things.

5. The poet made a(n) (analogy, farce, antipathy) between
(62, 66) his brother's hair and a mop.

6. James has more artistic talent than (I, me).
(53, 66)

7. Fernando and (me, myself, I) plan to run on the horse
(51, 53) trail today.

8. Of the three wild animals, the hyena is the (faster,
(42, 43) fastest).

9. The company might award a bonus to (we, us) cashiers.
(54, 66)

10. That milk shake is (yours, your's).
(56, 66)

11. The relative pronoun (who, which, that) may refer to
(64, 65) people, animals, or things.

12. The relative pronoun (who, which) may refer to animals
(64, 65) or things.

13. My brother ignores (me, my) practicing the tuba.
(56, 58)

14. The drama, (which, that) involved two porcupines, kept
(64, 65) all the children's attention.

15. The pronoun (who, whom) is in the nominative case.
(53, 64)

16. Rewrite the following, adding periods, commas, and
(35, 50) capital letters as needed and making necessary changes to
abbreviations for formal writing:

dear mr crockett

on fri sept 24 1834 judge snikity will be in town so
we can settle our dispute

meet me at the courthouse at ten am sharp or risk a
jail sentence

your neighbor

mr grump

17. Write the nominative case, first person, singular personal
(51, 53) pronoun.

18. Use an appositive to make one sentence from these two
(45, 46) sentences: Don was a United States citizen. Don served
twelve years as a consul in Panama.

19. Write the verb phrase from this sentence and label it
(25, 31) transitive or intransitive: Had the entire earth frozen?

20. From this sentence, write the dependent clause, circling
(24, 57) the subordinating conjunction: As cold temperatures
ravaged the earth, Davy sought a solution.

21. For a and b, write the plural of each noun.
(12, 13) (a) stitch   (b) cherry

22. Tell whether the underlined expression in this sentence
(64, 65) is essential or nonessential: The parrots, <u>which visit my
macadamia nut tree each fall</u>, are driving the crows away
from this area.

23. Tell whether the following is a phrase or a clause: after
(24, 57) trying to thaw the frozen pipes

24. Rewrite the following, adding periods, commas, capital
(11, 69) letters, and quotation marks as needed: davy crockett
sang a song called fire in the mountain

25. Write the superlative form of the adjective *bad.*
(42, 43)

26. Write the four principal parts of the verb *grin.*
(6, 15)

27. Write the participial phrase from this sentence, followed
(27, 48) by the word it modifies: I waved to several frontiersmen
roping steer.

Diagram sentences 28–30.

28. Walking is good exercise, but running is better exercise.
(19, 62)

29. He likes my cooking vegetables.
(19, 66)

30. Does drinking soda destroy the enamel on our teeth?
(19, 25)

LESSON 70

Demonstrative Pronouns

Dictation or Journal Entry

Vocabulary:

Drama, epithet, flashback, genre, and *gothic novel* are literary terms.

Drama is the category of literature known as plays. William Shakespeare wrote *drama.*

An *epithet* is a term used to characterize a person or thing in either a flattering or derogatory manner. "Honest Abe" was an *epithet* of Abraham Lincoln.

A *flashback* is the narrative technique of going backward in time, allowing the author to cover a greater time span and give important background details in a story. Esther Summerfield's *flashbacks* to her childhood helped the reader to understand her insecurities as a young adult.

A *genre* is a form or type of literature. Drama is one *genre,* and poetry is another.

A *gothic novel* contains mysterious, scary elements. The setting of this *gothic novel* is an old haunted castle.

Pointers   *This, that, these,* and *those* are **demonstrative pronouns.** Some people call them "pointing pronouns" because they seem to point out the person or thing being referred to, distinguishing it from others.

> *This* is a prolific writer.

> *That* is H.G. Wells.

> *These* are samples of his work.

> *Those* have already been categorized.

A demonstrative pronoun must agree in number with its antecedent (the noun that it points out).

SINGULAR:	*This* is a classic.
PLURAL:	*These* are classics.
SINGULAR:	*That* is a time machine.
PLURAL:	*Those* are time machines.

This, These   We use *this* and *these* to point out persons or things that are nearby in space, time, or awareness.

> *This* is a springer spaniel.

> *These* are border collies.

That, Those   We use *that* and *those* to point out persons or things that are farther away.

That is a Labrador retriever.

Those are dachshunds.

Errors to Avoid   We never add "here" or "there" to a demonstrative pronoun.

NO: This *here* is H.G. Wells's novel.
YES: This is H.G. Wells's novel.

NO: That *there* combines science and politics.
YES: That combines science and politics.

We do not use "them" in place of "these" or "those."

NO: *Them* taste delicious.
YES: *These* taste delicious.

NO: *Them* things make me laugh.
YES: *Those* things make me laugh.

Adjective or Pronoun   The demonstrative pronouns *this*, *that*, *these*, and *those* also function as demonstrative adjectives.

It is easy to tell the difference. If they stand alone, they are demonstrative pronouns. If they come before a noun, they are demonstrative adjectives.

These are not satisfactory. (pronoun)

These books are not satisfactory. (adjective)

The librarian recommended *this*. (pronoun)

The librarian recommended *this* book. (adjective)

Example   Choose the correct demonstrative pronoun for each sentence, and write the noun that it points to.

(a) (This here, This) is an author whose novels were made into motion pictures.

(b) Is (that, those) the reason people thought Earth was being invaded by Martians?

(c) (This, These) are the fantasies that launched the science fiction genre.

(d) (Them, Those) are novels devoted to space travel.

Solution   (a) **This author.** We do not add "here" to demonstrative pronouns.

(b) **that reason.** A demonstrative pronoun must agree in number with its antecedent.

(c) **These fantasies**

(d) **Those novels**

Practice   For a–e, replace each blank with the correct vocabulary word.

a. Short stories, poems, and plays are different _____ of literature.

b. *Women in White*, a _____ _____, has a plot full of mystery and ghosts.

c. "Stonewall" Jackson, a Confederate general during the Civil War, acquired his _____ because of his unflinching courage.

d. With the use of _____, the protagonist's motivation began to make sense.

e. A musical, such as *My Fair Lady*, is often performed live as a _____.

For f–k, choose the correct demonstrative pronoun, and write the noun it points to.

f. (This, These) is one of the largest and best examples of early English architecture.

g. (That, Those) are the monarchs who have been crowned in Westminster Abbey.

h. (This, These) is the place where poets such as Geoffrey Chaucer, Edmund Spenser, and Robert Browning are buried.

i. (These, That) are the statesmen who are interred in the Abbey.

j. (This, This here) tomb holds the "Unknown Warrior" of World War I.

k. Replace the blank with the correct word. A demonstrative pronoun is sometimes called a _____ _____ pronoun.

Review set 70   Choose the best word to complete sentences 1–14.

1. The Greek word *metron* means (large, passion, measure).
(67)

2. An altimeter (raises, measures, lowers) an aircraft's altitude.
(67)

3. (Network, Database, Hardware) refers to the physical parts of a computer, such as the hard drive and keyboard.
(68)

4. A kind, generous person is (benevolent, misogynic, aphonic).
(7, 65)

5. A (database, monitor) is an organized collection of information.
(68)

6. Lorenzo and (me, myself, I) fell into the mud.
(51, 54)

7. Dad laughed harder than (me, I).
(53, 66)

8. Those muddy shoes are (our's, ours).
(56, 66)

9. Of the two frontiersmen, Davy was the (braver, bravest).
(42, 43)

10. The tuba player gave free concert tickets to (we, us) band members.
(51, 54)

11. Andrew Burnett, (who, which) received a shower of mud from the horse, jumped up swinging in anger.
(64, 65)

12. The horse, (that, which) galloped recklessly through the mud puddles, spewed dirt in every direction.
(64, 65)

13. The horse (which, that) covered Andrew with mud has escaped into hiding.
(64, 65)

14. Write the verb phrase from this sentence and name its tense: More than one friendship has begun as a result of a fight.
(18, 52)

15. Which sentence is more polite? Write A or B.
(54, 66)
A. Alba enjoyed talking with me and him.
B. Alba enjoyed talking with him and me.

16. Rewrite the following, adding periods, commas, and
(35, 50) capital letters as needed and making necessary changes to abbreviations for formal writing:

dear mr grump

    by fri sept 24 1834 i will no longer reside in this territory

    i am headed for the wild west and i will take my pets with me

                sincerely

                crockett

17. Write the nominative case, third person, plural personal
(53, 55) pronoun.

18. Use an appositive to make one sentence from these two
(45, 46) sentences: "Daniel Boone's Rifle" is a short story by Stewart Edward. "Daniel Boone's Rifle" tells about two young men who learn to appreciate what they have.

19. Write the verb phrase from this sentence and label it
(4, 22) action or linking: Does Mario's curiosity seem obsessive?

20. Write the dependent clause from this sentence and circle
(24, 57) the subordinating conjunction: Grandma's eyes snapped and twinkled agelessly even though she had lived a long time.

21. For a and b, write the plural of each noun.
(12, 13) (a) mother-in-law   (b) stepfather

22. Write the correct verb form in this sentence: Mark and
(15, 21) Melissa (present progressive tense of *worry*) about the test instead of studying for it.

23. Tell whether the following is a phrase or a clause: since
(24, 57) he'd stored the information on a database

24. Rewrite the following, adding periods, commas, capital
(35, 68) letters, and quotation marks as needed: i think said russell that daniel boone gave his rifle to mr burnett

25. Write the superlative form of the adjective *hilarious*.
(42, 43)

(6, 15) **26.** Write the four principal parts of the verb *empty*.

27. Write the participial phrase in this sentence, followed by
(48, 59) the word it modifies: Having read the story about Daniel
Boone, Grandma closed the book and fell asleep.

Diagram sentences 28–30.

28. Most friends dislike our nagging them.
(19, 25)

29. Printers and monitors are peripherals.
(37, 39)

30. She drove her car, but I rode a horse with no saddle.
(57, 64)

LESSON 71

Indefinite Pronouns

Dictation or Journal Entry

Vocabulary:
The Greek noun *derma* means "skin" and is commonly found as a part of many English words.

Taxidermy is the art of stuffing and mounting the skins of animals so that they look lifelike. One must study *taxidermy* to make stuffed moose look "real."

Dermatology is the branch of medicine dealing with skin and its diseases. A doctor of *dermatology* can diagnose skin cancer.

The *epidermis* is the outer, nonvascular, nonsensitive layer of skin. I scratched the *epidermis* on my elbow, and it neither hurt nor bled.

A *pachyderm* is a thick-skinned animal like an elephant, hippopotamus, or rhinoceros. What type of *pachyderm* has a long trunk?

A *melanoderm* is a person with dark pigmentation of the skin. A *melanoderm* is somewhat less likely to develop skin cancer than a fair-skinned person.

A pronoun that does not have a known antecedent is called an **indefinite pronoun.** It refers to a person or thing only generally.

Singular   Some indefinite pronouns refer to only one person or thing. They are singular and take singular verbs:

another	*anybody*	*anyone*
anything	*neither*	*either*
everybody	*everyone*	*everything*
each	*nobody*	*no one*
nothing	*other*	*one*
somebody	*someone*	*something*
much		

Everybody <u>gets</u> hungry.

Each of the experiments <u>is</u> critical.

Neither of us <u>is</u> exhibiting at the fair.

Nothing <u>is</u> going to happen.

Plural   The following indefinite pronouns refer to more than one person or thing. They take plural verbs:

several	*both*	*few*
ones	*many*	*others*

Both of them <u>want</u> to be friends.

Few <u>were</u> confident.

Many <u>are</u> predictable.

Others <u>take</u> more time.

Either Singular or Plural   Some indefinite pronouns can be singular or plural depending on their use in the sentence:

all	*any*	*most*
none	*some*	

They are plural when they refer to things that can be counted.

Most of the cookies <u>were</u> gone by noon.

They are singular when they refer to things that cannot be counted.

Most of the sugar <u>was</u> used for baking.

Example 1   Write each indefinite pronoun and tell whether it is singular or plural in the sentence.

(a) Lately, much has been said about drug abuse.

(b) I believe each must make his or her own decisions.

(c) Today, many of the students desire help with their math.

(d) Most of the food has been eaten already.

(e) All are welcome to come.

(f) None of the doors are locked.

Solution   (a) ***Much,*** **singular**   (b) ***Each,*** **singular**

(c) ***Many,*** **plural**   (d) ***Most,*** **singular**

(e) ***All,*** **plural**   (f) ***None,*** **plural** (can be counted)

Example 2   Choose the correct verb form (singular or plural) to match the indefinite pronouns in each sentence.

(a) (Is, Are) *all* of you familiar with Oscar Wilde?

(b) *Few* here (have, has) read his works.

(c) *Many* of us (realize, realizes) that he has created several genres of literary work.

(d) (Is, Are) *anything* impossible if we try hard?

Solution   (a) **Are** *all* of you familiar with Oscar Wilde?

(b) *Few* here **have** read his works.

(c) *Many* of us **realize** that he has created several genres of literary work.

(d) **Is** *anything* impossible if we try hard?

Adjective or Pronoun?   Just like demonstrative pronouns, when indefinite pronouns are placed before nouns, they function as indefinite adjectives.

> *Some* recall Roger Williams. (indefinite pronoun)

> *Some* students recall Roger Williams. (adjective)

Agreement with Antecedents   If an indefinite pronoun is the antecedent for a personal pronoun, the personal pronoun must agree in number, person, and gender with its antecedent.

> SINGULAR: *Everything* has *its* purpose.

> (antecedent) (personal pronoun)

> PLURAL: *Both* have *their* purpose.

> (antecedent) (personal pronoun)

There is an exception. When writing, we do not use the plural *their* with the singular *everyone, everybody*, etc. When speaking, however, it has become acceptable to use *their* when *him* or *her* would sound awkward.

> SPOKEN: *Everybody* must do *their* part.

> WRITTEN: *Everybody* must do *his* or *her* part.

Example 3   Choose the correct personal pronoun to match the antecedent when writing.

(a) Most of the colonists appreciated (their, his/her) freedom.

(b) Everybody lived in (their, his/her) own way.

(c) Nobody criticized (their, his/her) neighbor.

Solution   (a) The antecedent *most* is plural; it refers to colonists, which can be counted. Therefore, we choose a plural personal pronoun—**their.**

Most of the colonists appreciated **their** freedom.

(b) The antecedent *everybody* is singular, so we choose a singular pronoun—**his/her.**

Everybody lived in **his or her** own way.

(c) The antecedent *nobody* is singular, so we choose a singular personal pronoun—**his or her.**

Nobody criticized **his or her** neighbor.

Practice   For sentences a and b, write the indefinite pronoun and tell whether it is singular or plural.

   a. All of us treasure our freedom.

   b. Nothing is fair in a dictatorship.

For sentences c–e, choose the correct verb form to match the indefinite pronoun.

   c. *None* of my friends (want, wants) to return to former bad habits.

   d. *Some* candidates (is, are) more radical than others.

   e. *Each* of them (has, have) admirable qualities.

For f–h, choose the correct personal pronoun and verb form to match the indefinite pronoun antecedent.

   f. *Several* of the leaders (follow, follows) the advice of (their, his/her) elders.

   g. *Everything* (deserve, deserves) to be purchased at (its, their) true value.

   h. *One* of my friends (try, tries) to walk (their, his/her) dog twice a day.

For i–n, replace each blank with the correct vocabulary word.

i. Elephants, rhinoceroses, and hippopotami are located in the _____ section of the zoo.

j. The Greek root meaning "skin" is _____.

k. The _____ saw no reason to visit the tanning salon.

l. The exhibit of lifelike animals made visitors aware of the art of _____.

m. Acne, the curse of many teenagers, frustrates doctors of _____ as well.

n. Our _____ protects our deeper layers of skin.

More Practice   Tell whether each indefinite pronoun is singular, plural, or either.

1. most	**2.** both	**3.** anybody	**4.** neither
5. either	**6.** some	**7.** everyone	**8.** few
9. everything	**10.** ones	**11.** each	**12.** many
13. something	**14.** nothing	**15.** others	**16.** some
17. another	**18.** several	**19.** none	**20.** all

Review set 71   Choose the best word to complete sentences 1–7.

1. Keyboards, mice, printers, and monitors are all (software, hardware).
(68)

2. The Greek word (*morphe, chronos, chroma*) means color.
(39, 69)

3. A chromosome determines your hair (length, style, color).
(69)

4. A barometer (affects, changes, measures) atmospheric pressure.
(67)

5. A computer network is an arrangement of (disconnected, interconnected) printers and computers.
(68)

6. The guinea pig came to my sister and (me, myself, I) for comfort.
(51, 54)

7. My aunt has more patience than (he, him).
(53, 66)

8. (Who's, Whose) car is that?
(28, 56)

9. The letter (which, that) Malia wrote to Quan arrived on
(64, 65) Tuesday.

10. I was embarrassed, for (us, we) singers sang off key.
(54, 66)

11. Did you appreciate (me, my) singing "Swing Low, Sweet
(54, 68) Chariot"?

12. Uther Pendragon chose Igraine of Cornall (hisself,
(60) himself).

13. (Them, Those) stallions are the finest.
(70)

14. Nobody (want, wants) fleas in his or her house.
(71)

15. Rewrite the following, adding periods, commas, capital
(11, 35) letters, and quotation marks as needed: in a short story
called the round table arthur requires his knights to be
present at five p m for an early supper

16. Write the verb phrase from this sentence and name its
(15, 18) tense: Had any knight or baron succeeded in pulling the
sword from the anvil?

17. Write the objective case, third person, plural personal
(54, 55) pronoun.

18. Use an appositive to make one sentence from these two
(45, 46) sentences: Beatrice Clay is the author. The author tells
about Arthur's birth and his rise to kingship.

19. Tell whether the underlined expression in this sentence
(64, 65) is essential or nonessential: The cake <u>that Mom made</u> had
pink frosting.

20. Write the dependent clause from this sentence and circle
(57) the subordinating conjunction: Since Sir Kay had no
sword, Arthur grabbed the one in the anvil.

For sentences 21 and 22, write the verb and label it action or linking.

21. Performing his knightly exercises, Arthur looked kingly.
(4, 22)

22. Sir Kay looked for his sword.
(4, 22)

23. Write the correct verb form in this sentence: Sadly, Sir
(15, 52) Kay (past perfect tense of *misplace*) his sword before the tournament.

24. Tell whether the following is a phrase or a clause:
(24, 57) promising Merlin his first born son

25. Write the comparative form of the adjective *quiet.*
(42, 43)

26. Write the four principal parts of the irregular verb *steal.*
(6, 15)

27. Write the participial phrase from this sentence, followed
(48, 59) by the word it modifies: Looking for his sword, Sir Kay felt helpless.

Diagram sentences 28–30.

28. Sorting socks bores Molly and me.
(19, 25)

29. Both Iowa and Illinois are Midwest states.
(36, 39)

30. Isabel, whom you have met, will teach knitting.
(19, 64)

LESSON 72

Italics or Underline

Dictation or Journal Entry

Vocabulary:

Pun, satire, soliloquy, stereotype, and *stream of consciousness* are literary terms.

A *pun* is a "play on words," sometimes on different meanings of the same word and sometimes on the similar meaning or sound of different words. The word "knead" is a *pun* in this sentence: I work as a baker because I knead dough.

Satire is a form of literature that makes fun of or ridicules mistakes and weaknesses. "The Emperor's New Clothes" is an example of *satire.*

A *soliloquy* is a speech given by a character alone on stage, as if he were talking to himself. Shakespeare's characters delivered many *soliloquies.*

A *stereotype* is an oversimplified image of a certain person, group, or issue usually held in common by some segment of society. The *stereotype* of a librarian is a stern person with glasses.

Stream of consciousness is the technique of telling a story through the thoughts of the characters. Victorian authors used *stream of consciousness* in their narrations to further their plots.

The word ***italics*** refers to a slightly slanted style of type that is used to indicate titles of larger literary works or to bring special emphasis to a word of phrase in a sentence. The book title below is in italics.

The Red Badge of Courage

When we handwrite material, or when the italic style of type is not available, we **underline** the word or words that require italics in print.

The Red Badge of Courage

Here are some of the main categories of words and phrases that should be italicized or underlined.

Longer Literary Works, Movies, CD's, etc. We italicize or underline titles of books, magazines, newspapers, pamphlets, plays, book-length poems, television shows, movies, films, record albums, tapes, and CDs.

The library has hundreds of old copies of *Life Magazine.*

Last night, we popped lots of popcorn and watched The Wizard of Oz.

Ships, Planes, and Trains   We italicize or underline the names of ships, planes, and trains. (Words such as "The" and "U.S.S." are not treated as part of the vehicle's name.)

> The world's first space satellite was named *Sputnik I*.

> The United States President flies on <u>Air Force One</u>.

Paintings and Sculptures   We italicize or underline the names of famous paintings, sculptures, and other works of art.

> The *Statue of Liberty* welcomes weary immigrants to the United States.

> Leonardo da Vinci painted the famous <u>Mona Lisa</u>.

Example 1   For sentences a–e, underline all words that should be italicized in print.

(a) The travelers sailed from England on a vessel called the Gray Duchess.

(b) Beowulf is a long epic poem passed down orally from generation to generation.

(c) Leonardo da Vinci also painted a mural called The Last Supper.

Solution   (a) We underline **<u>Gray Duchess</u>** because it is the name of a ship.

(b) **<u>Beowulf</u>** is a book-length poem.

(c) **<u>The Last Supper</u>** is a famous painting.

Words as Words   We italicize or underline a word when the sentence calls attention to the word **as a word.**

> Please don't use *yeah* when you mean *yes*.

> The word *project* can be either a verb or a noun.

> Virginia wrote *allude* when she meant *elude*.

This is also true for numerals and lowercase letters.

> Is this a *5* or an *s?*

> The model number began with a *p* and ended with a *3*.

Foreign Words and Phrases   We italicize or underline foreign words not commonly used in everyday English language.

French restaurants often serve *escargot*, or snails.

Mom often uses *hóla* as a greeting.

Genus and Species Names   We italicize or underline the scientific names for a genus, species, or subspecies.

The black-billed magpie is a member of the genus *Pica*.

Is *Convolvulus maruitanicus* the scientific name for morning glory?

Example 2   For sentences a and b, underline all words that should be italicized in print.

(a) The student missed several math problems because her 7's looked like 1's.

(b) In Spanish, padre means "father."

Solution   (a) We underline <u>7</u> and <u>1</u> because these numbers are used out of context.

(b) **<u>Padre</u>** is a foreign word.

Practice   For a–e, replace each blank with the correct vocabulary word.

a. The _____ of an athlete is big, clumsy, and ignorant.

b. "A dog not only has a fur coat but also pants" is an example of a _____.

c. In *David Copperfield*, David pours out his humiliation and despair in a _____ ____ _____.

d. In a _____ from Shakespeare's *Much Ado About Nothing*, Benedick says to himself, "When I said I'd die a bachelor, I did not think I should live till I were married."

e. Jonathan Swift's *Gulliver's Travels* is a _____ that ridicules human nature.

Write and underline the words that should be italicized in sentences f–j.

   f. Some homeowners enjoy reading a magazine called Traditional Homes.

   g. The public spokesperson said you know far too many times.

   h. Another name for the calf muscles is the gastrocnemius.

   i. Spanish speakers say Feliz Navidad for Merry Christmas.

   j. The Titanic was a famous British luxury liner that sank in 1912, after hitting an iceberg.

More Practice   See Master Worksheets.

Review set 72   Choose the best word(s) to complete sentences 1–13.

   1. One who pretends to be ill is a(n) (caricature, antagonist, $^{(50,\ 60)}$pseudoinvalid).

   2. Calvary is a(n) (army on horseback, place).
$^{(18)}$

   3. (Database, Network, Software) is made up of instructions $^{(68)}$ that tell a computer what to do.

   4. Monochrome means having one (eye, sound, color).
$^{(69)}$

   5. An (allegory, allusion, epithet) is a term used to $^{(61,\ 70)}$characterize a person or thing in either a flattering or derogatory manner.

   6. Trevor and (him, himself, he) repaired the computer $^{(53,\ 60)}$(themselves, theirselves).

   7. Mr. Tseng walks farther than (me, myself, I) each $^{(53,\ 66)}$morning.

   8. Not everybody (brush, brushes) (their, his/her) teeth after $^{(56,\ 71)}$ eating.

   9. The song, (which, that) sounded like a ballad, made me $^{(64,\ 65)}$sad.

10. Will you meet with (us, we) distance runners after the
(51, 54) race?

11. I enjoy (him, his) telling jokes.
(56, 58)

12. Did you see (them, those) shooting stars?
(56, 66)

13. Neither of us (like, likes) pulling weeds.
(6, 71)

Rewrite 14 and 15, adding periods, commas, capital letters, and quotation marks as needed.

14. each day before class begins the seventh graders at
(68, 69) cleminson school sing a song called america the beautiful

15. unfortunately said james i missed my flight from chicago
(68, 69) to new york city so i took the train instead

16. Write the verb phrase from this sentence and name its
(8, 18) tense: During the joust, Sir Pellinore's sword had injured
King Arthur's epidermis.

17. Write the nominative case, first person, plural pronoun.
(53, 55)

18. Use an appositive to make one sentence from these two
(45, 46) sentences: Jumbo the elephant is a pachyderm. A
pachyderm is an animal with thick skin.

19. Tell whether the underlined expression in this sentence
(64, 65) is essential or nonessential: The road, <u>which is bumpy
and unpaved</u>, winds around the mountain.

20. Write the dependent clause from this sentence, and
(24, 57) circle the subordinating conjunction: King Arthur
demonstrated his knightly courage when he resisted Lady
Annoure's offers of power and wealth.

21. Write the verb phrase from this sentence and label it
(25, 31) transitive or intransitive: Inside the castle walls, the
knights were jousting for sport and entertainment.

22. Write the indefinite pronoun in this sentence and label it
(71) singular, plural, or either: I don't know if either of the
construction workers has safety goggles.

23. Write the reflexive pronoun in this sentence: Merlin
$^{(51,\ 60)}$ suggests that King Arthur protect himself better in the
future.

24. Tell whether the following is a complete sentence,
$^{(1,\ 3)}$ sentence fragment, or run-on sentence: Seeing the depths
of treachery in Lady Annoure's heart.

25. Write the comparative form of the adjective *good.*
$^{(42,\ 43)}$

26. Write the four principal parts of the verb *slip.*
$^{(15,\ 52)}$

27. Write the participial phrase in this sentence, followed by
$^{(48,\ 59)}$ the word it modifies: Using soliloquies, Beatrice Clay
reveals the whirling thoughts and intentions of King
Arthur.

28. Write and underline each word that should be italicized
$^{(72)}$ in this sentence: Bonjour is a French greeting.

Diagram sentences 29 and 30.

29. Pat likes watching fireworks in the sky.
$^{(19,\ 25)}$

30. The jousting knight proved brave.
$^{(32,\ 39)}$

LESSON 73

Irregular Verbs, Part 3

We have already learned that there are no rules for forming the past tense and past participle of irregular verbs. In this lesson, we will look at some additional irregular verbs.

Remember that we must memorize the principal parts of irregular verbs. To test yourself, cover the past and past participle forms, then try to write or say the past and past participle for each verb. Make a new list of the ones you miss, and work to memorize them.

VERB	PAST	PAST PARTICIPLE
beat	beat	(has) beaten
bite	bit	(has) bitten
bring	brought	(has) brought
build	built	(has) built
burst	burst	(has) burst
buy	bought	(has) bought
catch	caught	(has) caught
come	came	(has) come
cost	cost	(has) cost
dive	dove	(has) dived
drag	dragged	(has) dragged
draw	drew	(has) drawn
drown	drowned	(has) drowned
drive	drove	(has) driven
eat	ate	(has) eaten
fall	fell	(has) fallen

feel	felt	(has) felt
fight	fought	(has) fought
flee	fled	(has) fled
flow	flowed	(has) flowed
fly	flew	(has) flown
forsake	forsook	(has) forsaken

Example 1   Write the past tense and past participle forms of each verb.

     (a) forsake   (b) eat   (c) draw   (d) catch

Solution   (a) forsake, **forsook, (has) forsaken**

     (b) eat, **ate, (has) eaten**

     (c) draw, **drew, (has) drawn**

     (d) catch, **caught, (has) caught**

Example 2   Write the correct verb form for each sentence.

     (a) Tennessee Williams (came, come) to be regarded as one of the foremost dramatists of the twentieth century.

     (b) Some critics (feeled, felt) that *A Streetcar Named Desire* was the best play ever written by an American.

     (c) Unfortunately, the dramatist (fell, fallen) under the influence of drugs and alcohol in his later years.

Solution   (a) Tennessee Williams **came** to be regarded as one of the foremost dramatists of the twentieth century.

     (b) Some critics **felt** that *A Streetcar Named Desire* was the best play ever written by an American.

     (c) Unfortunately, the dramatist **fell** under the influence of drugs and alcohol in his later years.

Errors to Avoid   People sometimes treat a regular verb as if it were irregular. For example, the past tense of *drag* is *dragged*, not "drug." The past tense of *drown* is simply *drowned*, not "drownded." Avoid these errors by memorizing the irregular verbs and consulting a dictionary when in doubt. If the dictionary does not list the verb's principle parts, the verb is regular.

Practice For a–h, write the past and past participle form of each verb.

    a. bite   **b.** drag   **c.** fight   **d.** fly

    e. flee   **f.** drive   **g.** dive   **h.** build

For i–p, write the correct verb form for each sentence.

  i. Woodrow Wilson (beat, beated) such Democratic reformers as William Jennings Bryant for the nomination to run for President.

  j. Woodrow Wilson (brought, brang) eloquence and perception to the office of the Presidency.

  k. Reform measures were (drove, driven) through Congress to protect the individual citizen from undue control by great financial enterprises.

  l. Wilson's diplomacy in foreign affairs (costed, cost) him the support of American people.

  m. After a strenuous national speaking tour aimed at winning public support for the League of Nations, Woodrow Wilson (falled, fell) ill.

  n. Virginia Woolf (builded, built) her novels around no plot.

For o–s, replace each blank with the correct vocabulary word.

  o. The basketball fan waited after the game to get his favorite player's _____.

  p. The _____ covers distances without human or animal muscle power.

  q. I plan to write an _____ so that others can learn from all my mistakes.

  r. The Greek prefix that means "self" is _____.

  s. An _____ transmission shifts gears without movement of a clutch.

More Practice See Master Worksheets.

**Review set
73**

Choose the best word(s) to complete sentences 1–13.

1. The Greek word *chroma* means (large, sound,
(69) color).

2. Dad stores all his financial records on a (software,
(68) database, peripheral).

3. Drama and poetry are different (flashbacks, epithets,
(70) genres) of literature.

4. The Greek word (*chroma*, *graphein*, *derma*) means
(69, 71) skin.

5. The (connotation, denotation) of the word "pond" is a
(61) small body of water.

6. King Arthur received help from two kings, King Ban and
(54, 66) (he, him).

7. Mr. Tseng (himself, hisself) arrived before (me, myself, I).
(51, 60)

8. *Several, both, few, ones, many,* and *others* are always
(66, 71) (singular, plural) indefinite pronouns.

9. The birch trees (which, that) grow along the river get
(64, 66) plenty of water.

10. Did you see (we, us) distance runners when we crossed
(54, 66) the finish line?

11. The group was tired of (him, his) bragging.
(56, 58)

12. This sword is his, not (their's, theirs).
(56, 66)

13. Either of them (is, are) acceptable.
(66, 71)

Rewrite 14 and 15, adding periods, commas, capital letters,
and quotation marks as needed.

14. mom read me a chapter titled the sword in the stone but i
(11, 69) don't remember it for i was sleeping

15. yes said andy ms williams read that chapter to me last
(35, 68) saturday

16. Write the correct verb form in this sentence: King Arthur
(15, 73) (present tense of *rely*) on Kings Ban and Bor, his allies.

17. Write the objective case, first person, plural pronoun.
(54, 55)

18. Write the verb phrase in this sentence and name its tense:
(8, 21) The lesser kings were fighting for the control of Britain.

19. Write whether the underlined expression in this sentence
(64, 65) is essential or nonessential: King Leodegance's wedding
gift, <u>which was a round table</u>, greatly pleased Arthur and
Guinevere.

20. Write the dependent clause from this sentence, and circle
(24, 57) the subordinating conjunction: Some lesser kings desire
the crown even though the Archbishop of Canterbury has
declared Arthur king.

21. Write each noun in this sentence and label it abstract or
(7, 9) concrete: King Arthur rebuilt towns and restored order.

22. Write the indefinite pronoun in this sentence and label it
(71) singular, plural, or either: Several of the knights receive
their places around the Round Table.

23. Write each prepositional phrase in this sentence, and star
(17, 32) the object of each preposition: Because of King Arthur's
proposal, King Leodegance consents to the marriage of
Arthur and Guinevere.

24. Write whether the following is a phrase or a clause:
(24, 57) riding a magnificent stallion with golden strands in his
shiny, chestnut mane.

25. Write the superlative form of the adjective *studious*.
(42, 43)

26. Write the four principal parts of the verb *bring*.
(15, 73)

27. In this sentence, write the infinitive used as an adjective:
(23, 48) Since he missed the train, he was looking for a place to
stay.

28. Write and underline each word that should be italicized
(72) in this sentence: Auguste Rodin, an artist who lived and

worked in France, designed a famous statue called The Thinker.

Diagram sentences 29 and 30.

29. One of the students despises diagramming sentences.
(19, 25)

30. Was the knight, whom I met, your brother?
(39, 64)

LESSON 74

Irregular Verbs, Part 4

Dictation or Journal Entry

Vocabulary:

Let us examine the literary terms *understatement, slapstick, slice of life, resolution,* and *plagiarism.*

An *understatement* is the opposite of an exaggeration. To say that Albert Einstein was smart is an *understatement.*

A *slice of life* is an accurate picture of everyday life. Charles Dickens presents a *slice of life* showing what life was like for children in the workhouse.

Slapstick is a type of comedy that uses exaggerated physical action to make people laugh. The Three Stooges movies used *slapstick* comedy.

The *resolution* of a story is the satisfying (but not necessarily happy) ending. Injun Joe's capture provides *resolution* in *The Adventures of Tom Sawyer.*

Plagiarism is claiming as one's own someone else's work or ideas. Students are warned against *plagiarism* when writing research papers.

In this lesson, we will review more irregular verbs, whose principal parts we must memorize. To test yourself, cover the past and past participle forms, then try to write or say the past and past participle for each verb. Make a new list for yourself of the forms you miss, and work to memorize them.

VERB	PAST	PAST PARTICIPLE
give	gave	(has) given
go	went	(has) gone
hang (execute)	hanged	(has) hanged
hang (dangle)	hung	(has) hung
hide	hid	(has) hidden, hid
hold	held	(has) held
lay	laid	(has) laid
lead	led	(has) led
lend	lent	(has) lent
lie (recline)	lay	(has) lain
lie (deceive)	lied	(has) lied
lose	lost	(has) lost
make	made	(has) made
mistake	mistook	(has) mistaken
put	put	(has) put
raise	raised	(has) raised
ride	rode	(has) ridden

rise	rose	(has) risen
run	ran	(has) run
see	saw	(has) seen
sell	sold	(has) sold

Example 1   Write the past and past participle forms of each verb.
(a) lie (recline)   (b) lie (deceive)

(c) hang (execute)   (d) hang (dangle)

Solution   (a) lie, **lay, (has) lain**

(b) lie, **lied, (has) lied**

(c) hang, **hanged, (has) hanged**

(d) hang, **hung, (has) hung**

Example 2   Write the correct verb form for each sentence.
(a) William Wordsworth (gave, given) English Romantic poetry its beginning.

(b) Despite criticism, Wordsworth (hold, held) to his belief that poetry should draw from the scenes and events of everyday life.

(c) He (seen, saw) beauty everywhere in nature.

Solution   (a) William Wordsworth **gave** English Romantic poetry its beginning.

(b) Despite criticism, Wordsworth **held** to his belief that poetry should draw from the scenes and events of everyday life.

(c) He **saw** beauty everywhere in nature.

Practice   For a–h, write the past and past participle form of each verb.
a. go   **b.** hide   **c.** lose   **d.** make
e. run   **f.** ride   **g.** raise   **h.** mistake

For i–l, write the correct verb form for each sentence.
i. The waiter (leaded, led) them to their table.

j. They (gone, went) past three dessert trays.

k. Hard work had (maked, made) them especially hungry.

l. What had the chef (put, putted) on their plates?

For m–q, replace each blank with the correct vocabulary word.

m. It is an _____ to say that Superman is a good jumper.

n. We avoid _____ by using quotation marks and giving credit to the author when we write someone else's thoughts or words.

o. In the story's _____, the hero and the heroine rode off into the sunset together.

p. Being hit in the face with a pie is an example of _____ comedy.

q. The TV special gave a _____ __ _____ showing living conditions in a third world country.

More Practice See Master Worksheets.

Review set 74 Choose the best word to complete sentences 1–14.

1. A bibliography is a list of (people, places, books).
(64)

2. To help his listeners understand his message, Devon
(45, 66) drew an (irony, analogy, epoch) between mental obstacles and a mountain range.

3. The (etymology, context, length) of a word refers to the
(66) words around it.

4. Polychrome means having many (angles, colors, sides).
(57, 69)

5. A (genre, flashback, drama) tells about former events and
(70) provides background for a story.

6. We use the relative pronoun (who, whom) for the subject
(64, 66) of a sentence.

7. If the relative pronoun functions as an object, we use
(64, 66) (who, whom).

8. Not everyone (want, wants) an alligator in (their, his/her)
(66, 71) house.

9. That walnut tree, (that, which) shades his entire
(64, 66) backyard, has termites.

10. (We, Us) family members try to help one another.
(53, 66)

11. The guide encouraged (us, our) taking pictures.
(54, 58)

12. (This, This here) Lady of the Lake protects King Arthur in
(66, 70) his time of need.

13. Lady of the Lake, (who, whom) the reader will soon meet,
(64, 65) extends her arm out from the center of the lake, revealing
Excalibur.

14. Merlin had (brung, bringed, brought) Arthur to the
(15, 74) palace.

Rewrite 15 and 16, adding periods, commas, capital letters,
and quotation marks as needed.

15. when mom read me the chapter called the candle in the
(26, 68) wind i was wide awake

16. as a matter of fact said andy i have never heard that part
(5, 68) of king arthur's story

17. Write the possessive case, first person, plural pronoun.
(55, 56)

18. Write the indefinite pronoun in this sentence and label it
(71) singular, plural, or either: Has everybody heard of King
Arthur and Queen Guinevere?

19. Tell whether the underlined expression in this sentence
(64, 65) is essential or nonessential: Excalibur, <u>which revealed
marvelous workmanship</u>, was held in a very ordinary
scabbard.

20. Write the dependent clause from this sentence, and circle
(24, 57) the subordinating conjunction: Historians confess that

most of the stories surrounding the Knights of the Round Table are fabrications.

21. Write the verb phrase in this sentence and label it
(25, 31) transitive or intransitive: Excalibur must have been gleaming in the rays of the setting sun.

22. Write the five indefinite pronouns from this list that can
(71) be either singular or plural depending on their use in the sentence: nobody, all, both, none, someone, many, any, some, most

23. Write the gerund phrase in this sentence and label its
(18, 19) tense present or perfect: Having received pardon from King Arthur allowed Sir Pellinor to become one of the Knights of the Round Table.

24. Tell whether the following is a complete sentence,
(1, 3) sentence fragment, or run-on sentence: Leaping into the boat, without an oar.

25. For a–c, write the plural of each noun.
(12, 13) (a) tankful   (b) Justice of the Peace (c) entity

26. Write the four principal parts of the irregular verb *build.*
(15, 73)

27. Use an appositive to make one sentence from these two
(45, 46) sentences: *The Starry Night* is one of Van Gogh's paintings. It shows a village under the night sky in southern France.

28. Write and underline each word that should be italicized
(20, 72) in this sentence: When viewed up close, Monet's painting called Bridge Over a Pool of Water Lilies looks like blobs and blotches of paint.

Diagram sentences 29 and 30.

29. Jousting was a favorite medieval pastime.
(19, 39)

30. Who was the knight brandishing his sword?
(39, 64)

LESSON 75

Irregular Verbs, Part 5

> **Dictation or Journal Entry**
>
> **Vocabulary:**
> The Greek root *pyro-* means "fire" or "heat."
>
> A *pyromaniac* is a person who compulsively sets fires. The *pyromaniac* was arrested for starting the forest fire.
>
> A *pyrogen* is a substance that causes a rise in human or animal temperature. Streptococcal bacteria sometimes acts as a *pyrogen* in people.
>
> *Pyrotechnics* is the manufacture or use of fireworks. On July 4, spectators watched a magnificent *pyrotechnics* display.
>
> *Pyrography* is the art of burning a design in leather or wood with a heated tool. Using *pyrography*, the artist crafted pictures on wooden planks.

In this lesson, we will review the last group of irregular verbs, whose principal parts we must memorize. To test yourself, cover the past and past participle forms, then try to write or say the past and past participle for each verb. Make a new list for yourself of the forms you miss, and work to memorize them.

VERB	PAST	PAST PARTICIPLE
set	set	(has) set
shake	shook	(has) shaken
shine (light)	shone	(has) shone
shine (polish)	shined	(has) shined
shut	shut	(has) shut
sit	sat	(has) sat
slay	slew	(has) slain
sleep	slept	(has) slept
spring	sprang, sprung	(has) sprung
stand	stood	(has) stood
strive	strove	(has) striven
swim	swam	(has) swum
swing	swung	(has) swung
take	took	(has) taken
teach	taught	(has) taught
tell	told	(has) told
think	thought	(has) thought
wake	woke	(has) woken
weave	wove	(has) woven
wring	wrung	(has) wrung
write	wrote	(has) written

Example 1   Write the past and past participle forms of each verb.
(a) swim   (b) swing   (c) wring   (d) slay   (e) shake

Solution   (a) swim, **swam, (has) swum**

(b) swing, **swung, (has) swung**

(c) wring, **wrung, (has) wrung**

(d) slay, **slew, (has) slain**

(e) shake, **shook, (has) shaken**

Example 2   Write the correct verb form for each sentence.
(a) A grateful person (thinked, thought) that the Unknown Soldier should be honored.

(b) The enemy had (slew, slain) this soldier.

(c) The soldier (stood, standed) for others who lost their lives in the war.

Solution   (a) A grateful person **thought** that the Unknown Soldier should be honored.

(b) The enemy had **slain** this soldier.

(c) The soldier **stood** for others who lost their lives in the war.

Practice   For a–f, write the past and past participle form of each verb.
a. set   **b.** shine (light)   **c.** shine (polish)

d. shut   **e.** sleep   **f.** spring

For g–n, write the correct verb form for each sentence.
g. The Queen of England has (sit, sat) in front of the tomb of the Unknown Soldier in Westminster Abbey.

h. We (taken, took) a taxi to the Arc de Triomphe, in Paris, where the French Unknown Soldier lies.

i. The professor (teached, taught) that the Belgian Unknown Soldier lies in a tomb in Brussels.

j. Has anyone ever (telled, told) you about the Unknown Soldier's tomb in Rome, Italy?

k. My friend has (wrote, written) a report about each country's Unknown Soldier.

l. The farmer's rooster has (waked, woken) everyone each morning at dawn.

m. Olympic athletes have (strove, striven) to do their best.

n. The tri-athlete has (swam, swum) the first portion of the triathlon.

For o–s, replace each blank with the correct vocabulary word.

o. The manufacture of fireworks is called _____.

p. The craftsman used _____ to make designs in the pine.

q. Licorice is a _____; it causes a rise in body temperature.

r. The Greek root _____ means "fire" or "heat."

s. The _____ was obsessed with matches and flames.

More Practice   See Master Worksheets.

Review set 75   Choose the best word(s) to complete sentences 1–14.

1. A (genre, epithet, gothic novel) contains mysterious, scary elements.
(70)

2. Taxidermy is the art of stuffing and mounting animal (genres, bones, skins).
(71)

3. Dermatology is a branch of medicine dealing with (ears, noses, skin).
(71)

4. The statement "The owls didn't give a *hoot* about the snowy weather," includes a (satire, pun, soliloquy).
(72)

5. (Satire, Soliloquy, Stereotype) ridicules mistakes and weaknesses.
(72)

(54, 67) **6.** To (who, whom) were you speaking?

7. That singer, (who, whom) we heard at the concert, gives
^(54, 64) voice lessons.

8. Each of the vocalists (need, needs) (their, his/her) own
^(66, 71) copy of the music.

9. The airplane (that, which) just departed is headed for
^(64, 65) Spain.

10. (We, Us) brothers and sisters are planning a party for our
^(53, 66) parents.

11. Bob appreciates (Jenny, Jenny's) painting the outside of
⁽⁵⁸⁾ the house.

12. (Those, Them) cousins played basketball together all day.
^(66, 70)

13. Are these car keys (her's, hers)?
^(56, 66)

14. Yesterday, I gathered my courage and (dived, dove) from
^(15, 73) the high diving board.

Rewrite 15 and 16, adding periods, commas, capital letters,
and quotation marks as needed.

15. collecting his horse his armor and his sword arthur
^(50, 61) prepares for battle

16. last monday said james i flew from chicago illinois to
^(63, 68) sacramento california

17. Write the possessive case, third person, singular
^(55, 56) (masculine) pronoun.

18. Write the indefinite pronoun in this sentence and label it
⁽⁷¹⁾ singular, plural, or either: Much is required of Sir
Lancelot.

19. Tell whether the underlined expression in this sentence
⁽⁶⁵⁾ is essential or nonessential: Blanca's flight, <u>which
departed on time</u>, should arrive in San Salvador before
noon.

20. Write the intensive personal pronoun in this sentence:
⁽⁶⁰⁾ Sir Lancelot himself must go to the Chapel Perilous to
save Sir Meliot de Logris.

21. Write the infinitive from this sentence and tell whether it
(23, 48) functions as a noun or an adjective: Sir Lancelot is the
knight to emulate.

22. Write each predicate adjective from this sentence: As a
(27, 41) knight, Sir Lancelot was always faithful and
trustworthy.

23. Write the participial phrase from this sentence, followed
(48, 59) by the word it modifies: Playing softly in the background,
the mandolinists are serenading the chess tournament
contestants.

24. Write the personal pronoun from this sentence and name
(49, 51) its antecedent: Sir Lancelot lived as righteously as he
could.

25. Write the comparative form of the adjective *little*
(42, 43) (amount).

26. Write the four principal parts of the irregular verb *eat*.
(15, 73)

27. Use an appositive to make one sentence from these two
(45, 46) sentences: Queen Victoria was a great monarch of Great
Britain. She reigned from 1837 until her death in 1901.

28. Write and underline each word that should be italicized
(72) in this sentence: The scientific name for dandelion, a
common weed in lawns and flower beds, is Taraxacum
officinale.

Diagram sentences 29 and 30.

29. The contest winners were Dan and she.
(28, 39)

30. Sherry, my sister, loves picking berries and making berry
(23, 45) pies.

LESSON 76

The Exclamation Mark • The Question Mark • The Dash

Dictation or Journal Entry

Vocabulary:

Let us discuss the literary term *point of view*, the position of the narrator in relation to the story.

A *first-person point of view* means that one of the characters is telling the story. The novel *David Copperfield* is told by David in the *first-person point of view.*

A *third-person point of view* means that someone outside the story is telling it. *The Lion, the Witch, and the Wardrobe* is told by an outsider in the *third-person point of view.*

There are three basic third-person points of view:

(1) The *unlimited* (omniscient) point of view permits the narrator to read the minds of the characters—to know their thoughts and feelings.

(2) The *limited* (limited omniscient) point of view allows the narrator to relate the thoughts and feelings of only one character.

(3) The *camera* point of view allows the narrator to see and relay the action from a neutral or impartial point of view.

Almost every sentence ends with one of three punctuation marks. The period, the exclamation mark, and the question mark are called final, or terminal, punctuation marks.

Exclamation Mark

We use an **exclamation mark** after an exclamatory sentence (a sentence showing strong emotion).

> Come quickly! It's snowing outside!

We can also use an exclamation mark after a word or phrase showing strong emotion. We call this an **interjection.**

> Ouch! That hurt!

> Wow! That's amazing!

Careful writers limit their use of exclamation marks. Think of it as shouting. Sometimes shouting is appropriate, but one who shouts all the time is soon ignored. Use exclamation marks sparingly.

Question Mark

We place a **question mark** at the end of an interrogative sentence (one that asks a question).

> Do you know which planet ranks seventh in order of distance from the sun?

> Is this the planet discovered in 1781 by Sir William Herschel?

With Quotation Marks   When using exclamation marks and question marks with quotation marks, we must decide whether to place the final punctuation mark *inside* or *outside* the quotation marks. We do this by determining if the final punctuation mark punctuates the whole sentence or just the part in quotation marks.

In the sentence below, only the words in quotation marks ask a question. The question mark punctuates only the direct quotation, so it goes *inside* the quotation marks.

> "Can you answer the question?" asked the astronomer.

In the next sentence, the question mark punctuates the whole sentence, so it goes *outside* the quotation marks:

> Do you remember your recitation of "Little Orphan Annie"?

Example 1   Rewrite sentences a–d, inserting exclamation and question marks as needed.

(a) Is it true that Uranus is the seventh planet in order of distance from the sun

(b) I can't believe you guessed it

(c) Isn't Uranus also the name of a Greek god

(d) Hey There goes a shooting star

Solution   (a) This interrogative sentence requires a question mark.

Is it true that Uranus is the seventh planet in order of distance from the sun?

(b) **I can't believe you guessed it!** (exclamatory sentence)

(c) This interrogative sentence requires a question mark.

Isn't Uranus also the name of a Greek god?

(d) **Hey! There goes a shooting star!** Interjections and exclamatory sentences require exclamation marks.

Dash   Another punctuation mark that we must use sparingly is the **dash.** The dash can indicate a sudden change in thought, an interruption in the flow of the sentence, faltering speech, or an abrupt halt to speech.

> Uranus was originally named *Georgium Sidus*—can you believe it?—after King George III of Great Britain.

> Uranus—um, I think I remember—has five rings and five satellites.

> The purpose of this lecture—please excuse the interruption—is to show the order of the planets in relation to the sun.

The dash can also offset a word or phrase for emphasis.

> Alpha, Beta, Gamma, Delta, and Epsilon—these are the names of Uranus's five rings.

> Uranus was also Greek god of the heavens—husband of Gaea, father of the Titans, father of the Cyclops, and father of the hundred-handed giants.

> It is a very bright planet—sixth-magnitude of brightness.

Errors to Avoid We do *not* use a dash in place of a period. The following is *incorrect*:

> Ursa Major appears prominently in the night sky—Most people know it as the "Big Dipper."

These are two separate sentences. They must be separated by a period, not a dash:

> Ursa Major appears prominently in the night sky. Most people know it as the "Big Dipper."

Example 2 Rewrite sentences a–c, inserting dashes where needed.

(a) The name of the book about Scrooge now let me think is *A Christmas Carol,* by Charles Dickens.

(b) Please be home early by five o'clock.

(c) "Don't drop your" said Pat as Len's plate crashed on the floor.

Solution (a) We use dashes to indicate a an interruption in the flow of the sentence. **The name of the book about Scrooge—now let me think—is *A Christmas Carol*, by Charles Dickens.**

(b) We use a dash for emphasis. **Please be home early—by five o'clock.**

(c) We use a dash to indicate an abrupt halt to speech. **"Don't drop your—" said Pat as Len's plate crashed on the floor.**

Practice   Rewrite sentences a–d, placing exclamation marks and question marks where they are needed.

   a. Wow Look at the "Big Dipper"

   b. Do you know another name for Ursa Minor

   c. Is it "Little Dipper"

   d. Brilliant You know your constellations

Rewrite sentences e–g, inserting dashes where needed.

   e. At one time, Rudolph Valentino was a famous actor the heartthrob of millions of American women.

   f. He played starring roles in the two motion pictures let me think *The Four Horsemen of the Apocalypse* and *The Sheik.*

   g. "Hold on to your" said Gary as the wind swept Mary's hat from her head.

For sentences h–n, replace each blank with the correct vocabulary word.

   h. The _____ of view is the position of the narrator in relation to the story.

   i. Because Esther Summerfield, the main character, tells the story in her own words, *Bleak House* is in the _____-person point of view.

   j. *The Old Curiosity Shop* begins in the first-person point of view but changes to the _____-person point of view when a person outside of the novel begins telling the story.

   k. The third-_____ point of view has three basic forms.

l. The narrator can reveal the thoughts and feelings of only Little Nell in *The Old Curiosity Shop*, so the story is in the _____ form of the third-person point of view.

m. The narrator knows the thoughts and feelings of all the characters in *Anne of Avonlea*, so the story is told in the _____ form of the third-person point of view.

n. A news article is often told from the _____ form of the third-person point of view, because it reveals only the facts without emotions or narrator involvement.

More Practice   See "Slapstick Story #4 in Master Worksheets.

Review set 76   Choose the best word to complete sentences 1–13.

1. When Brian said, "The lumberjack was *axed* from his job
(70, 72) because he couldn't *hack* it anymore," he used (drama, flashback, puns).

2. A pachyderm is an animal with thick (legs, hair, skin).
(71)

3. A (stereotype, pun, satire) is a play on words.
(72)

4. The Greek prefix (*eu-*, *caco-*, *auto-*) means self.
(13, 73)

5. An (allusion, anecdote, understatement) is the opposite
(61, 74) of exaggeration.

6. (Whoever, Whomever) serves the King becomes one of
(67, 71) his most trustworthy companions.

7. King Arthur will choose (whoever, whomever) Guinevere
(67, 71) desires.

8. Neither of the sisters (want, wants) that tarantula in
(66, 71) (their, her) room.

9. Tom's suitcase, (that, which) contained only gummy
(64, 65) bears, was stolen.

10. The teachers have been waiting for (us, we) students.
(54, 66)

11. Kerry dislikes (Petey, Petey's) chewing her good shoes
(58) and furniture.

12. (Those, Them) seats at the Round Table are for King
(28, 70) Arthur's knights.

13. Is this seat (your's, yours)?
(28, 56)

14. Oh dear, a bear has (bite, bit, bitten) a hole in our tent!
(73, 74)

Rewrite 15 and 16, adding periods, commas, capital letters, and quotation marks as needed.

15. if we have time we shall read the chapter entitled the
(20, 69) adventure of the chapel perilous

16. no said ms sweet i did not leave my gumdrops in the tent
(20. 68)

17. Write the possessive case, third person, singular
(55, 56) (feminine) personal pronoun.

18. For sentences a and b, write the verb phrase and label it
(4, 22) action or linking.

   (a) Has Ms. Sweet proved her point?

   (b) Did Ms. Sweet prove innocent?

19. Tell whether the underlined expression in this sentence
(64, 65) is essential or nonessential: The suitcase that contained the gummy bears was stolen.

20. Tell whether the following is a phrase or a clause: having
(24, 57) shrunk away from Sir Lancelot du Lac

21. Write the gerund phrase from this sentence: Your job, Ms.
(19, 58) Sweet, will be mending the tent.

22. Write whether the following is a complete sentence,
(1, 3) sentence fragment, or run-on sentence: When challenged by Sir Lancelot du Lac, the giants had shrunk away.

23. Write the correct verb form in this sentence: I believe Sir
(18, 73) Lancelot (past perfect tense of the verb *come*) to save Sir Meliot.

24. Write the dependent clause in this sentence, and circle
(24, 57) the subordinating conjunction: If Sir Lancelot du Lac had kissed the Lady of the Chapel Perilous, he would have died.

25. Write the predicate adjective from this sentence: The
(22, 41) Chapel Perilous was evil.

26. Write the four principal parts of the irregular verb *fall*.
(15, 74)

27. In this sentence, write each prepositional phrase, starring
(32, 33) the object of each preposition: According to the Lady of
the Chapel Perilous, Sir Gawain barely escaped her wiles.

28. Write and underline each word that should be italicized
(72) in this sentence: During the early 1900s, Grandma Angles
crossed the Atlantic on a famous ship named the Queen
Mary.

Diagram sentences 29 and 30.

29. Neither of the brothers knows the secret.
(25, 71)

30. Did you see the person who stole Tom's suitcase?
(25, 64)

LESSON
77

Subject-Verb Agreement, Part 1

> **Dictation or Journal Entry**
>
> **Vocabulary:**
> The Greek word *cosmos* means "world" or "universe."
>
> *Cosmopolitan* is an adjective meaning "at home all over the world." Knowing about different cultures helps one to become *cosmopolitan.*
>
> A *cosmopolis* is an important city inhabited by people of different races and cultures. New York City is a *cosmopolis.*
>
> A *cosmonaut* is a Russian astronaut. Russia provides rigorous training for its *cosmonauts* before they enter outer space.
>
> *Macrocosm* refers to the world as a whole, and *microcosm* refers to a miniature "world." Each state government is a *microcosm* of the federal government.

Just as a pronoun must agree with its antecedent, a verb must agree with the subject of the sentence in **person** and **number**.

Person   Verbs and personal pronouns are the only parts of speech that change their form to show person (point of view).

When we learned about the irregular verbs *to be, have,* and *do* in Lesson 14, we used a chart similar to the one below. Here we show two regular verbs (*talk* and *watch*) and one irregular verb (*to be*) in the first, second, and third person. (Most regular verbs form the third person singular by adding -*s* or -*es.* The irregular verbs must be memorized.)

	SINGULAR	PLURAL
1ST PERSON	**I** talk, watch, am	**we** talk, watch, are
2ND PERSON	**you** talk, watch, are	**you** talk, watch, are
3RD PERSON	**he** talks, watches, is	**they** talk, watch, are

If the subject of a sentence is in the **first person** (I, we), the verb must also be in the first person:

> *I* talk to her daily.   *We* watch each sunset.
>
> *I* am ambivalent.   *We* are ambidextrous.

If the subject of a sentence is in the **second person** (you), the verb must also be in the second person:

> *You* talk every evening.

If the subject of a sentence is in the **third person** (he, she, it, or any noun), the verb must also be in the third person:

He <u>talks</u> every evening.   *They* <u>talk</u> every evening.

Thad <u>watches</u> every sunset.   *People* <u>watch</u> every sunset.

The *door* <u>is</u> red.   The *doors* <u>are</u> red.

Number   If the subject of a sentence is **singular,** the verb must also be singular:

> The vampire *bat* <u>lives</u> in South America.

> In folklore, the *bat* <u>rises</u> from the grave at night.

If the subject of a sentence is **plural,** the verb must also be plural:

> *Vampires* <u>live</u> in South America.

> The *bats* <u>rise</u> during the night.

Notice that the pronoun *you* always takes a plural verb, even when it is singular.

> *You* <u>are</u> benevolent, Mr. Chen.

> *You* <u>are</u> both sympathetic people.

Compound Subjects   We must carefully determine whether the subject of a sentence is singular or plural.

Compound subjects joined by *and* are considered plural and require a plural verb.

> *Jan* and *Van* <u>stroll</u> through the streets.

> The *mason* and his *helpers* <u>repair</u> chimneys.

Compound subjects joined by *or, nor, either-or,* or *neither-nor* can be singular or plural, depending on the subjects themselves:

• If both subjects are singular, we use a singular verb.

> Neither *ham* nor *bologna* <u>pleases</u> the finicky eater.

> Either *jam* or *honey* <u>mixes</u> well with peanut butter.

• If both subjects are plural, we use a plural verb.

> Neither the *shoes* nor the *socks* <u>match</u>.

> Either *sodas* or *juices* <u>sell</u> well at sporting events.

• If one subject is singular and the other is plural, the verb should agree with the subject nearest it.

> Neither the *doctor* nor the *nurses* report for duty today.

> Either the *encyclopedias* or the *dictionary* contains the information.

Example   Choose the correct verb form for each sentence.

(a) Either pepper or salt (taste, tastes) delicious on potato chips.

(b) The attorneys-at-law (plead, pleads) their cases before the judge.

(c) Malt vinegar and salt (accompanies, accompany) fried cod fillets.

(d) Neither the firemen nor the policemen (receive, receives) enough pay for their responsibilities.

Solution   (a) When compound singular subjects are joined by *either-or*, we use a singular verb form: Either pepper or salt **tastes** delicious on potato chips.

(b) The subject, "attorneys-at-law," is plural, so we use the plural verb form: The attorneys-at-law **plead** their cases before the judge.

(c) A compound subject joined by *and* uses a plural verb form: Malt vinegar and salt **accompany** fried cod fillets.

(d) Compound plural subjects joined by *neither-nor* require a plural verb form: Neither the firemen nor the policemen **receive** enough pay for their responsibilities.

Practice   For a–f, choose the correct verb form for each sentence.

a. The vampire bat (derive, derives) nourishment from mammals' blood.

b. These bats rarely (exceed, exceeds) three inches long.

c. Their esophagus, stomach, and intestine (differ, differs) from other animals.

d. Either humans or other animals (is, are) victims of the vampire bat.

e. Neither the werewolf nor the vampire really (exist, exists).

f. Salmon or octopi (make, makes) a good menu entrée.

For g–l, replace each blank with the correct vocabulary word.

g. Chicago, with its diverse population, is an example of a
_____.

h. The state of California could be considered a
_____ of the world's land features because within its boundaries are mountains, deserts, and beaches.

i. War represents a _____ of the difficulty individuals have getting along with one another.

j. _____ is a Greek word meaning "world" or "universe."

k. A Russian _____ will walk on the moon again.

l. Well-traveled individuals appear to be more _____ in their tastes for different types of foods.

More Practice Choose the correct verb form for each sentence.

1. Neither the harmonica nor the banjos (sound, sounds) right.

2. Either the piano or the guitars (is, are) out of tune.

3. The lory and the parrot (live, lives) in groups.

4. The sparrow and the finch (grow, grows) to about five inches long.

5. All doves (is, are) monogamous.

6. They always (love, loves) their mates.

7. Either a dove or a pigeon (was, were) bathing in the puddle.

8. A dove and a pigeon (was, were) pecking for seeds.

9. Either the robin or the nightingales (was, were) laying eggs.

10. Mynas and starlings (has, have) soft bills.

Review set 77   Choose the correct word(s) to complete sentences 1–14.

1. An autobiography is a life story written by one's (friend, self, aunt).
(73)

2. A (satire, soliloquy, slice of life) is an accurate picture of everyday life.
(72, 74)

3. (Understatement, Slapstick) is a type of comedy that uses exaggerated action.
(74)

4. (Cliché, Stereotype, Plagiarism) is claiming as one's own someone else's work.
(52, 74)

5. The Greek root (*morphe*, *pyro-*, *derma*) means fire or heat.
(26, 75)

6. Did you see the person (who, whom) stole Tom's suitcase?
(67)

7. Tom had asked Amparo and (she, her) to guard it.
(51, 54)

8. Neither of the bears (has, have) (their, its, it's) claws out.
(38, 56)

9. The camera (that, which) I was using had no film.
(64, 65)

10. (We, Us) English students are discussing the tales of King Arthur.
(51, 53)

11. Petey dislikes (Kerry, Kerry's) chasing him out the back door.
(58, 66)

12. (Those, Them) upside-down shields belong to the knights who cowered at the sight of giants.
(70)

13. These were (their, there, they're) shields.
(56, 58)

14. By the end of the trip, John had (took, taken) nine hundred pictures.
(74, 75)

Rewrite 15 and 16, adding capital letters and correct punctuation marks as needed.

15. help yelled tom did you see who stole my suitcase
(20, 68)

16. did the portuguese lady with whom you spoke see the
(5, 68) thief asked tom

17. Write the possessive case, second person (either singular
(55, 56) or plural) pronoun.

18. In this sentence, write the verb phrase and label it
(25, 31) transitive or intransitive: Has Sir Lancelot unhorsed Gareth?

19. In this sentence, write whether the underlined clause is
(64, 65) essential or nonessential: My camera, <u>which has no film</u>, is over there.

20. In this sentence, write the pronoun and its antecedent:
(49, 56) The Red Knight smote Sir Gareth on the hand and knocked his sword away.

21. From this sentence, write the infinitive and label it a
(23, 48) noun or an adjective: Ms. Sweet has a book to read.

22. Write the superlative form of the adjective *pleasant.*
(42, 43)

23. In this sentence, write the indefinite pronoun and label it
(71) singular or plural: Some of the salad dressing has become rancid.

24. In this sentence, write the dependent clause, circling the
(24, 57) subordinating conjunction: Sir Gareth defeats the Red Knight when he wins the heart of Lady Liones.

25. Write the four principal parts of the irregular verb *tell.*
(15, 75)

26. Use an appositive to make one sentence from these two
(45, 46) sentences: Lady Linit is Lady Liones's sister. Lady Linit marries Sir Gaheris.

27. For a–c, write the plural of each noun.
(12, 13)

(a) shelf   (b) match   (c) lady

28. Write and underline each word that should be italicized
(72) in this sentence: In C.S. Lewis's great novel called The
Last Battle, I read about how evil came to Narnia.

Diagram sentences 29 and 30.

29. Saul slew many, but David slew more.
(59, 62)

30. Does either of the astronauts enjoy building model
(19, 38) spacecraft?

LESSON 78

Subject-Verb Agreement, Part 2

Dictation or Journal Entry

Vocabulary: Let us examine the literary terms *action, antithesis, dramatic monologue, epigram,* and *essay.*

The *action* of a story is everything that happens. Tolkien's stories capture our interest with fast-moving *action.*

An *antithesis* is an exact opposite. We use *antithesis* to contrast ideas in the same sentence. Patrick Henry's exclamation, "Give me liberty, or give me death!" uses *antithesis* for emphasis.

A *dramatic monologue* is a passage that reveals the character of the speaker by his comments to himself or to another character. In Robert Browning's "My Last Duchess," the Duke's *dramatic monologue* exposes his own arrogant, jealous, and materialistic nature.

An *epigram* is a short, clever saying. J. H. Goldfuss gives this *epigram* on humility: "Why, even I'm not perfect."

An *essay* gives a writer's opinion or ideas on a subject. The short *essay* was to include an introductory paragraph, a body of three paragraphs, and a concluding paragraph.

For subject-verb agreement, we must first identify the subject of the sentence and then determine whether it is singular or plural.

Words Between the Subject and Verb

Words that come between the subject and the verb must not distract us. We must be aware of prepositional phrases, appositives, and other words that might be mistaken for the subject of the sentence. Diagramming the simple subject and simple predicate helps us to determine which verb form to use.

The notice concerning truant students (was, were) sent to all parents.

notice	was (not were)

No one with pro-slavery sentiments (support, supports) Martin Van Buren for a second term.

one	supports (not support)

James K. Polk, like other Southern Democrats, (was, were) in favor in annexing Texas as another slave state.

James K. Polk	was (not were)

Example 1   Diagram the simple subject and simple predicate in order to show the correct verb form for each sentence.

(a) A pile of dirty clothes (remain, remains) on the floor.

(b) The exit of the theater's patrons (cause, causes) a traffic jam.

(c) In Presidential elections, the bickering between politicians (is, are) often vicious.

Solution   (a) A pile of dirty clothes **remains** on the floor.

$$\begin{array}{c|c} \text{pile} & \text{remains} \end{array}$$

(b) The exit of the theater's patrons **causes** a traffic jam.

$$\begin{array}{c|c} \text{exit} & \text{causes} \end{array}$$

(c) In Presidential elections, the bickering between politicians **is** often vicious.

$$\begin{array}{c|c} \textbf{bickering} & \text{is} \end{array}$$

Reversed Subject-Verb Order   If the subject follows the verb, we carefully identify the subject and make the verb agree with it.

Off the coast of the United States (lie, lies) an island called Vancouver.

$$\begin{array}{c|c} \text{island} & \text{lies} \end{array}$$

There in the city of Vancouver (live, lives) the Salish Native Americans.

$$\begin{array}{c|c} \text{Native Americans} & \text{live} \end{array}$$

Here (comes, come) some new settlers.

$$\begin{array}{c|c} \text{settlers} & \text{come} \end{array}$$

Now there (is, are) excellent highways in Vancouver, British Columbia.

$$\underline{\text{highways} \mid \text{are} \qquad}$$

Example 2 Diagram the simple subject and simple predicate in order to show the correct verb form for each sentence.

(a) Here (is, are) a photograph of the Vanderbilt Family.

(b) There, at Vanderbilt University, (live, lives) the memory of Cornelius Vanderbilt, a great American industrialist and philanthropist.

(c) Following his father's footsteps (was, were) another philanthropist, William Henry Vanderbilt who donated substantial sums to Columbia University.

Solution (a) Here **is** a photograph of the Vanderbilt Family.

$$\underline{\textbf{photograph} \mid \textbf{is} \qquad}$$

(b) There, at Vanderbilt University, **lives** the memory of Cornelius Vanderbilt, a great American industrialist and philanthropist.

$$\underline{\textbf{memory} \mid \textbf{lives} \qquad}$$

(c) Following his father's footsteps **was** another philanthropist, William Henry Vanderbilt, who donated substantial sums to Columbia University.

$$\underline{\textbf{philanthropist} \mid \textbf{was} \qquad}$$

Practice Diagram the simple subject and simple predicate in order to determine the correct verb form for sentences a–d.

a. There in the encyclopedia (was, were) descriptions of several famous Vanderbilts.

b. Among the benefactors of the Cathedral of Saint John (was, were) Cornelius Vanderbilt.

   c. Here (is, are) a partial list of institutions this family supported: Vanderbilt University, Columbia University, Yale University, Cathedral of Saint John, the New York Theological Seminary.

   d. Steamships, railroads, yacht cup races, and the game of contract bridge (is, are) all connected with the name of Vanderbilt.

For e–i, replace each blank with the correct vocabulary word(s).

   e. J. H. Goldfuss wrote this _____ on remorse: "To err is human; to forget, divine!"

   f. We learn something about Hamlet as he talks to himself in a _____ _____ saying, "To be, or not to be: that is the question: ...."

   g. Jesus gave this _____ in his Sermon on the Mount: "It was said, 'An eye for an eye, and a tooth for a tooth,' but I say to you, offer no resistance to one who is evil...."

   h. The thrilling _____ of the adventure story made it popular with people of all ages.

   i. The teacher assigned a written persuasive _____ on the benefits of a republican form of government.

More Practice Choose the correct verb form for each sentence.

   1. A bag of peanuts (sit, sits) near the elephant.

   2. The sack of onions (smell, smells) rancid.

   3. A truckload of bricks (is, are) coming today.

   4. There (go, goes) the racing cyclists!

   5. There (is, are) many shades of blue.

   6. The noise of the parrots (drive, drives) the neighbors crazy.

   7. The music from distant bagpipes (make, makes) Mrs. Anderson nostalgic.

   8. Every one of the bicycles (was, were) returned in good condition after the ride.

9. Around the corner (lives, live) two of my best friends.

10. Above the buildings (fly, flies) an American flag.

Review set 78

Choose the best word(s) to complete sentences 1–14.

1. The greek root *pyro* means (fire, self, far).
(73, 75)

2. Automatic means (rarely, always, self) starting.
(73, 75)

3. Cavalry is a(n) (army on horseback, place).
(18)

4. The (plagiarism, resolution, satire) of a story is the satisfying ending.
(74)

5. An outsider tells the story when the point of view is (first, third) person.
(76)

6. You may ride with (whoever, whomever) you want.
(64, 66)

7. Amparo and (she, her) felt sad for Tom.
(51, 53)

8. Not everyone (trust, trusts) (their, his/her) own judgment in choosing a college or university.
(71, 78)

9. My flowers, (which, that) once looked like dainty miniature bluebells, have withered.
(64, 65)

10. Dr. Westman has been lecturing (we, us) students about life in the South.
(53, 66)

11. The Peckbeak sisters seemed to appreciate (me, my) planting petunias around their home.
(56, 58)

12. Neither the guinea pigs nor the hamster (eat, eats) much zucchini.
(6, 73)

13. That snapping turtle is mine, but this one is (her's, hers).
(56, 66)

14. Have we (mistook, mistaken) Ms. Sweet for the thief?
(74, 75)

Rewrite 15 and 16, adding capital letters and correct punctuation marks as needed.

15. sir lancelot one of king arthur's knights admits to sir gareth you are a stout knight
(5, 35)

16. dear king arthur
(29, 50)

thank you for granting me my three requests how excited i am to be a knight sir lancelot knighted me

gratefully

sir gareth

17. Write the seven common coordinating conjunctions.
(36)

18. In this sentence, write the verb phrase and label it action or linking: Does Sir Gawain appear frustrated?
(4, 22)

19. In this sentence, write whether the underlined clause is essential or nonessential: The marble <u>that holds the sword</u> glistens in the moonlight.
(64, 65)

20. Write whether the following is a phrase or a clause: striving to attain the Holy Grail
(24, 57)

21. In this sentence, write the infinitive and label is a noun or an adjective: Do the knights need to prepare for the Quest of the Holy Grail?
(23, 48)

22. Write the three personal pronoun case forms.
(55)

23. In this sentence, write the indefinite pronoun and label it singular or plural: Each of the knights is searching for the Holy Grail.
(71)

24. In this sentence, write the dependent clause, circling the subordinating conjunction: The Holy Grail was a chalice that represented Christian purity during medieval times.
(24, 57)

25. Write the four principal parts of the irregular verb *go*.
(15, 73)

26. Write the participial phrase from this sentence followed by the noun it modifies: Grieving the lost and wounded, King Arthur knows that his knights must keep their oaths.
(57, 59)

27. In this sentence, write each prepositional phrase, starring the object of each preposition: A great army of warriors rides alongside of the Red Knight.
(32, 33)

28. Write and underline each word that should be italicized
(72) in this sentence: The weather forecast, according to the Los Angles Times, calls for sunshine and high clouds.

Diagram sentences 29 and 30.

29. Ms. Sweet has a tent to mend.
(23, 25)

30. That lady, the one with the curlers in her hair, might
(25, 33) have stolen Tom's suitcase.

LESSON 79

Subject-Verb Agreement, Part 3

Dictation or Journal Entry

Vocabulary: The Greek verb *therapeuein,* meaning "to treat medically, to cure," appears in English words with the root *therap-.*

Therapy is treatment for a disorder or disease. Speech *therapy* helps those who stutter.

A *therapist* is one who gives therapy. The physical *therapist* prescribed flexing and straightening the stiff knee joint for thirty minutes each day.

Therapeutic is an adjective meaning curative and referring to the treatment of disorders. Liquids and rest are *therapeutic* for the common cold.

Therapeutic index is the difference between a lethal dosage and a therapeutic dosage of a drug. The *therapeutic index* for codeine is very small, so physicians must prescribe it cautiously.

Indefinite Pronouns   We remember that some indefinite pronouns are singular, some are plural, and some can be either. If an indefinite pronoun is the subject of a sentence, the verb must agree with it in number. (See Lesson 71 for the complete list of indefinite pronouns.)

SINGULAR	*Nobody* <u>is</u> alert.
PLURAL	*Few* <u>are</u> awake.
SINGULAR	*Some* <u>was</u> flashback.
PLURAL	*Some* <u>were</u> sympathetic.

Sometimes people are confused when a prepositional phrase comes between the subject and predicate. Diagramming the simple subject and simple predicate helps us to see that the singular verb is correct.

Neither of the problems (require, requires) therapy.

| Neither | requires |

One of them (is, are) more serious than the other.

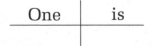

| One | is |

Each of the students (hope, hopes) to visit Rome.

| Each | hopes |

Somebody with glasses (is, are) taking photographs.

Somebody	is taking

Example 1 Choose the correct verb form for each sentence.

(a) Everyone (were, was) trying to see the parade.

(b) Neither of these tours (present, presents) the history of Rome.

Solution (a) The indefinite pronoun *everyone* takes a singular verb: Everyone **was** trying to see the parade.

(b) The indefinite pronoun *neither* takes a singular verb: Neither of these tours **presents** the history of Rome.

Special Plural Nouns Some nouns refer to a single "thing" but are still considered plural. We remember that words like *slacks, shears, scissors, tweezers,* and *pants* use a plural verb, for they are plural.

These pinking *shears* <u>leave</u> a jagged edge.

Her *pants* <u>were</u> too long.

Contractions We use contractions cautiously, expanding them, if necessary, to be sure the subjects and verbs agree.

The *boy* wasn't (<u>was</u> not) afraid of snakes.

The *boys* weren't (<u>were</u> not) afraid of snakes.

Guatemala isn't (<u>is</u> not) near Chile or Peru.

We aren't (<u>are</u> not) near Chile or Peru.

Robert doesn't (<u>does</u> not) have time.

They don't (<u>do</u> not) have time.

Yin hasn't (<u>has</u> not) answered my email.

Yin and *Kim* haven't (<u>have</u> not) answered my email.

Errors to Avoid We use the contraction *there's* ("there is" or "there has") only with singular subjects.

There's (there is) only one *man* on board.

There's (there has) been *upheaval* in Venezuela.

We do NOT use the contraction *there's* with plural subjects.

NO: There's several major *cities* in Italy.

YES: There <u>are</u> several major *cities* in Italy.

Ain't is not a word. We do not use it for *isn't, hasn't, aren't,* or *haven't.*

Venice isn't (NOT ain't) the only Italian seaport.

I haven't (NOT ain't) seen Venice in Italy.

Example 2   Choose the correct verb form for each sentence.

(a) My scissors (need, needs) sharpening.

(b) Lucy (don't, doesn't) want any help with the dishes.

(c) The businessman (hasn't, haven't) time for a canal tour.

(d) The artist (ain't, isn't) finished with his painting.

Solution   (a) *Scissors* is a plural subject, so we use a plural verb: My scissors **need** sharpening.

(b) *Lucy* is a singular subject, so we use the singular verb: Lucy **doesn't** want any help with the dishes.

(c) *Businessman* is a singular subject, so we use a singular verb: The businessman **hasn't** time for a canal tour.

(d) *Ain't* is not a word, so we choose *isn't*: The artist **isn't** finished with his painting.

Practice   For a–e, choose the correct verb form or contraction for each sentence.

a. Venus (ain't, isn't) the only planet in the solar system.

b. The binoculars (allows, allow) us to see Venus more clearly.

c. The Morning Star and the Evening Star (isn't, aren't) the only names for that bright planet.

d. (There's, There are) no other planets closer to Earth than Venus.

    e. Each of the planets (differ, differs) in diameter and mass.

For f–j, replace each blank with the correct vocabulary word.

    f. Joint replacements require both time and physical _____ in order to heal and return to normal.

    g. Anesthesiologists train for several years, for the _____ _____ of drugs requires skillful monitoring.

    h. The Greek root meaning "cure" is _____.

    i. Laughter is _____ for depression, discouragement, and disillusionment.

    j. The speech _____ prescribed exercises to improve the patient's pronunciation of *r*'s and *l*'s.

More Practice

Choose the correct verb form for each sentence.

    1. Tweezers (help, helps) remove splinters under the skin.

    2. The pants (has, have) a big hole in the knee.

    3. Business (isn't, ain't) good now.

    4. Everyone in sales (complain, complains) of being underpaid.

    5. Everybody at the Bowl Championship Series (pay, pays) an outrageous price for the ticket.

    6. Nobody in the upper grades (expect, expects) the rules to change.

    7. Either of them (perform, performs) well under pressure.

    8. Each of us (hope, hopes) to live a long, healthy life.

    9. Neither of the dogs (obey, obeys) the trainer.

    10. Of course, anyone (prefer, prefers) a well-trained pet.

    11. One of the athletic trainers (wrap, wraps) sprained ankles expertly.

    12. Jared (doesn't, don't) practice his harmonica enough.

    13. That orchestra (doesn't, don't) thrill the audience.

14. Republicans and Democrats (ain't, aren't) bickering as much as they were previously.

15. The farmer (ain't, isn't) happy about the ban on his most effective pesticide.

Review set 79   Choose the best word to complete sentences 1–16.

1. If King Arthur were narrating his own story, it would be
(76) in the (unlimited, camera, first-person) point of view.

2. A pyromaniac compulsively sets (tables, volleyballs,
(75) fires).

3. If you copy someone's writing and claim it as your own,
(11, 74) you are guilty of (misoneism, plagiarism, cacophony).

4. "A mechanic's job can be *wrenching*," contains a
(61, 72) (denotation, connotation, pun).

5. The Greek root (*pyro-, morph, cosmos*) means "world" or
(75, 77) "universe."

6. (Who, Whom) left the boa's cage open?
(67)

7. The boa frightened Ignacio and (I, me).
(51, 55)

8. Neither of the sisters (know, knows) (their, her) way
(38, 79) home.

9. Sir Galahad, (who, which) was destined to bear this
(63, 64) special sword, pulled it from the marble.

10. May (we, us) swimmers please use your swimming pool
(53, 66) today?

11. I am grateful for (him, his) teaching me to play the guitar.
(56, 58)

12. On top of the coop (sit, sits) two angry hens.
(77, 78)

13. Sir Gawain and Sir Percival have tried (there, they're,
(19, 56) their) best to remove the sword from the marble.

(74, 75) **14.** Sir Lancelot has (rode, ridden) deep into the forest.

Rewrite 15 and 16, adding capital letters and correct punctuation marks as needed.

15. during the 1930s millions of americans lost their jobs
(11, 35) their homes and their financial security

16. unfortunately said grandfather lucius the stock market
(26, 68) crashed so my investments became worthless

17. Write the gerund phrase in this sentence: Playing the
(19, 58) stock market led many people to ruin.

18. In this sentence, write the verb phrase and name its tense:
(18, 21) The Holy Grail had been appearing, from time to time, only to those pure in heart.

19. In this sentence, write whether the underlined clause is
(64, 65) essential or nonessential: The stock market, <u>which was like a big balloon</u>, finally burst in October of 1929.

20. Write whether the following is a complete sentence,
(1, 3) sentence fragment, or run-on sentence: Joseph of Arimathea had brought the Holy Grail to Britain could Sir Galahad find it?

21. Write the comparative form of the adjective *bad.*
(42, 43)

22. Write the objective case, first person, plural personal
(51, 54) pronoun.

23. In this sentence, write the indefinite pronoun and label it
(71) singular or plural: Do some of the soldiers march without their helmets?

24. In this sentence, write the pronoun and its antecedent:
(49) Monty insisted that he had shut the boa's cage.

25. Write the four principal parts of the irregular verb *give.*
(15, 73)

26. Use an appositive to make one sentence from these two
(45, 46) sentences: Sir Galahad is king of Sarras. Sir Galahad rules in faraway Babylon.

27. For a–c, write the plural of each noun.
(12, 13) (a) archetype   (b) wax   (c) elf

28. Write and underline each word that should be italicized
(72) in this sentence: In Sir Walter Scott's famous novel
Ivanhoe we meet such characters as Cedric the Saxon,
Lady Rowena, and Rebecca.

Diagram sentences 29 and 30.

29. Much of the fruit on the tree looks ripe and delicious.
(32, 39)

30. The lady who stole Tom's suitcase has false teeth.
(25, 64)

LESSON
80

Subject-Verb Agreement, Part 4

Dictation or Journal Entry

Vocabulary: We will expand our knowledge of literary terms.

Exposition usually occurs at the beginning of a novel or play and explains the background and setting of the story. Wilkie Collins gives an *exposition* and introduces the main characters in the first few chapters of the novel *Women in White*.

Figurative language, or "figures of speech," connote more than their literal meaning. Metaphors, similes, and personifications are types of *figurative language*.

Impressionism includes feelings and opinions of the author rather than just the facts. Newspaper editorials contain elements of *impressionism* because they give opinions of the writers.

Local color is detail that is specific to a certain area. Charles Dickens gives the *local color* of London with its dense fog and warehouses.

In this lesson, we will review agreement between subjects and verbs when the subject is a collective noun or a singular noun that seems to be plural.

Collective Nouns

A collective noun refers to a group or unit. The following words are collective nouns:

committee	*staff*	*faculty*	*team*
species	*army*	*pair*	*couple*

We use a singular verb if the collective noun refers to one unit.

The bicycling *group* <u>rides</u> together.

The *herd* <u>runs</u> wild when it hears thunder.

We use a plural verb if the collective noun refers to individuals within a group. The helping verb must also be plural.

The office *staff* <u>take</u> staggered summer vacations.

The *pair* <u>are purchasing</u> merchandise in different stores.

Special Singular Nouns

Some singular nouns appear to be plural, but they are not. The following singular nouns require a singular verb:

mumps	*measles*	*news*	*lens*

News <u>is</u> labeled "yellow journalism" if it exaggerates the facts.

Mumps <u>causes</u> one's cheeks to swell.

Special Singular or Plural Nouns   Some nouns have the same form whether they are singular or plural. *Corps*, *series*, *means*, *species*, and *gross*, as well as many animal names (*sheep*, *trout*, *bison*, *salmon*, etc.), are some examples. Use the meaning of the sentence to decide which verb form to use.

> SINGULAR: This *means* of transport <u>is</u> the best.
>
> PLURAL: Two other *means* <u>are</u> possible.
>
> SINGULAR: That *trout* <u>was</u> upstream.
>
> PLURAL: Several *trout* <u>were</u> downstream.

Finally, nouns that end in *-ics*, such as *mathematics*, *economics*, *ethics*, *athletics*, *acoustics*, and *politics,* can also be either singular or plural, depending on their meaning in the sentence. If we are referring to a body of knowledge, the noun is singular. If we are referring to a series of actions, the noun is plural:

> *Athletics* <u>is</u> her favorite class.
>
> Her *athletics* <u>are</u> amazing.

Example   Choose the correct verb form for each sentence.

(a) Mathematics (require, requires) patience and perseverance to understand all of the concepts.

(b) The jury (deliver, delivers) a verdict of guilt or innocence.

(c) The army (pitch, pitches) their tents in the wilderness.

(d) News (travel, travels) fast.

Solution   (a) Mathematics **requires** patience and perseverance to understand all of the concepts. ("Mathematics" is a singular noun in this sentence; it refers to a body of knowledge.)

(b) The jury **delivers** a verdict of guilt or innocence. ("Jury" is a collective noun referring to a unit.)

(c) The army **pitch** their tents in the wilderness. ("Army" is a collective noun referring to the individuals within the group in this case.)

(d) News **travels** fast. ("News" is a singular noun.)

Practice   Choose the correct verb form for sentences a–g.

a. The headquarters of the Salvation Army (remain, remains) in the United States.

b. Measles (cause, causes) an eruption of red blotches on the skin.

c. Athletics (is, are) a popular major at the university.

d. War news (capture, captures) the interest of almost any American.

e. The auxiliary (dress, dresses) in their finest uniforms on holidays.

f. The gaggle of geese (have, has) returned to the lake.

g. This gallows (hold, holds) suspected thieves until proper authorities arrive.

Vocabulary: For h–k, replace each blank with the correct vocabulary word.

h. The personification of leaves "dancing in the wind" is an example of _____ _____.

i. Sand dunes, a boardwalk, and the white caps of waves are examples of _____ _____ for a coastal story.

j. The author provided a thorough introduction or _____ of the backgrounds of the main characters.

k. Mark Twain uses _____ to inform the reader of his views on topics such as slavery, treatment of children, etc.

Review set 80   Choose the correct word(s) to complete sentences 1–15.

1. To say that the appearance of the Holy Grail was an unusual event is a(n) (euphony, heresy, understatement).
(13, 74)

2. An autograph is a signature written by one's (spouse, father, self).
(73)

3. Pyrography is the art of (painting, burning, tracing) a design in leather or wood.
(75)

4. A narrator reveals the thoughts and feelings of all the
(76) characters when the point of view is (unlimited, limited).

5. A cosmopolitan person feels at home all over the (oceans,
(77) mountains, world).

6. (Who, Whom) did the boa startle?
(67)

7. It startled (he and I, me and him, him and me).
(54, 66)

8. (Was, Were) either of the umpires wearing (their, his/her)
(77, 78) glasses?

9. The high fly ball (that, which) Monty hit flew over the
(64, 65) fence.

10. Please tell (we, us) swimmers the rules for this swim
(54, 66) meet.

11. Are you worried about (him, his) photographing reptiles
(56, 58) and arachnids in the desert?

12. Neither the hens nor the rooster (see, sees) me.
(38, 78)

13. Those hens are mine, but these are (her's, hers).
(56, 66)

14. My hens have (laid, lain) a dozen eggs this week.
(74, 75)

15. (There's, There are) eight planets in our solar system.
(79, 80)

16. Rewrite the following, adding capital letters and correct
(20, 46) punctuation marks as needed: william butler yeats an
irish poet wrote a short ballad called down by the salley
gardens

17. In this sentence, write the participial phrase followed by
(48, 59) the word it modifies: Entering the spacecraft, the
cosmonaut says good-bye to his Russian friends and
family.

18. In this sentence, write the verb phrase and label it
(25, 31) transitive or intransitive: Does Sir Lancelot grant the Fair
Maid of Astolat her last wish?

19. In this sentence, write whether the underlined clause is
(64, 65) essential or nonessential: The last pitch <u>that Jasmine threw</u> went over the batter's head.

20. From this sentence, write the dependent clause, circling
(24, 57) the subordinating conjunction: The people of Sarras made Galahad king after Estorause died.

21. Write the superlative form of the adjective *bad.*
(42, 43)

22. Write the objective case, third person, plural personal
(51, 54) pronoun.

23. In this sentence, write the indefinite pronoun and label it
(71) singular or plural: One of our tents has a hole in it.

24. Write the infinitive from this sentence and label it a noun
(23, 48) or an adjective: While walking around the park, Hillary likes to sing.

25. Write the four principal parts of the irregular verb *shake.*
(15, 75)

26. From this sentence, write each prepositional phrase,
(32, 33) starring the object of each preposition: According to rumors, the heathen ruler of the city of Sarras has thrown three knights into the dungeon.

27. Write whether the following is a phrase or a clause: about
(24) the Fair Maid's unrequited love for Sir Lancelot

28. Write and underline each word that should be italicized
(72) in this sentence: At the library, Molly likes to read magazines, especially National Geographic.

Diagram sentences 29 and 30.

29. A cosmopolis is a city inhabited by people from many
(33, 39) nations.

30. Helping people and curing diseases are therapists' main
(19, 37) objectives.

LESSON 81

Negatives • Double Negatives

Dictation or Journal Entry

Vocabulary: The Greek noun *hudōr* means "water," but appears in many English words as *hydro-* or *hydra-*.

Dehydrate is a verb meaning to deprive of water or to dry. An elevated body temperature will *dehydrate* an ill person.

Hydrophobia is the fear of water. *Hydrophobia* prevented him from learning to swim.

Hydrogen is a gas that becomes the liquid water when combined with oxygen. *Hydrogen* is a colorless, odorless, and flammable element.

A *hydrant* is a water faucet. Traffic laws prevent drivers from parking too close to fire *hydrants.*

Hydraulic is an adjective and refers to the use of water for motion. *Hydraulic* jacks provide an easier way to change a tire.

Negatives

Negatives are modifiers, usually adverbs, that mean "no" or "not." We will review adverbs later. In this lesson we will learn to recognize negatives and use them correctly. Negatives are italicized in the sentences below.

Steve *never* lies to his parents.

The lost puppy had *nowhere* to go.

He had *scarcely* finished when we arrived.

We do *not* know what the future holds.

Here is a list of common negatives:

no	*not*	*never*
hardly	*scarcely*	*barely*
nowhere	*none*	*no one*
nothing	*nobody*	

We see from the list above that the word *not* is a negative. Therefore, the contraction *n't* is also a negative:

Jasmine does*n't* understand Italian.

Perhaps she was*n't* listening.

I have*n't* studied for the test.

Example 1

Write each negative that you find in these sentences.

(a) I will barely have time to finish Jules Verne's novel.

(b) Hardly any of my friends enjoy science fiction.

(c) Juan did not remind anybody, so nobody remembered.

(d) The author was nowhere to be seen.

Solution (a) **barely**   (b) **Hardly**

(c) **not, nobody**   (d) **nowhere**

Double Negatives We use only one negative to express a negative idea. In the English language it is incorrect to use two negatives with one verb. We call this a **double negative,** and we avoid it.

NO: Mack *never* asks for *no* help. (double negative)
YES: Mack *never* asks for help.
YES: Mack asks for *no* help.

NO: Mr. Babikian has*n't no* beard. (double negative)
YES: Mr. Babikian has*n't* a beard.
YES: Mr. Babikian has *no* beard.

NO: A witness does*n't* need *no* lawyer. (double negative)
YES: A witness does*n't* need a lawyer.
YES: A witness needs *no* lawyer.

Example 2 Choose the correct word to complete each sentence. Avoid double negatives.

(a) The guests (would, wouldn't) hardly acknowledge the guards at the gate.

(b) Tobias doesn't bring (nothing, anything) to school.

(c) My new car doesn't need (no, any) gas.

Solution (a) The guests **would** hardly acknowledge the guards at the gate. (The words "wouldn't" and "hardly" are both negatives. We may use only one negative to express an idea, so we choose "would.")

(b) Tobias doesn't bring **anything** to school. (The words "doesn't" and "nothing" are both negatives. To avoid double negatives, we choose "anything.")

(c) My new car doesn't need **any** gas. (The words "doesn't" and "no" are both negatives. To avoid double negatives, we choose "any."

Correcting Double Negatives To correct a double negative, we can replace one of the negatives with a positive word. Study the positive forms of the negatives below:

NEGATIVE		POSITIVE
hardly	→	almost
no	→	any, a
nobody	→	anybody
nowhere	→	anywhere
never	→	ever
neither	→	either
none	→	any
no one	→	anyone
nothing	→	anything

Ben didn't eat ~~nothing~~ anything.

Lucille hasn't ~~no~~ a toothbrush.

Mack never wants ~~no~~ any advice.

Example 3 Rewrite this sentence and correct the double negative:

We couldn't find nobody.

Solution We replace the second negative, *nobody*, with a positive form—*anybody*:

We couldn't find *anybody*.

Remember that a sentence can contain more than one negative, as long as they are not in the same clause. The sentence below is not an example of a double negative because each negative is in a different clause.

She *didn't* work, so she has *no* money.

Rare Exceptions On rare occasions, we might use a double negative for effect. Look at the following sentences:

I was so eager to see you, I *couldn't not* come!

We had *barely, barely* enough money.

The double negative is deliberate in these sentences. Most double negatives, however, are unintended and incorrect. They are often heard in speech, but that is no excuse for using them.

Practice Choose the correct word to complete sentences a–e.

a. Mrs. Connor hardly (ever, never) travels to France.

b. Mallory (could, couldn't) find no cities on the map.

c. I've never seen (anything, nothing) like the mineral spa in Vichy, France.

d. Jake hasn't (ever, never) photographed Vichy.

e. I haven't bought (no, any) imported Vichy water.

For f–k, replace each blank with the correct vocabulary word.

f. Of all the elements, _____ is the lightest.

g. People with _____ often do not like to travel by ship over the ocean.

h. _____ machinery is powered by water.

i. Fire _____ are often painted bright yellow for high visibility.

j. The Greek root meaning water is _____.

k. On hot days, athletes may _____ if they don't drink large quantities of water.

More Practice Choose the correct word to complete these sentences.

1. Aaron doesn't have (no, a) job.

2. I didn't understand (nothing, anything) you said.

3. Kerry hasn't gone (nowhere, anywhere) today.

4. The potential witness screeched, "I didn't see (nothing, anything)!"

5. The starving peasant had hardly (no, any) food.

6. Moses had scarcely (no, any) time to sleep.

7. Cinderella hadn't (ever, never) attended a ball before.

8. The baby didn't touch (none, any) of the vegetables.

9. The bride and groom haven't left (no one, anyone) off the guest list.

10. Esther doesn't like (either, neither) color.

Review set 81 Choose the correct word(s) to complete sentences 1–15.

1. The narrator knows the thoughts and feelings of only one *(76)* character when the point of view is (unlimited, limited).

2. A cosmopolis is a city inhabited by people from all over *(77)* the (state, country, world).

3. An antithesis is an exact (replica, opposite, synonym). *(78)*

4. An (essay, epigram, antithesis) is a short, clever saying. *(78, 79)*

5. The Greek root (*cosmos, pyro-, therap-*) means *(77, 79)* cure.

6. For (who, whom) are you waiting? *(64, 66)*

7. (Me and him, Him and me, He and I) are waiting for (you *(53, 54)* and he, you and him).

8. One of the coaches (is, are) using (their, his/her) *(79, 80)* binoculars.

9. A high fly ball, (that, which) Allison hit, crashed through *(64, 65)* the Stern's window.

10. (We, Us) baseball players apologized to the Stern Family. *(53, 66)*

11. I think that Mr. Stern is tired of (us, our) playing baseball *(58, 66)* near his house.

12. The committee of experts (want, wants) my opinion. *(6, 15)*

13. He has his, but he (don't, doesn't) have (your's, yours). *(14, 56)*

(74, 75) **14.** Have you (swam, swum) the English Channel?

15. The tuxedo pants (is, are) neatly pressed.
(79)

16. Rewrite the following, adding capital letters and correct
(63, 68) punctuation marks: all right replied jim i will practice the cello feed the fish and wash the dishes while you mom are vacationing in wisconsin

17. In this sentence, write the gerund phrase: Is fighting with
(19, 58) people the best way to solve our problems?

18. In this sentence, write the verb phrase and name its tense:
(18, 21) For many months, the Fair Maid of Aslot had been searching for Sir Lancelot and her brother.

19. In this sentence, write whether the underlined clause is
(64, 65) essential or nonessential: The opossums <u>that live in the attic</u> kept me awake all night.

20. From this sentence, write the dependent clause, circling
(24, 57) the subordinating conjunction: Have you tried to wake an opossum after it has gone to sleep?

21. Write the comparative form of the adjective *generous*.
(42, 43)

22. Write the nominative case, third person, plural personal
(51, 53) pronoun.

23. In this sentence, write the indefinite pronoun and label it
(71) singular or plural: Undoubtedly, much of the work is too difficult for elementary school students.

24. In this sentence, write the pronoun and its
(49, 53) antecedent: Mr. Hake doesn't know if he will have time to play today.

25. Write the four principal parts of the irregular verb *sleep*.
75)

26. Use an appositive to make one sentence from these two
(45, 46) sentences: Piet Mondrian is a Dutch artist known for his nonrepresentational art. Piet Mondrian painted *Broadway Boogie-Woogie* to express his reactions to the world around him.

27. For a–c, write the plural of each noun.
(12, 13) (a) Harry   (b) baby   (c) son-in-law

28. Write and underline each part that should be italicized in
(72) this sentence: In the index, we find many entries under S
due to the many Sirs.

Diagram sentences 29 and 30.

29. A knight of noble character serves his king.
(25, 32)

30. Do you have time to relax?
(23, 25)

LESSON 82

The Hyphen: Compound Nouns, Numbers

The **hyphen** is a punctuation mark used in connecting elements of compound words and in expressing numbers.

Compound Nouns

We have learned that some compound nouns are hyphenated. There are no absolute rules for spelling a compound noun as one word, as two words, or hyphenated. However, certain categories of compound nouns are usually (but not always) hyphenated.

- Compound nouns that end in prepositional phrases:

right-of-way	father-in-law	stick-in-the-mud
tiger-at-large	man-about-town	attorney-at-law

- Compound nouns containing the prefix *ex-* or *-self* or the suffix *-elect*:

ex-President	self-discipline	President-elect

- Compound nouns that are units of measurement:

board-foot	man-hour	light-year

- Compound nouns that end with the prepositions *in, on,* or *between*:

check-in	stand-in	trade-in
add-on	goings-on	go-between

Nouns without Nouns? The English language is so flexible that we can create nouns from almost any part of speech. Look at the last category (compound nouns that end with prepositions) and notice that some of them don't contain an actual noun. Following are more examples of compound nouns formed from other parts of speech. We join the elements (words) with hyphens.

go-getter	know-it-all	has-been
get-together	look-alike	hand-me-down
sit-up	cure-all	merry-go-round

The dictionary lists many of these words. But no dictionary can show every single combination of words that might make up a compound noun. If you have the need for a unique combination, do what experienced writers do: use any similar words you can find in the dictionary to decide how to punctuate your compound noun.

Example 1 Write the words that should be hyphenated in sentences a–c.

(a) Casper has state of the art machinery in his shop.

(b) Several passers by noticed that the motorist needed help.

(c) How many man hours will be required for the project?

Solution These compound words need hyphens:

(a) **State-of-the-art** is a compound ending in a prepositional phrase.

(b) We check the dictionary and find that **passers-by** requires a hyphen to connect the preposition *by* to the first part of the compound word.

c) We use a hyphen in **man-hours** because it is a unit of measurement.

Numbers Hyphens are often used to join elements in the expression of numbers, inclusive sets or sequences, and fractions.

Numbers as Words We use a hyphen in compound numbers from twenty-one to ninety-nine:

forty-nine, seventy-six, thirty-three, etc.

A Range of Numbers   We use a hyphen to indicate a range of numbers or an inclusive set or sequence.

pages 14–29   the years 1985–1995

40–50 percent   the week of April 12–19

scores 98–107

Because the hyphen takes the place of pairs of words such as *from/through*, *from/to*, or *between/and*, we do not use one of the words and a hyphen.

INCORRECT: between 1995–2003

CORRECT: between 1995 and 2003

Example 2   Write the numbers and fractions that should be hyphenated in sentences a–d.

(a) Danny Cozak was still riding his bike when he was ninety seven years old.

(b) Junior celebrated his twenty second birthday yesterday.

(c) The set scores of the tennis match were 6 4, 3 6, and 4 6.

Solution   (a) **ninety-seven** is hyphenated because it is a number between 21 and 99.

(b) **twenty-second** is hyphenated because it is a number between 21 and 99.

(c) **6-4, 3-6, 4-6** are hyphenated because they are set scores from a tennis match.

Practice   For a–e, replace each blank with the correct literary term.

a. An omniscient _____ tells the reader the inner thoughts and feelings of all the characters.

b. The _____ of the story about the tortoise and the hare is to keep working steadily at a task even if it seems pointless.

c. There is a _____ explaining how the elephant got his unusual trunk.

d. Often, a beautiful _____ of the Christmas story accompanies a Christmas pageant.

   e. Saying, "You're on shallow ground there!" when you really mean, "You're on hallowed ground there!" is an example of a _____ .

For f–j, write each expression that should be hyphenated.

   f. Twenty one plus thirty one is fifty two.

   g. The check in time is three o'clock.

   h. Twenty four minutes and thirty two seconds remained on the phone card.

   i. A thirteen year old ice skater won the gold medal for the United States.

   j. Use words to write this number: 98

More Practice

For 1–4, use words to write each number.

   1. 26   **2.** 44   **3.** 81   **4.** 39

Write each expression that should be hyphenated in sentences 5–8.

   5. The University of Southern California beat its cross-town rival, the University of California at Los Angeles, 97 94 in last night's basketball game.

   6. My friend's follow up visit to the doctor revealed complete healing of the broken bone.

   7. Each passenger is allowed two pieces of luggage and one carry on.

   8. On her cruise, Aunt Bertha hardly noticed the up and down motion of the ship.

Review set 82

Choose the best word(s) to complete sentences 1–15.

   1. A therapist tries to (analyze, cure, discuss) a disease.
     (79)

   2. An example of figurative language is the (cliché, metaphor, satire).
     (72, 80)

   3. "Her legs collapsed like a folding chair" is an example of (irony, figurative language, empathy).
     (66, 80)

   4. Impressionism gives the author's (address, feelings, income) rather than just the facts.
     (80)

5. The Greek root (*pyro-*, *cosmos*, *hydra-*) means
(75, 81) water.

6. There are three kinds of verbals: the gerund, the
(19, 48) infinitive, and the (preposition, participle).

7. (Me and her, Her and me, She and I) will travel with (you
(53, 54) and he, you and him).

8. Neither of the artists (have, has) finished (their, his/her)
(79, 80) work yet.

9. I don't see (no, any) clouds in the sky at the moment.
(81)

10. Nancy has ridden horses more than (me, I).
(53, 66)

11. She said she likes (me, my) riding along with her.
(56, 66)

12. That group of spectators (cheer, cheers) louder than the
(78, 79) others.

13. (Wasn't, Weren't) there any scissors during the Middle
(77, 80) Ages?

14. Carolyn has (wove, woven) several colorful blankets.
(74, 75)

15. Sir Lancelot calls (himself, hisself) "The Knight of the
(60) Crimson Sleeve."

16. Rewrite the following, adding capital letters and correct
(5, 44) punctuation marks: in westminster england king arthur
and queen guinevere discover a letter dated wednesday
september 3 1250

17. In this sentence, write the infinitive and label it a noun or
(23, 48) an adjective: Sleeping peacefully, the weary maiden
began to dream.

18. In this sentence, write the verb phrase and name its tense:
(8, 18) Among the lords and ladies of the kingdom, poisonous
gossip had been mistaken for the truth.

19. In this sentence, write whether the underlined clause is
(64, 65) essential or nonessential: The opossums, <u>which kept me
awake last night</u>, are living in my attic.

20. From this sentence, write the dependent clause, circling
(24, 57) the subordinating conjunction: After running in the heat,
I felt dehydrated even though I had drunk plenty of
water.

21. Write the four common pairs of correlative conjunctions.
(38)

22. Write the nominative case, third person, singular (neuter
(53, 55) gender) personal pronoun.

23. In this sentence, write the indefinite pronoun and label it
(71) singular or plural: I see that most of the banana cream pie
has been eaten.

24. In this sentence, write each prepositional phrase, starring
(32, 33) the object of each preposition: Mordred, the dishonorable
nephew of King Arthur, holds onto his jealousy and rage
towards Lancelot.

25. Write the four principal parts of the irregular verb *run.*
(15, 75)

26. In this sentence, write the verb phrase and label it action
(4, 22) or linking: Does Mordred look suspicious?

27. Write whether the following is a complete sentence,
(1, 3) sentence fragment, or run-on sentence: Refusing to
believe Mordred's lies or to fall into his trap.

28. Write and underline each word that should be italicized
(72) in this sentence: Broadway is a street in New York City,
but Broadway Boogie-Woogie is a painting by Piet
Mondrian.

Diagram sentences 29 and 30.

29. Was fighting the solution to all the knights' problems?
(19, 39)

30. Picasso liked painting, but Poe enjoyed writing.
(19, 25)

LESSON 83

Adverbs that Tell "How"

Dictation or Journal Entry

Vocabulary: The Greek word *psychē* means "mind" or "soul."

Psychology is the science of the mind. One learns about basic human needs in a *psychology* class.

Psyche refers to a person's psychological or mental structure. The *psyche* of a schizophrenic is fractured and unstable.

A *psychic* is a person who is supposedly sensitive to the forces of the mind. A *psychic* is also known as a medium.

A *psychosis* is a serious mental disorder that causes one to lose touch with reality. In *Miracle on Thirty-fourth Street,* the psychiatrist thought that Kris Kringle, believing he was Santa Claus, suffered from *psychosis.*

Psychotherapy is the professional treatment of mental disorders or maladjustments. Alcoholics Anonymous is a form of *psychotherapy,* for it teaches its participants the reasons for their alcohol abuse.

Adverbs are descriptive words that "modify" or add information to verbs, adjectives, and other adverbs. They answer the questions "how," "when," "where," and "how much" (or "to what extent"). The italicized adverbs below modify the verb *dressed*:

HOW: The President dressed *meticulously.*

WHEN: He dressed *promptly.*

WHERE: He dressed *here.*

HOW MUCH: He dressed *frequently.*

"How"   In this lesson we will focus on adverbs that tell "how." An adverb that tells "how" usually modifies the verb or verb phrase and often ends in *ly*. For example, let's think about how Wendy surfs:

Wendy surfs *fanatically.*

Wendy might also surf *beautifully, clumsily, recklessly, cautiously, expertly,* or *uncertainly.* These adverbs answer the question "how" she surfs.

Example 1   Write the adverbs that tell "how" from this sentence:

The elderly gentleman walked carefully and slowly with his cane.

Solution   The adverbs **carefully** and **slowly** tell "how" the gentleman walked.

Suffix -*ly* We remember that descriptive adjectives often end with suffixes such as *-able*, *-ful*, *-ive*, or *-ous*. Below are the adjective and adverb forms of some nouns. Notice that the adverb is formed by adding *-ly* to the adjective.

NOUN	ADJECTIVE	ADVERB
truth	*truthful*	*truthfully*
beauty	*beautiful*	*beautifully*
grace	*graceful*	*gracefully*
peace	*peaceful*	*peacefully*
joy	*joyful*	*joyfully*
patience	*patient*	*patiently*
sincerity	*sincere*	*sincerely*
love	*loving*	*lovingly*

Of course, not every word that ends in *-ly* is an adverb. *Ghastly, chilly, lovely, orderly,* and *friendly* are all adjectives.

Adjective or Adverb? Some words, such as *hard, fast, right, early,* and *long,* have the same form whether they are used as adjectives or adverbs. However, we can always tell how the word is being used because an adjective modifies a noun or pronoun, and an adverb modifies a verb, adjective, or other adverb.

ADJECTIVE: I fell on *hard* ice. (modifies the noun "ice")
ADVERB: I skated *hard*. (modifies the verb "skated")

ADJECTIVE: It was a *fast* car. (modifies the noun "car")
ADVERB: Leopold drove *fast*. (modifies the verb "drove")

ADJECTIVE: Make a *right* turn at the stop sign.
ADVERB: Please turn *right* at the stop sign.

ADJECTIVE: We attended an *early* class.
ADVERB: We attended class *early*.

We look carefully to distinguish between an adverb and a predicate adjective. Consider the following sentence:

The new student felt lonely.

It might seem that *lonely* tells "how" the student felt. But we remember that we can identify a predicate adjective by replacing a possible linking verb (felt) with a "to be" verb:

The new student *was* lonely. (lonely student)

The word *lonely* describes the student, not the act of feeling. It is an adjective. Compare this to a sentence containing an action verb:

The new student works silently.

If we replace an action verb with a "to be" verb, the sentence no longer makes sense:

The new student *is* silently? (silently student?)

Silently does not describe the student. It describes the act of working. It is an adverb.

Example 2 Tell whether the italicized word in each sentence is an adjective or adverb. Also, tell which word or phrase it modifies.

(a) Please stand *still*.

(b) The *still* air seemed eerie after the hurricane.

(c) Sometimes the air grows *still* before a storm.

Solution (a) The word *still* is an **adverb that modifies the verb "stand."** *Still* tells "how" to stand.

(b) The word *still* is an **adjective. It modifies the noun "air."** *Still* tells "what kind" of air.

(c) The word *still* is a predicate **adjective modifying the noun "air."**

Practice For sentences a–c, write each adverb that tells "how" and tell what word or phrase it modifies.

a. In the Lipari Islands near Sicily, the volcano, Stromboli, erupts violently and frequently.

b. Paroxysmal eruptions spew stones and ashes explosively and forcefully.

c. Volcanoes in Hawaii erupt quietly and continually.

For d–g, tell whether the italicized word is an adjective or an adverb, and give the word or phrase it modifies.

d. While in France, Jen felt *chilly*.

e. The French writer and philosopher, Voltaire, wrote *brilliantly* and *sarcastically*.

f. The bust of Voltaire appears *homely*.

g. Voltaire's writings *accurately* revealed the heinous crimes of the French regent, Philippe II.

For h–l, replace each blank with the correct vocabulary word.

h. George Bailey thought his angel, who had lost touch with reality, suffered from _____.

i. The Old Testament forbids the use of a _____ to read people's minds or look into the future.

j. Group therapy is a form of _____ and helps those who are grieving over the death of a loved one.

k. When we study _____ we learn how complex our minds are.

l. The athlete's _____ included a determination to keep on trying.

Review set 83   Choose the correct word(s) to complete sentences 1–15.

1. To dehydrate is to become deprived of (food, shelter, water).
(81)

2. A person's diary is written in the (first-, third-) person point of view.
(76)

3. The Greek word *cosmos* means (fire, form, world).
(75, 77)

4. Cowardice is the antithesis of (fear, drama, bravery).
(70, 78)

5. Mr. Pecksniff used a (vulgarity, malapropism, myth) when he said that changes in life are *inedible*.
(63, 82)

6. Words like *no, hardly, none, scarcely,* and *barely* are examples of (appositives, adjectives, negatives).
(27, 81)

7. Sir Gawain and (they, them) refuse to believe Mordred's lies.
(53, 66)

8. Each of the opossums (have, has) (their, its) own stash of
(79, 80) fruit.

9. We haven't (ever, never) seen a white buffalo on this
(81) prairie.

10. (Me and him, He and I, Him and me) tried harder than
(53, 66) you and (her, she).

11. Please send (us, we) cooks your favorite recipes.
(54, 66)

12. That huge box of science books (is, are) still sitting on the
(77, 78) floor of the library.

13. Chicken pox (was, were) a serious communicable disease
(79, 80) during medieval times.

14. I (saw, seen) some interesting critters in the attic.
(73, 74)

15. Sir Gareth and (me, myself, I) told King Arthur about
(53, 60) Mordred's lies.

16. Rewrite the following, adding capital letters and correct
(26, 82) punctuation marks, including hyphens: half of my class
has already completed the first twenty five lessons of the
english grammar book said mrs smith

17. In this sentence, write the participial phrase followed by
(48, 59) the word it modifies: Sleeping peacefully, the weary
maiden began to snore.

18. In this sentence, write the verb phrase and name its tense:
(8, 21) The knights were riding out the castle gates and into
perilous unknown territory.

19. In this sentence, write whether the underlined clause is
(64, 65) essential or nonessential: The opossum _that woke me_ was
hanging by its tail and munching a crispy apple.

20. From this sentence, write the dependent clause, circling
(24, 57) the subordinating conjunction: Sir Gawain became more
enraged when Sir Lancelot refused to fight back.

21. For a–c, write the plural of each noun. Use the dictionary
(12, 13) if you are not sure.

(a) shovelful   (b) staff   (c) axis

22. Write the objective case, third person, singular
(54, 55) (masculine gender) personal pronoun.

23. In this sentence, write the indefinite pronoun and label it
(71) singular or plural: Strangely, some of the left-over
spaghetti has disappeared from the refrigerator.

24. Write the superlative form of the adjective *tasty.*
(42, 43)

25. Write the four principal parts of the irregular verb *lose.*
(15, 73)

26. In this sentence, write the verb phrase and label it
(25, 31) transitive or intransitive: Is the fallen Sir Gawain crying
loudly?

27. Write whether the following is a complete sentence,
(1, 3) sentence fragment, or run-on sentence: Sir Lancelot
refuses to fight back Sir Gawain becomes more enraged.

28. Write and underline each word that should be italicized
(72) in this sentence: On Saturday, my family and I are going
to see a musical play called Camelot.

Diagram sentences 29 and 30.

29. Having learned the truth, Sir Lancelot feels discouraged.
(39, 59)

30. The artist whom you met likes painting penguins.
(19, 64)

LESSON 84

Using the Adverb *Well*

Good The words *good* and *well* are frequently misused. *Good* is a descriptive adjective or a predicate adjective. It describes a noun or pronoun as in these sentences:

James Fenimore Cooper is a *good* novelist.
(descriptive adjective modifying "novelist")

He wrote some *good* books.
(descriptive adjective modifying "books")

That novel sounds *good.*
(predicate adjective describing "novel")

Well The word *well* is usually an adverb. It modifies an action verb and explains "how" someone does something.

That tenor sings *well.*

Monty and Tom play football *well.*

How *well* do you play this game?

We do not use the word *good* as an adverb. Instead, we use *well.* See these examples:

NO: Kerry cooks *good.*
YES: Kerry cooks *well.*

NO: This invention works *good.*
YES: This invention works *well.*

Example 1   Replace each blank with *well* or *good.*

(a) Did you sleep _____ last night?

(b) James Fenimore was a _____ man with a great love for his family.

        (c) His books sold _____ in the United States.

        (d) Natty Bumppo's _____ qualities include independence and skill.

Solution   (a) Did you sleep **well** last night? *Well* is an adverb telling "how" you did sleep.

        (b) James Fenimore was a **good** man with a great love for his family. *Good* is an adjective which modifies the noun "man."

        (c) His books sold **well** in the United States. *Well* is an adverb which modifies the verb "sold." It tells "how" his books sold.

        (d) Natty Bumppo's **good** qualities include independence and skill. *Good* is an adjective which modifies the noun "qualities."

Feeling Well?   The word *well* is used as an adjective when referring to the state of one's health. You feel *good* about passing a test, for example, but when you wish to state that you are in good health, it is preferable to say that you are *well*.

I feel *well* today.

Is Buster *well*, or is he still sick?

Example 2   Choose either *well* or *good* to complete each sentence.

        (a) Kate had a (good, well) feeling when she finished the psychology research paper.

        (b) Today I am ill; yesterday, I felt (good, well).

Solution   (a) Kate had a **good** feeling…. (We use *good* because it is an adjective modifying "feeling." Also, it does not refer to one's health.)

        (b) Today I am ill; yesterday, I felt **well.** (It is preferable to use the word *well* to describe how one feels.)

Practice   Choose the correct descriptive word for sentences a–e.

        a. The neighbors worked together (good, well) to build the bridge.

b. Dale did a (good, well) job sawing the lumber.

c. They prefer their potatoes baked (good, well).

d. Emerson's philosophic essays gave him a (good, well) reputation.

e. His wife, Ellen Tucker, did not feel (good, well), for she had tuberculosis.

Replace each blank with the correct literary term.

f. The climax came too early in the _____ _____ to make the story interesting.

g. A character's flat tire on the way to work is an example of _____ if it is included in a story.

h. The moral of the _____ was to use the gifts that you have rather than to wish that you had more.

i. Did you notice the meter and stanza pattern in this piece of _____?

j. "Wash your face, comb your hair, and brush your teeth" uses the literary technique of _____.

More Practice

Choose the correct descriptive word for each sentence.

1. Glasses look (good, well) on most people.

2. How (good, well) do you know the life story of Ralph Waldo Emerson?

3. Did he dance (good, well)?

4. He may have been a (good, well) dancer.

5. The macaroni casserole smelled (good, well).

6. Judy is feeling (good, well) today.

7. Emerson argued (well, good) with boys his own age.

8. Emerson had a (good, well) voice for preaching.

9. Rumpelstiltskin spun straw very (good, well).

10. Indeed, he spun a (good, well) skein of gold.

**Review set
84**

Choose the correct word(s) to complete sentences 1–15.

1. The statement "Aunt Clara sipped her tea and *medicated*
(70, 82) about the events of her day" includes a (genre, resolution, malapropism).

2. Hydraulic machines use (oil, coal, water) for motion.
(81)

3. The Greek root (*morphe, therap-, psychē*) means "mind"
(79, 83) or "soul."

4. (Exposition, Impressionism, Antithesis) explains the
(78, 80) background and setting of a story.

5. (Stream of consciousness, Point of view, Slice of life) is
(72, 76) the narrator's position in relation to the story.

6. *Now, then, soon, often,* and *here* function in sentences as
(83, 84) (nouns, adverbs, adjectives).

7. (Her and me, Me and her, She and I) walked farther than
(53, 66) you and (him, he).

8. Dad appreciates (us, our) washing and waxing the car.
(54, 58)

9. "Dogs don't train (theirselves, themselves)," said the
(60) obedience instructor.

10. (Isn't, Ain't, Aren't) there any hedge clippers in the shed?
(81)

11. Molly has (her's, hers), but she (don't, doesn't) have
(56, 77) (their's, theirs).

12. The young artist (who, whom) we met at the exhibition
(64, 65) has become famous for his penguin paintings.

13. The penguin (that, which) he painted yesterday has
(64, 65) funny-looking ears.

14. The squirrels have (ate, eaten) all the sunflower seeds.
(73, 74)

15. Of the two horses, King Arthur's was the (taller, tallest).
(42, 43)

16. Rewrite the following, adding capital letters and correct
(35, 82) punctuation marks, including hyphens: last tuesday dr getz spent forty five minutes reading us his favorite short

story about king arthur its title was how king arthur and sir gawain went to france

17. For a–c, write whether the *-ing* word in each sentence is a verb, participle, or gerund.

(15, 19) (a) Battling consumes Sir Gawain.

(27, 48) (b) Sir Lancelot subdues the battling Sir Gawain.

(4, 15) (c) Sir Gawain is battling against Sir Lancelot.

18. In this sentence, write the verb phrase and name its tense:
(8, 18) Has the band of knights ridden into an enemy snare?

19. In this sentence, write whether the underlined clause is
(64, 65) essential or nonessential: That silly sentence, <u>which contained a malapropism</u>, made me laugh.

20. From this sentence, write the dependent clause, circling
(24, 57) the subordinating conjunction: Before Sir Gawain dies, he begs Sir Lancelot's forgiveness.

21. Write the seven common coordinating conjunctions.
(36)

22. Write the nominative case, third person, singular
(53, 55) (masculine gender) personal pronoun.

23. For sentences a and b, write whether the italicized word
(27, 83) functions as an adjective or an adverb.

(a) Benito runs *fast*.

(b) He is a *fast* runner.

24. From this sentence, write the pronoun followed by its
(49, 53) antecedent: After Debby fed the cats, dogs, and horses, she edited the company newsletter.

25. Write the four principal parts of the irregular verb *catch*.
(15, 73)

26. Write whether the following is a phrase or a clause: from
(24, 57) the perspective of a nineteenth century coal miner in Holland

27. From this sentence, write each prepositional phrase,
(17, 32) starring the object of each preposition: In spite of the thunderstorm, we drove throughout the night across the desert to Mom's hometown.

28. Write and underline each word that should be italicized
(72) in this sentence: Beowulf is the first English epic poem
written down in the Anglo-Saxon tongue between 800
and 900 A.D.

Diagram sentences 29 and 30.

29. Sir Gawain was stubborn and vindictive.
(37, 41)

30. The flustered receptionist asked me to wait.
(23, 25)

LESSON 85

The Hyphen: Compound Adjectives

Dictation or Journal Entry

Vocabulary: The Greek word *thermos* means "hot" or "heat."

Hypothermia is a subnormal body temperature. Swimmers use wet-suits in cold water to avoid *hypothermia.*

Hyperthermia is an elevated body temperature. The body fights disease with *hyperthermia.*

A *thermostat* is a device to automatically maintain a certain temperature. The gas company encourages consumers to set their *thermostats* at sixty-eight degrees.

A *thermometer* measures the temperature. The nurse placed a *thermometer* under the patient's tongue to measure the body temperature.

A *thermos* is an insulated bottle intended to keep liquids hot or cold.

We have seen how hyphens are used in compound nouns and with numbers. In this lesson we will discuss more uses for hyphens.

Compound Adjectives

Just as we combine words to form compound nouns, we can combine words to form **compound adjectives**. A compound adjective is a group of words that works *as a unit* to modify a noun with a single thought. It is not a list of adjectives, each modifying a noun in its own way.

COMPOUND ADJECTIVE:	*cheese-filled* crust
TWO ADJECTIVES:	*crisp, flaky crust*
COMPOUND ADJECTIVE:	*handwoven* basket
TWO ADJECTIVES:	*colorful wicker* basket
COMPOUND ADJECTIVE:	*blue* and *white* shirt
THREE ADJECTIVES:	*clean white dress* shirt

As shown above, compound adjectives can be spelled as one word, left as separate words, or hyphenated. How they appear is sometimes a matter of rule but is often a matter of custom or style. The following guidelines will help you form many compound adjectives confidently.

Clarity

Our goal is to make our meaning as clear as possible to the reader. When we use hyphens to join two or more words, it helps the reader understand that the words are to be read as a single unit. This prevents confusion. Consider this sentence:

The company sponsored teams of athletes are here.

The reader, seeing a subject (company), a verb (sponsored), and a direct object (teams), is likely to misread the sentence. So we hyphenate the compound adjective for greater clarity:

The company-sponsored teams of athletes are here.

Borrowed phrases and clauses One of the ways we modify nouns is by borrowing descriptive phrases and clauses and using them as compound adjectives. Hyphens help join words that work as a unit to modify a noun.

Prepositional phrases When we use a prepositional phrase to modify a noun, it is functioning as a compound adjective. If it comes *before* the noun, it should be hyphenated.

An *up-to-date* dictionary is preferable.
(The dictionary is *up to date*.)

He made an *off-the-record* comment.
(They took the comment *off the record*.)

Words out of order When we borrow a descriptive phrase or clause and place it before a noun, we often eliminate or rearrange some of the words. To help them express a single thought, words that are out of their normal order can be held together by hyphens.

A *mud-covered* dog sat in my lap.
(The dog was *covered with mud*.)

The *happy-looking* mutt wagged its tail.
(The mutt *looked happy*.)

An exception We *do not* use a hyphen in a compound adjective that begins with an adverb ending in *-ly*.

some *nicely kept* yards, a *securely fastened* latch

the *newly married* couple, my *painfully swollen* wrist

Number + unit of measure We use a hyphen when joining a number to a unit of measure to form a compound adjective.

12-foot pipe, *five-mile* hike, *three-year* project

We *do not* use a hyphen when the number alone modifies the noun:

12 feet, five miles, three years

Fractions We use a hyphen in a fraction that functions as an adjective.

Sam won the election by a *two-thirds* majority.

The container is *three-fifths* full.

If the numerator or the denominator of a fraction is already hyphenated, *do not* use another hyphen:

A *five twenty-fifths* increase equals a *one-fifth* increase.

We *do not* use a hyphen if the fraction functions as a noun.

Three fourths of my relatives live nearby.

Example 1   Write the words that should be hyphenated in sentences a–e.

(a) The gel filled capsule dissolved easily in water.

(b) We enjoyed the after dinner mints.

(c) Sweet smelling roses covered the trellis.

(d) I need a six inch piece of tape.

(e) Three eighths of the tomato plants survived the storm.

Solution   (a) We hyphenate **gel-filled** because the words work as unit to modify the noun *capsule* with a single thought: filled with gel.

(b) We hyphenate **after-dinner** because it is a prepositional phrase that comes before and modifies the noun *mints.*

(c) We hyphenate **sweet-smelling** to help it retain its meaning (something that smells sweet).

(d) We hyphenate **six-inch** because it is a compound adjective formed by a number and a unit of measure.

(e) **None.** We do not hyphenate the fraction three eighths because it is functioning as a noun.

Dictionary clues   Remember, dictionaries cannot contain all the compound words we can create. But if you are faced with an unfamiliar compound, you can search the dictionary for similar compounds and use them as clues.

Other uses for hyphens   We use hyphens to avoid confusion or awkward spelling, and to join unusual elements.

With prefixes and suffixes   If you add a prefix or suffix to a word, and the resulting word is misleading or awkward, use a hyphen for clarity.

Sam will *re-press* (not *repress*) his suit before he wears it.

A *shell-like* (not *shelllike*) material covered the surface.

I must *re-educate* (not *reeducate)* myself.

Also, use a hyphen to join a prefix to any proper noun.

pro-American, mid-November, post-World War II

Letter + word, number + number
Hyphens are used to combine unusual elements into single expressions.

When a letter (or group of letters) modifies a word in a compound noun or adjective, a hyphen is often used.

C-clamp, U-turn, y-coordinate, t-shirt, B-rated

We can also use a hyphen to join numbers in expressions such as the following:

The final score was *89-97*.

I have a *fifty-fifty* chance of flipping heads.

Example 2 Write the words, if any, that should be hyphenated in sentences a–d. Be prepared to use the dictionary.

(a) She must research her office for her keys.

(b) Why are they antiAmerican?

(c) The builder will use an a frame for the roof.

(d) They will divide the cost sixty forty.

Solution (a) We hyphenate **re-search** to avoid misleading the reader.

(b) We hyphenate **anti-American** because we are joining a prefix and a proper noun.

(c) We consult the dictionary and find that **a-frame** is a hyphenated term.

(d) We use a hyphen to form the expression **sixty-forty**.

Practice Write the words, if any, that should be hyphenated in sentences a–e.

a. Parents should evaluate PG 13 rated movies before giving permission for their teenagers to see them.

b. A pro American advertising company is urging consumers to purchase American made products.

c. The self appointed division manager resigned all the checks and documents.

d. A rapidly moving forest fire engulfed the canyon.

e. I'll need a six yard length of ribbon for the gift.

For f–k, replace each blank with the correct vocabulary word.

f. According to the _____, the temperature was one hundred degrees outside.

g. If you put your soup in a _____, it will stay hot until lunchtime.

h. The unfortunate boater suffered _____ after she fell into the icy water.

i. Strep throat is often accompanied by _____.

j. The air conditioner cycles "on" when the _____ registers seventy-eight degrees.

k. The Greek word meaning "heat" is _____.

Review set 85

Choose the correct word(s) to complete sentences 1–15.

1. A hydrant is a source of (soda, hydrogen, water).
(81)

2. When Hank said, "The car went out of control and crossed the *comedian* strip," he used a (narration, moral, malapropism).
(82)

3. Psychology is the science of the (earth, mind, universe).
(83)

4. A (plot line, parable, psychic) is a short story with a moral.
(83, 84)

5. (Impressionism, Local color) is detail that is specific to a certain area.
(80)

6. After the picnic, I (could, couldn't) eat no more watermelon.
(81)

7. Sam thinks that physics (is, are) difficult to comprehend.
(4, 14)

8. A flock of sheep (has, have) been grazing in the meadow.
(14, 80)

9. (Us, We) volunteers would like another opportunity to
(53, 66) help you.

10. (Her and me, Me and her, She and I) usually work as late
(53, 66) as (he, him).

11. He (don't doesn't) have (no, any) time to waste.
(14, 81)

12. One of the opossums (leave, leaves) (their, its) tracks in
(77, 78) the garden soil each night.

13. Sometimes I can see the raccoons and (they, them) in the
(25, 54) moonlight.

14. My sleeping beagle has not (drove, driven) these
(73, 74) nocturnal creatures from my vegetable patch.

15. Debby, please help Christie and (me, myself, I) with our
(25, 54) grammar.

16. Rewrite the following, adding capital letters and correct
(11, 85) punctuation marks, including hyphens: this recipe said
aunt bea calls for three and three fourths cups of well
sifted flour it makes twenty four pancakes

17. For a–c, write whether the *-ing* word in each sentence is a
(15, 19, 48) verb, participle, or gerund.

    (a) Laughing improves our health.

    (b) Mordred scowled at the laughing children.

    (c) The children were laughing at Mordred.

18. In this sentence, write the verb phrase and name its tense:
(8, 21) The villain was attacking King Arthur's cavalry on the
shores of Dover.

19. In this sentence, write whether the underlined clause is
(64, 65) essential or nonessential: The Tower of London, <u>which
housed Queen Guinevere</u>, protected her until King
Arthur returned to England.

20. From this sentence, write the dependent clause, circling
(24, 57) the subordinating conjunction: I shall bring you some
gummy bears as soon as I find Tom's suitcase.

21. For a–c, write the plural of each noun.
(12, 13) (a) Curtis   (b) sheaf   (c) father-in-law

22. Write the nominative case, third person, singular
(51, 53) (feminine gender) personal pronoun.

23. For sentences a and b, write whether the italicized word
(27, 83) functions as an adjective or an adverb.
    (a) We are working *hard.*
    (b) This is *hard* work.

24. Use an appositive to make one sentence from these two
(45, 46) sentences: Grandpa frequently tells me his favorite old
saying. Grandpa's favorite old saying is, "A rolling stone
gathers no moss."

25. Write the four principal parts of the irregular verb *cost.*
(15, 75)

26. Write the comparative form of the adjective *tasty.*
(42, 43)

27. In this sentence, write each infinitive, labeling it an
(27, 48) adjective or a noun: This is Sir Gawain's opportunity to
forgive and to forget.

28. Write and underline each word that should be italicized
(72) in this sentence: Professor Fidget is looking in the
classified section of the New York Times for a used
washing machine.

Diagram sentences 29 and 30.

29. Laughing, Maristela handed Lilibet a gorilla costume.
(25, 31)

30. Sir Gawain regrets having doubted the integrity of Sir
(19, 25) Lancelot.

LESSON 86

Adverbs that Tell "Where"

Dictation or Journal Entry

Vocabulary: Let us discuss more literary terms.
Rising action refers to those problems that occur before the climax of a story. In the *Prince and the Pauper*, the *rising action* includes the boys' identity switch.

Romance is writing that pictures life as the writer might like it to be rather than as it really is. The exciting life of James Bond is an example of *romance*.

Sarcasm is the use of sharp, cutting remarks or language intended to mock, wound, or ridicule. "That was a smart thing to say!" is *sarcasm*, if the speaker really means, "That was a stupid statement."

The *structure* of a written piece is its form. The required *structure* of the writing assignment was a poem.

A *symbol* is a concrete object used to represent an idea. The American flag is a *symbol* of the United States of America.

We have identified adverbs that tell "how." In this lesson, we will review adverbs that tell "where." Again, let's think about how the President dresses:

> The President dresses *meticulously*.

"Where" Now, let's think about **where** the President dresses:

> The President dresses *inside*.

He might also dress *somewhere, here, there,* or *anywhere*.

Here are some common adverbs that tell "where:"

nearby	*anywhere*	*up*	*in*
far	*everywhere*	*here*	*out*
down	*nowhere*	*there*	*home*
uptown	*somewhere*	*upstream*	*inside*
downtown	*around*	*downstream*	*outside*

We remember that words like *in, out*, and *down* can also be prepositions. But in order to function as a preposition, a word must have an object. When a word like *in, out, up,* or *down* does not have an object, it is an adverb.

PREPOSITION: He climbed *up* the stairs. (object "stairs")

ADVERB: He climbed *up*. (no object)

Example 1   For sentences a–d, write each adverb that tells "where," and give the verb or verb phrase that it modifies.

(a) The legend of William Tell is known everywhere.

(b) William Tell proceeded outside and shot an arrow through an apple on his young son's head.

(c) Tell was imprisoned somewhere for opposing Gessler, the despotic Austrian governor of Uri.

(d) Gessler sat nearby and watched William Tell perform his punishment.

Solution (a) The adverb **everywhere** tells "where" the legend of William Tell **is known**.

(b) The adverb **outside** modifies the verb **proceeded**, telling "where" William Tell proceeded.

(c) The adverb **somewhere** modifies the verb **was imprisoned**, telling "where" Tell was imprisoned.

(d) The adverb **nearby** modifies the verb **sat**, telling "where" Gessler sat.

Diagramming We diagram adverbs just as we do adjectives. We write the adverb on a slanted line under the word it modifies. Here we diagram a sentence containing an adverb:

The President dresses *inside*.

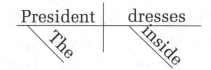

Example 2 Diagram this sentence: The raft floated downstream.

Solution We see that the adverb *downstream* tells "where" the raft floated, so we diagram the sentence like this:

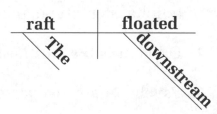

Practice Write each adverb that tells "where" in sentences a–d, then write the verb or verb phrase it modifies.

a. The bear lumbered inside to eat.

b. Bessie has gone nowhere.

c. Eric might have been working there.

d. Squirrels scampered around.

Diagram sentences e and f.

e. Brian and Kim searched everywhere.

f. Tucker had dropped his wallet somewhere.

For g–k, replace each blank with the correct vocabulary word.

g. Dredging the river in search of "dead" Tom Sawyer is an example of the _____ _____ in a story.

h. When everyone is lazily lying around, the comment, "Well, aren't we a lively group today!" is _____.

i. An example of _____ in literature is the changing of the Beast into a handsome prince.

j. The lion is a _____ of strength, majesty, and power.

k. The dramatic _____ of the play included soliloquies by the main characters.

Review set 86 Choose the correct word(s) to complete sentences 1–15.

1. Have you heard the old saying, "A rolling stone gathers no moss"? When Hank said, "A rolling stone gathers no *moths*," he used a (satire, antipathy, malapropism). *(82)*

2. Hydrophobia is fear of (people, heights, water). *(81)*

3. "The pickle *relishes* being part of a sandwich," contains a (cliché, stereotype, pun). *(52, 72)*

4. Diligent is the antithesis of (lazy, hard-working, wise). *(78)*

5. Psyche refers to a person's (eyes, body, mind). *(83)*

6. This spaghetti that you made tastes (good, well). *(22, 84)*

7. Can (me and him, him and me, he and I) meet you and (she, her) for dinner? *(53, 54)*

8. I think he resents (me, my) beating him in chess.
(56, 58)

9. Inez and (me, myself, I) play chess daily.
(51, 53)

10. Mathematics (isn't, ain't, aren't) difficult if you practice
(80) the concepts.

11. You don't have (your's, yours), and she (don't, doesn't)
(56, 81) have (her's, hers).

12. The artist (who, whom) sold me a penguin painting has
(64, 65) become famous in Maine.

13. The exhibit, (that, which) opened last Tuesday, has
(64, 65) attracted tourists from all over the world.

14. The cavalry has (rode, ridden) twelve miles today.
(73, 74)

15. Of all the horses, mine was the (more, most) spirited.
(42, 43)

16. Rewrite the following, adding capital letters and correct
(63, 85) punctuation marks, including hyphens: excuse me dad
but isn't this a self cleaning oven asked tom

17. For a–c, write whether the *-ing* word in each sentence is a
verb, participle, or gerund.

(27, 48)(a) The whistling wind signaled the onset of another
storm.

(4, 6) (b) The wind was whistling through the tall redwoods.

(19, 25)(c) Jasmine enjoys whistling show tunes.

18. In this sentence, write the verb phrase and name its tense:
(8, 18) King Arthur and his fourteen knights had desired to make
a treaty with Sir Mordred.

19. In this sentence, write whether the underlined clause is
(65) essential or nonessential: The tower <u>that housed Queen
Guinevere</u> lies on the north bank of the Thames River.

20. From this sentence, write the dependent clause, circling
(24, 57) the subordinating conjunction: A thief ran off with the
suitcase while Tom was not looking.

21. From this sentence, write the indefinite pronoun and
(71) label it singular or plural: Most of us have heard of the
Tower of London.

22. Write the nominative case, second person, personal
(53, 55) pronoun.

23. For a–c, write whether the italicized word functions as an
(27, 83) adjective or an adverb.
   (a) King Arthur and his knights fought *valiantly*.
   (b) Sir Mordred was *slovenly* in appearance.
   (c) The *lonely* Sir Mordred will reap what he has sowed.

24. Write whether the following is a phrase or a clause:
(24, 33) before the invention of the light bulb

25. Write the four principal parts of the irregular verb *feel*.
(15, 73)

26. In this sentence, write each prepositional phrase, starring
(16, 32) the object of each preposition: In addition to Sir
Bedivere, many other knights gathered around King
Arthur during his time of need.

27. In this sentence, write the infinitive, labeling it an
(23, 48) adjective or a noun: Now we have several new ideas to
explore.

28. Write and underline each word that should be italicized
(72) in this sentence: When something is overly or
unpleasantly familiar, we might call it déjà vu, a French
expression meaning "already seen."

Diagram sentences 29 and 30.

29. Rescuing the king is Sir Bedivere's mission.
(39, 59)

30. Fighting a strong current, Sal rowed frantically upstream.
(28, 59)

LESSON
87

Word Division

Dictation or Journal Entry

Vocabulary: The Greek root physio- refers to things in their natural form, order, or origin.

A *physiocrat* believes that there is a natural, inherent order for properly governing society. The *physiocrat* approves of free trade.

Physiognomy is the features or expressions of a face. Frankenstein's *physiognomy* frightened the town's citizens.

Physiography is the study of the earth's features. We learned about the earth's landforms and climates in our *physiography* class.

Physiology studies the natural chemical and physical functions of living organisms. In my *physiology* class, I learned that the brain sends signals to the heart to make it beat.

Physiometry measures the functions of the body. The *physiometry* part of his check-up included a measurement of his resting heart rate.

When writing, we use a hyphen to divide a word if we run out of room at the end of a line. It is important to know *where* (or *whether*) to divide a word. Using a computer does not free us from this responsibility. Many "automatic" word divisions are unacceptable in good writing.

We observe the following guidelines when dividing a word.

Between syllables   Words can be divided only between syllables. We check the dictionary if we are in doubt about how a word is divided. The hyphen always appears with the first half of the word.

nor- mal   cap- tive   rib- bon   for- get

One-letter syllables   A one-letter syllable should not be divided from the rest of the word.

uku- lele (not u- kulele)

acad- emy (not a- cademy or academ- y)

Because of this, two-syllable words such as the following are never divided:

amaze   lucky   evolve   icon

When a word contains a one-letter syllable, we divide the word *after* that syllable.

presi- dent (not pres- ident)

nega- tive (not neg- ative)

experi- ence (not exper- ience)

Compound words Divide a compound word between its elements. If the word is already hyphenated, divide it *after* the hyphen.

silver- ware (not sil- verware)

super- market (not supermar- ket)

mid- January (not mid- Janu- ary)

Prefixes and suffixes Divide a word after a prefix or before a suffix.

pre-fabricate (not prefabri-cate or prefab-ricate)

penni- less (not pen- niless)

Longer words Some longer words contain more than one possible dividing place. We divide them as needed to fit the line.

car- nivore   *or*   carni-vore

fan- tastic   *or*   fantas- tic

Do not divide Some words and expressions are never divided.

One-syllable words One-syllable words cannot be divided, no matter how many letters they contain. Remember that even when you add *-ed*, some words are still one syllable.

breathe   cleansed   phrased   straight

Short words Words with four letters should not be divided even if they are more than one syllable.

many   liar   tiny   very

Also, we do not divide contractions or abbreviations.

shouldn't   they're

Example Use hyphens to divide each of the words. Remember that not all words should be divided. Use the dictionary if necessary.

(a) hyphen   (b) abort   (c) epigram

(d) glamorous   (e) stepdaughter   (f) dreamed

Solution (a) We divide between syllables: **hy- phen**

(b) We do not divide a one-letter syllable from the rest of the word. **Abort** cannot be divided.

(c) We divide a word *after* a single-letter syllable: **epi- gram**

(d) We divide a word *before* a suffix: **glamor- ous**

(e) We divide a compound word between its elements: **step-daughter**

(f) We do not divide one-syllable words. **Dreamed** cannot be divided.

Practice Use a hyphen to divide words a–f. Not all the words should be divided. Use a dictionary if you are not sure.

a. inept   **b.** origin   **c.** coalition

d. quail   **e.** couldn't   **f.** forty-nine

For g–k, replace each blank with the correct vocabulary word.

g. _____ studies the process of oxygenating blood.

h. _____ includes the measurement of blood pressure, working heart rate, resting heart rate, body temperature, etc.

i. The _____ of California includes deserts, mountains, and valleys.

j. Matt's _____ revealed his surprise and pleasure when he saw his long-lost friend.

k. A _____ is not a socialist.

More Practice Hyphenate each word correctly. Use the dictionary if you are not sure.

1. thought   **2.** hasn't

3. substance   **4.** crime

5. hemoglobin   **6.** antidote

7. won't   **8.** pentagon

9. religion   **10.** semiarid

11. imbecile   **12.** finger

13. picture   **14.** hexagon

15. stepfather   **16.** kilometer

17. matron-of-honor   **18.** gentility

19. hemisphere   20. atmosphere

Review set 87 Choose the correct word(s) to complete sentences 1–15.

1. A psychosis is a (digestive, respiratory, mental) disorder.
(83)

2. A parable is a short story with a (myth, moral, satire).
(72, 82)

3. (Impressionism, Realism, Parallelism) repeats words or
(80, 84) phrases in a pattern.

4. The Greek word (*therap-*, *cosmos*, *thermos*) means
(77, 85) "heat."

5. Hypothermia is subnormal body (strength, fitness,
(85) temperature).

6. He (don't, doesn't) have (no, any) mosquito bites.
(14, 81)

7. Measles (is, are) a miserable disease.
(79, 80)

8. A swarm of wasps (was, were) pestering us during our
(78, 79) picnic.

9. Please allow (us, we) volunteers to assist you.
(54, 66)

10. Kurt and (him, he) have as much musical talent as (we,
(53, 66) us).

11. Kurt and he (sing, sings) (good, well).
(75, 84)

12. Each of the band members (have, has) (their, his/her) own
(77, 78) instrument.

13. (Them, Those) knights have kept their vows.
(28, 70)

14. The swallows have (flew, flown) south for the winter.
(73, 74)

15. Fred and (them, themselves, they) were marching in
(53, 60) formation.

16. Rewrite the following, adding capital letters and correct
(63, 68) punctuation marks: yes tom replied his father this oven is
self cleaning ouch it's hot

17. For a–c, write whether the *-ing* word in each sentence is a
(27, 48) verb, participle, or gerund.

  (a) Honking horns broke the silence.

  (b) All the drivers were honking their horns.

  (c) Shall we practice honking our horns?

18. In this sentence, write the verb phrase and name its tense:
(18, 21) Mrs. Madison has been raising the American flag each
morning at sunrise.

19. Write whether this sentence is true or false: In adjective
(64, 65) clauses, the use of "that" or "which" depends on whether
the clause is essential or nonessential.

20. From this sentence, write the dependent clause, circling
(24, 57) the subordinating conjunction: Unless we can locate that
woman with curlers in her hair, we might never recover
Tom's suitcase.

21. Use an appositive to make one sentence from these two
(45, 46) sentences: The Tower of London is a historic fortress in
the city of London. The tower was used as a royal
residence and as a prison until Elizabethan times.

22. Write the possessive case, second person, personal
(55, 56) pronoun.

23. For a and b, write whether the italicized word functions
(27, 83) as an adjective or an adverb.

  (a) Several *lively* puppies frolic in the fenced yard.

  (b) They romp *happily* beneath the elm tree.

24. Write whether the following is a phrase or a clause:
(24, 57) before the light bulb was invented

25. Write the four principal parts of the irregular verb *put.*
(15, 74)

26. Write the superlative form of the adjective *tentative.*
(42, 43)

27. For a–c, write the plural of each noun.
(12, 13) (a) allegory   (b) bonus   (c) analogy

28. Write and underline each word that should be italicized
(72) in this sentence: Pablo Picasso surprised everyone when

he painted his abstract work called The Ladies of Avignon.

Diagram sentences 29 and 30.

29. The airport detectives asked me to help.
(23, 25)

30. Pablo Picasso, a cubist, led the way in experimental art
(25, 45) forms.

LESSON 88

Adverbs that Tell "When"

Dictation or Journal Entry

Vocabulary: Let us discuss a few more computer terms.

A *peripheral* is an external hardware device that is connected to a computer, usually by a cable. Keyboards, mice, printers, and monitors are all *peripherals.* How many *peripherals* does your computer have connected to it?

A *backup* is a duplicate or copy for the purpose of avoiding loss in case the original is corrupted, destroyed, or lost. We can make a *backup* of the information from our hard drive by copying it onto a disk.

Compression is the process of making a file or group of files use less storage space. Using *compression* software, John condensed his music files so that they were one-tenth their original size.

We have reviewed adverbs that tell "how" and "where." In this lesson, we will review adverbs that modify a verb and tell "when." Again, let us think about how and where the President dresses:

> HOW: The President dresses *splendidly.*

> WHERE: The President dresses *inside.*

"When" Now we will think about "when" the President dresses:

> WHEN: The President dresses *early.*

He might also dress *later, daily, soon, nightly*, or *today.*

The following are common adverbs telling "when:"

before	*when*	*late*	*soon*
yearly	*tonight*	*after*	*monthly*
hourly	*early*	*today*	*tomorrow*
now	*then*	*nightly*	*daily*

Adverb Position An adverb can appear almost anywhere in a sentence.

> *Daily* I walk around the park.

> I walk *daily* around the park.

> I walk around the park *daily.*

Even though the adverb *daily* modifies the verb *walk* in each of the sentences above, it is not necessarily placed near the verb. Since the placement of the adverb can vary, we must learn to identify adverbs even when they are separated from the verbs they modify.

Example 1   For each sentence, write the adverb that tells "when" and the verb or verb phrase it modifies.

(a) Salem, Massachusetts, was then a leading seaport in the United States.

(b) Now we will study the author, Nathaniel Hawthorne.

(c) Hawthorne worked daily on his best novel, *The Scarlet Letter*

(d) Eventually, Nathaniel Hawthorne married his sweetheart, Sophia Peabody.

Solution   (a) The adverb **then** tells "when" Salem **was** a leading seaport. *Then* modifies the verb *was.*

(b) The adverb **now** modifies the verb **will study.**

(c) The adverb **daily** modifies the verb **worked.**

(d) The adverb **eventually** modifies the verb **married.**

Example 2   Diagram this sentence: Will you write a novel soon?

Solution   We place the adverb *soon* under the verb *will write*:

Practice   For sentences a–d, write the adverb that tells "when" and the verb or verb phrase it modifies.

a. Earlier, Hawthorne had been interested in the impact of sin on men and women.

b. President Franklin Pierce later rewarded Hawthorne for writing his campaign biography.

c. Yearly, Hawthorne visited Liverpool, England, as American consul.

d. He met in Boston monthly with other literary figures like Henry Wadsworth Longfellow and Oliver Wendell Holmes.

Diagram sentences e and f.

   e. Eppie weeds her garden daily.

   f. Her tomatoes will soon ripen.

For g–i, replace each blank with the correct computer term.

   g. Wassim created a _____ of his homework file by duplicating it on a disk.

   h. _____ of his files allowed Mr. Cheung to use less storage space in his computer.

   i. The lab technician purchased new _____ such as keyboards, mice, and monitors for the computer lab.

Review set 88 Choose the correct word(s) to complete sentences 1–15.

1. Exposition, rising action, climax, falling action, and
(70, 84) resolution are the five parts of the (parable, epithet, plot line).

2. Hyperthermia is elevated body (height, weight,
(85) temperature).

3. Rising action occurs (before, after) the climax of a story.
(86)

4. An automobile is a (fast-, slow-, self-) moving vehicle.
(73)

5. (Soliloquy, Satire, Stereotype) is a lone character's
(72) speech.

6. James plays volleyball (well, good).
(84)

7. Will Oscar and (he, him) help (me and her, she and I, her
(53, 54) and me) to prepare the meal?

8. The grazing cattle ignored (us, our) taking their pictures.
(56, 58)

9. Inez plays chess with either Gretchen or (me, myself, I).
(54, 66)

10. My scissors (isn't, ain't, aren't) sharp enough.
(77, 78)

11. Tom (don't, doesn't) have his suitcase, so he'll borrow
(14, 56) (your's, yours).

12. The artist from (who, whom) we bought the penguin
(64, 65) painting lives in Maine.

13. The luggage (that, which) Tom lost contains his
(64, 65) souvenirs.

14. Yesterday, they (flew, flown) home from Germany.
(73, 74)

15. Maxine is the (less, least) spirited of the two horses.
(42, 43)

16. Rewrite the following, adding capital letters and correct
(29, 50) punctuation marks:

dear sir bedivere

    please take me to the waterside and place me on the barge i shall sail to the east for there lies the valley of avalon the current will carry me in an easterly direction

gratefully

king arthur

17. For a–c, write whether the *-ing* word in each sentence is a verb, participle, or gerund.

(18, 21) (a) Your Chihuahua has been barking all evening.

(19, 58) (b) Barking at strangers is a watchdog's job.

(27, 48) (c) Did my barking Chihuahua disturb you?

18. In this sentence, write the verb phrase and name its tense:
(8, 18) Had Sir Bedivere chosen to keep the sword?

19. Write whether each underlined clause is essential or
(64, 65) nonessential: The long poem <u>that you wrote</u> reminds me of an epic <u>that I once read</u>.

20. From this sentence, write the dependent clause, circling
(24, 57) the subordinating conjunction: After the magnificent hall was completed, Hrothgar hosted a sumptuous feast.

21. From this sentence, write the indefinite pronoun and
(71) label it singular or plural: Was either of the landmarks visible?

22. Write the possessive case, first person, singular personal
(56, 66) pronoun.

23. For a–c, write the question answered by the italicized
(86, 88) adverb. The first one is done for you.

    (a) The three queens wept *mournfully.*   (How?)

    (b) King Arthur had been to the lake *before.*

    (c) Was the Lady of the Lake waiting *there?*

24. In this sentence, write the infinitive and label it an
(23, 48) adjective or a noun: Professor Braine has a new theory to
explain.

25. Write the four principal parts of the irregular verb *stand.*
(15, 75)

26. In this sentence, write the pronoun and its antecedent:
(49, 53) Because Grendel refused to accept a peace offer, he
waged war for twelve years.

27. For a–c, hyphenate each word correctly.
(85, 87) (a) clothes   (b) mother-in-law   (c) earthworm

28. Write and underline each word that should be italicized
(72) in this sentence: The National Geographic magazine had
an interesting article about a shipwreck from Greece's
Golden Age.

Diagram sentences 29 and 30.

29. Rob wants to work, but he needs to sleep.
(23, 62)

30. Eluding authorities, the lady with curlers in her hair fled
(33, 59) upstairs.

LESSON 89

Adverbs that Tell "How Much"

Dictation or Journal Entry

Vocabulary: The Greek root *osteo-* means "bone."

An *osteoblast* is a bone-forming cell. Healthy *osteoblasts* are needed for strong bones.

Osteochondritis is inflammation of the bone and cartilage. Knees are often affected by *osteochondritis.*

Osteocope is severe pain in the bones. *Osteocope* is symptomatic of certain diseases.

Osteogenesis refers to the formation of the bone. *Osteogenesis* occurs early in the embryo.

"How Much" or "To What Extent"

Some adverbs tell "how much" or "to what extent." These adverbs are sometimes called **intensifiers** because they add intensity (either positive or negative) to the words they modify.

Notice how the "intensifiers" in the sentences below add intensity to the words they modify:

Irving felt *very* honored.

Rip Van Winkle awoke *extremely* puzzled.

They were *too* tired to continue.

The flight assistant had been *most* kind.

We were *so* relieved.

Some adverbs that tell "how much" or "to what extent" are easy to identify because they end in *-ly*. However, many others do not. Here are some common intensifiers:

absolutely	*almost*	*altogether*
awfully	*barely*	*completely*
especially	*even*	*extremely*
fully	*hardly*	*highly*
incredibly	*just*	*least*
less	*most*	*not*
partly	*quite*	*rather*
really	*so*	*somewhat*
terribly	*thoroughly*	*too*
totally	*vastly*	*very*

An adverb that tells "how much" or "to what extent" usually modifies an adjective or another adverb. However, it occasionally modifies a verb.

MODIFYING AN ADJECTIVE

Irving was *extremely* appreciative.

The adverb *extremely* modifies the adjective *exhausted* and tells "how appreciative" Irving was.

MODIFYING ANOTHER ADVERB

Washington Irving was named *rather* creatively.

The adverb *rather* modifies the adverb *creatively* and tells "how creatively" Irving was named.

MODIFYING A VERB

My friend has *highly* recommended that book.

The adverb *highly* modifies the verb *recommended* and tells "to what extent" the book has been recommended.

Example 1 For each sentence, write the adverb that tells "how much" or "to what extent" and give the word it modifies.

(a) Washington Irving was totally enamored with Matilda Hoffman.

(b) Knickerbocker and Washington Irving became quite famous.

(c) The stories about Rip Van Winkle and Ichabod Crane are based slightly on German legend.

(d) The state of New York most proudly commends Washington Irving.

Solution (a) The adverb **totally** modifies the verb **"was enamored."**

(b) The adverb **quite** modifies the predicate adjective **"famous."**

(c) The adverb **slightly** modifies the verb **"are based."**

(d) The adverb **most** modifies the adverb **"proudly."**

not Notice that the word *not* is an adverb. In contractions like couldn't, *n't* is an adverb. When we diagram contractions, we show *not* as an adverb as in the example below:

Didn't you experience hyperthermia?

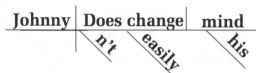

Example 2 Diagram this sentence:

Doesn't Johnny change his mind easily?

Solution We place the adverbs *n't* and *easily* underneath the verb "does change."

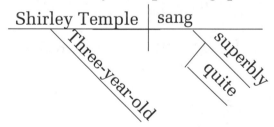

Diagramming Adverbs that Modify Adjectives or Other Adverbs We have diagrammed adverbs that modify verbs. Now we will diagram adverbs that modify adjectives or other adverbs. As shown in the examples below, we place the adverb on a line underneath the adjective or other adverb which is modified:

Three-year-old Shirley Temple sang quite superbly.

Shirley Temple | sang

An adverb may be a part of a prepositional phrase as in the sentence below:

Shirley Temple is one of the most famous child performers.

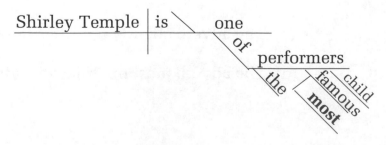

In the sentence above, notice that the adverb *most* modifies the adjective "famous" which modifies "performers" which is the object of the preposition "of."

Example 3 Diagram this sentence:

> Extremely successful child stars aren't guaranteed adult careers.

Solution We place the adverb *extremely* underneath the adjective it modifies, *successful*, which describes "stars." We remember that *not* is also an adverb, so we place *n't*, the contraction for "not," under the verb "are guaranteed."

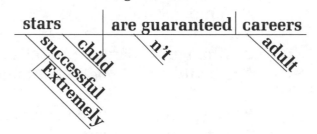

Practice For sentences a–e, write each adverb that tells "how much" or "to what extent" and the word it modifies.

a. Tetanus is a very serious disease of the nervous system.

b. The tetanus toxin attacks rather viciously the jaws and facial muscles.

c. Immunization against tetanus is quite effective.

d. Tetanus boosters are absolutely crucial.

e. My brother didn't know this.

Diagram sentences f and g.

f. Immunizations are really important.

g. We must very diligently protect our health.

For h–l, replace each blank with the correct vocabulary word.

h. Running may aggravate _____ in the *talus*, or anklebone.

i. The Greek root meaning "bone" is _____.

j. Many _____ are needed for bone growth to occur.

k. Calcium provides nourishment for _____, or bone formation.

l. Arthritis causes pain, or _____, in some people.

More Practice   See Master Worksheets.

Review set 89   Choose the best word to complete sentences 1–15.

1. A thermostat maintains a certain (weight, attitude, temperature).
(85)

2. (Romance, Sarcasm, Realism) pictures life as the writer might like it to be rather than as it really is.
(86)

3. A (romance, symbol, parable) is a concrete object that represents an idea.
(86)

4. The Greek root (*therap-*, *thermos*, *physio-*) refers to things in their natural form, order, or origin.
(85, 87)

5. Physiognomy is the (natural, ugly, pleasant) features of a face.
(87)

6. Mrs. Poovey (doesn't, don't) ask (no, any) questions.
(14, 81)

7. (Ain't, Aren't, Isn't) your tuxedo pants too long?
(14, 80)

8. A can of home-grown peaches (sits, sit) on the shelf.
(74, 75)

9. (Us, We) shepherds shall protect our sheep.
(53, 66)

10. Benito and (her, she) speak Spanish more fluently than (me, I).
(53, 66)

11. Aunt Steph and Uncle Bill (make, makes) (good, well) enchiladas.
(77, 84)

12. None of the volunteers (understand, understands) (their, his/her) tasks.
(78, 79)

13. I (saw, seen) (them, those) knights with their shining armor.
(70, 74)

14. Using chalk and construction paper, the artist (drew,
(74, 75) drawn) two white doves sitting on a tree branch.

15. The artist gave the drawing to Jake and (me, myself, I).
(32, 54)

16. Rewrite the following, adding capital letters and correct
(35, 44) punctuation marks: on july 26 2002 a class of thirty two
geology students traveled to tucson arizona to
photograph rock formations

17. For a–c, write whether the *-ing* word in each sentence is a
verb, participle, or gerund.
(27, 48) (a) A group of singing hikers trekked along the mountain
trail.
(73, 74) (b) Were the hikers singing until sunset?
(19, 27) (c) Singing fun songs makes time pass more quickly.

18. In this sentence, write the verb phrase and name its tense:
(19, 21) For centuries, historians have been examining epic
poetry for clues to early civilizations.

19. Write whether the underlined clause is essential or
(64, 65) nonessential: Daisy's autobiography, <u>which talks about
her school days in Detroit</u>, lies covered with dust in her
attic.

20. From this sentence, write the dependent clause, circling
(24, 57) the subordinating conjunction: The Danes suffer as
Grendel attacks their homeland.

21. Write the comparative form of the adjective *persnickety*.
(42, 43)

22. Write the possessive case, first person, plural personal
(28, 56) pronoun.

23. For a and b, write the adjective and adverb forms of each
(27, 83) noun.

(a) peace   (b) harm

24. Write whether this sentence is simple or compound:
(36, 62) Stories about Grendel spread far and wide, so Beowulf
eventually heard them.

25. Write the four principal parts of the irregular verb *sit*.
(15, 77)

26. Use an appositive to make one sentence from these two
(45, 46) sentences: Frank Lloyd Wright was a famous American architect. He designed houses to fit in with the features of the surrounding landscape.

27. For a–c, write the plural of each noun.
(12, 13) (a) merry-go-round   (b) glassful   (c) child

28. Write and underline each word that should be italicized
(72) in this sentence: Christina's World, a realistic painting by Andrew Wyeth, shows a lone woman sitting on a grassy field.

Diagram sentences 29 and 30.

29. We must catch the fleeing lady, or Tom will never see his
(25, 62) suitcase again.

30. The woman who took the suitcase has already left the
(28, 62) airport.

LESSON 90

Comparison Adverbs

Like adjectives, some adverbs can express the three degrees of comparison: positive, comparative, and superlative. Below are examples of the positive, comparative, and superlative forms of some adverbs:

POSITIVE	COMPARATIVE	SUPERLATIVE
slow	*slower*	*slowest*
late	*later*	*latest*
quick	*quicker*	*quickest*

Positive   The positive form describes an action without comparing it to anything.

Peng finished *late.*

Comparative   The comparative form compares the action of **two** people, places, or things.

Peng finished *later* than Eng.

Superlative   The superlative form compares the action of **three or more** people, places, or things.

Of the three, Peng finished *latest.*

Example 1   Choose the correct adverb form for each sentence.

(a) Of the two sisters, Priscilla climbed (higher, highest).

(b) Of all choir members, Sergio sang (louder, loudest).

Solution   (a) Of the two sisters, Priscilla climbed **higher.** (We use the comparative form since there are two people.)

(b) Of all the choir members, Sergio sang **loudest.** (We use the superlative form since we are comparing more than two voices.)

Forming Comparison Adverbs We form comparison adverbs the same way we form comparison adjectives. How we create the comparative and superlative forms of an adverb depends on how the adverb appears in its positive form. There are two main categories to remember.

One-Syllable Adverbs We create the comparative form of most one-syllable adverbs by adding *er* to the end of the word. We create the superlative form by adding *est*.

POSITIVE	COMPARATIVE	SUPERLATIVE
hard	*harder*	*hardest*
soon	*sooner*	*soonest*
deep	*deeper*	*deepest*

Two or More Syllables Most two-syllable adverbs do not have comparative or superlative forms. Instead, we put the word "more" (or "less") in front of the adverb to form the comparative, and the word "most" (or "least") to form the superlative.

POSITIVE	COMPARATIVE	SUPERLATIVE
slovenly	*more slovenly* *less slovenly*	*most slovenly* *least slovenly*
gracefully	*more gracefully* *less gracefully*	*most gracefully* *least gracefully*

Since most adverbs are formed by adding the suffix *-ly* to an adjective, the rule above applies to most adverbs.

Irregular Comparison Adverbs Some adverbs have irregular comparative and superlative forms. We must learn these if we haven't already.

POSITIVE	COMPARATIVE	SUPERLATIVE
well	*better*	*best*
badly	*worse*	*worst*
far	*farther*	*farthest*
little	*less*	*least*
much	*more*	*most*

We check the dictionary if we are unsure how to create the comparative or superlative form of a two-syllable adverb.

Example 2   Complete the comparison chart by adding the comparative and superlative forms of each adverb.

POSITIVE	COMPARATIVE	SUPERLATIVE
(a) much	_____	_____
(b) truthfully	_____	_____
(c) little	_____	_____
(d) lovingly	_____	_____

Solution

POSITIVE	COMPARATIVE	SUPERLATIVE
(a) much	**more**	**most**
(b) truthfully	**more truthfully**	**most truthfully**
(c) little	**less**	**least**
(d) lovingly	**more lovingly**	**most lovingly**

Practice   Write the correct adverb form for sentences a–e.

a. Of the four long jumpers, Slater jumped (short, shorter, shortest).

b. Erika completed the algebra problems (more quickly, most quickly) than Danika.

c. Louisa liked the chocolate mousse (well, better, best) than the crème brulee.

d. Of all the performers, Dustin dressed (appropriately, more appropriately, most appropriately).

e. Doctor Raven squawks (badly, worse, worst) than Doctor Robin, but Doctor Crow squawks (badly, worse, worst) of all.

For f–j, replace each blank with the correct computer term.

f. Is this program compatible with your computer's _____ _____?

g. The computer is capable of _____, for it can do many things simultaneously.

h. Ruthie is learning to use a new _____ for computer animation.

More Practice

Write the correct comparison adverb for each sentence.

1. Of the three dancers, Meaghan glides (gracefully, more gracefully, most gracefully) across the stage.

2. Lindsay practiced (little, less, least) than Stephan.

3. Of the two, Chef Crocker cooks (well, better, best).

4. Molly crawled (fast, faster, fastest) than Holly.

5. Nick studies (long, longer, longest) than Rick.

6. Kurt whistles (well, better, best) than Bert.

7. Of all the art students, Chloe paints (well, better, best).

8. Becca throws (far, farther, farthest) than Heather.

9. Fido barks (little, less, least) in the morning than he does in the afternoon.

10. Of all the dogs, he barks (much, more, most).

Review set 90

Choose the correct word(s) to complete sentences 1–15.

1. The (protagonist, antagonist, narrator) is the person who (50, 54) tells the story.

2. Psychotherapy attempts to cure (spiritual, physical, (83) mental) disorders.

3. The dove is often used as a (romance, symbol, parable) (86) for peace.

4. Physiography is the study of the earth's (man-made, (87) natural) features.

5. A (backup, compression, peripheral) is an external (88) hardware device connected to a computer.

6. We use (good, well) when talking about one's health or (84) how one feels.

7. Beowulf and (them, they) intend to overcome Grendel, (51, 53) the terrible fiend.

8. Beowulf and his men are (well-equipped, well equipped)
(85, 87) for the task.

9. The (well-equipped, well equipped) army appears
(85, 87) formidable.

10. The neighbor complained about (us, our) noisily mowing
(56, 58) the grass at five a.m.

11. Perhaps she (doesn't, don't) realize that the suitcase
(14, 81) (isn't, ain't) (her's, hers).

12. The man (who, whom) bought the first penguin painting
(64, 65) has sold it for thousands of dollars.

13. The souvenirs, (that, which) disappeared with the
(64, 65) luggage, have little cash value.

14. Has your team ever (beat, beaten) their team?
(73, 74)

15. Of all the horses on the farm, Maxine can jump (higher,
(42, 90) highest).

16. Rewrite the following, adding capital letters and correct
(68, 76) punctuation marks: stop cried mrs. poovey to the taxi
driver please wait for me i need to feed the cat get my
purse and lock the door before i go

17. In this sentence, write the participial phrase followed by
(48, 59) the word it modifies: Having approached Hrothgar on
friendly terms, the Goths offered their help.

18. In this sentence, write the verb phrase, name its tense,
(18, 31) and label it transitive or intransitive: Centuries ago, a
pirate ship had sunk near the island of Tatakoto.

19. Write whether this sentence is simple or compound:
(3, 62) Through the years, many groups of curious explorers
have dived to the sunken ship in search of lost treasure
and interesting artifacts.

20. Write whether the following is a complete sentence,
(1, 3) sentence fragment, or run-on sentence: My scuba
equipment is ready I'm going to join the divers.

21. Write the relative pronoun in this sentence: Hrothgar,
$^{(64,\ 65)}$who greatly appreciates Beowulf, reports that Beowulf
has the strength of thirty men.

22. Write the objective case, first person, plural personal
$^{(54,\ 55)}$pronoun.

23. For a and b, write the adjective and adverb forms of each
$^{(42,\ 90)}$noun.

    (a) truth   (b) care

24. In this sentence, write the infinitive and label it an
$^{(23,\ 48)}$adjective or a noun: My workload was large, but Esther
offered to help.

25. Write the four principal parts of the irregular verb *write.*
$^{(15,\ 75)}$

26. In this sentence, write the indefinite pronoun and label it
$^{(71)}$ singular or plural: Everyone is waiting patiently to
purchase his or her theater ticket.

27. Write and hyphenate each part as needed in this
$^{(82,\ 85)}$sentence: Word of mouth communication spread
Beowulf's reputation throughout the land.

28. Write and underline each word that should be italicized
$^{(72)}$ in this sentence: This morning I read a portion of Oswald
Chambers's devotional classic book called My Utmost for
His Highest.

Diagram sentences 29 and 30.

29. The savior of the severely oppressed Scyldings arrived
$^{(32,\ 33)}$today.

30. Beowulf, a doughty leader, carefully plans his attack on
$^{(25,\ 45)}$Grendel.

LESSON 91

The Semicolon • The Conjunctive Adverb

Dictation or Journal Entry

Vocabulary: Knowing the numerical values of the Greek prefixes *proto-,* *deutero-,* and *tri-* helps us with word meanings.

Proto- means "first" or "earliest form." A *Prototype* is the earliest model, or original, of something. The glider served as a *prototype* for the airplane.

Deutero- means "second." *Deuteronomy* is the second statement of Mosaic law in the Old Testament. The Mosaic laws set forth in the book of Exodus are repeated in the book of *Deuteronomy.*

Tri- means "three." *Triarchy* refers to government by three people. The king, the queen, and the prince formed the nation's *triarchy.*

The **semicolon** (;) is sometimes called a "mild period." It is used as a connector. It indicates a pause longer than a comma yet shorter than a colon. In this lesson we will learn how to use the semicolon correctly.

Related Thoughts In a compound sentence, we can use a semicolon instead of a coordinating conjunction (*and, but, or, for, nor, yet, so*) between the two independent clauses. However, these clauses must contain related thoughts.

> YES: Termites can cause great damage to wooden structures; they feed mainly on the wood of houses or furniture. (related thoughts)

> NO: Building foundations should not be made of wood; termites are sometimes called "white ants." (not related thoughts)

Example 1 Use a semicolon instead of the coordinate conjunction in this sentence:

> I started the building project, but Steve finished it.

Solution We replace the coordinate conjunction with a semicolon:

> I started the building project; Steve finished it.

With Other Commas If an independent clause contains other commas, we use a semicolon to show where one independent clause ends and where another one begins.

> UNCLEAR: Felix travels to California, Oregon, and Arizona, and Gerard visits Colorado, New Mexico, and Texas.

> CLEAR: Felix travels to California, Oregon, and Arizona; and Gerard visits Colorado, New Mexico, and Texas.

Semicolons can also be used to separate phrases or dependent clauses that contain commas.

> The month of February has many holidays including Valentine's Day, February 14; Abraham Lincoln's birthday, February 12; and George Washington's birthday, February 22.

> Today, Debby has to feed the cats, dogs, and chickens; neatly trim the hedges, bushes, and trees; and wash her car until it sparkles.

Example 2 Place semicolons where they are needed in sentences a and b.

(a) James will tour Philadelphia, Pennsylvania, Princeton, New Jersey, and New York City, New York.

(b) Izumi enjoys tacos, enchiladas, and burritos, and Carlos prefers sushi, chop suey, and chow mein.

Solution (a) We separate each "city, state" pair of words with a semicolon for clarity.

> James will tour Philadelphia, Pennsylvania; Princeton, New Jersey; and New York City, New York.

(b) Because the independent clauses in this sentence already contain commas, we separate the two clauses with a semicolon.

> Izumi enjoys tacos, enchiladas, and burritos; and Carlos prefers sushi, chop suey, and chow mein.

Conjunctive Adverbs An adverb used as a conjunction is called a **conjunctive adverb.** Below are some examples.

however	*therefore*	*consequently*
accordingly	*for this reason*	*for example*
on the other hand	*furthermore*	*besides*
moreover	*still*	*likewise*
in addition	*at the same time*	*nevertheless*
otherwise	*thus*	*hence*

We place a semicolon before a conjunctive adverb.

YES: William Thackerary competed with his great contemporary, Charles Dickens; however, his novel, *Vanity Fair*, never achieved the popularity of *David Copperfield*.

Using a comma where a semicolon is needed results in a run-on sentence:

NO: William Thackerary competed with his great contemporary, Charles Dickens, however, his novel, *Vanity Fair*, never achieved the popularity of *David Copperfield*.

Example 3 Place a semicolon where it is needed in this sentence:

We have learned the meaning of many Greek prefixes, however, there are many more that we need to study.

Solution A semicolon is necessary before the conjunctive adverb, *however*. So we write,

We have learned the meaning of many Greek prefixes; however, there are many more that we need to study.

Practice Rewrite sentences a–c, and replace commas with semicolons where they are needed.

a. We recognize Greek numerical prefixes like "proto," first, "deutero," second, and "tri," three.

b. Khaki pants, shorts, and skirts are acceptable, they are all part of the school uniform.

c. The student is wearing purple pants, therefore, she is out of school uniform.

For d–i, replace each blank with the correct vocabulary word.

d. The Greek prefix meaning "three" is _____.

e. Alexander Graham Bell built a _____ for the telephone.

f. The Greek prefix meaning "first" is _____.

g. The United States is not governed by three people, or a _____; instead it is governed by three branches—the executive, legislative, and judicial.

    h. The Greek prefix meaning "second" is _____.

    i. In the book of _____, we can read the Mosaic law for the second time.

More Practice   See Master Worksheets.

Review set 91

Choose the correct word to complete sentences 1–15.

1. A (backup, compression, peripheral) is a computer term
(88) meaning "duplicate copy."

2. We can condense computer files using (backup,
(88) peripheral, compression) software.

3. The Greek root (*cosmos, morphe, osteo*-) means
(77, 89) bone.

4. Physiometry is a (measurement, alteration, surgery) of
(87) bodily functions.

5. (Monochrome, Polychrome) means having many colors.
(69)

6. Mr. Poovey and his poodle (isn't, ain't, aren't) home yet.
(14, 81)

7. Mrs. Poovey (could, couldn't) see no reason for the delay.
(81)

8. A bushel of apples (make, makes) several large pies.
(77, 78)

9. Please wake (us, we) shepherds if you see a wolf.
(54, 66)

10. Kurt and (him, he) learned the game rules more quickly
(51, 53) than (me, I).

11. (Good, Well) is usually an adverb that modifies an action
(27, 84) verb and explains "how."

12. (Good, Well) is a descriptive adjective or predicate
(27, 84) adjective that describes a noun or pronoun.

13. One of the players (promise, promises) to forfeit (their,
(79, 80) his/her) turn.

14. Earlier, the guard had (lead, led) Beowulf and his men to
(73, 74) Hrothgar's court.

15. Jake and (me, myself, I) will proudly display the penguin
$^{(51,\ 53)}$painting on our living room wall.

16. Rewrite the following, adding capital letters and correct
$^{(63,\ 68)}$punctuation marks: never mind said mrs poovey to the
taxi driver you are in a hurry therefore i shall drive my
own vehicle

17. In this sentence, write the gerund phrase: I thanked Ms.
$^{(58)}$ Sweet for mending the tent so well.

18. In this sentence, write the verb phrase, name its tense,
$^{(8,\ 21)}$and label it action or linking: For defeating Grendel,
Beowulf will be receiving eternal gratitude from the
Danes.

19. In this sentence, write the dependent clause, circling the
$^{(24,\ 57)}$subordinating conjunction: I remember the hero Beowulf
whenever I think of Denmark.

20. Write whether the following is a phrase or a clause: using
$^{(24,\ 57)}$the computer application for word processing and
desktop publishing

21. Write whether the underlined part in this sentence is
$^{(64,\ 65)}$essential or nonessential: My neighbor <u>Mr. Poovey</u> has
purchased his wife a new car.

22. Write the seven common coordinating conjunctions.
$^{(36,\ 62)}$

23. Write the comparative form of the adverb *well*.
$^{(90)}$

24. Use an appositive to make one sentence from these two
$^{(45,\ 46)}$sentences: Grover Cleveland was the twenty-second and
the twenty-fourth President of the United States. He
began his political career as Erie County sheriff in New
York.

25. Write the four principal parts of the irregular verb *swing*.
$^{(74,\ 75)}$

26. For a and b, write the adjective and adverb forms of each
$^{(27,\ 83)}$noun.

    (a) faith   (b) joy

27. Write and hyphenate each part as needed in this
(82, 85) sentence: The fast growing company hired twenty six
people today.

28. Write and underline each part that should be italicized in
(72) this sentence: The most common English word is the, and
the most frequently used letter is e.

Diagram sentences 29 and 30.

29. Knowing the numerical value of some Greek prefixes
(19, 58) increases our vocabulary.

30. The tales in this epic poem about Beowulf seem rather
(33, 39) unlikely.

LESSON 92

Descriptive Adverbs
• Adverb Usage

Dictation or Journal Entry

Vocabulary: Let us learn the numerical meaning of the Greek prefixes *tetra-*, *penta-*, and *hexa-*.

Tetra- means "four," so a *tetragon* is a polygon with four angles and four sides. A rectangle is a *tetragon*.

Penta- means "five," so a *pentad* is a period of five years. The patient had been taking anti-cancer drugs for a *pentad*.

Hexa- means "six," so a *hexapod* is a six-legged creature. Another name for an insect is a *hexapod*.

Improving Our Writing

Without adverbs, our sentences would be dull. This sentence has no adverbs:

The President dresses.

In order to express ourselves in a vivid and colorful manner, we can use **descriptive adverbs.** The sentence above is more interesting when we add adverbs to describe how the President dresses:

The President dresses *elegantly*.

He might also dress *patiently, frantically, quickly, clumsily, casually, formally,* or *conservatively*.

Example 1 Replace each blank with at least one adverb to make the sentence more descriptive.

(a) Darren _____ hired his staff for the summer months.

(b) Sir Knight rode _____ on his horse through the forest.

Solution Our answers will vary. Here are some examples.

(a) Darren **carefully, quickly, responsibly, hurriedly, promptly, wearily, skillfully, expertly** hired his staff for the summer months.

(b) Sir Knight rode **wildly, frantically, gallantly, energetically, confidently, slowly, cautiously** on his horse through the forest.

Sure or Surely?   We often use the word *sure* incorrectly. It is an adjective and not an adverb. *Sure* should not take the place of the adverbs *surely, certainly,* or *really.*

> NO: Bernie is *sure* struggling.
>
> YES: Bernie is *surely* struggling. (modifies verb "is struggling")
>
> NO: I'm *sure* exhausted.
>
> YES: I'm *really* exhausted. (modifies p. adjective "exhausted")
>
> NO: You are *sure* helpful.
>
> YES: You are *certainly* helpful. (modifies p. adjective "helpful")

We remember that *sure* is an adjective, and we use it only as an adjective or predicate adjective as in the sentences below:

> Max was *sure* of his success. (predicate adjective)
>
> Is vitamin C a *sure* cure for the common cold? (adjective)
>
> We were *sure* the storm was over. (predicate adjective)

Example 2   Replace each blank with *sure* or *surely.*

(a) Are you _____ the answer is correct?

(b) The recipe _____ calls for spices like rosemary, sage, and thyme.

Solution   (a) Are you **sure** the answer is correct? (predicate adjective)

(b) The recipe **surely** calls for spices like rosemary, sage, and thyme. (adverb modifying the verb "calls")

Real or Really?   Like *sure,* the word *real* is an adjective and should not take the place of the adverb *really. Real* modifies a noun or pronoun, while *really* modifies a verb, adjective, or adverb.

> NO: I'm *real* happy to meet you.
>
> YES: I'm *really* happy to meet you. (modifies p. adj. "happy")
>
> NO: That's a *real* nice shirt.
>
> YES: That's a *really* nice shirt. (modifies adjective "nice")
>
> NO: Kim sings *real* well.
>
> YES: Kim sings *really* well. (modifies adverb "well")

We remember that *real* is an adjective, and we use it only as an adjective or predicate adjective as in the sentences below:

> The man in the uniform looked like a *real* policeman. (adjective modifying the noun "policeman")

> Is the policeman *real*, or is he an imposter? (predicate adjective)

Example 3 Replace each blank with *real* or *really*.
(a) Mr. Cabrera ran (real, really) fast.

(b) Those artificial flowers look (real, really).

Solution (a) Mr. Cabrera ran **really** fast. ("Really" is an adverb that modifies another adverb, "fast."

(b) Those artificial flowers look **real.** ("Real" is a predicate adjective that follows the linking verb "look" and describes the subject "flowers.")

Bad or Badly? The word *bad* is an adjective. It describes a noun or pronoun, and often follows linking verbs like *feel, look, seem, taste, smell,* and *is.* The word *badly* is an adverb that tells "how." We do not use *bad* as an adverb.

> NO: I ran *bad* in the race.
> YES: I ran *badly* in the race. (adverb that tells "how")

> NO: The President dressed *bad.*
> YES: The President dressed *badly.* (adverb that tells "how")

> NO: Dad golfed *bad* today.
> YES: Dad golfed *badly* today. (adverb that tells "how")

We remember that *bad* is an adjective, and we use it only as an adjective or predicate adjective as in these sentences:

> Miss Priss felt *bad* this morning. (predicate adjective)

> The thunderstorm looks *bad.* (predicate adjective)

> Did you receive a *bad* grade on your test? (adjective that describes "grade")

Example 4 Replace each blank with *bad* or *badly.*
(a) The *Titanic* was damaged _____ by striking an iceberg.

(b) Loss of life on the *Titanic* was _____.

Solution   (a) The *Titanic* was damaged **badly** by striking an iceberg. ("Badly" is an adverb that tells "to what extent" the *Titanic* "was damaged.")

(c) Loss of life on the *Titanic* was **bad**. ("Bad" is a predicate adjective that follows the linking verb "was" and describes the subject "loss.")

Practice   For a–f, replace each blank with the correct vocabulary word.

a. The Greek prefix meaning "six" is _____.

b. Rectangles, squares, and parallelograms are quadrilaterals or _____.

c. The Greek prefix meaning "four" is _____.

d. A child spends a _____ at home before entering school.

e. The Greek prefix for "five" is _____.

f. The insect has six legs; therefore, it is a _____.

For g and h, replace each blank with at least one adverb to make the sentence more descriptive.

g. Vivian paddled her canoe _____ down the canal.

h. Grandma usually drives _____.

Choose the correct word to complete sentences i–m.

i. The sinking of the *Titanic* was (sure, surely) tragic.

j. Rescuers tried (real, really) hard to save as many lives as possible.

k. It was (real, really) sad.

l. Does your injured knee hurt (bad, badly)?

m. This morning our team played basketball very (bad, badly).

More Practice Choose the correct word to complete each sentence.

1. The band (sure, surely) performed well today.

2. I'm (sure, really) relieved.

3. The committee (sure, certainly) gave generously of their time.

4. Freddy is (real, really) tired.

5. My dog obeys (real, really) well.

6. Audrey broke both arms (bad, badly).

7. A toothache is a (bad, badly) ailment.

8. His tooth hurt (bad, badly).

9. The basketball player shot (bad, badly) in the last game of the season.

10. It was a (bad, badly) day for the team.

Review set 92 Choose the correct word(s) to complete sentences 1–15.

1. An osteoblast is a (hair-, bone-, skin-) forming cell.
   (89)

2. Physiology studies the (unusual, natural, abnormal) chemical and physical functions of living organisms.
   (87)

3. We use an (analogy, application, anecdote) to do word processing, desktop publishing, or computer artwork.
   (66, 90)

4. The Greek prefix (*pre-, pro-, proto-*) means "first" or "earliest form."
   (91)

5. The Greek prefix (*eu-, miso-, deutero-*) means "second."
   (7, 91)

6. Nam and (she, her) saddled the horses (theirselves, themselves).
   (60)

7. I haven't (never, ever) (rode, ridden) with Nam and (they, them).
   (75, 81)

8. Do you have (up-to-date, up to date) information about the space program?
   (82, 85)

9. Yes, my information is (up-to-date, up to date).
   (82, 85)

10. Are you in agreement with (me, my) writing to the
(56, 58) governor about noisy lawn mowers?

11. Quan (doesn't, don't) know that those horses (isn't, ain't,
(56, 81) aren't) (our's, ours).

12. The applicant (who, whom) the company hired will start
(64, 65) work next week.

13. Hrothgar feels (good, well) today.
(84)

14. Have you ever (flew, flown) in a helicopter?
(77, 78)

15. Of the two horses, Maxine prances (more, most)
(90) gracefully.

16. Rewrite the following, adding capital letters and correct
(63, 68) punctuation marks: help screamed mrs poovey to the
police officer can't you see that i need help i didn't see
the stop sign so my car is wrecked

17. In this sentence, write the infinitive and label it an
(23, 48) adjective or a noun: Detective Onsworth has a perplexing
case to investigate.

18. In this sentence, write the verb phrase, name its tense,
(10, 31) and label it transitive or intransitive: Will Beowulf and
his brave seamen find Grendel in the hall?

19. In this sentence, write the dependent clause, circling the
(24, 57) subordinating conjunction: Please use compression
software so that this computer file will use less space.

20. For a–c, write whether the -ing word is a gerund,
participle, or verb.
(19, 58) (a) Conquering the wicked Grendel is Beowulf's goal.
(8, 21) (b) Beowulf is conquering the fiend.
(27, 48) (c) The conquering hero deserves praise.

21. Write whether the underlined part in this sentence is
(65) essential or nonessential: Our history teacher, <u>Mr. Minos</u>,
has been discussing the Minoan civilization of Crete.

22. Write the nominative case, first person plural personal
(53, 55) pronoun.

23. Write the superlative form of the adverb *well*.
(84, 90)

24. Write whether this sentence is simple or compound: The
(3, 62) Danes praise Beowulf, for he is their hero.

25. Write the four principal parts of the irregular verb *teach*.
(79, 80)

26. Write the conjunctive adverb in this sentence: I am very
(91) tired; nevertheless, I shall finish my chores.

27. Rewrite this sentence, adding a dash where it is
(91) appropriate: Lorna baked my three favorite kinds of pie
fresh peach, banana cream, and French apple.

28. Write and underline each part that should be italicized in
(72) this sentence: Have you read The Horse and his Boy, the
fifth book in C.S. Lewis's series about the land of Narnia?

Diagram sentences 29 and 30.

29. Has your neighbor Mr. Poovey forgiven his wife yet?
(25, 45)

30. Forgiving his wife will be difficult, but he will succeed
(19, 62) eventually.

LESSON 93

The Colon

Dictation or Journal Entry

Vocabulary: Three more Greek numerical prefixes include *hepta, octo,* and *ennea.*

Hepta means seven. A *heptose* is a molecule containing seven atoms of carbon. A *heptose* does not react with water to create a new compound.

Octo means eight. An *octoroon* is a person with one-eighth black ancestry. The *octoroons* displayed great pride in their African heritage.

Ennea means nine. An *ennead* is a group of nine persons. A baseball team consists of an *ennead* on the field.

The **colon** (:) signals to the reader that more information is to come. In this lesson we will learn to use the colon correctly.

Between Independent Clauses

We have learned that a semicolon can join two independent clauses that contain related thoughts. A colon can join two independent clauses when the first clause introduces the second or the second clause illustrates the first.

> I have one more request: pray for me.

> My dog Remington looked awful: his fur was matted, his ears were drooping, and his paws were caked with mud.

Example 1   Insert colons where they are needed in these sentences.

(a) She still has a concern she is afraid it might rain.

(b) His desk was tidy the papers were stacked neatly, and the pencils stood upright in their holder.

Solution   (a) The first independent clause introduces the second, so we place a colon between them:

> She still has a concern: she is afraid it might rain.

(b) The second independent clause illustrates the first. We place a colon between them:

> His desk was tidy: the papers were stacked neatly, and the pencils stood upright in their holder.

Salutation of a Business Letter

We use a colon after a salutation in a business letter.

> Ladies:

> Dear Mr. Frappe:

Time When we write the time of day with digits, we use a colon to separate the hours and minutes.

> The space shuttle departs at 10:00 a.m.

Example 2 Insert colons where they are needed in these sentences.

(a) Please be at work at 800 a.m. sharp!

(b) Dear Dr. Hare
I wish to inquire about the carrots...

Solution (a) We place a colon between the hours and minutes when we write about time, so we write **8:00** a.m.

(b) We use a colon after the salutation in a business letter, so we write **Dear Dr. Hare:**

Introducing a List We use a colon at the end of a sentence to introduce a list.

> Here are some American authors: William Faulkner, Jack London, Mark Twain, Ralph Waldo Emerson, and Ernest Hemingway.

> We will study these works by Charles Dickens: *The Old Curiosity Shop, Bleak House, Oliver Twist, David Copperfield,* and *Great Expectations.*

We do not use a colon if the sentence is grammatically correct without it.

> No: You should bring: a pencil, a book, and an eraser.

> Yes: You should bring these things: a pencil, a book and an eraser.

The Following, As Follows We often use a colon with the words *the following* or *as follows* when they introduce a list. Sometimes the list will begin on a separate line.

> The recipe calls for *the following* ingredients: flour, sugar, eggs, and milk.

> We bathe a dog as follows:
> Fill a tub with lukewarm water.
> Gently lift the dog into the water.
> Shampoo the dog...

Quotations We can use a colon to introduce a citation or quotation.

> Many of us can recite the Preamble to the Constitution of the United States:
>
>> We the people of the United States, in order to form a more perfect union, establish justice, insure domestic tranquility, provide for the common defense, promote the general welfare...
>
> Aunt Bertha continued her story: "During the night, I heard a thump..."

Bible References We use a colon between the chapter and verse in a Bible reference.

> Our assignment was to read from Psalm 1:1 to Psalm 150:6.

Example 3 Insert colons where they are needed in these sentences.

(a) For the Bible class, each student was asked to memorize John 3 16.

(b) To paint the chair, you will need the following items sandpaper, paint brush, rags, drop cloth, and paint.

(c) Please tell me who said these words "Ask not what your country can do for you; ask what you can do for your country!"

Solution (a) We use a colon between the chapter and verse in a Bible reference, so we write **John 3:16.**

(b) We use a colon to introduce a list, so we write the sentence as follows:

To paint the chair, you will need the following items: sandpaper, paint brush, rags, drop cloth, and paint.

(c) We can use a colon to introduce a quotation, so we write the sentence as follows:

Please tell me who said these words: "Ask not what your country can do for you; ask what you can do for your country!"

Practice   Rewrite a–e and insert colons where they are needed

    a. This airplane flight arrives at 7 35 p.m. daily.

    b. Bible verses on trust can be found in Proverbs 3 5–6.

    c. To take the standardized test, you will need the following items picture I.D., #2 pencil, dictionary, calculator, and scratch paper.

    d. Dear Assemblyman Mountjoy

    This household would like you to vote "no" on…

    e. Paul Revere is famous for these words "The British are coming!"

For f–k, replace each blank with the correct vocabulary word.

    f. A person with one-eighth African ancestry is a(n) _____

    g. The Greek prefix meaning "seven" is _____.

    h. The Greek prefix meaning "eight" is _____.

    i. The _____ of judges consisted of four men and five women.

    j. The Greek prefix meaning "nine" is _____.

    k. A _____ molecule contains seven atoms of carbon.

More Practice   See "Slapstick Story #5" in Master Worksheets.

Review set 93   Choose the best word to complete sentences 1–11.

    1. Osteochondritis is inflammation of the (liver, kidney, bone).
    (89)

    2. Keyboards, mice, and printers are all computer (backups, peripherals, compressions).
    (88)

    3. A prototype is the (latest, earliest, best) model of something.
    (91)

4. The Greek prefix (*eu-, miso-, deutero-*) means "second."
(91)

5. The Greek prefix (*micro-, ortho-, tri-*) means "three."
(91)

6. Mr. Poovey and his poodle (wasn't, weren't) (ever, never) home on time.
(14, 81)

7. (Those, Them) lazy pirates don't do (anything, nothing) all day long.
(70, 81)

8. A large bag of potato chips (feed, feeds) the entire family.
(73, 74)

9. Whenever (we, us) shepherds see a wolf, we panic.
(53, 66)

10. Max and (they, them) are as hungry as (me, I).
(53, 66)

11. *Well* is usually an (adjective, adverb) modifying an action verb and explaining "how."
(42, 84)

12. She swept the floor (real, really) (good, well) after the party.
(84, 92)

13. Each of those clowns (have, has) (their, his/her) shoes on the wrong feet.
(77, 78)

14. Debby has (strove, striven) for excellence in editing.
(74, 75)

15. Will you please fix Jake and (me, myself, I) a sandwich?
(25, 54)

16. There are three types of verbals: the gerund, the infinitive, and the (appositive, participle, antecedent).
(19, 48)

17. A(n) (antecedent, gerund, infinitive) ends in *-ing* and functions as a noun.
(19, 23)

18. Rewrite the following, adding capital letters and correct punctuation marks: whew exclaimed mrs poovey to the driver whose car she had hit i did not injure you however i badly dented your car
(63, 68)

19. Write whether the following is a phrase or a clause: with an angry, fire-spewing dragon ravaging the kingdom
(24, 57)

20. In this sentence, write the verb phrase, name its tense,
(6, 22) and label it action or linking: The dragon guarding the
heathen gold seems furious.

21. In this sentence, write the dependent clause, circling the
(24, 57) subordinating conjunction: The Goths will not live in
safety unless Beowulf can destroy the dragon.

22. In this sentence, write the indefinite pronoun and label it
(71) singular or plural: Was either of the detectives carrying a
magnifying glass?

23. Write the comparative form of the adverb *carefully*.
(90)

24. Write the four principal parts of the irregular verb *think*.
(74, 75)

25. Write whether the following is a complete sentence,
(1, 3) sentence fragment, or run-on sentence: Beowulf carries a
bright sword this is his dependable weapon.

26. Write the conjunctive adverb in this sentence: The fiery
(91) dragon appears fearsome; on the other hand, Beowulf
looks well prepared for the battle.

27. For a and b, write the word from each pair that is divided
(87) correctly.

(a) wouldn't, would-n't   (b) cobble-stone, cob-blestone

28. Rewrite this sentence, replacing a comma with a
(91) semicolon as needed: Jenny will bring lettuce, tomatoes,
and condiments, and Beth will bring meat, buns, and
chips.

Diagram sentences 29 and 30.

29. Don't give me a reason to worry.
(23, 25)

30. The jealous Unferth deserts Beowulf and hatefully
(25, 62) discredits him.

LESSON 94

The Prepositional Phrase as an Adverb • Diagramming

> **Dictation or Journal Entry**
>
> **Vocabulary:** Both Greek and Latin have the same numerical prefix *deca-* (spelled with a K in Greek), that means "ten."
>
> A *dekameter* is a measure of length equal to ten meters. The yard is five *dekameters* wide.
>
> A *decapod* is any crustacean with five pairs of legs. Crabs, lobsters, and shrimp are *decapods.*
>
> A *decade* is a period of ten years. One hopes to live at least eight *decades.*
>
> A *decathlon* is a series of ten track and field events. The United States hopes to win the *decathlon* in the upcoming Olympics.

Adverb Phrase

We have learned that a prepositional phrase can function as an adjective by modifying a noun or a pronoun. A prepositional phrase can also function as an adverb. A prepositional phrase that modifies a verb, an adjective, or another adverb is called an **adverb phrase.** It answers the questions "how," "when," "where," "why," and "to what extent." The italicized adverb phrases below modify the verb "dressed."

HOW
The President dressed *like a sophisticated leader.*

WHEN
The President dressed *before the press conference.*

WHERE
The President dressed *in the White House.*

WHY
The President dressed *for the occasion.*

TO WHAT EXTENT
The President dressed *in his finest clothes.*

Most adverb phrases modify verbs. However, an adverb phrase can also modify an adjective or another adverb as in the examples below.

The President is loyal *to his political party.* (modifies predicate adjective "loyal")

The President spoke confidently *from the beginning to the end of his inaugural speech.* (modifies the adverb "confidently")

Example 1   Write the adverb phrase, and tell which word it modifies.

(a) Jim Thorpe is remembered for his athletic ability.

(b) Jim Thorpe was spectacular at both the pentathlon and the decathlon.

(c) His Olympic medals are displayed there between the two trophies.

Solution   (a) The adverb phrase **for his athletic ability** modifies the verb **is remembered.** It tells "why."

(b) The adverb phrase **at both the pentathlon and the decathlon** modifies the adjective **spectacular.**

(c) The adverb phrase **between the two trophies** modifies the adverb **there.**

Diagramming   We diagram a prepositional phrase under the word it modifies. Therefore, we place an adverb phrase under a verb, adjective, or other adverb. Let us diagram this sentence:

The President dressed in the White House.

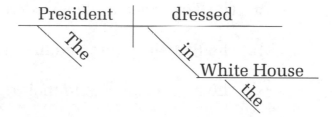

In the sentence above, the adverb phrase *in the White House* modifies the verb. It tells where the President dressed.

Example 2   Diagram the three sentences from Example 1.

Solution   (a) Jim Thorpe is remembered for his athletic ability.

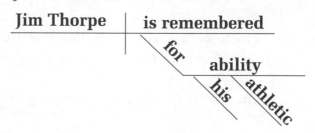

(b) Jim Thorpe was spectacular at both the pentathlon and the decathlon.

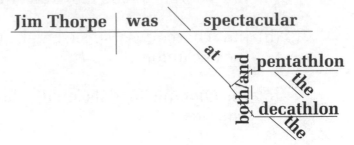

(c) His Olympic medals are displayed there between the two trophies.

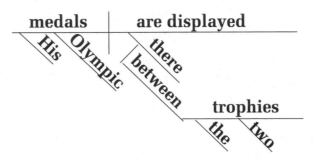

Practice   For a–d, write each adverb phrase and tell which word or phrase it modifies.

   a. The Thugs acted like murderous barbarians.

   b. The British suppressed the Thugs in the 1830s.

   c. Thugs were sincere in their rituals.

   d. The British marched high into the hills.

Diagram sentences e and f.

   e. Spats wandered far from home.

   f. Nancy found him in the meadow.

For g–l, replace each blank with the correct vocabulary word.

   g. She was fifty years old; she had lived five _____.

   h. *Deka* is a Greek numerical prefix meaning _____.

   i. A _____ requires athletic training for ten different events.

   j. The Greek prefix _____ means "ten."

k. Look at that _____ with ten legs!

l. A _____ is ten meters long.

More Practice

Diagram sentences 1–3.

1. Christina glided across the ice.

2. Are you knowledgeable concerning nutrition?

3. The driver swerved far to the left.

Write each prepositional phrase from sentences 4 and 5, and star the object of each preposition.

4. The newly fallen snow melted fast in the warm rays of the sun.

5. At the shore of the Sea of Galilee, Toby searched for turtles and sand fleas.

Review set 94

Choose the best word to complete sentences 1–9.

1. A triarchy is a government by (two, three, ten) people.
(91)

2. Deuteronomy is the (first, second, fifth) statement of Mosaic law.
(91)

3. The Greek prefix (*tetra-*, *penta-*, *hexa-*) means "four."
(92)

4. The Greek prefix (*tetra-*, *penta-*, *hexa-*) means "five."
(92)

5. The prefix (*tetra-*, *penta-*, *hexa-*) means "six."
(92)

6. Henri and (him, he) are (sure, really) excited.
(53, 92)

7. We haven't (ever, never) (ate, eaten) *escargot.*
(73, 81)

8. The (terror stricken, terror-stricken) Grendel knew his days had come to an end.
(82)

9. Grendel was (terror stricken, terror-stricken).
(82)

10. Would you prefer (me, my) contacting the governor by phone?
(56, 58)

11. She (doesn't, don't) know how to feed a guinea pig or clean (its, it's) cage.
(56, 81)

12. In the end, (who, whom) do you think stays behind to
$_{(66, 67)}$ fight alongside Beowulf?

13. Christina skates (real, really) (well, good).
$_{(84, 92)}$

14. Has Beowulf (slew, slain) Grendel?
$_{(74, 75)}$

15. Blanca works (harder, hardest) of all the cooks in the
$_{(90)}$ kitchen.

16. In this sentence, write the infinitive and label it a noun or
$_{(23, 48)}$ an adjective: Will Beowulf's ally Wiglaf find the strength
to fight?

17. In this sentence, write and underline each part that
$_{(72)}$ should be italicized: In Germany, people greet each other
with guten Morgen in the morning and gute Nacht in the
evening.

18. Rewrite the following, adding capital letters and correct
$_{(29, 50)}$ punctuation marks:

dear king beowulf

    you defeated grendel so we have been spared much
evil nevertheless the furious dragon is now ravaging our
kingdom

                with concern
                your loyal subjects

19. Rewrite this sentence, making it an interrogative sentence
$_{(1, 3)}$ instead of a demonstrative sentence: Beowulf and Wiglaf
will fight the dragon courageously.

20. In this sentence, write the verb phrase, name its tense,
$_{(18, 31)}$ and label it transitive or intransitive: With its sharp teeth,
the dragon has enclosed Beowulf's neck.

21. In this sentence, write the dependent clause, circling the
$_{(24, 57)}$ subordinating conjunction: Evil will triumph unless they
strike down the foe.

22. In this sentence, write whether the underlined part is
$_{(64, 65)}$ essential or nonessential: The story mentions a firedrake,
<u>another name for a mythical fiery dragon</u>.

23. Write the objective case, third person, singular,
(54, 55) masculine gender personal pronoun.

24. Write the four principal parts of the irregular verb *buy*.
(73, 74)

25. Write whether the following sentence is simple or
(3, 62) compound: Wiglaf's armor fails to protect him, yet he maintains his courage.

26. Write the conjunctive adverb in this sentence: Nam
(91) bought the food for the picnic; in addition, he will supply the paper goods.

27. From this list, write the word that is divided correctly: a-
(87) bandon, ab-andon, aban-don

28. Rewrite the following, adding a colon where it is needed:
(93) Erika has purchased these items sponges, soap, car wax, and tire cleaner.

Diagram sentences 29 and 30.

29. Does raging increase the dragon's effectiveness?
(19, 25)

30. Beowulf gave him and me iron shields to carry.
(23, 32)

LESSON
95

Preposition or Adverb?
• Preposition Usage

Dictation or Journal Entry

Vocabulary: Let us discuss three more computer terms.

To *download* means to retrieve a file from the World Wide Web or other Internet source. I will *download* that free application to my new computer.

Cache, pronounced "cash," is a storage place on the hard drive for recently-used Internet information that needs to be accessed quickly. Mieko's computer automatically stores her Internet family photo galleries in a *cache* so that she can view the pictures without waiting for them to download.

Encryption is the coding or scrambling of information in a file so that it can only be decoded and read by someone who has the correct decoding key. Web sites use *encryption* to prevent anyone from intercepting personal information like credit card numbers.

Preposition or Adverb?   Most prepositions can be used as adverbs as well. We remember that an adverb stands alone, but a preposition always has an object.

> ADVERB: The kitten climbed *down.*
> PREPOSITION: The kitten climbed *down the *tree.*

> ADVERB: The kitten climbed *over.*
> PREPOSITION: The kitten climbed *over the *fence.*

> ADVERB: The kitten fell *off.*
> PREPOSITION: The kitten fell *off the *branch.*

Diagramming can help us determine whether a word is being used as an adverb or a preposition. Look at the word "down" in these two sentences:

> ADVERB: Fido knocked *down* the vase.

(We can see that "vase" is a direct object telling what Fido knocked. It is not an object of a preposition. "Down" is an adverb telling where.)

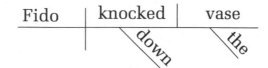

> PREPOSITION: Then he dashed *down the stairs.*

(In this sentence, "stairs" is the object of the preposition "down.")

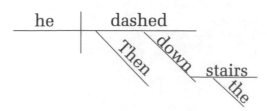

Example 1 Tell whether the italicized word in each sentence is an adverb or a preposition.

(a) You may wait *inside.*

(b) The bus stop is *outside* the building.

(c) The puppy wiggled *underneath* the gate.

(d) The excited toddler is jumping *around.*

Solution (a) "Inside" is an **adverb** telling where you "may wait."

(b) We see that "outside" is a **preposition** because it has an object—"building."

(c) We see that "underneath" is a **preposition** because it has an object—"gate."

(d) "Around" is an **adverb** telling where the toddler "is jumping."

Preposition Usage Certain pairs of prepositions are frequently misused. In this lesson, we will learn to use these prepositions correctly:

in and *into*

between and *among*

beside and *besides*

In or into? The preposition *in* means you are already there.

We were *in* the office.

He was *in* the theater.

The preposition *into* refers to moving from the outside to the inside.

We went *into* the office.

He stepped *into* the theater.

Between or Among? We use *between* when referring to two people, places, or things.

The two friends divided the peanuts *between* them.

We'll keep the secret *between* you and me.

We use *among* when referring to three or more people, places, or things.

> Junior was one *among* many who worked on the project.

> He is *among* the greatest performers of all time.

Beside or Besides? The preposition *beside* means "at the side of."

> The bride stood *beside* the groom.

> They parked the car *beside* their apartment.

Besides means "in addition to" or "as well as."

> *Besides* the lions, I'd like to see the tigers.

> What animal *besides* the lion does the tiger resemble?

Example 2 Choose the correct preposition for each sentence.

(a) The sports fans entered (in, into) the Baseball Hall of Fame.

(b) Joseph Bert Tinker was (between, among) the best infield baseball players of all time.

(c) John Joseph Evers, a second baseman, stood (beside, besides) Joseph Bert Tinker, a shortstop.

Solution (a) The sports fans entered **into** the Baseball Hall of Fame.

(b) Joseph Bert Tinker was **among** the best infield baseball players of all time.

(c) John Joseph Evers, a second baseman, stood **beside** Joseph Bert Tinker, a shortstop.

Practice For sentences a–d, tell whether the italicized word is an adverb or a preposition.

a. The whales swam *by*.

b. The seals circled *around* the boat.

c. The whale watchers jumped *over* the side.

d. The seasick passenger settled *down*.

For e–g, choose the correct preposition.

e. The hungry whale watcher sauntered (in, into) the snack bar.

f. The baby whale swam (between, among) the pod of whales

g. Would anyone (beside, besides) the crew like to get closer to the whales?

For sentences h–j, replace each blank with the correct computer term.

h. Did you _____ that encyclopedia file to your computer?

i. _____ makes the transfer of data secure; it keeps others from viewing information.

j. Her computer automatically placed the Internet information in a _____ to make it quicker to access.

Review set 95

Choose the correct word(s) to complete sentences 1–16.

1. Six-legged insects, or (pentagons, tetragrams, hexapods),
(92, 94) infest our garden shed.

2. King Hrothgar, Queen Wealtheow, and their son reign as
(91, 92) a (prototype, triarchy, cosmopolis) in Scylding.

3. The prefix (*hepta-, octo-, ennea-*) means seven.
(92, 93)

4. The prefix (*hepta-, octo-, ennea-*) means eight.
(92, 93)

5. The prefix (*hepta-, octo-, ennea-*) means nine.
(92, 93)

6. Neither the Pooveys nor their poodle (is, are) home.
(78, 79)

7. Neither the poodle nor the Pooveys (is, are) home.
(78, 79)

8. (Does, Do) a pile of gold coins lie in the dragon's den?
(14, 80)

9. Beowulf gave (us, we) Goths hope for a safe future.
(54, 66)

10. Max and (they, them) (eat, eats) more than (us, we).
(53, 66)

11. A(n) (gerund, participle, infinitive) is a verbal that is the
(19, 23) basic form of the verb, usually preceded by the preposition "to."

12. She is (sure, surely) tired, for she didn't sleep (good, well)
(84, 92) last night.

13. Neither of Beowulf's weapons (prove, proves) effective
(79, 80) against the dragon's deadly breath.

14. How many penguins has the artist (drew, drawn)?
(74, 75)

15. The circus, (that, which) will be here for two weeks,
(64, 65) opens a week from Tuesday.

16. Here (come, comes) a busload of tourists.
(78, 79)

17. In this sentence, write and underline each part that
(72) should be italicized: Mariya and Irina named their guinea pigs Cavia and Porcellus after the scientific name for guinea pig, Cavia porcellus.

18. Rewrite the following, adding capital letters and correct
(29, 50) punctuation marks:

dear mrs poovey

the auto body shop will charge me forty five hundred dollars to repair my car please write the check to rondo's auto body before monday may 22

sincerely

tom curtis

19. Use an appositive to make one sentence from these two
(45, 46) sentences: Duke Ellington was a great American composer. He became the leader of a jazz band during the Roaring Twenties.

20. Write whether the following is a complete sentence,
(1, 3) sentence fragment, or run-on sentence: Ruthlessly plundering the dragon's hoard.

21. In this sentence, write the dependent clause, circling the
(24, 57) subordinating conjunction: The cowardly warriors appear repentant and sheepish as they desert the battlefield.

22. In this sentence, write whether the underlined part is
(64, 65) essential or nonessential: The chapter <u>that tells about Beowulf and the dragon</u> may have been sung long ago.

23. Write the superlative form of the adverb *carefully.*
(90)

24. Write the four principal parts of the irregular verb *sell.*
(74, 75)

25. In this sentence, write the indefinite pronoun and label it
(71) singular or plural: We are staying close to the nest, for one of the goose eggs is hatching!

26. Write the conjunctive adverb in this sentence: Detective
(91) Onsworth continues to investigate; at the same time, Tom has nearly given up the search for his suitcase.

27. Rewrite this sentence, adding dashes where they are
(93) appropriate: The lady with the curlers I don't know her name was last seen in the airport parking lot.

28. Rewrite this sentence, placing a semicolon where it is
(91) needed: The soil looks dry as a bone the pansies have withered and died.

Diagram sentences 29 and 30.

29. Beowulf and Wiglaf fought and defeated the dragon
(33, 62) guarding the hoard in the cave at Eagle's Ness.

30. Noisily chewing bright pink gum, the batter stepped up
(59, 94) to the plate.

LESSON 96

The Infinitive as an Adverb • The Infinitive Phrase • Diagramming

---

Dictation or Journal Entry

Vocabulary: The Latin prefix *multi-* means "many."

To *multiply* means to make many or to increase the number. Fleas *multiply* rapidly if they are not exterminated.

A *multivitamin* contains several vitamins in one capsule. The doctor recommended a daily *multivitamin* for all his patients.

Multiped means many-footed. The centipede is a *multiped*.

A *multitude* is a great many. A *multitude* of supporters rallied behind the candidate for governor.

The Infinitive as an Adverb
We remember that the infinitive is the basic form of the verb, usually preceded by the preposition "to." Thus far, we have examined infinitives that function as nouns or adjectives in a sentence. In this lesson, we will see that the infinitive can also function as an adverb. Infinitives that function as adverbs are italicized in the sentences below.

To travel, save your money. (modifies the verb; tells "why" save)

The tourists are eager *to travel*. (modifies the adjective "eager")

He's strong enough *to travel*. (modifies the adverb "enough")

Example 1
Write the infinitive from each sentence and tell whether it functions as a noun, an adjective, or an adverb.

(a) Snowboarding is difficult to learn.

(b) Important things to remember are warm clothes, spending money, and a good attitude.

(c) To snowboard requires balance and patience.

Solution
(a) **To learn** functions as an **adverb.** It modifies the adjective "difficult."

(b) **To remember** functions as an **adjective** and modifies the noun "things."

(c) **To snowboard** is a **noun.** It functions as the subject of the sentence.

Example 2   The sentences below contain infinitives that function as adverbs. For each sentence, write the infinitive and tell whether it modifies a verb, an adjective, or another adverb.

(a) To excel, you must practice many hours.

(b) The van is ready to leave.

(c) Josie is well enough to come.

Solution   (a) **"To excel" modifies the verb "must practice."**

(b) **"To leave" modifies the adjective "ready."**

(c) **"To come" modifies the adverb "enough."**

The Infinitive Phrase   An **infinitive phrase** is an infinitive along with its objects and modifiers. The phrase may contain adverbs, adjectives, predicate nominatives, direct objects, indirect objects, and prepositional phrases.

The infinitive phrase may function as a noun, an adjective, or an adverb.

INFINITIVE PHRASE AS A NOUN:

> *To snowboard in the Olympics* is the boarder's goal. (subject)

> The skiers began *to use snowboards.* (direct object)

> My goal was *to race down the mountain.* (predicate nominative)

> He would do anything except *to work many hours.* (object of the preposition)

INFINITIVE PHRASE AS AN ADJECTIVE:

> It is time *to excel in your sport.* (modifies the noun "time")

> Fred needs someone *to train him.* (modifies the pronoun)

INFINITIVE PHRASE AS AN ADVERB:

> We came *to cheer for you.* (modifies the verb; tells "why")

> The skiers were brave *to try the steep slope.*
> (modifies the adjective "brave")

> The beginner was good enough *to ride the ski lift.*
> (modifies the adverb "enough")

Diagramming   We remember that we place the infinitive on stilts. We diagram the infinitive along with its objects and modifiers in the location that shows how the infinitive phrase functions in the sentence. The sentence below contains an infinitive phrase that functions as an adverb.

To exercise more consistently, Kotomi ran daily.
(modifies the verb "ran")

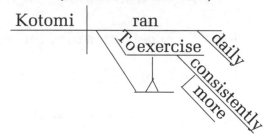

Example 3   Diagram each sentence.

(a) To golf with success requires practice.

(b) Briana is well enough to go with us.

(c) Tuesday is the day to play miniature golf.

Solution   (a) The infinitive phrase, "to golf with success," is the subject of the sentence.

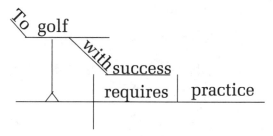

(b) The infinitive phrase, "to go with us," functions as an adverb, for it modifies another adverb, "enough."

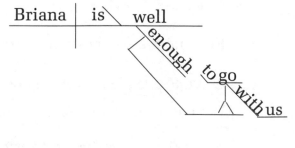

(c) The infinitive phrase, "to play miniature golf," functions as an adjective, for it modifies the noun "day."

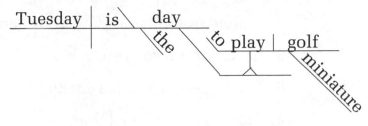

Practice For a–e, replace each blank with the correct vocabulary word.

a. The Latin prefix _____ means "many."

b. The elephant, a _____, has four feet.

c. The _____ listed vitamins A, D, and C.

d. Stagnant water provides a place for mosquitoes to _____ quickly.

e. Having a _____ of friends gave him the sense that he was loved.

For f–h, write whether the infinitive phrase functions as a noun, an adjective, or an adverb.

f. Sheung loves *to golf on Saturday mornings.*

g. *To golf on Saturday mornings,* call for an early tee-off time.

h. José appointed someone *to golf with Sheung.*

For i–l, write the infinitive phrase that functions as an adverb. Then, write the word it modifies.

i. Sheung is good enough to enter a tournament.

j. Bonnie is hopeful to watch the tournament.

k. To view the competitors, you must arrive early at the golf course.

l. Diagram this sentence: To practice his golf, Sheung enters a tournament monthly.

More Practice   Diagram each sentence.

1. Max is eager to fly home.

2. I came to help you with your chores.

3. To open the can, press here.

4. He leaped to avoid a snake.

5. I am happy to meet you.

6. To play drums well, practice daily.

Review Set 96   Write the correct word(s) to complete sentences 1–16.

1. A tetragon is a polygon with (four, five, six) sides and
$^{(92, 94)}$ angles.

2. A pentad is a period of (four, five, six) years.
$_{(92, 94)}$

3. A heptose is a molecule containing (seven, eight, nine)
$^{(92, 93)}$ atoms of carbon.

4. A decapod is a crustacean with (six, eight, ten) legs.
$_{(93, 94)}$

5. Osteocope is pain in the (back, head, bones).
$_{(89)}$

6. I promised Jorge and (she, her) that I would try (real,
$^{(54, 92)}$ really) hard to swallow the *escargot*.

7. Lilly (doesn't, don't) have (nobody, anybody) to help her
$^{(77, 81)}$ with the project.

8. A (fast-moving, fast moving) train thunders down the
$^{(27, 82)}$ tracks.

9. The noisy locomotive is (fast-moving, fast moving).
$_{(27, 82)}$

10. Do you remember (our, us) telling you about the
$^{(56, 58)}$ compression software?

11. (There's, There are) enough cars without (her's, hers).
$_{(56, 78)}$

12. The grandmother (who, whom) called the police could
$^{(64, 67)}$ not be reached for comment.

13. Kerry and Robert (sure, surely) play drums (good, well).
$_{(84, 92)}$

14. The moon had (rose, risen) over the lake.
(79, 80)

15. Of the two new employees, Kim drives (farther, farthest)
(90) to work.

16. Ms. Sweet sneaked (in, into) the laboratory and worked
(95) on her gumdrop experiment (between, among) several
unsuspecting technicians.

17. Write the six adverbs from this list that tell "how much"
(89) or "to what extent": not, quite, quiet, very, vain, rather,
somewhat, somewhere, two, to, too

18. Rewrite this paraphrased dialogue, adding capital letters
(63, 68) and punctuation marks as needed:

> i will win the gold by my valor or battle shall destroy
> me beowulf told his companions
> wiglaf reminded him you must defend yourself with
> all your might

19. For a–c, write the plural of each noun.
(12, 13) (a) busload   (b) goose   (c) pocketknife

20. In this sentence, write the verb phrase, name its tense,
(18, 22) and label it action or linking: Has Beowulf grown weary
of fighting the dragon?

21. Write whether this sentence is simple or compound:
(3, 62) Making something loosely resembling music, the
orchestra attempted to follow the conductor.

22. Write the seven common coordinating conjunctions.
(36)

23. Write the objective case, third person, plural personal
(54, 55) pronoun.

24. Write the four principal parts of the irregular verb *make.*
(73, 74)

25. Write the word from this list that is divided correctly: an-
(87) tidote, anti-dote, antid-ote

26. Write the conjunctive adverb in this sentence: Our
(91) washing machine is broken; for this reason, we shall take
our dirty clothes to the laundromat.

27. Write and underline each part that should be italicized in
(72) this sentence: In the 1950s, we traveled across the United
States on a train called Superchief.

28. Rewrite the following, adding a colon where it is needed:
(93) This book covers the eight parts of speech adjectives,
adverbs, conjunctions, interjections, nouns, prepositions,
pronouns, and verbs.

Diagram sentences 29 and 30.

29. Each of us must learn to see through the eyes of the other.
(23, 33)

30. Seeing through the eyes of others gives us more
(19, 25) compassion.

LESSON 97

The Apostrophe: Possessives

Dictation or Journal Entry

Vocabulary: The Latin prefix *ambi-* means "both" or "around."

The adjective *ambisinister* means clumsy with both hands. The *ambisinister* painter could not make a straight line with either hand.

Ambidextrous means skillful with both hands. The *ambidextrous* batter could hit a home run while batting either right or left-handed.

Ambilateral refers to both sides. The flaws on the plywood were *ambilateral,* so the carpenter could not use either side of this wood for the countertop.

Ambiversion is a personality that exhibits both extroversion and introversion. Hank's *ambiversion* allowed him to enjoy either solitude or crowds.

Ambivalent means having conflicting feelings or attitudes about an object, person, or idea. The family was *ambivalent* about their upcoming move to another state.

We use the apostrophe to show possession.

Singular Possessive

To give a singular noun ownership, we add an apostrophe and an *s* (*'s*). The noun then becomes a **singular possessive noun** as in the examples below.

SINGULAR NOUN	POSSESSIVE NOUN
skier	*skier's* gloves
instructor	*instructor's* manual
antelope	*antelope's* horns
bride	*bride's* bouquet

In a compound noun, possession is formed by adding *'s* to the last word.

maid-of-honor	maid-of-honor's dress
track team	track team's victory
grandparent	grandparent's advice

Shared or Separate Possession

When more than one noun shares possession, we add *'s* to the last noun as in the example below.

Natasha, Nadia, and Nicole's baseball game

When the nouns each possess something separately, we add *'s* to each noun.

Debby's and Scot's autographs

Example 1

Use the apostrophe to make each singular noun possessive.

(a) Holly   (b) Uncle Morris

(c) attorney-at-law   (d) boss

(e) Yin, Kim, and Kari (group project)

Solution (a) **Holly's**   (b) **Uncle Morris's**

(c) **attorney-at-law's**   (d) **boss's**

(e) **Yin, Kim, and Kari's** group project

Plural Possessive To give a regular plural noun ownership, we add only an apostrophe. The noun then becomes a **plural possessive noun,** as in the examples below.

PLURAL NOUN	PLURAL POSSESSIVE
parrots	*parrots'* squawks
monkeys	*monkeys'* squeals
hens	*hens'* clucks

Irregular Plurals To give an irregular plural noun ownership, add *'s.*

PLURAL NOUN	PLURAL POSSESSIVE
children	*children's* clothing
mice	*mice's* tails
gentlemen	*gentlemen's* cloaks
oxen	*oxen's* harnesses

Many people make errors when forming plural possessive nouns. To avoid this, form the plural noun first. Then apply the guidelines above to make it possessive.

Example 2 Use the apostrophe to form a plural possessive noun from each plural noun.

(a) sheep   (b) trout

(c) dolphins   (d) nurses

(e) matrons-of-honor

Solution (a) **sheep's**   (b) **trout's**

(c) **dolphins'**   (d) **nurses'**

(e) **matrons-of-honor's**

Practice For a–f, replace each blank with the correct vocabulary word.

    a. Tucker could not decide whether to use a snowboard or skis; he felt _____.

    b. The Latin prefix _____ means "around" or "both."

    c. Molly was sometimes shy and sometimes outgoing because of her _____.

    d. Larry pitches well with either arm because he is _____.

    e. I would not like an _____ surgeon to operate on me!

    f. The damage to the car was _____, for the car had plowed between two trucks.

For g–l, write the possessive form of each italicized noun.

    g. The two *brothers-in-law* children were the same age.

    h. *Denny, Daisy,* and *Donny* canopy protected them from the sun's rays.

    i. Did you notice the *geese* flying formation?

    j. The *duck* quacking awoke a sleeping swan.

    k. She is combing the *lice* eggs from her hair.

    l. *Hoss* horse bolted from the corral into the open field.

More Practice For 1–8, write the possessive form of each singular noun.

    1. parable   **2.** consul   **3.** louse   **4.** statue

    5. ally   **6.** hypocrite   **7.** machinist   **8.** platoon

For 9–16, write the possessive form of each plural noun.

    9. moose   **10.** ants   **11.** caterpillars **12.** criteria

    13. caddies   **14.** children   **15.** women   **16.** syllabi

Review Set 97 Choose the correct word(s) to complete sentences 1–16.

    1. An ennead is a group of (seven, eight, nine) persons.
    (93)

2. A dekameter is a measure of length equal to (one
(94) hundred, ten, eight) meters.

3. A decade is a period of (twenty, fifty, ten) years.
(94)

4. For security, we use (encryption, foreshadowing) to code
(50, 95) or scramble computer information.

5. To (antedate, download) is to retrieve a file from the
(31, 95) Internet.

6. The ten cowards didn't have (nothing, anything) to do
(81) with slaying the dragon.

7. Either the students or the teacher (pay, pays) for the
(79, 80) pizza.

8. (Isn't, Aren't, Ain't) there a pallet of bricks in the yard?
(78, 79)

9. (Us, We) Goths shall forever remember Beowulf.
(53, 66)

10. Max and (we, us) (sleeps, sleep) less than (they, them).
(53, 66)

11. The word *not* is an (adverb, adjective, preposition).
(81, 83)

12. Wiglaf is (sure, surely) overwhelmed by the hoard in the
(92, 95) dragon's cave.

13. One of the robots (diagram, diagrams) sentences quite
(77, 84) (good, well).

14. Yesterday, the Poovey's poodle (lay, lain) in the shade all
(73, 74) afternoon.

15. The camel (which, that) Molly rode was swaying from
(64, 65) side to side.

16. Through the door (bolt, bolts) two lively springer
(77, 78) spaniels.

17. Write the five adverbs from this list: lonely, friendly,
(83, 89) here, still, almost, lovely, now, quite

18. Rewrite the following, adding capital letters and
(29, 50) punctuation marks as needed:

dear tom curtis

enclosed is a check for twenty three hundred dollars to cover the cost of repairs on your car i will send you the remaining twenty two hundred when i return from heidelberg germany on april 1 2017

sincerely

mrs poovey

19. In this sentence, write the infinitive phrase and label it a
(96) noun, adjective, or adverb: Isn't she too honest to tell a lie?

20. In this sentence, write the verb phrase, name its tense,
(18, 21) and label it transitive or intransitive: Someone has been perpetuating rumors about Mrs. Poovey's intentions.

21. In this sentence, write the dependent clause, circling the
(24, 57) subordinating conjunction: According to the Welsh tale, whatever Kilhuch desires, King Arthur grants him.

22. In this sentence, write whether the underlined part is
(64, 65) essential or nonessential: The lance <u>that proved most effective</u> belonged to Sir Bedour.

23. In this sentence, write the indefinite pronoun and label it
(71) singular or plural: Has anyone seen that lady with the curlers in her hair?

24. Write the four principal parts of the irregular verb *hold*.
(73, 74)

25. Write the comparative form of the adverb *gently*.
(90)

26. Write the conjunctive adverb in this sentence: For over a
(91) year, Kilhuch has been searching for Olwen; consequently, he has become discouraged.

27. Rewrite the following, adding a dash where it is needed:
(76) Beowulf's faithful followers traveled to view the wonders of Eagle's Ness the strange creature, the doughty king, the flagons, and the swords.

28. Rewrite the following, replacing a comma with a
(91) semicolon where it is needed: Wiglaf was indefatigable, moreover, he encouraged Beowulf to remain strong to the end.

Diagram sentences 29 and 30.

29. Gallantly, the wounded servant galloped his horse into
(25, 94) the presence of the king.

30. Did he arrive early enough to warn the king?
(23, 94)

LESSON 98

The Apostrophe: Contractions, Omitting Digits and Letters

Dictation or Journal Entry

Vocabulary: Here are four more computer terms.

A *template* is a pre-formatted file that is used as a starting point for a new document. For his business letter, Quan used a *template* which had a place for his name and address in the upper right, a place for the recipient's address a little below that on the left side, an area for the body of the letter below that, and a space for his signature at the bottom.

Pixels, short for "picture elements," are the tiny dots that make up the pictures on computer displays. The screen is divided up into a matrix of thousands or even millions of *pixels*.

Resolution describes how fine an image a monitor can display and a printer can print. A printer's *resolution* is measured by the number of pixels per square inch it can print.

A *server* is a computer that serves information to other computers connected to it. My computer is connected to a *server* that allows me to access the web and e-mail.

Contractions When we combine two words and shorten one of them, we form a **contraction.** We insert an apostrophe to take the place of the letter or letters taken out.

Sometimes a verb is shortened as in the examples below.

you have	→	you've
we would	→	we'd
he will	→	he'll
that is	→	that's

Other times we combine the verb and the word *not*. We shorten the word *not*, and use an apostrophe where the letter *o* is missing.

did not	→	didn't
was not	→	wasn't
is not	→	isn't
are not	→	aren't
cannot	→	can't
could not	→	couldn't
were not	→	weren't
has not	→	hasn't
does not	→	doesn't
have not	→	haven't

Note: the contraction *won't* (will not) is spelled irregularly.

Example 1   Use an apostrophe to write the contractions of a–d.

(a) he is   (b) we are

(c) should not   (d) is not

Solution   (a) **he's**   (b) **we're**

(c) **shouldn't**   (d) **isn't**

Omitted Digits   We use an apostrophe when the first two digits are omitted from the year.

2002	→	'02
1999	→	'99
1968	→	'68
1930	→	'30

Omitted Letters   We use an apostrophe to show that we have taken letters out of a word. In informal writing, we can leave out letters to indicate the way we imagine the words being spoken.

good morning	→	good mornin'
best of luck	→	best o' luck
until later	→	'till later
walking, talking	→	walkin', talkin'

Plurals of Lowercase Letters and Words Used as Nouns   We use an apostrophe to form the plurals of lowercase letters and words used as nouns. Notice that the letters or words may be italicized or underlined.

Take care that your *g*'s do not look like *y*'s.

Doby uses too many *you know*'s when he talks.

This is one of the few times when an apostrophe is used to form a plural. Be especially careful not to form regular plurals with apostrophes.

Plurals of numbers and capital letters are usually formed by adding only an *s*.

Geraldine earned all *B*s on her report card.

She received four *1*s and two *2*s in citizenship.

Example 2   Write the expression that needs an apostrophe in each sentence.

(a) She hoped to attend the winter Olympics in 06.

(b) The poem begins, "Twas the night before Christmas, and all through the house...."

(c) There are too many *Is* and *mes* in this research paper.

Solution (a) She hoped to attend the winter Olympics in **'06.**

(b) The poem begins, "**'Twas** the night before Christmas, and all through the house...."

(c) There are too many ***I's*** and ***me's*** in this research paper.

Practice For sentences a–e, write each expression that needs an apostrophe.

a. Arent you surprised that there really is a place called Timbuktu?

b. As of 02, Timbuktu remained of little economic importance in the Sahara Desert.

c. George Eliot writes, "And so Ill go now, Master Marner ... and I wish you the best o luck, and its my belief as itll come to you, if you do whats right by the orphan child..."

d. Shes always sayin that ain't isnt a word.

e. The *ahs* of delight encouraged the performers.

Make contractions for f and g.
f. would not   **g.** they are

For h–k, replace each blank with the correct computer term.
h. A resolution of 640 × 480 is comprised of a matrix of 640 × 480 _____.

i. A greater number of pixels per square inch creates better _____.

j. Our history teacher suggested that we create a _____ for writing our weekly homework assignments on the computer.

k. Since the _____ had crashed, I was not able to receive my e-mail.

**More
Practice**   See Master Worksheets.

**Review set
98**   Choose the best word to complete sentences 1–10.

1. A decathlon is a series of (seven, six, ten) track and field
$^{(93, 94)}$events.

2. A (heptose, decapod, cache) is a storage place for
$^{(93, 95)}$computer information.

3. The Latin prefix *multi-* means (ten, many, long).
$^{(96)}$

4. A (soliloquy, satire, stereotype) is an oversimplified
$^{(72, 99)}$image of a certain person or group of people.

5. The epidermis is the outer layer of (rock, crust, skin).
$^{(71)}$

6. Jorge and (he, him) were (real, really) hungry.
$^{(53, 95)}$

7. *Really* is an (adjective, adverb).
$^{(28, 95)}$

8. Daniel has a (full-time, full time) job.
$^{(82, 85)}$

9. He works (full-time, full time).
$^{(82, 85)}$

10. Have you forgotten (us, our) signing the contract?
$^{(54, 58)}$

11. They can't find (their's, theirs) (anywhere, nowhere).
$^{(56, 86)}$

12. The plumber (who, whom) I called (doesn't, don't) fix
$^{(64, 77)}$refrigerators.

13. (Bad, Badly) is an adverb.
$^{(92)}$

14. Several tiny zebra finches (flew, flown) into the willow
$^{(73, 74)}$tree.

15. Of all the knightly legends, which one do you like (more,
$^{(89, 90)}$most)?

16. Who (beside, besides) Richard wants to stand (between,
$^{(95, 33)}$among) the two pillars for this photo shot?

17. For a–c, write the possessive form of each noun.
$^{(97)}$ (a) The Curtises   (b) Jenny   (c) mother-in-law

Rewrite 18 and 19, adding capital letters and punctuation marks, including apostrophes, as needed.

18. (63, 68) i need your help for my suitcase is still missing said tom to detective onsworth a woman with curlers in her hair took it but i dont know this womans identity

19. (44, 97) at my mothers school in detroit michigan sister mary taught the following subjects mathematics music latin and history

20. (45, 46) Use an appositive to make one sentence from these two sentences: John Dalton was an English schoolteacher in the early 1800s. He proposed the idea that all matter is composed of atoms.

21. (3, 62) Write whether the following sentence is simple or compound: Kilhuch is discouraged, so he blames King Arthur.

22. (24, 57) In this sentence, write the dependent clause, circling the subordinating conjunction: If Samson has a haircut, he will lose his strength.

23. (53, 55) Write the nominative case, third person, singular, feminine gender, personal pronoun.

24. (49, 53) Write the antecedent of the italicized pronoun in this sentence: After Kilhuch had searched everywhere, *he* asked for help from his friends.

25. (24, 57) Write whether the following is a phrase or a clause: wearing dirty white sneakers with holes in the bottom

26. (87) Write the word from this list that is divided correctly: hex-apod, hexap-od, hexa-pod

27. (91) Write the conjunctive adverb in this sentence: Trials and difficulties filled my day; nevertheless, I shall sleep peacefully tonight.

28. (72) Write and underline each word that should be italicized in this sentence: Arthur's personal sailing ship might have been named Lady Guinevere.

Diagram sentences 29 and 30.

29. Kilhuch's tasks might prove too difficult to perform.
(23, 39)

30. To win Olwen, Kilhuch must find the boar, Truith.
(23, 96)

LESSON
99

The Adjective Clause •
The Adverb Clause •
The Noun Clause

Dictation or Journal Entry

Vocabulary: The Latin word *solus* means "alone, single, sole" and often appears in English as the prefix *soli-*.

We remember that a *soliloquy* is a discourse in which one is speaking to oneself. Lady Macbeth's *soliloquy* reveals her innermost thoughts.

Solitude is the state of being or living alone. The *solitude* of the forest appealed to the lone hiker.

Solitaire is a card game played by only one person. Because his friend was not available to play cards, Marco played *solitaire*.

A *solo* is a performance or action done by one person. During his *solo* flight from San Diego to Los Angles, David felt lonely.

Like a phrase, a subordinate clause acts as a single part of speech—as an adjective, an adverb, or a noun. In this lesson we will learn to identify the adjective clause, the adverb clause, and the noun clause.

The Adjective Clause

An **adjective clause** is a subordinate clause that, like an adjective, modifies a noun or pronoun. We have italicized adjective clauses in the sentences below. An arrow points to the word that the clause modifies. We have underlined the relative pronouns, which connect the clause with the rest of the sentence.

The book, *which I read for my science class,* is about Mars.

Let's listen to someone *whom we can trust.*

Please show me the picture *that you are painting.*

This is the work *for which you are responsible.*

The Adverb Clause

An **adverb clause** is a subordinate clause that, like an adverb, modifies a verb, an adjective, or an adverb. We have italicized adverb clauses in the sentences below. We see that the first four adverb clauses below modify the verb "paints" and tell *how, when, where,* and *why.* The last clause modifies the adverb "more" and tells *how much.*

He paints *as though his life depended on it.* [how]

He paints *whenever he has time.* [when]

He paints *wherever he goes.* [where]

He paints *because he loves the result.* [why]

He paints more *than most artists do.* [how much]

We remember that adverb clauses may modify adjectives as well as verbs and other adverbs. See the examples below.

James feels certain *that he can succeed.* [modifies the adjective "certain"]

She seems *smarter than I am.* [modifies the adjective "smarter"]

The Noun Clause

A **noun clause** is a subordinate clause used as a noun. It may function as a subject, object, or predicate nominative. We have italicized noun clauses in the sentences below, and we explain how the clause functions in the sentence.

Whoever arrives first will have the best seat. [sentence subject]

We learned *that Longfellow is a poet.* [direct object]

Here is a prototype of *what I am proposing.* [object of the preposition "of"]

This is *what I have been looking for.* [predicate nominative]

Example

Write whether the italicized clause is an adjective clause, an adverb clause, or a noun clause.

(a) Dan was uncertain *that he would make the team.*

(b) I know *whose keys these are.*

(c) The lady *who arrived last* left first.

Solution

(a) "That he would make the team" is an **adverb clause** that modifies the adjective "uncertain."

(b) "Whose keys these are" is a **noun clause** that functions as the direct object of the sentence.

(c) "Who arrived last" is an **adjective clause** that modifies the noun "lady."

Practice For a–e, replace each blank with the correct vocabulary word.

a. Authors use a literary technique called _____ to reveal a character's deepest thoughts.

b. The Latin prefix _____ means "alone."

c. The soprano performed her _____ beautifully.

d. With a deck of cards, one person can play _____.

e. She preferred the _____ of the country to the hustle and bustle of the city.

For f–j, write whether the italicized clause is an adjective clause, an adverb clause, or a noun clause.

f. *Whoever knows the song* may sing along.

g. The teacher chose Tedmond *who is a conscientious student.*

h. I remember *where I was standing.*

i. She dances *whenever the music plays.*

j. Dancing is *what she likes most.*

Review Set 99 Choose the correct word(s) to complete sentences 1–16.

1. A multivitamin contains (strong, many, both) vitamins.
(96)

2. The Latin prefix *ambi-* means (color, measure, both).
(97)

3. Osteogenesis refers to the formation of (teeth, bone, muscles).
(89)

4. An (operating system, application, anecdote) is another computer term for "program."
(47, 90)

5. Ambidextrous means skillful with (no, one, both) hand(s).
(97, 99)

6. Kilhuch couldn't find Olwen (anywhere, nowhere).
(81)

7. Neither the brother nor the sisters (like, likes) dumping
^(77, 78)the trash.

8. Economics (is, are) essential for the business student to
^(79, 80)understand.

9. Even (those, them) Welsh tales idolize King Arthur!
^(56, 70)

10. (We, Us) old folk have had more birthdays than (they,
^(53, 66)them).

11. A(n) (transitive, intransitive) verb has a direct object.
^(25, 31)

12. Robin Hood and his Merry Men ride (real, really) far into
^(89, 95)the forest.

13. Each of the Merry Men (carry, carries) (their, his) own
^(77, 78)water for the journey.

14. Have you (strove, striven) for excellence in your
^(74, 75)academic endeavors?

15. Whispering Forest Road, (that, which) winds through the
^(64, 65)mountains, will take us to Big Bear City.

16. Across the corn fields (come, comes) a black tornado.
^(77, 78)

17. For a–c, write the possessive form of each noun.
⁽⁹⁷⁾ (a) brothers-in-law(b) James(c)The Rivases

Rewrite 18 and 19, adding capital letters and punctuation marks as needed.

18. after reading mrs pooveys letter tom shouted dadgummit
^(63, 68)i cannot wait until april 1 2017 to repair my car is this
lady crazy

19. olwen will become kilhuchs bride and theyll live happily
^(11, 63)ever after

20. Write the superlative form of the adverb *loudly*.
⁽⁹⁰⁾

21. In this sentence, write the indefinite pronoun and label it
⁽⁷¹⁾ singular or plural: No one wants to have his beard shaved
by an enemy.

22. In this sentence, write the dependent clause, circling the
(24, 57) subordinating conjunction: John misplaced some crucial software while he was setting up the office computer network.

23. Write the seven common coordinating conjunctions.
(36)

24. Write the four principal parts of the irregular verb *wake*.
(74, 75)

25. In this sentence, write the participial phrase and the
(59) word it modifies: The young man drinking his tea through a straw has offered to pay for my sandwich.

26. Write the word from this list that is divided correctly:
(87) dek-ameter, dekam-eter, deka-meter

27. Write the conjunctive adverb in this sentence:
(91) Unfortunately, I've found the story gory and offensive; hence, I shall read no further.

28. In this sentence, write the verb phrase, name its tense,
(18, 22) and label it action or linking: Yspaddaden, the antagonist in the story, has proven unbelievably wicked and deceitful.

Diagram sentences 29 and 30.

29. Chewing her last bite of macaroni, Opal left the
(19, 33) restaurant in a hurry.

30. Has Opal discovered a recipe for grilling pasta with
(25, 59) cheese?

LESSON
100

The Complex Sentence •
The Compound-Complex Sentence
• Diagramming the Adverb Clause

> **Dictation or Journal Entry**
>
> **Vocabulary:** The Latin prefix *circum-* means "around" or "round about."
>
> The *circumference* is the boundary around a circular area. In geometry, we often calculate the *circumference* of a circle.
>
> To *circumvent* means to go around. A cat will *circumvent* a mud puddle whenever possible.
>
> *Circumspect* is an adjective meaning watchful and prudent of every action. The *circumspect* behavior of the stranger made everyone edgy.
>
> To *circumnavigate* is to fly or sail around something. The sailor's goal was to *circumnavigate* the world.

We have learned how to join two simple sentences, or independent clauses, with a coordinating conjunction to form a compound sentence.

José writes beautifully, **for** he practices every day.

independent clause   coordinating conjunction   independent clause

In a compound sentence, each of the independent clauses can stand alone. They are equal grammatical parts.

José writes beautifully. = He practices every day.

Subordinate Clauses Not all sentences are composed of equal parts. Sometimes a dependent clause is connected to an independent clause. We remember that we can turn an independent clause into a dependent clause, or **subordinate clause**, by adding a subordinating conjunction such as *after*, *although*, *because*, *even though*, *if*, *since*, or *unless*.

José writes beautifully *because he practices every day*.

independent clause   subordinating conjunction   dependent clause

The subordinate clause "because he practices every day" cannot stand alone; it is dependent on the main clause, "José writes beautifully."

Complex Sentence A **complex sentence** contains one independent clause and one or more dependent, or subordinate, clause. In the sentence below we have underlined the independent (main)

clause and italicized the subordinating conjunction that introduces the dependent clause.

> <u>Tintern Abbey ranks as one of the most beautiful churches in England</u> *even though* it is a monastic ruin.

Notice that the subordinate clause above is an *adverb clause* modifying the verb "ranks." A complex sentence might also contain a dependent *adjective* or *noun clause.* In the complex sentences below, we have underlined the main clauses and italicized the dependent clauses.

> ADJECTIVE CLAUSE:
>
> <u>Christie is a writer</u> *who has shown remarkable dedication.*

> NOUN CLAUSE:
>
> <u>I know</u> *that she works hard.*

Compound-complex Sentence

A **compound-complex sentence** contains two or more independent clauses and one or more dependent clauses. In the compound-complex sentence below, we have underlined the two independent clauses and italicized the subordinating conjunction that introduces the two dependent clauses.

> <u>Visitors still come</u>, for <u>the abbey remains</u> *although* its roof has vanished, and its tower has crumbled.

Example 1   For a–d, tell whether each sentence is simple, compound, complex, or compound-complex.

(a) In Greek mythology, the Titans were the children and grandchildren of Heaven and Earth.

(b) Because they supposedly ruled the universe for many ages, the Titans were known as the Elder Gods.

(c) Cronus was the most important of the Titans, and he ruled the universe until Zeus dethroned him.

(d) Oceanus was the god of the river flowing around the earth, but Atlas was the god with the world on his shoulders.

Solution   (a) This is a **simple** sentence—one independent clause.

(b) This sentence is **complex.** It has one independent clause ("the Titans were known as the Elder Gods") and one dependent clause ("*Because* they supposedly ruled the universe for many ages").

(c) This is a **compound-complex** sentence. It has two independent clauses ("Cronus was the most important of the Titans" and "he ruled the universe") and one dependent clause ("*until* Zeus dethroned him").

(d) This is a **compound** sentence—two independent clauses ("Oceanus was the god of the river flowing around the earth" and "Atlas was the god with the world on his shoulders") joined by the coordinating conjunction "but."

Diagramming the Adverb Clause   Notice that we diagram the subordinating conjunction on a dotted vertical line connecting the dependent clause (subordinate clause) to the independent clause (main clause). We place the adverb clause below the word that it modifies in the main clause, and diagram it as if it were a separate sentence. The dotted line connects the verb in the dependent clause with the word that the clause modifies.

While the dog munched his treat, the veterinarian checked the dog's ears.

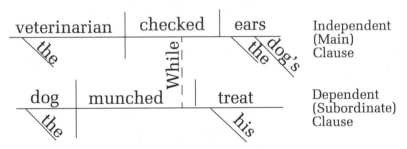

Example 2   Diagram this sentence:

Since Fido was sitting so quietly, the veterinarian gave him a shot.

Solution   We connect the dependent clause to the independent clause with a dotted vertical line upon which we place the subordinating conjunction, "since."

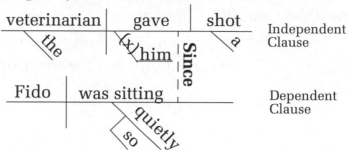

Practice   For a–c, tell whether each sentence is simple, compound, complex, or compound-complex.

    a. Do you remember Tethys, the wife of Oceanus?

    b. Although I had forgotten her, Mnemosyne was the goddess of memory.

    c. Zeus received punishment because he had overthrown Cronus, and reconciliation did not occur for many years.

    d. Diagram this sentence: Though the biker felt exhausted, she had promised to finish the race. Hint:

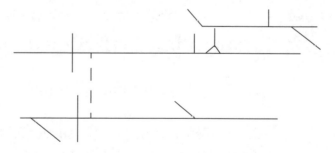

For e–i, replace each blank with the correct vocabulary word.

    e. The motorist detoured ten miles in order to _____ the flooded area.

    f. He claims he will _____ the world in a hot air balloon in eighty days.

    g. The formula for finding the _____ of a circle is πd.

    h. The Latin prefix _____ means "around."

      i. The _____ cat eyed the dog suspiciously.

More For 1–5, tell whether the sentence is simple, compound,
Practice complex, or compound-complex.

 1. The teacher marked "wont" wrong on the spelling test because there was no apostrophe.

 2. I used the word "ain't," so the contraction cops indicted me.

 3. The talented, creative grandmother fashioned porcelain dolls and wedding cakes for her friends and family.

 4. When the track events finished, the awards ceremony began, and many athletes departed.

 5. The circumspect buyer investigated all his options before he purchased the property.

 6. Diagram this compound-complex sentence: As I ran, horns blew, and people cheered.

Additional See Master Worksheets.
Diagramming
Practice

Review set Choose the best word to complete sentences 1–16.
100

 1. A multiped has (large, few, many) feet.
 (96)

 2. Ambilateral refers to (opposite, flat, both) sides.
 (97)

 3. A (template, pixel, server) is a pre-formatted computer
 (98) file used as a starting point for a new document.

 4. (Pixels, Servers, Templates) are tiny dots that make up
 (98) the pictures on computer displays.

 5. (Archaic, Colloquial, Profane) diction is old-fashioned.
 (63)

 6. The two heroes, Lancelot and (he, him), are familiar
 (45, 53) figures to most Britons.

 7. Fernando was sick last week, but now he is feeling (real,
 (84, 92) really) (good, well).

8. The little girl on the beach had (sun bleached, sun-
$^{(27, 85)}$bleached) hair.

9. The four types of sentences include declarative,
$^{(1, 3)}$ interrogative, imperative, and (transitive, exclamatory, important).

10. I appreciate (John, John's) fixing my computer.
$^{(58, 97)}$

11. King Arthur hasn't (no, a) choice but to enter the cave
$^{(60, 81)}$(himself, hisself).

12. The electrician (who, whom) installs wiring (doesn't,
$^{(64, 77)}$don't) install electrical tooth brushes.

13. The law (that, which) Hammurabi devised is the most
$^{(64, 65)}$complete code ever written.

14. I looked up to see that the stars (shone, shined) in the
$^{(74, 75)}$night sky.

15. Of the two Welsh tales, which did you like (better, best)?
$^{(90, 92)}$

16. We use (between, among) when referring to two people,
$^{(16, 95)}$places, or things.

17. For a–c, write the possessive form of each noun.
$^{(9, 97)}$(a) fox   (b) foxes   (c) Charles Dickens

Rewrite 18 and 19, adding capital letters and punctuation marks as needed.

18. i   the case of the missing suitcase
$^{(20, 35)}$ a   clues
      b   suspects
      c   evidence

19. detective onsworth must consider the evidence moreover
$^{(11, 91)}$he must question all the suspects

20. Write the comparative form of the adverb *loudly*.
$^{(83, 90)}$

21. In this sentence, write whether the underlined part is
$^{(64, 65)}$essential or nonessential: Demna, <u>Cumhal's youngest son</u>, was valiant and generous.

22. In this sentence, write the dependent clause, circling the
(24, 57) subordinating conjunction: Although those elderly men
look pitiful and ragged, their eyes reveal fiery pride and
zeal.

23. Write the nominative case, first person, singular personal
(53, 55) pronoun.

24. Write whether the following sentence is simple or
(3, 62) compound: Wild boar, wolves, and giant deer ran
throughout Europe during the times of the Fianna, the
mighty hunters for Ireland's High King.

25. Write whether the italicized clause is a noun clause, an
(99) adjective clause, or an adverb clause: We learned *that the
ancient epic literature of Ireland* is divided into three
great cycles: the Mythological, the Ulster or Red Branch,
and the Finn or Ossianic cycle.

26. Write and underline each word that should be italicized
(72) in this sentence: The abbreviation e.g. stands for the Latin
words exempli gratia, meaning "for example."

27. Write the conjunctive adverb in this sentence: Mrs.
(91) Poovey is rather eccentric; for example, she always wears
sparkling purple dancing shoes with lime-green socks
underneath.

28. In this sentence, write the verb phrase, name its tense,
(21, 31) and label it transitive or intransitive: The Clan Morna has
been envying the power and glory of Cumhal, son of
Trenmor.

Diagram sentences 29 and 30.

29. Will eating fish give you exceedingly great wisdom?
(19, 94)

30. Both Finn and his followers promise to protect the aged
(23, 25) warriors.

LESSON 101

Parallel Structure

Dictation or Journal Entry

Vocabulary: The Greek prefix *para-* means "beside" or "near."

A *parasite* is an animal or plant that lives on or in another organism of a different species, from which the parasite obtains its food. Mistletoe is a *parasite* found in trees.

Parallel means "extending in the same direction and remaining the same distance apart at every point." The rails on a train track are *parallel*. *Parallel* also means "similar," "corresponding," or "having the same grammatical form." I found *parallel* statements in both books.

A *paragon* is a model of excellence. The boy remained a *paragon* of strength, even through life's difficulties.

A *paradigm* is a pattern or example. The advent of e-mail created a new *paradigm* for rapid communication.

Similar Parts   When ideas are similar, they should be expressed in similar form. Parts of sentences that are similar in function should also be expressed in similar form. The balance, consistency, and symmetry resulting from **parallel structure** produces simplicity, elegance, and logic in our writing. Important words strike the eye at once. *The Constitution of the United States* provides a perfect example of parallel structure in its "Preamble":

> We the people of the United States, in order to
> <u>form</u> a more perfect Union,
> <u>establish</u> justice,
> <u>insure</u> domestic tranquility,
> <u>provide</u> for the common defense,
> <u>promote</u> the general welfare, and
> <u>secure</u> the blessings...

Notice that the "Preamble" uses a series of verbs that have the same tense and form. Since the grammatical parts in the series are equal in form and function, we call them **parallel.**

Examine the structure of these sentences:

NON-PARALLEL

> Archibald <u>marched</u> across the room, <u>stood</u> at attention, and <u>salutes</u> the general. (mixes past and present verb tenses)

PARALLEL

> Archibald <u>marched</u> across the room, <u>stood</u> at attention, and <u>saluted</u> the general. (series of past tense verbs)

NON-PARALLEL

He likes <u>diving</u>, <u>swimming</u>, and <u>to hike</u>. (two gerunds and an infinitive)

PARALLEL

He likes <u>diving</u>, <u>swimming</u>, and <u>hiking</u>. (series of gerunds)

or

He likes <u>to dive</u>, <u>to swim</u>, and <u>to hike</u>. (series of infinitives)

or

He likes to <u>dive</u>, <u>swim</u>, and <u>hike</u>. (It is acceptable to drop the *to* in the second and third parts because it is "understood.")

Example 1 Write which sentence has parallel structure. Choose A or B.

A. I go to the mountains to study my grammar, to read the newspaper, and for relaxing in the hammock.

B. I go to the mountains to study my grammar, to read the newspaper, and to relax in the hammock.

Solution Sentence **B** has parallel structure; it contains a series of infinitive phrases—"to study...," "to read...," "to relax...." Sentence *A* is not parallel because it mixes two infinitive phrases with the gerund phrase "relaxing in the hammock."

Articles and Prepositions We apply an article or a preposition to *all* the parts in the sentence or *only to the first part.*

PARALLEL

Ida Hung was thrilled <u>with</u> the schedule of classes, <u>with</u> the extracurricular activities, and <u>with</u> the diversified student population. (The preposition is applied to *all* the parts.)

or

Ida Hung was thrilled <u>with</u> the schedule of classes, the extracurricular activities, and the diversified student population. (The preposition is applied *only to the first part.*)

PARALLEL

They drove through <u>the</u> deserts, <u>the</u> mountains, and <u>the</u> farmlands. (The article is applied to *all* the parts.)

or

They drove through <u>the</u> deserts, mountains, and farmlands. (The article is applied *only to the first part.*)

NON-PARALLEL

> They drove through <u>the</u> deserts, mountains, and <u>the</u> farmlands. (To make a sentence parallel, we apply the article to *all* the parts or *only to the first part*.)

Example 2 Rewrite each sentence so that it has parallel structure:

(a) I ate a sandwich, peach, and a cupcake.

(b) Bob is thankful for his hardworking wife, for his respectful sons, and his compassionate daughter.

Solution (a) **I ate <u>a</u> sandwich, <u>a</u> peach, and <u>a</u> cupcake.** We apply the article to *all* the parts.

or

I ate <u>a</u> sandwich, peach, and cupcake. We apply the preposition *only to the first part.*

(b) **Bob is thankful <u>for</u> his hardworking wife, <u>for</u> his respectful sons, and <u>for</u> his compassionate daughter.** We apply the preposition to *all* the parts.

or

Bob is thankful <u>for</u> his hardworking wife, his respectful sons, and his compassionate daughter. We apply the preposition *only to the first part.*

Correlative Conjunctions If we write a sentence using a pair of correlative conjunctions (either/or, neither/nor, not only/but also, both/and, whether/or), we must match the parts after each conjunction. Each member of the conjunction pair must be followed by the same kind of construction. For example, if a prepositional phrase follows one correlative conjunction, a prepositional phrase should follow the other.

NON-PARALLEL

> The athletic club offered *either* <u>cycling</u> on a stationary bike *or* <u>one could step</u> on an elevated bench. (The first conjunction is followed by a gerund phrase, the second by a clause.)

PARALLEL

> The athletic club offered *either* <u>cycling</u> on a stationary bike *or* <u>stepping</u> on an elevated bench. (Both conjunctions are followed by gerund phrases.)

Non-parallel

His brother *not only* <u>was strong</u> *but also* <u>brave</u>. (The first conjunction is followed by a linking verb and a predicate adjective, the second by only a predicate adjective.)

Parallel

His brother *not only* <u>was strong</u> *but also* <u>was brave</u>. (Both conjunctions are followed by a linking verb and a predicate adjective.)

or

His brother was *not only* <u>strong</u> *but also* <u>brave</u>. (Both conjunctions are followed by a predicate adjective.)

Example 3   Write which sentence has parallel structure. Choose A or B.

A. His job is both to design the house and its construction.

B. His job is both to design the house and to construct it.

Solution   Sentence **B** has parallel structure. Both conjunctions are followed by an infinitive. Sentence A is not parallel because the parts following the conjunctions are not similar. The first conjunction is followed by an infinitive, but the second is followed by a noun.

Practice   For a–c, write which sentence has parallel structure. Choose A or B.

a. A. James is always running, biking, or he'll play the piano.

B. James is always running, biking, or playing the piano.

b. A. He ran through the snow, wind, and hail.

B. He ran through the snow, wind, and the hail.

c. A. She desires neither to help you nor hinder you.

B. She desires neither to help you nor to hinder you.

Rewrite sentences d and e so that they have parallel structure.

d. For her birthday, Malia asked for a fish, horned toad, and a rabbit.

e. In his dream, Quan fought against dragons, thieves, and against monsters.

For f–k, replace each blank with the correct vocabulary word.

f. The red and white stripes on the American flag arc _____.

g. His presentation included a _____ for the new amusement park, which would be built in the future.

h. Danny's honesty and integrity made him a _____ of virtue.

i. The Greek prefix _____ means "beside" or "near."

j. Animals often need to be treated for _____.

k. His sentence flowed smoothly because its structure was _____.

More Practice With a teacher or friend, read each sentence and note its non-parallel structure. Then reword the sentence so that its structure is parallel. (There is more than one correct answer.) This may be either an oral or a written exercise.

1. Stephen stuck sticky notes around his desk, inside his books, and put them onto his computer.

2. He will stick notes either outside the door or post them inside the house.

3. John has neither the patience nor does he have time to repair the computer.

4. Elspeth studied her Spanish, called her friend, and feeds her fish.

5. This afternoon, she will begin shopping, cleaning, and to plan for the party.

6. My cousin has the strength of an ox, the speed of a cheetah, and is wise as an owl.

7. I lack the stamina, courage, and the desire to run a marathon.

8. During her travels, she learned that she could survive without her favorite television programs, without fast-food restaurants, and her comfortable home.

9. In her free time, she likes to read mystery novels, to draw anteaters, and working crossword puzzles.

10. Debby bought not only a cherry pie but also she bought a banana cream pie.

Review Set 101   Choose the correct word(s) to complete sentences 1–16.

1. Marco could not decide whether or not to swim in the
$^{(44, 97)}$ ice-cold mountain stream; he felt (ingenious, ambivalent, heterogeneous).

2. A printer's (server, template, resolution) is measured by
$^{(98)}$ the number of pixels per square inch it can print.

3. A computer screen is divided up into a matrix of
$^{(98)}$ thousands of (servers, templates, pixels).

4. The Latin prefix (*soli-, circum-, ambi-*) means "alone."
$^{(97, 99)}$

5. Solitude is the state of being (sad, intelligent, alone).
$^{(99)}$

6. Robbie (don't, doesn't) have (no, any) math homework.
$^{(14, 81)}$

7. Either the cats or the dog (eat, eats) my leftover food.
$^{(78, 79)}$

8. My hair clippers (is, are) in the closet.
$^{(77, 78)}$

9. I've read several of (those, them) Welsh tales.
$^{(70)}$

10. You set an excellent example for (us, we) teenagers.
$^{(54, 66)}$

11. A(n) (transitive, intransitive) verb has no direct object.
$^{(25, 31)}$

12. Scot was (sure, surely) sorry that he hit me with a water
$^{(92)}$ balloon!

13. One of the Merry Men (has, have) two feathers in (their,
$^{(79, 80)}$ his) hat.

14. The sun (shone, shined) in my eyes so that I could not
$^{(74, 75)}$ see.

15. The road (which, that) veers to the right will take you to
(64, 65)Running Springs.

16. From beneath the sofa (scampers, scamper) three little
(77, 78)mice.

17. For a–c, write the possessive form of each noun.
(97) (a) commander-in-chief   (b) gentlemen   (c) actress

Rewrite 18 and 19, adding capital letters and punctuation marks as needed.

18. finn searched for saba his true love in remote glens dark
(44, 46)forests and deep chasms

19. dear saba
(50, 98)   im thankful that my two hounds bran and sceolaun found you youre one of the fairest maidens ive ever seen would you consider being my wife
                    all my love
                    finn

20. Write the word from this list that is divided correctly:
(87) multit-ude, mu-ltitude, multi-tude

21. In this sentence, write the personal pronoun and its
(49, 56)antecedent: The Celtic heroes Finn and Oisin achieve their fame from a story about the Land of Youth.

22. Write the four principal parts of the irregular verb *beat.*
(73, 74)

23. Write the four common pairs of correlative conjunctions.
(38)

24. Write whether the following sentence is simple,
(62, 100)compound, complex, or compound-complex: The story takes place long ago on a misty summer morning as Finn and Oisin are out hunting on the shores of Loch Lena.

25. Write whether the italicized clause is a noun clause, an
(64, 99)adjective clause, or an adverb clause: The horse *that Oisin rode* was fast but gentle.

26. In this sentence, write the participial phrase and the
(59) word it modifies: Wearing the garb of a queen, a beautiful maiden rides on a snow-white steed.

27. Write the conjunctive adverb in this sentence: We have
(91) examined ancient literature from several countries;
however, we have an abundance of material yet to study.

28. In this sentence, write the verb phrase, name its tense,
(18, 22) and label it action or linking: On his flight to the Land of
Youth, Oisin has observed a shore of yellow sand, the
ripples of a summer sea, and wooded hills with stately
trees.

Diagram sentences 29 and 30.

29. Is Oisin mature enough to accompany Finn on his
(23, 39) adventures?

30. Will you continue reading *Beowulf* until you finish the
(19, 25) book?

LESSON 102

Active or Passive Voice

Dictation or Journal Entry

Vocabulary: Here are four more computer terms.

Upload, the opposite of download, means to send a file from your computer to a server usually connected to the Internet. Perhaps I can *upload* this grammar file to the company's server so that my sister-in-law can download it.

Spam, which originates from the name of Hormel's canned meat, is a noun that has come to mean unsolicited, or "junk" e-mail. It is also used as a verb meaning to send unsolicited mail via e-mail. It took Eriden twenty minutes to filter through all of the *spam* in search of his friend's e-mail message.

A *webmaster* is the person in charge of maintaining a web site. The *webmaster* organizes the web site's structure and responds to e-mails about the web site.

A *firewall* is a security feature, which protects a networked server from damage by users. The CIA's *firewall* prevents unauthorized personnel from accessing its secure computer network.

A transitive verb can be used in either **active voice** or **passive voice.** When the subject acts, the verb is in the **active voice.**

John <u>repaired</u> the computer.

When the subject is acted upon, the verb is in the **passive voice.**

The *computer* <u>was repaired</u> by John.

Verbs that are in the passive voice contain a form of "to be." Often the sentence contains a prepositional phrase beginning with "by." The subject *receives* the action; it does not *do* the action.

PASSIVE: The *poem* <u>was read</u> by Miss Farris.

ACTIVE: *Miss Farris* <u>read</u> the poem.

Active Voice   Writing is more exciting and powerful in the active voice. We try to use the active voice as much as possible.

WEAK PASSIVE:
Longfellow <u>had been disappointed</u> by the tragedies.

STRONG ACTIVE:
The *tragedies* <u>had disappointed</u> Longfellow.

WORDY PASSIVE:
Longfellow's first *wife* <u>was mourned</u> by him for many years.

CONCISE ACTIVE:
Longfellow <u>mourned</u> his first wife for many years.

INDIRECT PASSIVE:
The *idea* <u>was presented</u> to the class by Miss Farris.

DIRECT ACTIVE:
Miss Farris <u>presented</u> the idea to the class.

**Passive
Voice**   We see that the passive voice can be wordy and indirect. It can confuse the reader and tends to be dull. However, the passive voice does have a purpose. We use the passive voice in order to leave something unsaid. When the doer is unimportant or unknown, or when we want to emphasize the receiver of the action, we use the passive voice.

The *forest* <u>was</u> completely <u>burned</u>.

All the *animals* <u>had been rescued</u> from the flames.

The national *anthem* <u>had been sung</u>.

The *prototype* <u>had been tested</u>. (doer unknown)

Example   Tell whether the verb in each sentence is active or passive voice.

(a) Longfellow wrote "the Village Blacksmith."

(b) "The Village Blacksmith" was written by Longfellow.

(c) Initially, Longfellow's marriage proposal was rejected by Fanny Appleton.

(d) Initially, Fanny Appleton rejected Longfellow's marriage proposal.

Solution   (a) The verb is **active voice.** The subject (Longfellow) acts.

(b) The verb is **passive voice.** The subject ("The Village Blacksmith") is acted upon.

(c) The verb is **passive voice.** The subject (proposal) is acted upon.

(d) The verb is **active voice.** The subject (Fanny Appleton) acts.

Practice   Tell whether the verb in each sentence a–d is active or passive voice.

    a. Longfellow and Fanny were married eight years after his first wife's death.

    b. Longfellow married Fanny eight years after his first wife's death.

    c. Fanny's dress was engulfed by flames from a lighted match.

    d. Flames from a lighted match engulfed Fanny's dress.

Vocabulary: For e–h, replace each blank with the correct computer term.

    e. In order to share my information with you, I will _____ my file to the server so that you can download it to your computer.

    f. Defensive coding software created a _____ to protect the computer network from damage or intrusion from users.

    g. Please contact the _____ if you have problems with this web site.

    h. It is not polite to clutter other people's mailboxes with _____.

More Practice   Write whether the verb in each sentence is active or passive voice.

    1. Longfellow was devastated by the loss of his second wife.

    2. The loss of his second wife devastated Longfellow.

    3. Longfellow discusses the soul in "A Psalm of Life."

    4. The soul is discussed by Longfellow in "A Psalm of Life."

    5. The book of Genesis is alluded to in the second stanza.

    6. The second stanza alludes to the book of Genesis.

    7. An optimistic view of life is proposed by the poem.

    8. Without doubt, the poem proposes an optimistic view of life.

Review set 102   Choose the correct word(s) to complete sentences 1–16.

1. Solitaire is a game played by (ten, one, many) person(s).
(94, 99)

2. The Latin prefix *circum-* means (under, through, around).
(100)

3. The circumference is the distance (around, through, under) a circle.
(100)

4. Ambiversion is a personality with (strong, little, both) extroversion and introversion.
(97)

5. A solo is a performance by (fifty, many, one).
(99)

6. My two sisters-in-law, Steph and (her, she) made salads for our picnic.
(45, 53)

7. Kurt (sure, surely) has learned quickly how to swim (well, good).
(84, 92)

8. A (compound, simple, complex) sentence contains one independent clause and one or more dependent clauses.
(100)

9. Dependent clauses are sometimes called (independent, subordinate) clauses.
(57, 100)

10. I can't see (anything, nothing) in this fog.
(81, 89)

11. Had you forgotten (us, our) asking for a map?
(58)

12. The electrician (who, whom) I called never showed up.
(64, 65)

13. Two simple sentences joined with a (preposition, adverb, coordinating conjunction) form a compound sentence.
(62, 100)

14. Of the two banana packers, who works (harder, hardest)?
(89, 90)

15. Jonathan (shined, shone) his shoes before the wedding.
(74, 75)

16. I noticed genuine compassion (between, among) the three friends.
(17, 95)

17. For a–c, write the possessive form of each plural noun.
(97)
    (a) steeds   (b) maidens   (c) youths

Rewrite 18 and 19, adding capital letters and punctuation marks as needed.

18. dear mrs poovey
(29, 50)

   if you wish to settle this case out of court please contact my personal attorney mr chatwell at the following address 42 leisurely lane anaconda texas

                              sincerely

                              tom curtis

19. turbos father stanley has fleas ticks and mange but his
(62, 97) mother sasha does not

20. For a–c, write the plural of each singular noun.
(12, 13) (a) sovereignty   (b) Jones   (c) bay

21. Write whether the underlined part of this sentence is an
(65) essential part or a nonessential part: Tomorrow, the couple, <u>Oisin and she</u>, will go hunting together in the forest.

22. Write the superlative form of the adverb *imaginatively*.
(90)

23. Write the objective case, first person, singular personal
(54, 55) pronoun.

24. Write whether the following sentence is simple,
(3, 100) compound, complex, or compound-complex: With a mighty effort, Finn rouses himself from his dreams and tears the cover from his spearhead.

25. In the sentence below, write the dependent clause,
(57, 99) circling the subordinating conjunction. Then write whether the clause functions as a noun, adjective, or adverb.

   I will feed the dogs as soon as you have bathed them.

26. Write and underline each word that should be italicized
(72) in this sentence: The Odyssey of Homer is the great epic of Greek literature.

27. Write the conjunctive adverb in this sentence: Oisin has
(91) enjoyed victory; consequently, he begs to return to Erinn.

28. Rewrite this sentence so that it has parallel structure:
[101] Allison likes to ride bikes, swim laps, and playing basketball.

Diagram sentences 29 and 30.

29. Fovor, who has imprisoned a maiden, faces Oisin in
[25, 64] combat.

30. After I finish *Beowulf*, I shall begin to read American
[23, 25] novels.

**LESSON
103**

Dangling or Misplaced Modifiers

Dictation or Journal Entry

Vocabulary: The Latin root *audi-* refers to sounds within the range of human hearing.

Audible means capable of being heard. Although he whispered, his voice was *audible.*

An *audience* is a group of listeners at a public event. The *audience* appreciated the orchestra's fine performance.

An *audition* is a trial hearing given to a vocalist or actor. She will sing in an *audition* for the leading role of the cast.

An *audiologist* evaluates one's hearing. The *audiologist* reported that I have a slight hearing loss.

**Dangling
Modifiers**

A **dangling modifier** is a participle, infinitive, or gerund that has no clear subject to modify. Consider the sentence pairs below. Modifiers are underlined.

UNCLEAR—DANGLING MODIFIER

<u>Having played a game of chess</u>, it was time to leave.
(Which word does the phrase modify?)

CLEAR

<u>Having played a game of chess</u>, *we* had to leave. (The phrase modifies the subject, "we.")

UNCLEAR—DANGLING MODIFIER

The sun went down <u>while playing basketball</u>. (Was the sun playing basketball?)

CLEAR

The sun went down while *we were* <u>playing basketball</u>. (The phrase now has a subject, "we.")

**Misplaced
Modifiers**

Some modifiers cause confusion when they are out of place. We place modifiers as close as possible to the words or phrases they modify. Examine the **misplaced modifiers** in the sentences below.

**Participle
Phrases**

We are especially careful to place participal phrases near the words they modify.

MISPLACED MODIFIER

I saw a ferocious dog <u>skateboarding this afternoon</u>.
(Was the dog skateboarding?)

CORRECTED SENTENCE

<u>Skateboarding this afternoon</u>, I saw a ferocious dog.
(We move the participle phrase closer to the subject, "I.")

MISPLACED MODIFIER

> Constructed of pine, Bob sanded and varnished the table. (Was Bob constructed of pine?)

CORRECTED SENTENCE

> Bob sanded and varnished the table constructed of pine. (Ahhhhh, yes, the *table* was constructed of pine.)

Prepositional Phrases We also place prepositional phrases close to the words they modify.

MISPLACED MODIFIER

> Josh tried to explain before lunch what his friend had done. (Does *before lunch* tell when Josh tried to explain, or does it tell when his friend had done something?)

CORRECTED SENTENCE

> Before lunch, Josh tried to explain what his friend had done. (Now it is clear that Josh tried to explain *before lunch*.)

> or

> Josh tried to explain what his friend had done before lunch. (Now it is clear that his friend had done something *before lunch*.)

MISPLACED MODIFIER

> Without experience, the job overwhelmed the new employee. (Was the *job* inexperienced?)

CORRECTED SENTENCE

> The job overwhelmed the new employee without experience. (Clearly, *the new employee* lacked experience.)

Example For each pair of sentences, tell which is more clear. Choose A or B.

(a) A. I found a ten dollar bill walking down the street.

   B. Walking down the street, I found a ten dollar bill.

(b) A. With the support of many friends, the task became manageable.

   B. With the support of many friends, he found the task manageable.

(c) A. Racing up the hill, I noticed that my shoe fell off.

   B. Racing up the hill, my shoe fell off.

Solution (a) Sentence **B** is more clear. The participal phrase, "walking down the street," is close to the subject, "I," the person doing the walking. Sentence *A* says that a *dollar bill* was walking down the street! The sentence has a misplaced modifier.

(b) Sentence **B** is more clear. The prepositional phrase, "with the support of many friends," modifies the subject, "he." In sentence *A*, the prepositional phrase is dangling; it has no subject to modify.

(c) Sentence **A** is more clear. The participle phrase, "racing up the hill," is near the subject, "I." In sentence *B*, the participle phrase is dangling; it has no subject to modify. It sounds like the *shoe* was racing up the hill!

Practice For a–d, tell which sentence is more clear. Choose A or B.

a. A. Swimming in the pool, the cool water refreshed me.

B. Swimming in the pool, I felt refreshed by the cool water.

b. A. At school, Sam remembered what had happened.

B. Sam remembered at school what had happened.

c. A. I recognized the king snake researching reptiles.

B. Researching reptiles, I recognized the king snake.

d. A. Moth-eaten and torn, he found his old sweater.

B. He found his old sweater moth-eaten and torn.

For e–i, replace each blank with the correct vocabulary word.

e. The _____ used both high and low tones to determine the patient's hearing capacity.

f. The Latin prefix _____ refers to sounds that are within the range of human hearing.

g. _____ were offered to all who were interested in performing in the opera.

    h. The _____ clapped enthusiastically after the drummer's solo.

    i. Harriet was so tired that her voice was barely _____.

More Practice

With your teacher or with a friend, read each sentence and answer these questions orally for each sentence: (1) What is wrong with this sentence? (2) What do you think the writer meant to say?

    1. Rushing to class, Harriet's book fell out of her backpack.

    2. Having been written and revised, I was ready to publish the paper.

    3. We saw a huge bull on the way to our hotel.

    4. Singing in the choir, a bat swooped overhead.

    5. Tying my shoe, the other player made a point against our team.

    6. Leaving church, the pews were empty.

    7. He found a little sparrow mowing the lawn.

    8. While rushing to get ready for school, the phone rang.

    9. Being completely untamed, Josh suggested we stay away from his python.

    10. Jared wanted to know after class what the teacher said to his friend.

    11. Making a sandwich, two ants crawled out of the bread bag.

    12. Beating on the roof steadily, I could hardly wait till the rain stopped.

Review Set 103

Choose the correct word(s) to complete sentences 1–16.

    1. To circumvent means to go (over, under, around).
    (100)

    2. A person who is looking around might be called
    (26, 100) (endomorphic, circumspect, forcible).

3. The Greek prefix *para-* means "near" or (alone, good,
(101) beside).

4. (Circumspect, Parallel, Ambidextrous) means similar or
(100, 101) corresponding.

5. A (template, pixels, parasite) lives on another organism.
(98, 101)

6. There (ain't, aren't) (no, any) gray-haired people in the
(14, 81) Land of Youth.

7. Everyone in the Land of Youth (remain, remains) young
(77, 78) forever.

8. I have larger feet than (her, she).
(53, 66)

9. Grandma gave me a (hand-stitched, hand stitched) quilt.
(82)

10. (Us, We) teenagers want to thank you for your excellent
(53, 66) guidance.

11. A sentence containing two or more independent clauses
(57, 100) and one or more dependent clauses is called a (simple,
compound, complex, compound-complex) sentence.

12. We were (real, really) cold and hungry after watching the
(89, 92) football game.

13. Both the mice and the cat (live, lives) under my bed.
(73, 74)

14. The sun had already (rose, risen) when I woke up.
(74, 73)

15. A gold crown, (that, which) sparkled in the moonlight,
(63, 64) sat on Niam's head.

16. Over the fence (jump, jumps) that cat with the black
(79, 80) spots.

17. For a–c, write the possessive form of each noun.
(9, 97)
    (a) Sherry   (b) The Gregorys   (c) Mr. Cruz

Rewrite 18 and 19, adding capital letters and punctuation marks, and making necessary changes to abbreviations for formal writing.

18. dr yokoi i believe will offer her seminar on figurative
(63, 68) language in epic literature on fri oct 12 at 10 am

19.   lets go mrs poovey shouted to her husband i dont
(11, 68) want to miss my flight

    must you always go out in public wearing curlers in your hair asked mr poovey

20. Write the four principal parts of the irregular verb *lead.*
(73, 74)

21. Use an appositive to make one sentence from these two
(45, 46) sentences: Alfred Lord Tennyson was a great English poet during the Victorian age. He wrote a series of twelve stories, called *Idylls of the King,* about King Arthur and his knights.

22. Write the word from this list that is divided correctly:
(87, 101) par-adigm, para-digm, parad-igm

23. In this sentence, write each personal pronoun and its
(49, 53) antecedent: Oisin needs the white steed to carry him across the sea to his homeland.

24. Write whether the following sentence is simple,
(62, 100) compound, complex, or compound-complex: Yesterday, Oisin was a young man, but today he is very old.

25. In the sentence below, write the dependent clause,
(57, 99) circling the subordinating conjunction. Then write whether the clause functions as a noun, adjective, or adverb.

The thought that you might move away troubles me deeply.

26. In this sentence, write whether the verb is in the active or
(4, 102) passive voice: Niam was devastated by Oisin's decision to return to Erinn.

27. Write the conjunctive adverb in this sentence: Oisin
(91) foolishly leaves Niam; moreover, he arrogantly brags to
his countrymen.

28. Rewrite this sentence so that it has parallel structure: The
(101) job includes preparing the surface, taping the edges, and
to paint the top.

Diagram sentences 29 and 30.

29. Telling his heroic deeds to St. Patrick was one of Oisin's
(19, 58) last joys.

30. Oisin instantly grew old when he returned to the land of
(41, 100) Erinn.

LESSON
104

Parentheses • Brackets

Dictation or Journal Entry

Vocabulary: The Latin preposition *cum,* meaning "with" or "together" changes form when used as a prefix. It becomes *con-, com-, co-, col-,* and *cor-,* and the letter following the prefix usually determines which prefix is used.

Con-, as in *convene,* comes before most consonants. *Convene* means to come together. The meeting will *convene* at 8 a.m. on Friday.

Com-, as in *commingle,* comes before *b, p,* and *m. Commingle* means to mix together or combine. At the conference, the math teachers were asked to *commingle* with teachers of history and English.

Co-, as in *coadjutor,* comes before a vowel, *h,* or *gn.* A *coadjutor* works with another as an assistant. The employer and the *coadjutor* hired several new employees.

Col-, as in *collateral,* comes before *l. Collateral* is the security provided when applying for a loan. The loan application included an insurance policy to be used as *collateral* for the borrowed money.

Cor-, as in *correlate,* comes before *r.* To *correlate* means to show a meaningful connection between. Let us *correlate* each name with a certain number.

Parentheses

We use **parentheses** to enclose a thought only loosely related to the main idea of the sentence. Parentheses can enclose additional or explanatory information, personal commentary, figures, or examples that are not essential to the sentence and are not intended to be a part of it grammatically. A single word or figure, a phrase, or an entire sentence can be enclosed in parentheses. (The singular form of *parentheses* is *parenthesis.* Remember, however, that parentheses are always used in pairs.)

Additional Information

In the sentences below, the information enclosed in parentheses is additional, but nonessential, information.

> In America, Alexis de Tocqueville studied democracy (in addition to other things).

> *Democracy in America* (although critical of some aspects) explains what conditions stimulated the growth of democracy in America.

Clarifying Meaning or Figures

We use parentheses around words or figures that are included to explain or clarify meaning.

> The peak of the dormant volcano Mount Shasta (Northern California) is over fourteen thousand feet above sea level.

> Lori prefers citrus fruits (oranges, lemons, limes, etc.) for decorating her tables.

> Bananas were on sale for thirty-three cents (33¢) per pound.

Personal Commentary   In informal writing, we can use parentheses around words that express our personal thoughts about something in the sentence.

> Kilani's dog Jeb (he's always frightened me) rescued some lost hikers on Mount Wilson.

> I finally finished my homework (are you proud of me?) and went out to play basketball.

Punctuation with Parentheses   All of the *sentence's* punctuation marks are placed outside the parentheses.

> YES: Please send it to Tom (Bob's son).

> NO: Please sent it to Tom (Bob's son.)

If the *words in parentheses* require a question mark or exclamation mark, we place it inside the parentheses. However, we never include a period if the parentheses are within a sentence.

> YES: Our new camera (it's digital!) arrived yesterday.

> NO: Monty (you'll remember him from the wedding.) will be taking pictures.

If parentheses are inserted into a sentence where a comma, colon, or semicolon would normally occur, the punctuation is placed after the parentheses.

> YES: If Ilbea is elected (please vote for her), things will be better.

> YES: I was not able to shop yesterday (Sunday); the stores were closed.

Example 1   Rewrite sentences a and b below and add parentheses where they are needed.

(a) Last weekend we visited a town today called El Monte that once marked the end of the Santa Fe Trail.

(b) Mr. Martin paid four hundred dollars $400 for each new saxophone for the band.

(c) When the driver slammed his finger in the car door ouch! I felt sorry for him.

Solution   (a) The words "today called El Monte" provide additional but nonessential information, so we enclose them in parentheses.

Last weekend we visited a town (today called El Monte) that once marked the end of the Santa Fe Trail.

(b) We enclose $400 in parentheses to confirm the number.

Mr. Martin paid four hundred dollars ($400) for each new saxophone for the band.

(c) We enclose the personal commentary in parentheses. The comma goes after the parentheses.

When the driver slammed his finger in the car door (ouch!), I felt sorry for him.

Brackets   We use **brackets** to insert our own words (additions, explanations, comments, etc.) into quoted material.

Professor Noir explained, "Henry de Tonti was known as 'Iron Hand' because of his artificial hand [a substitute hand for the one he lost in battle]."

"Further," shared Professor Noir, "the Indians [a superstitious group] believed that Tonti's artificial hand gave him magical powers."

"I [Martin Luther King, Jr.] have a dream…"

The Rabbi Shapiro taught, "The Pentateuch [first five books of the Torah] is the cornerstone of Jewish religion and law."

Example 2   In the sentence below, use brackets to enclose words that are not a part of the direct quotation.

Lucy said, "He Robert Andrew Hooper saw the thief leave the building carrying the stolen goods."

Solution   **[Robert Andrew Hooper]** is not a part of the direct quotation. These words were inserted by the writer to make clear who "he" was.

Practice   For sentences a–d, insert parentheses or brackets as needed.

a. The lecturer said, "She Anne Frank was a Dutch Jewish girl and a victim of the Holocaust."

b. The farmer's tomato crop was worth at least twelve thousand dollars $12,000 .

c. We will all bring something a book to read or a toy to help entertain the younger children.

d. Jamana won a car wow! in an essay contest.

For e–i, replace each blank with the correct vocabulary word.

e. At the party the Republicans and Democrats will _____.

f. We will _____ each letter of the alphabet with a number.

g. The _____ stood near the dentist to help with each procedure.

h. The court will _____ tomorrow morning at 9 a.m.

i. A credit card was required as _____ to rent skis and boots.

Review Set 104

Choose the best word(s) to complete sentences 1–16.

1. A (solo, paragon, server) is a model of excellence.
(99, 101)

2. A (paradigm, webmaster, bonus) is a pattern or example.
(101, 102)

3. To (circumvent, spam, upload) is to send a file from your computer.
(100, 102)

4. (Bonanza, Spam, Epidermis) has come to mean junk e-mail.
(71, 102)

5. A (template, pixel, webmaster) organizes a website.
(98, 102)

6. Tonight, I will call my brothers, Bob and (he, him).
(45, 54)

7. The puppies behaved (real, really) (good, well) today.
(89, 92)

8. We try to use (passive, active) voice whenever possible.
(102)

9. Verb phrases in the (passive, active) voice contain a form of "to be."
(102)

10. Niam didn't have (anything, nothing) to do with Oisin's
(81) return to the land of Erinn.

11. Did you enjoy (me, my) telling you the jokes?
(56, 58)

12. The electrician (who, whom) gave me an estimate will
(64, 65) return on Monday.

13. The verb *hesitate* is (transitive, intransitive).
(25, 31)

14. Of all the banana packers, who works (harder, hardest)?
(89, 90)

15. The city lights (shined, shone) from afar.
(72, 73)

16. A lasting friendship grew (between, among) the five
(16, 95) classmates.

17. For a–c, write the possessive form of each noun.
(97) (a) Mrs. Campos　　(b) The Camposes　　(c) Saturday

18. Rewrite this sentence, adding the necessary punctuation
(72) marks and underlining each word that should be
italicized: Marco comforted the anxious Guatemalan
family with the following words Jamás duerme el que te
cuida

19. Rewrite this sentence, adding capital letters and
(63, 68) punctuation marks as needed: i wear curlers to style my
hair and i dont care what others think declared mrs
poovey

20. For a–c, write the plural form of each noun.
(12, 13) (a) Thomas　　(b) liberty　　(c) lady-in-waiting

21. Which sentence is clearer? Choose A or B.
(103) A. James watched a woodpecker using his binoculars.

B. Using his binoculars, James watched a woodpecker.

22. Write the comparative form of the adverb *clearly*.
(90)

23. Write the possessive case, first person, plural personal
(55, 56) pronoun.

24. Write whether the following sentence is simple,
(62, 100) compound, complex, or compound-complex: Since
Chuchulain has gained favor, he wears the king's armor
and drives the king's chariot.

25. In the sentence below, write the dependent clause,
(57, 99) circling the subordinating conjunction. Then write
whether the clause functions as a noun, adjective, or
adverb.

We watched as Chuchulain skillfully drove the horses
and chariot.

26. In this sentence, write whether the verb is in the active or
(102) passive voice: Oisin's decision to return to Erinn has
devastated Niam.

27. Write the conjunctive adverb in this sentence:
(91) Chuchulain lacks experience and maturity; on the other
hand, he has confidence and determination.

28. Rewrite this sentence so that it has parallel structure: He
(101) said he would need a horse, chariot, and a rider.

Diagram sentences 29 and 30.

29. Driving furiously, Chuchulain recognizes a sturdy
(25, 58) chariot.

30. Not only Ivar but also Conall had begged Setanta to turn
(25, 38) from danger.

LESSON 105

Interjections

Dictation or Journal Entry

Vocabulary: The Latin prefix *contra-* means "against."

To *contradict* means to speak against. The accountant *contradicted* the company's earning statement.

Contraband is goods that are illegally exported or imported. The U.S. Coast Guard seizes shipments of *contraband.*

To *contravene* means to go against or oppose something. A traitor *contravenes* the principles of loyalty and patriotism.

A *contrast* is a comparison which shows the differences. A school counselor presented the occupational *contrast* between those who received a college degree and those who didn't.

Contralateral refers to parts of the human body on opposite sides. The biceps are *contralateral* to the triceps.

Interjections

A word or short phrase used to show strong emotion is called an **interjection.** An interjection is one of the eight parts of speech. It can express excitement, happiness, joy, rage, surprise, pain, or relief. Interjections are italicized below.

Boo! Did I scare you?

Yippee! Today is Saturday, my day to relax.

Oh dear, I lost my keys again.

Oh, pardon me. I didn't understand what you said.

An interjection is not a sentence and has no relationship with the words around it. For this reason, it is usually set apart from the rest of the sentence by some sort of punctuation. Generally, an exclamation point follows an interjection, but, if the emotion is not very intense, a comma follows the interjection.

INTENSE: *Yuck!* There's mold growing on that bread.

NOT INTENSE: *Shh*, the librarian allows no talking.

Below is a list of common interjections. Notice that sounds can be interjections too.

ah	*oh dear*	*ugh*	*man*
aha	*oh my*	*uh oh*	*drat*
bam	*oh yes*	*well*	*oops*
boy	*far out*	*yippee*	*bravo*
oh no	*whee*	*good grief*	*okay*
whoops	*goodness*	*ouch*	*wow*
hey	*ow*	*yikes*	*hooray*

| phew | yuck | hurrah | pow |
| boo | oh | shh | whew |

We must not overuse interjections. They lose their effectiveness when used too frequently.

Example 1   Write each interjection that you find in a–d.

(a) Ow! I stepped on a thorn.

(b) I forgot to bring my homework to school. Drat!

(c) Uh oh, the weather has turned cool, and I am dressed for summer.

(d) We won the league championship. Bravo!

Solution   (a) **Ow**   (b) **Drat**

(c) **Uh oh**   (d) **Bravo**

Diagramming   We diagram interjections like this:

Whee! This roller coaster is really fast.

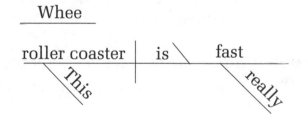

Example 2   Diagram this sentence:

Whoops, I didn't intend to reveal the secret.

Solution   We place the interjection on a line apart from the rest of the sentence.

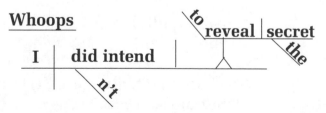

Practice   Write the interjection that you find in a–d.

a. Ah, that explains it.

b. The two cars crashed. Bam!

c. Hey, that's not fair!

d. You can ride your new bike to the beach. Cool!

Diagram e and f.

e. Oh dear, I forgot your birthday.

f. Good grief, try to be on time.

For g–l, replace each blank with the correct vocabulary word.

g. Drugs, such as marijuana and cocaine, are _____.

h. Harold does not like to _____ his wife in public.

i. Our hamstrings are _____ to our quadriceps.

j. In our political science class, we will see the _____ between a dictatorship and a democracy.

k. The Latin prefix _____ means "against."

l. The hoodlums intended to _____ the law by smuggling contraband into the country.

Review set 105

Choose the best word to complete sentences 1–15.

1. A (server, firewall, pixel) is a computer security feature.
(98, 102)

2. The Latin prefix (*soli-, circum-, audi-*) refers to sound.
(100, 103)

3. (Archaic, Colloquial, Profane) diction is old-fashioned.
(63)

4. A(n) (analogy, farce, irony) is written to make people laugh.
(66)

5. An audiologist evaluates one's (vision, hearing, cholesterol).
(103)

6. There (isn't, ain't, aren't) (anyone, no one) in the office on Sundays.
(71, 81)

7. One of Robin Hood's Merry Men (leave, leaves) (their, his) shoes beside the stream.
(56, 71)

8. He has smaller feet than (me, I).
(53, 66)

9. The quilt that Grandma gave me was (hand-stitched,
(82, 85) hand stitched).

10. The lecture on reptiles gave (us, we) campers something
(54, 66) to think about.

11. A phrase that does not clearly modify a certain word is
(103) called a (direct quotation, dangling modifier, passive
voice).

12. Your cross-country team (sure, surely) raced (well, good)
(89, 92) last week.

13. Either the mice or the cat (wakes, wake) me during the
(77, 78) night.

14. The crown (that, which) Niam wore sparkled brilliantly.
(63, 64)

15. Later, an argument developed (between, among) two of
(16, 95) the classmates.

16. In this sentence, write the verb phrase, name its tense,
(21, 22) and label it action or linking: Today, Aunt Bea has been
making grim prognostications about the consequences of
poor nutrition.

17. For a–c, write the possessive form of each noun.
(97) (a) chariot   (b) Fergus   (c) horses

18. Rewrite the following, underlining each word that should
(72, 104) be italicized and adding punctuation marks (including
brackets or parentheses) as needed:
According to the Monrovia Muse the police apprehended
Mrs Poovey as a suspect in the suitcase theft but she is
out on ten thousand dollars $10,000 bail

19. Rewrite the following, adding capital letters and
(63, 68) punctuation marks as needed: i think said mr poovey to
his wife that your hair curlers attracted the attention of
the authorities

20. Use an appositive to make one sentence from these two
(44, 45) sentences: Kitty Hawk, North Carolina, is now a national

historical monument. Kitty Hawk, North Carolina, was the site of Orville and Wilbur Wright's first airplane flight.

21. Which sentence is clearer? Choose A or B.
(103)

A. Quan looked under a rock for the garter snake wearing his cowboy hat.

B. Wearing his cowboy hat, Quan looked under a rock for the garter snake.

22. In this sentence write whether the underlined part is an
(45, 65) essential or nonessential part: Debby's dog <u>Lilibet</u> has five puppies.

23. Write the four principal parts of the irregular verb *rise*.
(74, 75)

24. Write whether the following sentence is simple,
(3, 100) compound, complex, or compound-complex: Queen Meave and her husband, Ailill, listened to the telling of "The Boyhood of Chuchulain."

25. In the sentence below, write the dependent clause,
(57, 99) circling the subordinating conjunction. Then write whether the clause functions as a noun, adjective, or adverb.

I did not realize that my fencing opponent was ambidextrous.

26. Rewrite this sentence using active voice: The chariot was
(4, 102) driven by Chuchulain.

27. Rewrite this sentence, adding punctuation as needed and
(63, 91) circling the conjunctive adverb: Only a few Egyptian papyrus rolls have survived however scholars can learn much from them

28. Rewrite this sentence so that it has parallel structure: The
(101) Hittites conquered Anatolia (Turkey), forced out foreign traders, and take over the metal trade.

Diagram sentences 29 and 30.

29. The Mycenaeans, whom I read about, sailed great
(23, 64) distances to trade their goods.

30. Both Chuchulain and Finn are Irish epic heroes, but
(39, 62) Beowulf is a Danish hero.

LESSON
106

Spelling Rules: Silent Letters
k, g, w, t, d, and *c*

Dictation or Journal Entry

Vocabulary: The Latin prefix *dis-* means "apart," "away," or "the opposite of."

Disarray means out of order. The shoppers left the merchandise in *disarray* because they were in a hurry.

To *disappoint* means to fail to meet the expectations. Friends *disappoint* one another when they do not keep promises.

Disbelief is a lack of belief or refusal to believe. Henry stared in *disbelief* at his dog's aggressive behavior.

To *dishearten* is to discourage. Life *disheartens* us all at times.

To *disown* is to refuse to recognize as one's own. Henry wanted to *disown* his ferocious dog.

Why Are Some Letters Silent?   The English language contains many words that are spelled differently than they are pronounced. There are several reasons for this.

As the language changed and grew through the centuries, the way people pronounced a word often changed, yet the way the word was spelled remained the same.

Some early scholars insisted on applying Latin rules of spelling to English words. (Since English borrowed the Latin alphabet, this idea wasn't illogical.)

More words were borrowed from other languages, and their foreign spellings were kept.

In the midst of this, the printing press appeared. It helped to "freeze" the spelling of all these words, no matter how irregular. Most English words are spelled today just as they were in the 1500s. As a result, there are many words that contain letters we no longer (or never did) pronounce.

The Letter *k*   A silent *k* at the beginning of a word is always followed by an *n.*

*k*napsack   *k*nead   *k*nickers   *k*nock

The Letter *g*   A silent *g* may also be followed by an *n* at the beginning or the end of a word.

*g*narl   *g*naw   si*g*n   rei*g*n

The Letter *w*   A silent *w* can come before the letter *r.*

*w*rap   *w*reck   *w*rench   *w*rist

Sometimes the silent *w* comes before *h*:

*wh*ole   *wh*om   *wh*ose   *wh*oever

Other silent *w*'s appear in the words *answer, sword,* and *two.*

The Letter *t* A silent *t* can follow the letter *s*.

ne*st*le   bri*st*le   jo*st*le   ca*st*le

A silent *t* can also come before the letters *ch*.

no*tch*   ba*tch*   clu*tch*   fe*tch*   gli*tch*

Not all words that end with the "ch" sound have a silent *t* (touch, which, rich, attach, detach, such, much, sandwich, etc.). When in doubt, check the dictionary.

Other silent *t*'s appear in words borrowed from the French such as *ballet, depot, debut, gourmet,* and *mortgage.*

The Letter *d* The letters *ge* usually follow a silent *d*.

bu*d*ge   he*d*ge   ri*d*ge   lo*d*ge   ba*d*ge

We also find silent *d*'s in these words:

a*d*jective   a*d*jacent   a*d*just   We*d*nesday

The Letter *c* A silent *c* can follow the letter *s*.

*sc*issors   *sc*ene   *sc*ience   *sc*ent   *sc*epter

Example Rewrite these words and circle each silent letter.

(a) stitch   (b) gnaw   (c) dredge

(d) wring   (e) sword   (f) knave

Solution (a) sti**t**ch   (b) **g**naw   (c) dre**d**ge

(d) **w**ring   (e) s**w**ord   (f) **k**nave

Practice For a–h, rewrite the words and circle each silent letter.

a. trestle   **b.** whom   **c.** gnu   **d.** know

e. knit   **f.** knelt   **g.** Gnostic   **h.** wrangler

For i–n, replace each blank with the correct vocabulary word.

i. The unorganized librarian left the books in _____, so I couldn't find the one I wanted.

j. The Latin prefix _____ means "apart" or "opposite of."

k. Mom had a look of _____ when I told her I would clean the entire house and take out the trash for a year.

l. Constant failure may _____ even the most determined individual.

m. If my cat brings home another dead rat, I will _____ him!

n. It will _____ Grandma if we don't come to her birthday party.

Review set 106   Choose the correct word(s) to complete sentences 1–15.

1. Audible means capable of being (seen, smelled, heard).
(103)

2. An audition is a trial (race, test, hearing).
(103)

3. The Latin prefix *audi-* refers to (measure, sound, speed).
(103)

4. To circumnavigate means to go (over, through, around).
(100)

5. The Latin prefixes *con-, com-, co-, col-,* and *cor-* mean
(104) (almost, good, together).

6. My two cousins, John and (him, he) scuba dive off the
(45, 53) coast of Catalina Island.

7. They (sure, surely) observe the safety rules.
(89, 92)

8. The following is a (phrase, clause): having alluded to
(24, 57) some long-lost relatives in Austria

9. (Beside, Besides) reading about Robin Hood, I'd like to
(95) read "The Boyhood of Chuchulain."

10. Sadly, I didn't win (none, any) of the games or contests.
(81)

11. Do the people of Erinn resent (Oisin, Oisin's) bragging
(58, 97) about his victories?

12. The scuba diver (which, who) found Freddy's wedding
(64, 65) ring has flown to Hungary.

13. The verb in this sentence is (transitive, intransitive): Can
(25, 31) Setanta protect himself against Culain's vicious mastiff?

14. Of the two banana packers, Harold comes to work
(90) (earlier, earliest).

15. There was never (any, no) jealousy (between, among) the
(81, 95) two sisters.

16. In this sentence, write the verb phrase, name its tense,
(18, 31) and label it transitive or intransitive: Has Count Don
Gomez insulted Don Diego?

17. For a–c, write the possessive form of each noun.
(97) (a) Jerry and Iris   (b) materials   (c) Egyptians

18. Rewrite the following, adding capital letters and
(29, 50) punctuation marks as needed:

dear mother

    i am asking you and my wife to love one another for
my sake the king has ordered me to go into the royal
service so you must take care of each other

              love

              cid

19. Rewrite the following, adding a colon where it is needed:
(93) Some of the Egyptian gods and goddesses had these
names Hathor, Taweret, Ptuh, Apis, and Thoth.

20. For a–c, write the plural of each noun.
(12, 13) (a) Gomez   (b) Henry   (c) parenthesis

21. Which sentence is clearer? Choose A or B.
(103)
A. The scholar found an iron tool walking through the
archeological site.

B. Walking through the archeological site, the scholar
found an iron tool.

22. Write the superlative form of the adverb *clearly*.
(90)

23. Write the possessive case, third person, plural, neuter
(55, 56) gender personal pronoun.

24. Write whether the following sentence is simple,
(62, 100) compound, complex, or compound-complex: Nelda drank weak tea with cream and sugar, but Vernley drank strong black coffee.

25. In the sentence below, write the dependent clause,
(57, 99) circling the subordinating conjunction. Then write whether the clause functions as a noun, adjective, or adverb.
As they studied the stars and planets, the Egyptians worked out the 365-day calendar.

26. Rewrite this sentence using active voice: The leper was
(4, 102) given food and shelter by Cid.

27. Rewrite this sentence, adding a semicolon and a comma
(91) as needed and circling the conjunctive adverb: Cid had conquered five Moorish kings nevertheless he sent them back to their own country without a ransom.

28. Rewrite this sentence using parallel structure: I am
(101) thankful for family, shelter, and for food.

Diagram sentences 29 and 30.

29. During the first century, Cid won several cities for his
(25, 64) king, who reigned for thirty-one years.

30. No, I don't like to pull weeds.
(23, 105)

LESSON 107   Spelling Rules: Silent Letters *p, b, l, u, h, n* and *gh*

Dictation or Journal Entry

Vocabulary: The Latin prefix *extra-* and its English counterpart *extro-* mean "outside of," and "beyond."

Extracurricular means outside of the regular school curriculum. Band, drama, and basketball are usually *extracurricular* activities.

An *extrovert* is an outgoing, sociable person. *Extroverts* enjoy most social events.

Extraordinary is an adjective meaning "not usual." Some firemen showed *extraordinary* courage on September 11, 2001.

Extrasensory refers to things outside of one's normal perception. At times, his *extrasensory* perception seemed to give him intuitive knowledge about unseen things.

Extrospection is the observation of things outside of oneself. Through *extrospection*, he saw that other people had more serious needs and problems than he did.

The Letter *p*   The Greek language is a source of many words that contain a silent *p*. The silent *p* occurs only before the letters *t*, *s*, and *n*.

    *p*salm   *p*neumonia   *p*terodactyl   *p*sychology

The Letter *b*   Many words contain the letter *m* followed by a silent *b*.

    plu*mb*   cli*mb*   succu*mb*   la*mb*

Other silent *b*'s are found in the words *debt, doubt,* and *subtle.*

The Letter *l*   Many words that contain a silent *l* follow a similar pattern: an *l* followed by a consonant that makes the *l* difficult to pronounce.

    ba*l*k   cau*l*k   wa*l*k   yo*l*k   fo*l*k

    ba*l*m   psa*l*m   wou*l*d   shou*l*d

    ca*l*ves   ha*l*f

The Letter *u*   A silent *u* usually follows the letter *g*. It reminds us to pronounce the *g* with a "hard" sound (*g*) rather than a "soft' sound (*j*), at either the beginning or the end of a word.

    g*u*illotine   g*u*est   g*u*arantee   dialog*u*e   vag*u*e

The Letter *h*   A silent *h* usually follows *c, r,* or *g*, as in these words:

    sc*h*eme   ac*h*e   r*h*ythm

    ag*h*ast   g*h*ost   r*h*apsody

An initial *h* can also be silent, as in the words *honor, hour, herb* and *heir.*

The Letter *n* Sometimes the letter *m* is followed by a silent *n*, as in these words:

colu*mn*   conde*mn*   hy*mn*   sole*mn*

The Letters *gh* The letter combination *gh* is always silent when it comes before the letter *t.*

strai*gh*t   brou*gh*t   ei*gh*t   fou*gh*t

mi*gh*t   ou*gh*t   kni*gh*t   sou*gh*t

A *gh* at the end of a word can be silent as well:

nei*gh*   thorou*gh*   wei*gh*   si*gh*

slei*gh*   dou*gh*   bou*gh*   hi*gh*

Example Rewrite each word and circle each silent letter.

(a) neighbor   (b) could   (c) chalk   (d) succumb

(e) earache   (f) limb   (g) through   (h) thumb

(i) should   (j) balk   (k) psalter   (l) guild

Solution (a) **neighbor**   (b) **could**   (c) **chalk**   (d) **succumb**

(e) **earache**   (f) **limb**   (g) **through**   (h) **thumb**

(i) **should**   (j) **balk**   (k) **psalter**   (l) **guild**

Practice Rewrite words a–l, and circle each silent letter.

a. guarantee   **b.** thorough   **c.** charisma   **d.** rhinoceros

e. would   **f.** half   **g.** alms   **h.** caulk

i. debt   **j.** pneumatic   **k.** bomb   **l.** yolk

For m–r, replace each blank with the correct vocabulary word.

m. Having a "feeling" that something is about to happen is an example of _____ perception.

n. The Latin prefix _____ means "outside of."

o. An _____ is not shy.

p. An eight-foot tall man has _____ height.

q. After school, Holly participated in the _____ activities of tennis and band.

r. Because of his constant _____, Harry could not see his own faults.

Review set 107   Choose the correct word to complete sentences 1–14.

1. Convene means to come (here, apart, together).
(104)

2. A coadjutor works (against, with) another person.
(104)

3. The Latin prefix *contra-* means (with, good, against).
(105)

4. Commingle means to mix (chemicals, together, signals).
(104)

5. To contravene means to (encourage, oppose, appreciate) something.
(104)

6. There is scarcely (no, any) food in the refrigerator.
(81)

7. Each of the divers (have, has) (their, her/his) own air tank.
(77, 78)

8. We dove as skillfully as (they, them).
(53, 66)

9. The (self-reliant, self reliant) girl did her own laundry.
(82, 85)

10. (Us, We) divers found a sunken pirate ship.
(53, 66)

11. A (phrase, clause) may contain nouns and verbs, but it does not have both a subject and a predicate.
(24, 57)

12. Ivar knows the landscape very (good, well).
(84)

13. We usually place punctuation marks (before, after) parentheses.
(104)

14. The two companions have some disagreement (between, among) themselves.
(16, 95)

15. Rewrite this sentence, adding parentheses as needed:
(104) Rodrigo also called Cid, Chief, and the Perfect One had a successful and happy life.

16. For a–c, rewrite each word, circling the silent letters.
(106) (a) whistle   (b) badge   (c) knowledge

17. For a–c, write the possessive form of each noun.
(97) (a) lass   (b) Cid and the leper   (c) garments

18. Rewrite the following, adding punctuation marks and underlining each word that should be italicized: In May 2002 Luxuriant Landscaping magazine featured an article titled Propagating Perennials for Pennies
(72)

19. Rewrite the following, adding capital letters and punctuation marks as needed: there is in fact a story explaining gods protection over cid as he traveled to compostella to pay homage to saint mary on january 12 1026
(11, 50)

20. Use an appositive to make one sentence from these two sentences: John Keats was a gifted 19th-century Romantic poet. He was the son of a livery stable owner in London.
(45, 46)

21. Which sentence is clearer? Choose A or B.
(103) A. Balancing a tall stack of dinner plates, his foot slipped on a banana peel.

B. While he was balancing a tall stack of dinner plates, his foot slipped on a banana peel.

22. In this sentence, write whether the underlined part is an essential or nonessential part: I think my friend <u>Debby</u> has more than a hundred pets.
(64, 65)

23. Write the four principal parts of the irregular verb *raise*.
(74, 75)

24. Write whether the following sentence is simple, compound, complex, or compound-complex: Nelda slurped her tea as Vernley sipped his hot coffee.
(3, 100)

25. In the sentence below, write the dependent clause,
(57, 99) circling the subordinating conjunction. Then write
whether the clause functions as a noun, adjective, or
adverb.

On the lonely mountain road, I didn't know where I was
going.

26. Rewrite this sentence using active voice: Miss Petunia
(4, 102) Schnootz was driven to the bus station by Uncle Richard.

27. Rewrite this sentence, adding a semicolon and a comma
(91) as needed and circling the conjunctive adverb: Mrs.
Poovey will write Tom a letter of apology in addition she
will pay for his car repairs.

28. Rewrite this sentence using parallel structure: You may
(101) use that new computer for playing games, for
communicating with your friends, and to write your
papers.

Diagram sentences 29 and 30.

29. While Moe is very gregarious, his brother is as friendly as
(39, 57) a marble statue.

30. Moe's brother has graciously accepted my teasing him.
(23, 25)

LESSON
108

Spelling Rules: Suffixes, Part 1

> **Dictation or Journal Entry**
>
> **Vocabulary:** The Latin prefix inter- means "between" or "among."
>
> *Interscholastic* means between schools. High schools within a twenty-five-mile radius comprised the *interscholastic* tennis league.
>
> To *interfere* means to concern oneself with other people's affairs without having been asked. Do you *interfere* in matters that don't concern you?
>
> To *intervene* is to come between certain events or points in time. Several months *intervened* before they communicated again. To *intervene* also means to act as a mediator. Police *intervene* if a crowd becomes unruly.
>
> To *intercept* means "to catch between," seize, or delay on the way. A football player might *intercept* a pass.

Words Ending in y   A final *y* usually changes to *i* when suffixes (except for the suffix *-ing*) are added:

$$\text{deny} + \text{ed} = \text{denied}$$
$$\text{modify} + \text{er} = \text{modifier}$$
$$\text{exemplify} + \text{ed} = \text{exemplified}$$
$$\text{pity} + \text{ful} = \text{pitiful}$$
$$\text{pry} + \text{s} = \text{pries}$$
$$\text{worry} + \text{some} = \text{worrisome}$$
$$\text{cloudy} + \text{ness} = \text{cloudiness}$$
$$\text{foggy} + \text{er} = \text{foggier}$$
$$\text{ready} + \text{ly} = \text{readily}$$
$$\text{sporty} + \text{est} = \text{sportiest}$$
$$\text{glory} + \text{ous} = \text{glorious}$$
$$\text{plenty} + \text{ful} = \text{plentiful}$$

but: *denying, modifying, exemplifying, pitying, prying, worrying, glorying*

When preceded by a vowel, the final *y* does not change to *i*.

$$\text{enjoy} + \text{able} = \text{enjoyable}$$
$$\text{play} + \text{er} = \text{player}$$
$$\text{annoy} + \text{ed} = \text{annoyed}$$
$$\text{ray} + \text{s} = \text{rays}$$
$$\text{gray} + \text{est} = \text{grayest}$$

Exceptions   Important exceptions include the following:

$$\text{lay} + \text{ed} = \text{laid}$$
$$\text{pay} + \text{ed} = \text{paid}$$

$$\text{say} + \text{ed} = \text{said}$$
$$\text{day} + \text{ly} = \text{daily}$$

Example 1 Add suffixes to these words ending in *y*.

(a) toy + ed = _____

(b) shiny + er = _____

(c) tardy + ness = _____

(d) mercy + less = _____

(e) happy + ly = _____

Solution (a) toy + ed = **toyed** (The *y* is preceded by a vowel, so it does not change to an *i*.

(b) shiny + er = **shinier** (The final *y* usually changes to *i* when suffixes are added.)

(c) tardy + ness = **tardiness**

(d) mercy + less = **merciless**

(e) happy + ly = **happily**

Words Ending in a Silent *e* We generally drop the silent *e* before adding a suffix beginning with a vowel (including the suffix -*y*).

$$\text{nerve} + \text{ous} = \text{nervous}$$
$$\text{rose} + \text{y} = \text{rosy}$$
$$\text{wire} + \text{y} = \text{wiry}$$
$$\text{blame} + \text{ing} = \text{blaming}$$
$$\text{explore} + \text{ation} = \text{exploration}$$
$$\text{love} + \text{able} = \text{lovable}$$
$$\text{achieve} + \text{able} = \text{achievable}$$

However, we keep the final *e* when we add a suffix beginning with a consonant.

$$\text{arrange} + \text{ment} = \text{arrangement}$$
$$\text{like} + \text{ness} = \text{likeness}$$
$$\text{care} + \text{less} = \text{careless}$$
$$\text{sure} + \text{ly} = \text{surely}$$
$$\text{grace} + \text{ful} = \text{graceful}$$

Exceptions Exceptions to the rules above include the following words:

$$\text{judge} + \text{ment} = \text{judgment}$$
$$\text{argue} + \text{ment} = \text{argument}$$
$$\text{wise} + \text{dom} = \text{wisdom}$$
$$\text{gentle} + \text{ly} = \text{gently}$$
$$\text{true} + \text{ly} = \text{truly}$$

Also, when adding *ous* or *able* to a word ending in *ge* or *ce*, we keep the final *e* to indicate the soft sound of the *c* (as in *celery*) or *g* (as in *giant*).

$$\text{manage} + \text{able} = \text{manageable}$$
$$\text{trace} + \text{able} = \text{traceable}$$
$$\text{change} + \text{able} = \text{changeable}$$
$$\text{outrage} + \text{ous} = \text{outrageous}$$
$$\text{courage} + \text{ous} = \text{courageous}$$

Example 2 Add suffixes to these words ending in a silent *e*.

(a) conceive + able = _____

(b) shave + ing = _____

(c) glare + ing = _____

(d) live + ly = _____

(e) lame + ly = _____

(f) trace + able = _____

(g) true + ly = _____

Solution (a) conceive + able = **conceivable** (We usually drop the silent *e* when the suffix begins with a vowel.)

(b) shave + ing = **shaving**

(c) glare + ing = **glaring**

(d) live + ly = **lively** (We usually keep the final *e* when the suffix begins with a consonant.)

(e) lame + ly = **lamely**

(f) trace + able = **traceable** (We keep the silent *e* after the *c* to retain the soft *c* ("*s*") sound.

(g) True + ly = **truly** (This is an exception to the rule.)

Practice   Add suffixes to words a-k.

    a. blame + less = _____

    b. drowsy + ness = _____

    c. weary + est = _____

    d. steady + ly = _____

    e. force + ful = _____

    f. slave + ing = _____

    g. late + ly = _____

    h. tame + er = _____

    i. fame + ous = _____

    j. rate + ing = _____

    k. plenty + ful = _____

For l–q, replace each blank with the correct vocabulary word.

    l. The Latin prefix _____ means "between" or "among."

    m. The _____ speech meet involved students from four different schools.

    n. She is polite; she does not _____ with other people's business.

    o. The teacher might _____ any correspondence that is passed between students during class.

    p. Three days of study will _____ before our final test.

q. During the argument, he tried to _____ in her behalf.

Choose the correct word(s) to complete sentences 1–14.

1. To contradict means to speak (clearly, well, against).
(105)

2. The Latin prefix (soli-, audi-, contra-) means against.
(103, 105)

3. The Latin prefix *dis-* means "the (best, same,
(106) opposite)."

4. Disbelief is the (lack, strength) of belief.
(106)

5. Beauty and the Beast living happily ever after is an
(84, 86) example of (realism, romance, satire).

6. Alba and David bought snorkeling gear for Freddy and
(32, 54) (her, she) three years ago.

7. Freddy and (her, she) were (real, really) pleased with the
(53, 92) snorkeling equipment.

8. The following is a (phrase, clause): when Hank alluded to
(24, 57) those long-lost relatives in Austria

9. We walked (beside, besides) the creek and listened to the
(16, 95) croaking of many frogs.

10. There were scarcely (any, no) trout in the stream.
(81)

11. (Oisin, Oisin's) bragging about his victories probably
(58, 97) drove his friends away from him.

12. The ring (which, that) Freddy lost in the ocean was never
(64, 65) recovered.

13. Tassoula has not (forsook, forsaken) her Greek heritage.
(73, 74)

14. Of all the banana packers, Harold comes to work (earlier,
(90) earliest).

15. Rewrite this sentence, adding parentheses as needed:
(104) Mrs. Poovey still owes Tom a hundred dollars $100 and a suitcase full of gummy candy.

16. For a–c, rewrite each word, circling the silent letters.
(106, 107)(a) lamb   (b) gnash   (c) psalm

17. For a–c, write the possessive form of each noun.
(97) (a) charters   (b) geese   (c) cattle

18. Rewrite the following, adding punctuation marks and (72) underlining each word that should be italicized: Buon compleanno an Italian birthday greeting appeared on the card that came with my roses

19. Rewrite the following, adding capital letters and (63, 68) punctuation marks as needed: alvar fanez said yes i am forced to be content with only partial pardon for cid

20. For a–c, write the plural of each noun.
(12, 13)(a) gentleman   (b) octopus   (c) fly

21. Which sentence is clearer? Choose A or B.
(103)   A. Trembling and frightened, the battle horrified Cid's wife and daughters.

    B. The battle horrified the trembling and frightened wife and daughters of Cid.

22. Write the comparative form of the adverb *reluctantly*.
(90)

23. Write the possessive case, third person, plural personal (55, 56) pronoun.

24. Write whether the following sentence is simple, (62, 100)compound, complex, or compound-complex: Nelda knits, and Opal plays solitaire while Erwin sleeps.

25. In the sentence below, write the dependent clause, (57, 99) circling the subordinating conjunction or relative pronoun. Then write whether the clause functions as a noun, adjective, or adverb.
When the bear cub saw us, it scampered up a tree.

26. Rewrite this sentence using active voice: Uncle Richard (4, 102)had been driven crazy by Miss Petunia Schnootz.

27. Rewrite this sentence, adding a semicolon and a comma (91) as needed and circling the conjunctive adverb: You should buy me lunch because we're friends besides it's my birthday.

28. Rewrite this sentence using parallel structure: In case of
(101) invasion, Cid stored provisions, strengthened walls, and arms the citizens.

Diagram sentences 29 and 30.

29. Throughout his campaign, Cid acted honorably towards
(25, 64) those whom he defeated.

30. Oops, the king made a big mistake in banishing Cid.
(58, 105)

LESSON 109

Spelling Rules: Suffixes, Part 2

Dictation or Journal Entry

Vocabulary: The Latin prefix *trans-* means "across," "beyond," or "through."

To *transmit* means to send or to forward. The Internet allows a sender to *transmit* messages to a receiver.

Transcontinental is an adjective meaning "crossing a continent." The first *transcontinental* railroad ran from New York on the east coast to San Francisco on the west coast.

To *transcend* is "to rise above" or "to go beyond." The idea of eternity *transcends* human understanding.

One meaning of *transfix* is "to pierce through" or "to impale." With a pin, he will *transfix* the insect to a display board.

Doubling Final Consonants

When a one-syllable word ends with a single consonant preceded by a single vowel, we double the final consonant before adding a suffix that begins with a vowel.

$$\text{chop} + \text{ed} = \text{chopped}$$
$$\text{plan} + \text{er} = \text{planner}$$
$$\text{drip} + \text{ing} = \text{dripping}$$
$$\text{wrap} + \text{ing} = \text{wrapping}$$
$$\text{split} + \text{ing} = \text{splitting}$$
$$\text{big} + \text{est} = \text{biggest}$$
$$\text{run} + \text{y} = \text{runny}$$

Exceptions include the words *bus* (bused), *sew* (sewing), *bow* (bowed), and *tax* (taxing).

When a word of two or more syllables ends with a single consonant preceded by a single vowel, we double the final consonant if the word is accented (stressed) on the last syllable.

$$\text{begin} + \text{ing} = \text{beginning}$$
$$\text{confer} + \text{ed} = \text{conferred}$$
$$\text{submit} + \text{ed} = \text{submitted}$$

Do Not Double

We **do not** double the final consonant of any of the words described above (words ending with a single consonant preceded by a single vowel) when adding a suffix that begins with a consonant.

$$\text{mad} + \text{ly} = \text{madly}$$
$$\text{sad} + \text{ly} = \text{sadly}$$
$$\text{glad} + \text{ness} = \text{gladness}$$

We **do not** double the final consonant if it is preceded by two vowels or another consonant:

$$rain + ed = rained$$
$$great + ly = greatly$$
$$cold + est = coldest$$
$$bash + ful = bashful$$

Words Ending in *ful*   All words ending in *ful* have only one *l*.

successful	beautiful	cupful
cheerful	bountiful	handful
graceful	hopeful	spoonful

Example   Add suffixes to these words.

(a) wrap + ing = _____

(b) tan + er = _____

(c) submit + ed = _____

(d) hot + ly = _____

(e) ear + full = _____

Solution   (a) wrap + ing = **wrapping** (In most one-syllable words, we double the final consonant when we add a suffix beginning with a vowel.)

(b) tan + er = **tanner**

(c) submit + ed = **submitted**

(d) hot + ly = **hotly** (When the suffix begins with a consonant, we do not double the final consonant before adding the suffix.)

(e) ear + full = **earful** (Words ending in *ful* have only one *l*.)

Practice   Add suffixes to words a–e.

  a. chip + ed = _____

  b. flop + ing = _____

c. bad + ly = _____ _____

d. eye + full = _____

e. sad + ness = _____

For f–j, replace each blank with the correct vocabulary word.

f. The Latin prefix _____ means "across," "beyond," or "through."

g. The villain's evil stare _____ the helpless maiden and left her unable to flee.

h. The telegraph made _____ communication much faster.

i. The glider _____ the clouds and flew smoothly several miles.

j. Voting precincts were required to _____ election results quickly to party headquarters.

Review set 109   Choose the correct word(s) to complete sentences 1–14.

1. The Latin prefix (*soli-*, *audi-*, *dis-*) means the opposite
(103, 106) of.

2. The Latin prefix *extra-* and the English *extro-* mean
(107) beyond and also (ten, both, outside of).

3. Extracurricular means (within, beyond) the regular
(107) school curriculum.

4. An extrovert is (shy, outgoing, timid).
(107)

5. The Latin prefix *inter-* means (good, beyond, between).
(108)

6. There wasn't (anyone, no one) home this afternoon.
(71, 81)

7. One of the banana packers (give, gives) me (their, his/her)
(71, 73) over-ripe bananas.

8. I eat more bananas than (her, she).
(53, 66)

9. A (fast-moving, fast moving) flock of sheep passed before
(82, 85) my eyes.

10. Please join (us, we) shepherds in the pasture.
(54, 66)

11. Within a quotation, we use (brackets, semicolons) to
(104) insert our own explanations.

12. Cid didn't feel (good, well) after his interview with the
(84) king.

13. Cid was (real, really) angry at the knights for their false
(89, 92) accusations.

14. Is there agreement (between, among) the four students?
(16, 95)

15. For a–c, combine each word and suffix to make one word.
(108, 109) (a) flame + ing   (b) blame + less   (c) modify + ed

16. For a–c, rewrite each word, circling the silent letters.
(106) (a) knuckle   (b) sleigh   (c) batch

17. For a–c, write the possessive form of each noun.
(97) (a) Mr. Jones   (b) The Joneses   (c) Debby

18. Rewrite the following, adding punctuation marks and
(72) underlining each word that should be italicized:
Didelphis virginiana is the scientific name for opossum a
nocturnal mammal that often lives in trees

19. Rewrite the following, adding capital letters and
(20, 69) punctuation marks as needed: the infantes of carrion is
the title of the chapter depicting the characters of diego
and ferrando

20. Use an appositive to make one sentence from these two
(45, 46) sentences: Ferrando and Diego are the future sons-in-law
of Cid. They behave selfishly and pathetically.

21. Which sentence is clearer? Choose A or B.
(103)
A. Riding my bike around the park, I found my
neighbor's missing tortoise.

B. I found my neighbor's missing tortoise riding my bike
around the park.

22. In this sentence, write whether the underlined part is
(65) essential or nonessential: My neighbor's tortoise, <u>Ezekiel</u>,
often wanders away from home.

23. Write the four principal parts of the irregular verb *hang*
(73, 74) (dangle).

24. Write whether the following sentence is simple,
(3, 100) compound, complex, or compound-complex: Neither the
Infante Diego nor the Infante Ferrando was a respectable,
trustworthy young man.

25. In the sentence below, write the dependent clause,
(57, 99) circling the subordinating conjunction or relative
pronoun. Then write whether the clause functions as a
noun, adjective, or adverb.
The spider that dangled above me appeared harmless.

26. Rewrite this sentence using active voice: Diego and
(102) Ferrando were frightened by a pet lion.

27. Rewrite this sentence, adding a semicolon and a comma
(91) as needed and circling the conjunctive adverb: Those
observing the cowardly behavior of Ferrando and Diego
began laughing and making fun of the brothers however
Diego and Ferrando failed to see the humor in the
situation.

28. Rewrite this sentence using parallel structure: Tortoises
(101) don't like swimming, surfing, or to water ski.

Diagram sentences 29 and 30.

29. Aha, Ferrando has scrambled under a bench to escape a
(23, 59) pet lion.

30. The rude robot serving popcorn asked me to leave the
(25, 34) theater.

LESSON
110

Spelling Rules: *ie* or *ei*

> **Dictation or Journal Entry**
>
> **Vocabulary:** The Latin adjective *omnis-* means "all" and appears in English words as the prefix *omni-*.
>
> *Omniscient* is an adjective that means "having all knowledge or understanding." An *omniscient* narrator knows all the thoughts and actions of the characters in a story.
>
> *Omnipotent* means having complete or unlimited power. Was the king *omnipotent*?
>
> *Omnifarious* means all kinds, types, or forms. The market's *omnifarious* collection of flowers impressed the florists.
>
> *Omnivorous* means eating all types of foods. An *omnivorous* beast feeds on both plants and animals.

To determine whether to use *ie* or *ei* to make the long *e* sound in a word, we recall this rhyme:

Use *i* before *e*

Except *after* c

Or when sounded like *ay*

As in *neighbor* and *weigh*.

USE *i* BEFORE *e*:

ach*ie*ve	w*ie*ld	sh*ie*ld
th*ie*f	pr*ie*st	p*ie*ce

EXCEPT AFTER *c*:

c*ei*ling	dec*ei*ve	conc*ei*t
conc*ei*ve	rec*ei*pt	perc*ei*ve

OR WHEN SOUNDED LIKE *ay*:

n*ei*ghbor	v*ei*n	*ei*ght	r*ei*gn

Exceptions   The following words are exceptions to the rule. We must memorize them.

either	leisure	neither	seize
conscience	height	forfeit	weird
sovereign	omniscient	counterfeit	feisty

Example   Write the words that are spelled correctly.

(a) feild, field   (b) beleif, belief

(c) recieve, receive   (d) acheive, achieve

(e) freight, frieght   (f) niether, neither

Solution   (a) **field** (Use *i* before *e*.)   (b) **belief** (Use *i* before *e*.)

(c) **receive** (Except after *c*.)   (d) **achieve** (Use *i* before *e*.)

(e) **freight** (Or when sounded as *ay*.)

(f) **neither** (exception)

Practice   For a–f, write the words that are spelled correctly.
  a. neice, niece   **b.** sieze, seize

  c. reprieve, repreive   **d.** reciept, receipt

  e. weight, wieght   **f.** sliegh, sleigh

For g–k, replace each blank with the correct vocabulary word.
  g. The Latin prefix _____ means "all."

  h. The dictator wanted to be _____.

  i. A vegetarian is not _____.

  j. His _____ butterfly collection included all kinds.

  k. Most people believe that God is _____.

Review set   Choose the correct word(s) to complete sentences 1–15.
110   **1.** Extraordinary means (very, beyond, always) ordinary.
    (107)

    2. Interscholastic means (good, between, interesting)
    (108) schools.

    3. The Latin prefix *trans-* means (across, between, five).
    (109)

    4. The Latin prefix *omni-* means (against, sound, all).
    (110)

    5. The transcontinental railroad went (under, over, across) a
    (109) continent.

    6. Isabel invited Harriet and (they, them) to swim in her
    (54, 66) pool.

7. Harriet and (they, them) swam for a (real, really) long
$^{(53, 92)}$time.

8. The following is a (phrase, clause): after a succession of
$^{(24, 57)}$battles with the Moors

9. The sheep in the pasture were noisy and (fast-moving,
$^{(82, 85)}$fast moving).

10. I have barely (any, no) time for fishing today.
$^{(81)}$

11. The beauty of this sunset transcends the beauty in (them,
$^{(28, 70)}$those) photographs.

12. The ring, (that, which) was brand new, fell off while
$^{(64, 65)}$Freddy was swimming.

13. Manny has (strove, striven) for excellence in archery.
$^{(74, 75)}$

14. Of the twin sisters, Anela seems the (more, most) reliable.
$^{(90)}$

15. Did you (recieve, receive) my letter?
$^{(110)}$

16. For a–c, rewrite each word, circling the silent letters.
$^{(106, 107)}$(a) guarantee   (b) plumber   (c) yolk

17. For a–c, write the possessive form of each plural noun.
$^{(97)}$ (a) bees   (b) fleas   (c) oxen

18. Rewrite the following, adding punctuation marks and
$^{(72, 97)}$underlining each word that should be italicized: Jack
      Londons most famous novel The Call of the Wild was
      published in 1903

19. Rewrite the following, adding capital letters and
$^{(44, 91)}$punctuation marks as needed: on january 4 1076 an all
      knowing sage confronted a self righteous hypocrite
      moreover the sage exposed the hypocrite to public
      scrutiny

20. For a–c, write the plural of each noun.
$^{(12, 13)}$(a) suffix   (b) morning glory   (c) Dennis

21. For a–c, combine each word and suffix to make one word.
$^{(108, 109)}$(a) shop + ing   (b) mad + ly   (c) strap + ed

22. Write the superlative form of the adverb *reluctantly*.
(90)

23. Write the objective case, third person, plural personal
(51, 54) pronoun.

24. Write whether the following sentence is simple,
(62, 100) compound, complex, or compound-complex: Cid wants
justice, so he will demand it.

25. In the sentence below, write the dependent clause,
(57, 99) circling the subordinating conjunction or relative
pronoun. Then write whether the clause functions as a
noun, adjective, or adverb.
The news that his future sons-in-law were proud and
scornful troubled Cid deeply.

26. Rewrite this sentence using active voice: That entire two-
(102) story house was painted by Jenny and her father.

27. Write whether this sentence is true of false: When we
(105) write, we should use as many interjections as we possibly
can.

28. Which sentence has parallel structure? Choose A or B.
(101) A. Pero Bermudez was not only brave but also had a hot
temper.

B. Pero Bermudez was not only brave but also hot-
tempered.

Diagram sentences 29 and 30.

29. Oh behalf of his daughters, Cid demands an opportunity
(23, 25) to express his complaints to the king.

30. While Cid's men fight against the dishonorable brothers,
(23, 94) two kings plan on marrying Cid's daughters.

Appendix

Dictations

At the beginning of class each Monday, students will copy their dictation to study and prepare for a test on Friday.

Week 1   A book of fiction portrays imaginary characters and events. When we read fiction, we consider these factors: plot, setting, theme, characterization, style, and format. The plot is the plan of the story. It tells what the characters do and what happens to them. It is the glue that holds the story together and makes the reader want to continue reading.

Week 2   The setting of a piece of literature is the time and place. It tells where and when the action occurs. The setting may be in the past, present, or future. The story may take place in a specific setting, or in a deliberately vague place and time, only hinting at a big city or rural community. The action, the characters, and the theme are all affected by the setting.

Week 3   Pearl S. Buck (1892–1973) was the first woman ever to receive the Nobel Prize. Growing up in China with missionary parents, she traveled in other Asian countries as well. Therefore, she chose the East as the setting for her stories and novels. Her popular novel, *The Good Earth*, tells the story of a peasant named Wang Lung and of the land that sustained him throughout his lifelong struggles.

Week 4   The theme of a book reveals the author's purpose for writing the story. It adds a dimension to the story beyond the action of the plot. For young people, an appropriate theme might be growing up, accepting others or oneself, or overcoming prejudice or fear. Books of lasting value depict sound moral and ethical principles. The theme adds depth and meaning to the story.

Week 5   Characters are another aspect of a story. The author tries to make characters convincingly real and lifelike by showing their true natures, strengths, and weaknesses. To present a credible character, the author may narrate the character's appearance and personality, record the character's conversation with others, describe the character's thoughts, or show the character's actions. Good character development makes the reader feel well-acquainted with the people in the story.

Week 6   Style is another variable in a literary work. The selection and arrangement of words defines the author's style. Effective writing style creates and reflects the mood of the story. It is not excessively descriptive or patronizing. The chosen point of view as well as the language pattern is appropriate for the plot, characters, and setting. A unique and identifiable style characterizes many successful writers and enhances the story.

Week 7   Thus far, we have discussed five considerations for evaluating fiction: a well-constructed plot, an authentic setting, a significant theme, a convincing group of characters, and an appropriate style. The final criterion is the format. The format of a book includes the quality of paper, the binding, the typography, the illustrations, the size, and shape, and the design of the pages. Because of the fabulous format and illustrations in many books, we discover that books can be fine works of art as well as of literature.

Week 8   Literature expresses people's concern about their human strengths, weaknesses, and their relationships to other people and to the world. Traditional literature forms the foundation of our understanding of life and includes parables, fables, proverbs, classical myths, folklore, and sacred writings. A myth is a narrative that reveals a significant truth about people, their origins, or their interactions with natural or supernatural beings. A group of myths that is particular to a culture is called a mythology.

Week 9   The folk tale is a written or oral narrative handed down through the years. One type of folk tale, the "formula tale," follows a distinct pattern. It has no plot but is used to tease or to end a storytelling session. Another type has a complex plot with a conflict that is resolved through several episodes. The "wise beast—foolish beast" folk tale follows this pattern. There are also romantic folk tales in which the heroes must meet a monster or prove their bravery. Finally, there are the "why" stories, which explain certain animal or human idiosyncrasies.

Week 10   Fables are short, educational tales in which an animal or inanimate object speaks like a human. The story usually includes only one incident, and the lesson may be implied or stated directly. Some fables have more than one interpretation. Fables are usually associated with a Greek slave named Aesop, although some scholars doubt that Aesop even existed. We know, however, that fables come from several different sources.

Week 11   Joel Chandler Harris (1848–1908) a native of Georgia, was a journalist and fiction writer remembered for his Uncle Remus tales. These fables were narrated in Negro dialect by an elderly slave, Uncle Remus, to the seven-year-old son of "Miss Sally," his mistress. The Uncle Remus tales are an example of local color writing. Set in pre-Civil War days, they give insight into life on the Southern plantation.

Week 12   Joel Chandler Harris gave this advice to writers for the newspaper:

> When you've got a thing to say,
> Say it! Don't take half a day.
> When your tale's got little in it,
> Crowd the whole thing in a minute!
> Life is short—a fleeting vapor—
> Don't you fill the whole blamed paper
> With a tale which, at a pinch,
> Could be cornered in an inch!
> Boil her down until she simmers,
> Polish her until she glimmers.

Week 13   The epic, a long, narrative poem, uses the adventures of an epic hero to express the moral values of a society. Bards and poets weave into a tale the complete life cycle from birth to death of an ideal hero. These songs, ballads, or sagas contain a mythical element since the heroes interact with gods. The epic illustrates the history of man's thoughts about goals and values of human life. Because the epic hero is portrayed with both his strengths and his weaknesses, the common man gains hope in an alien, hostile world.

Week 14   Henry Ward Beecher, a famous American pulpit orator and lecturer, said these words during the 1800s:

> It is not work that kills men; it is worry.
> Work is healthy; you can hardly put more
> upon a man than he can bear. Worry is rust
> upon the blade. It is not the revolution that
> destroys the machinery, but the friction.
> Fear secretes acids; but love and trust are
> sweet juices.

Week 15   Good listening is an acquired skill and requires practice. We must think of the other person and keep our minds on what he or she is saying rather than on our own affairs. We listen with our minds and our ears, and we show interest with our faces. Whether or not we agree with the speaker, our interest will help the speaker communicate better. Sitting back with a phony smile is no way to listen. Listening requires our full attention. We listen to others the way we desire others to listen to us.

Week 16   Let us discuss some techniques for listening in order "to learn." First, we choose a seat as near to the speaker as possible in order to hear better and avoid distraction. Listening carefully to oral directions and explanations, we take notes and ask questions if anything is unclear. With our minds focused on what the speaker is saying, we pay close attention to reports, announcements, discussions, and instructions. Remembering class assignments is especially crucial, so we write down the details of the assignment and the due date.

Week 17   Conversing well in a group of people also takes practice. First, we try to be thoughtful of others and sensitive to their feelings. We avoid saying things that might hurt or embarrass people around us. If we disagree with something that is said, we disagree graciously. We exercise patience and do not interrupt anyone. As we speak, we include everyone in the group by looking at each one. Finally, we ask questions to bring out the special interests of others in the group rather than talking only about ourselves.

Week 18   Many of us dread oral reports, yet we are often required to give them. Let us discuss tips to improve our oral reports. First, we aim for a pleasing, effective voice that is not harsh, hoarse, shrill, or high-pitched. We vary our tone, emphasis, loudness, and speed to make our meaning clearer and capture our listeners' attention. We pronounce each word carefully and accurately, and we avoid letting our voice fade at the end of a sentence. Breathing regularly and smoothly, looking at the audience, and standing tall make us appear relaxed and confident even if we do not feel that way.

Week 19   Following some simple rules of etiquette while using the telephone will enhance our reputations and our relationships with other people. First we turn down the radio or television before answering the phone. We keep paper and a pencil near the phone so that we can take a message if someone calls for a person who is unavailable. Holding the mouthpiece about one-half inch away from our mouth, we speak clearly, politely, and pleasantly, making sure that we are understood. Of course, we try to call people at times that are convenient for them rather than during mealtimes or while they are sleeping. No one likes to answer the phone unnecessarily, so we dial the numbers carefully. Good phone manners are a way of demonstrating consideration and respect for others.

Week 20   Let us discuss some simple rules for introducing people to one another. We begin by saying the name of the person that we wish to honor. For instance, if we were introducing our grandmother, we would say, "Grandmother, this is Erin Chung. Erin, this is my grandmother, Mrs. Angles." Common courtesy specifies that a younger person be introduced to an older one. It is also polite to introduce a man to a woman: "Mrs. Ireland, this is my brother, Pancho." When people are about the same age, it does not matter who is introduced first: "Sherry, this is our new neighbor, Marsha."

Week 21   When making introductions, we say each name clearly so that no one has to say, "I am sorry, but I didn't hear the name." If we are introducing people who share common interests, we try to help them begin a conversation by talking about things that interest both of them. When people are introduced to us, we listen carefully for the name of the person, and then we try to use the name in conversation.

Polite comments like, "I have been hoping to meet you," "I have heard many nice things about you," or "How do you do?" are appropriate after we have been introduced. These social skills help us to form friendships and good business relationships throughout our lives.

Week 22   Those of us who have ever been lost know the importance of giving accurate directions to someone who is looking for a certain location. First, we must determine whether the person knows which way is north, south, east, and west. If not, we should use "left" or "right" when giving our explanation. We give the directions from where the person will start, and we say each directional step in order, mentioning any landmarks or buildings that might serve as guides. If possible, we carefully sketch a map on paper. However, if we are giving directions orally, we ask the person to repeat the directions back to us for clarity. Of course, we never give directions unless we are sure of the way.

Week 23   Making clear explanations might seem like an easy task, but it takes special care and thought. Before we begin to explain something, we must thoroughly understand the concept or process ourselves; therefore, we research all the facts. Next, we make an outline, in a logical order, of every necessary detail or step. Finally, we put the explanation into words that the hearers or readers can understand. Illustrations, drawings, or charts may add additional clarity. After an oral explanation, we allow time for questions and answers.

Week 24   With practice, we can improve our test-taking skills if we follow some simple guidelines. Before a test, we prepare thoroughly. Good nutrition and plenty of rest help us. On test day, we pay close attention to instructions. Failure to read directions often causes careless mistakes. In order to do well on tests, we read instructions carefully and ask questions about anything we do not understand. Next, we clearly write the answers to the questions, in the form that is required. Finally, we proofread our work for errors by reading both the questions and our answers over again.

Week 25   An official meeting holds no surprises if we are aware of *parliamentary procedure.* The chairman of a meeting usually sits except to call a meeting to order, to state a motion, or to take a vote. Members must rise and ask permission to speak unless they second a motion or call for a vote by saying, "Question!" The commonest method of voting is by saying "Aye" or "Nay." There is a definite order of events: call to order; reading and approval of minutes; reports from committees; old business; new business; program; and adjournment.

Week 26

Trees

by Joyce Kilmer (1886–1918)

I think that I shall never see
A poem lovely as a tree.

A tree whose hungry mouth is prest
Against the sweet earth's flowing breast;

A tree that looks at God all day,
And lifts her leafy arms to pray;

A tree that may in summer wear
A nest of robins in her hair;

Upon whose bosom snow has lain;
Who intimately lives with rain.

Poems are made by fools like me.
But only God can make a tree.

Week 27

The Purist

by Ogden Nash (1902–1971)

I give you now Professor Twist,
A conscientious scientist.
Trustees exclaimed, "He never bungles!"

And sent him off to distant jungles.
Camped on a tropic riverside,
One day he missed his loving bride.
She had, the guide informed him later,
Been eaten by an alligator.
Professor Twist could not but smile.
"You mean," he said, "a crocodile."

Week 28   Edward Everett Hale, an American writer and clergyman, was born in Boston in 1822 and educated at Harvard University. From 1903 until his death in 1909, he served as chaplain of the U.S. Senate. He is famous for these wise words:

I am only one,
But still I am one.
I cannot do everything,
But still I can do something;
And because I cannot do everything
I will not refuse to do the something that I can do.

Week 29   Ralph Waldo Emerson (1803–1882) wrote the following poem entitled "A Nation's Strength":

Not gold, but only man can make
    A people great and strong;
Men who, for truth and honor's sake,
    Stand fast and suffer long.

Brave men who work while others sleep,
    Who dare while others fly—
They build a nation's pillars deep
    And lift them to the sky.

Week 30   A group of related sentences that makes a specific idea or subject understandable to the reader is called a paragraph. There are four types of paragraphs: descriptive, narrative, expository, and persuasive. A descriptive paragraph gives a focused, clear picture of a person, place, thing, or idea. A narrative paragraph provides the details of an event or experience. An expository paragraph explains ideas, defines terms, or gives directions. A persuasive paragraph presents an opinion and attempts to convince the reader that this opinion is valid. Each type of paragraph performs a function in literature.

Journal Topics

At the beginning of class on Tuesday, Wednesday, and Thursday, students will spend five minutes writing in their journals. Each entry should be at least three sentences long. The following are suggested topics.

Topic # 1. Write about a creative person you admire. Tell how that person expresses his or her creativity.

2. Think about a friend or family member's eyes. Describe them in detail.

3. Would you like to adopt a tortoise? Explain why or why not.

4. Think about a person's eyebrows. Describe how the eyebrows can show emotion.

5. Describe the most beautiful flower you have ever seen.

6. Tell about the sounds you hear on a warm summer evening.

7. Describe your house or apartment.

8. Write about going barefoot. Is there anything special that you like or don't like to feel with your bare feet?

9. Describe how you can show love to a dog or a cat. If you have a different animal, describe how you can show it love.

10. Have you ever seen snow? Describe how it looks and feels.

11. Have you ever had to adapt to changes in your life? Tell about these changes and explain how you adapted to them.

12. Have you ever sat near a campfire? Describe the sight, sound, and smell of the fire.

13. "Don't judge a book by its cover," is an old saying. Does it have a deeper meaning? Tell what it means to you.

14. "No man is an island," is another old saying. What does it mean to you?

15. Some people say, "Honesty is the best policy." Do you agree? Explain.

16. An old saying warns us, "All that glitters is not gold." Tell what this means to you.

17. Someone once said, "The best things in life are free." What do you think that person meant?

18. Think about cotton candy. Describe its appearance, taste, and feel.

19. Imagine what you might see and hear if you sat on the beach at sunset. Describe it.

20. Describe a sea horse. If you have never seen one, look at a picture in the encyclopedia.

21. Describe your bedroom.

22. Tell about a travel experience on an airplane, jet, train, boat, or in a car or bus.

23. Describe your dream vacation.

24. Write about a rainy day.

25. Some people say, "A dog is man's best friend." Do you agree? Why or why not?

26. "The early bird catches the worm," is an old, familiar saying. What does it mean to you? Do you believe it is true?

27. Some people say, "Every cloud has a silver lining." What might this mean? Do you agree?

28. You have previously described your bedroom. Now describe your "ideal" bedroom.

29. Tell about your household chores.

30. Write about things you can do to support your country.

31. Write about things you can do to make the world a better place.

32. What are some things that cause dissension in the United States of America?

33. Describe ways that people show their patriotism.

34. Write about a time when you or someone you know demonstrated courage.

35. Why is it important to maintain a good reputation?

36. What holiday is your favorite, and why?

37. Describe your dream vehicle.

38. Some people say, "Don't cry over spilled milk." What does this mean to you? Do you agree? Explain.

39. "Haste makes waste," is an old saying. Do you agree? Explain.

40. "April showers bring May flowers" is an old, familiar saying. Might it have a deeper meaning? Tell what it means to you.

41. If you could travel anywhere in the world, what country would you visit? Why?

42. Describe a baby. How does this little person look, smell, sound, and feel? How does he or she move?

43. Write about your favorite things to do at a waterfront (beach, bay, lake, river, stream, etc.).

44. Sometimes people say, "Cross that bridge when you come to it," when there are no bridges in sight. What do they mean? Is this good advice? Why or why not?

45. "Don't put all your eggs in one basket," is another common saying. What does it mean to you? Do you consider it good advice? Why or why not?

46. People say, "Rome wasn't built in a day." Are they talking only about Rome, or are they talking about something else? Write what this statement means to you and explain how you might apply it to your life.

47. When people say, "Beauty is only skin deep," what do they mean? Do you agree? Why or why not?

48. Write about a relative, either living or dead, that you admire. Describe their good qualities.

49. Write about the things you like to do in your free time.

50. Write about a time when someone did something nice for you.

51. Write about a time when you had sympathy for someone.

52. Antipathy is a strong dislike or an aversion to something. Have you antipathy toward anything? Explain.

53. Discuss a skill you would like to acquire in the future. Explain how you will develop this skill.

54. Write about a person, place, or thing that makes you happy.

55. If you were to write under a pseudonym, what name would you choose? Why?

56. Describe your vision of a perfect life.

57. What kind of weather do you enjoy most? Why? Describe this weather in detail.

58. Write about a book or collection of books you would like to own and explain why you would like to have them.

59. If you were allowed to redecorate one room in your house, how would you do it? Write about the paint or wall-paper, floor-covering, furniture, artwork, window-covering, etc. that you would use in the room.

60. Imagine that you are on a boat at sea. What do you see? How do you feel? What do you hear?

61. Most families have "traditions." Share one of your favorite family traditions.

62. What is the most memorable "special event" (game, play, parade, etc.) you have attended? Write about it.

63. Write about the best gift you have ever received.

64. Write about a piece of clothing that is special to you (Example: hat, jacket, dress, shoes, etc.)

65. Write about the qualities that a good friend should have.

66. Describe how your family welcomes in a new year.

67. Describe the most beautiful sunset that you have ever seen.

68. If you were President of the United States, what change would you try to make in our country?

69. Have you ever seen an eclipse? A comet? A constellation? A shooting star? The moon or a planet through a telescope? Describe what you saw.

70. Write about your favorite kind of tree, plant, or flower.

71. Describe your favorite board game or video game.

72. Write about your ideas for the ideal career or occupation.

73. Apples come in a variety of colors and tastes. Describe your favorite kind of apple.

74. Write about an animal or insect that you consider interesting.

75. Describe how you might care for a small bird with a broken leg.

76. Create a silly character in your mind. Give the person a name, and describe his or her appearance and personality.

77. Describe an orange.

78. Have you, or has anyone you know, ever broken a bone? Tell about the experience.

79. If you could live during any period of history, what period would you choose? Why?

80. Describe an ocean creature that interests you.

81. What is your favorite way to travel? Why?

82. Describe a banana.

83. Write about a funny story, song, or movie that has made you laugh.

84. Write about a story, song, or movie that has made you sad.

85. Describe a palm tree or another kind of tree, if you prefer.

86. Write about the kindest person you know.

87. Write about the wisest person you know.

88. Describe a watermelon.

89. Some people are optimists; some are pessimists. Which are you? Explain.

90. Describe a giraffe or another animal, if you prefer.

91. Do you celebrate Valentine's Day? How?

92. If you could play any musical instrument in the world, which one would you play? Why?

93. Some people are extroverts; some are introverts. Which are you? Explain.

94. There are many different kinds of salads. Explain how you would make a salad that you would enjoy.

95. Have you ever wiggled your toes in sand? Describe how sand feels.

96. Describe broccoli or another vegetable, if you prefer.

97. Write about your favorite short story, poem, or novel.

98. Have you ever had an unwanted bug or animal in your house? Write about your experience.

99. Have you ever had a difficult time sleeping? Write about your experience.

100. Do you like dogs? Tell why or why not.

Index